DISCOVERING LOND **S**

With
twelve
walks

DISCOVERING LONDON'S BUILDINGS

With twelve walks

by John Bold and Tanis Hinchcliffe
with photographs by Scott Forrester
and maps by Andrew Donald

FRANCES LINCOLN LIMITED
PUBLISHERS

Frances Lincoln Limited
4 Torriano Mews
Torriano Avenue
London NW5 2RZ
www.franceslincoln.com

Discovering London's Buildings
Copyright © 2009 Frances Lincoln Limited
Text copyright © John Bold and Tanis Hinchcliffe
Photographs copyright © Scott Forrester

First Frances Lincoln edition 2009
First published in US and Canada 2009

British Library Cataloguing in Publication Data
A catalogue record for this book is available from the British Library

ISBN: 978-0-7112-2918-1

Designed by Gillian Greenwood
Printed in Singapore

9 8 7 6 5 4 3 2 1

HALF TITLE   Holland House, 32 Bury Street.
TITLE PAGE   View from Monument with Tower Bridge.
THESE PAGES View from Greenwich Park.

CONTENTS

ACKNOWLEDGEMENTS

Highpoint One, North Hill, Highgate, Berthold Lubetkin, 1933–5.

In the preparation of this book we have incurred many debts. We are grateful to the custodians and staff of monuments for access to buildings for research and photography, particularly at the Greenwich Foundation for the Old Royal Naval College, London Transport, Somerset House, Southwark Cathedral, All Saints Margaret Street, the Crossness Engines Trust and the City churches. We are especially grateful to Patricia and Peter Kenyon for providing repeated access and hospitality at their flat in Shakespeare Tower, Barbican. We thank the staff of the British Library, the British Architectural Library, the Guildhall Library and the London Library for enabling research in their collections. We also wish to thank English Heritage, the Guildhall Library, the London Transport Museum, the Minneapolis Institute of Arts, the National Maritime Museum and Solo Syndication for permission to reproduce photographs of items from their collections. Thanks also to Fleur Jago of the British Library for supplying a disk of *Street Knowledge* – London from the taxi driver's point of view. We are grateful also to Faber and Faber Ltd for permission to publish lines from Samuel Beckett on the Monument.

For insights and rewarding discussions we wish to thank Michael Althorpe, Monique Chatenet, Kerry Downes, Peter Guillery, Bernard Herman, Delcia Keate and Ann Robey, who in addition made a major contribution to the development of the walks. Thanks are due to students at New York University in London, International Education of Students London and the University of Westminster for their participation and contribution to the development of these walks. For practical advice on the view from the air, we wish to thank Andrew Cook (University of Westminster) and British Airways pilots Captain Nick Lamont and First Officer Peter Clark. For practical help we thank Martha Forrester, Sarah Hokanson, Chris Salewicz, Natalie Vieira and Rachel Yarmolinsky. Throughout the project we have had the encouragement of our colleagues at the University of Westminster, Nick Bailey, Murray Fraser and Kate Heron, and we are grateful also to the University for financial contributions towards the costs of research and illustrations. We are particularly indebted to Sarah Bold for her consistent support and encouragement of a time-consuming endeavour, and to Richard Hill for his constant interest and many suggestions.

FOREWORD

London is a world city with a population and significance beyond the confines of mere nationality, and with a long history of distinguished architecture. It is richly varied, not unplanned but without an overall plan, employing a range of styles for different purposes, and juxtaposing old and new in such a way that it is very difficult to gain an understanding of the development of the whole. It is also very large and can no longer be encapsulated in a single view or narrated in a single story. Rather than producing a sequential history, we have attempted to give a general picture of the development of the capital by approaching it selectively and thematically, looking at elements of London's architecture and servicing: domestic, commercial, religious and institutional. The themes are supported by twelve walks which provide illustrative slices of London's architectural and social development in the City and Westminster and the inner suburbs. Apart from the walk through Legal London, these walks do not follow a single theme or a single broad time period. This is a vibrant city in which functions, styles and dates of buildings are juxtaposed in an apparently random manner, making it extremely rewarding and exciting to explore on foot. The walks necessarily, and the thematic chapters to a great extent, place their emphasis on what can be seen, although it does not follow that the buildings mentioned are open to the public. Some of them are, but the majority are not, and current security concerns, commercial interests and the privatisation of public spaces are reducing or inhibiting access still further. This is a regrettable if sometimes unavoidable trend, since architecture plays a fundamental role in maintaining the quality of life in an open society, and that sustaining role is diminished where there are constraints.

There still is, however, an enormous amount to see and appreciate in London's buildings and open spaces, and this book is intended as a way into the subject: an aid towards gaining an informed appreciation of the architectural development of the capital. The approach adopted has been developed in teaching an MA course on London Architecture at the University of Westminster, and some of the walks have also been developed in the company of American students on study abroad programmes at New York University in London and International Education of Students London. Such courses can be neither comprehensive nor definitive, and indeed the size, scope and complexity of London would defy any such objective. Here, therefore, are aspects of London's architecture: some important buildings but not all of them, selected in some cases because they are undeniably significant, in others because they are illustrative of approaches. The work of great architects is considered from Jones and Wren in the seventeenth century, Hawksmoor and Chambers in the eighteenth, Barry and Scott in the nineteenth, and Lasdun and Stirling in the twentieth, coming up to date with the work of Foster and Rogers. All of these have produced great and potentially enduring buildings, but there is more to London than great architecture alone. It is the gallimaufry of styles and forms which engages interest; the accumulation of the ordinary which provides the day-to-day backdrop for the working population and the visitor; the spaces between buildings which provide sudden, unexpected views of the familiar; the glimpses of an unknown which then demands exploration. It is difficult to see London at street level since it is too built-up and shy of grand boulevards, but the attempt should be made, and if weariness overcomes the walker, then there are always the parks, semi-rural idylls offering an entirely different and calmer perspective.

INTRODUCTION
The built heritage

Exploring London prompts consideration not only of its architectural development but also of perceptions of significance and value which have evolved over the past century. The idea of a built heritage that we identify, nurture, protect and pass on, attempting to save it from its inevitable disintegration, is a relatively new concept in legislation. It was not until the 1970s that the idea of heritage came into official usage, applicable to the built environment as well as the natural landscape, and crucially, if defined at all, defined by threat. It became axiomatic that the heritage, however broadly or narrowly considered, is in danger. In 1975 the declaration of European Architectural Heritage Year gave a powerful spur to the notion of a built heritage at risk and in need of protection. Lord Duncan-Sandys, chairman of the international organising committee and prime mover in the establishment of the Civic Trust in 1957, offered the view that

> *the conservation of our architectural heritage is not simply a nostalgic attachment to the past. Nor again is it a wish to preserve old buildings as museums. It serves a much wider purpose ... it contributes to the quality of life. It gives variety, colour and interest to the surroundings in which we live ... In an age of oppressive uniformity, it preserves for our towns and villages their individual identity and inspires pride and fellowship among their citizens.*

European Architectural Heritage Year culminated in the Amsterdam Declaration, which affirmed the role of the architectural heritage in giving a consciousness of a common history and a common future destiny; it stressed the great breadth of the built heritage, and insisted that since these treasures are the joint possession of all the peoples in Europe, we all have a responsibility to protect them. It declared that conservation and rehabilitation should be a major objective of planning rather than a marginal activity and, moreover, that programmes of education should increase public appreciation of the architectural heritage. New architecture also has its place in the Amsterdam Declaration – it should be of high quality because it is the heritage of tomorrow.

By 1975, the protection of landscapes, buildings and sites had been proceeding in England for many years, but it was the threat to the built environment by neglect or large-scale redevelopment in what many saw as unsympathetic styles, inimical to traditional ideas about how places should look, that prompted the next quarter century of heritage protection. The modern concept of heritage may be interpreted as a function of the perceived failures of post-war modernisation and reconstruction – a defensive response to too much rapid change. This recent phase was analogous to previous periods in which the threat to a well-loved scene or building proved to be the occasion for the establishment of mechanisms to record and protect. We were not first on the scene in England in enacting protective legislation, not least because of something which Andrew Saint has identified as Britain's 'fetishising the rights of private ownership'. The protection of ancient monuments and historic buildings proceeded hesitantly. Now, with over 500,000 listed buildings in England, we have one of the furthest reaching legal systems of architectural conservation to be found anywhere in the world.

The rights of private ownership ensured that the early Ancient Monuments Acts excluded inhabited buildings. The first such Act, in 1882, was concerned with

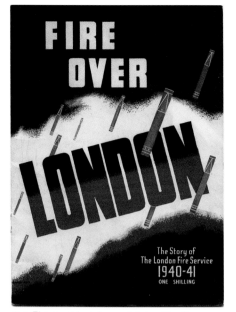

0.1 *Fire over London*, published by the London County Council, 1941.

prehistoric and Roman sites; in 1900 this was extended to medieval abbeys and castles, with further extensions in 1913 and 1931. The Town and Country Planning Act of 1932 was the first to include inhabited houses; this was followed by important legislation in 1944 and 1947. Accompanying legislation was the establishment of bodies devoted to protection – the National Trust in 1895 – and to recording historic buildings and sites as a spur to protection: the Survey of London in 1894; the Royal Commission on Historical Monuments in 1908; the National Buildings Record in 1940, set up in response to the threat of destruction in the Second World War. In 1983 the National Heritage Act established the Historic Buildings and Monuments Commission for England, soon to rebrand itself as 'English Heritage'. This body is responsible, among other things, for making recommendations for the classification and protection (listing) of historic buildings and archaeological sites, for research into buildings and building types, and for the compilation of registers of buildings at risk that are in search of new uses. (The Royal Commission on the Historical Monuments of England, with the accompanying National Monuments Record – formerly the National Buildings Record – was absorbed by English Heritage in 1999 when it also took over responsibility for the Survey of London.)

English Heritage does not define what it means by the word heritage, preferring to refer to 'this inheritance', which recalls its original definition – that which we inherit from our predecessors. This carries with it the connotation of ownership – in this case something owned by society as a whole as well as by the nominal owners of buildings and sites – but although historic buildings may be deemed worthy of protection, the idea of the heritage of which they form a part remains nebulous. 'Heritage' has become a portmanteau term which in its current usage embraces artefacts, histories, perceptions and feelings, given clarity only through process: the act of defining and making inventories of its component parts.

In the definition, celebration and protection of the built heritage, it is not just the national institutions which have occupied the key roles. Private individuals have played a significant part in the establishment of pressure groups inspired by threat, which later, as amenity societies, were absorbed into official consultation procedures: the Society for the Protection of Ancient Buildings, founded by William Morris in 1877 to counteract the brutal restoration of medieval buildings; the Ancient Monuments Society, 1924, which moved from Manchester to London in 1953; the Georgian Group, 1937; the Victorian Society, 1957; the Thirties Society, 1979, which became the Twentieth Century Society in 1993; and SAVE Britain's Heritage, 1975, which is a rather different, very effective, case-led organisation that does not have members. Over the span of a century the area of interest has steadily widened, a nationwide broadening in which the regular rebuilding and continuing development of London and the consequent need to protect the historic fabric have played a formative role. Buildings and building types whose destruction we would now regard as unthinkable have only come to be so regarded following threats to their existence, which have been countered by public opinion and pressure through the actions of organised groups and the media mobilised at critical moments.

The saving of St Paul's Cathedral during the Blitz was recorded in a commemorative booklet, *Fire over London: The Story of the London Fire Service 1940–41*, published for the London County Council (LCC) and depicting dramatic black and white photographs of burning buildings and heroic firemen (fig. 0.1). The morning after, 30 December 1940, 'Historic churches designed centuries before by the master hand of Christopher Wren lay shattered, their very altars choked with the black mud of sodden ember and ash. And yet with all this melancholy toll of destruction, the heart of the City, together with its great Cathedral, had been saved.' St Paul's Cathedral had already been enlisted as a symbol of national identity, but the City churches had taken longer to achieve an equivalent status, perhaps because there were so many of them. Wren and his office had rebuilt fifty-one of them after the Great Fire of 1666: an embarrassment of cumulative riches. They have not been regarded always as sacrosanct. Some were impediments to traffic and were demolished as new streets were cut through the City in the nineteenth century. They were not loved by a Church establishment which favoured the Gothic; also, with population shifts, the Church supported the idea of selling valuable building plots in order to finance new churches in the godless suburbs. In 1854, there was a proposal to demolish twenty-nine churches by Wren and others: fourteen had gone by 1888. In 1919, there was a further proposal by the Bishop of London to demolish another nineteen, including St Vedast (fig. 0.2) and Hawksmoor's St Mary Woolnoth (p. 140). The City Corporation was opposed and the plan was quashed by Parliament in 1926. Following the Second World War, they have joined St Paul's as symbols of survival, restored and in use but short of money. Since the Church of England is an arm of the state as well as of religion, and the churches themselves part of our common heritage, we perhaps need a new dispensation to arrange for their continuing upkeep.

As Gavin Stamp has shown, the threatened demolition of historic buildings in London has been consistently the major driver in the establishment of preservation pressure groups. The case of Mornington Crescent in Camden is indicative. Here, in a district whose accessibility had been increased through the coming of the railways and the Underground, the asymmetrical garden in front of an early nineteenth-century crescent of thirty-six houses was sold to a developer in 1919, and sold on again in 1926. A new factory – the Arcadia Works for Carreras, makers of Craven A cork-tipped (said to be kind to the lips and harmless to the throat) and Black Cat cigarettes – was built on the site to the design of M. E. and O. H. Collins, adapting plans by A. G. Porri, destroying the view from the houses (fig. 0.3). The newly fashionable Egyptian-style decoration followed the discovery of Tutankhamun's tomb in 1922. Production of 1,300 cigarettes per minute ceased in 1959 when the factory moved, and the works were sold for offices, to be refitted in 1960–2 as Greater London House. All the Egyptian decoration, condemned by modernists, was stripped off, before changes in fashion and ideas of heritage

0.2 St Vedast Foster Lane, 1695–1701, with spire of 1709–12.

0.3 Mornington Crescent, 1821–32, overshadowed by the Carreras factory of 1926.

0.4 The Carreras façade restored in 1998, with one of the pair of black cats.

0.5 Bedford Square, 1775–86, east side.

0.6 Euston Arch, 1834–8, demolished 1962; watercolour by G. F. Sargent, c.1847 (Guildhall Library, City of London).

prompted its restoration in 1998 (fig. 0.4). The loss of these and other gardens led to the establishment of a Royal Commission on London squares in 1927, and in due course to the founding of the Georgian Group. Although no more gardens were lost, there was continuing rebuilding within squares: even Bedford Square was at risk when the British Museum proposed the redevelopment of the east side in 1937–8 (fig. 0.5).

The demolition of the Euston Arch, even in defeat, was one of the great spurs to the conservation movement (fig. 0.6). A new station was proposed in 1937 as a perverse celebration of the centenary of the first London terminus. The Georgian Group accepted that Philip Hardwick's Great Hall had to go, but believed that his superb Doric propylaeum of 1834–8 could be saved by moving it south. This was agreed in 1938 by the London Midland and Scottish railway company, but war intervened and the proposals lapsed. In the 1950s the Great Hall was restored, but in 1959 the British Transport Commission decided to rebuild and neither it nor the LCC, the Ministry of Works or the Treasury was prepared to pay the £180,000

needed to re-site the arch. Prime Minister Harold Macmillan was petitioned in vain. The demolition contractor, Frank Valori, offered to number the stones for re-erection elsewhere; he later presented the Victorian Society with a model of the demolished arch. This defeat, together with the loss of J. B. Bunning's Coal Exchange of 1846–9 in the City in the same year, 1962, concentrated minds. The proposed demolition by British Rail of both King's Cross and St Pancras stations in 1966, for a single new terminus, was met with public protest and defeat. This was in part a recognition of the magnificent engineering of the train-sheds (fig. 0.7), and also of the architectural value of George Gilbert Scott's Midland Grand Hotel at St Pancras, which hitherto had not enjoyed universal support (fig. 0.8). Mark Girouard, teetering on the parapet, later put up a memorable defence of the building in the 1975 BBC television series *Spirit of the Age* (with accompanying book), which no doubt helped influence opinion. Scott's Foreign and Commonwealth Office, also discussed by Girouard, had been saved at the same time as the stations when an LCC scheme to rebuild Whitehall, approved in 1963, was defeated in 1966 with the help of the Civic Trust.

It was the Civic Trust again – together with considerable public pressure, local government resistance and a shift in favour of the retention of historic townscapes – which eventually helped to secure the future of Covent Garden Market at a public inquiry in 1973, before the removal of the market south of the river to a site more accessible for wholesale traders. Although redevelopment had been accepted in principle, the canny listing during the same year of 245 buildings led to small-scale restoration and to the ambitious conversion of the nineteenth-century market buildings, including scooping out the basement to allow for small shops and restaurants. The restoration, undertaken by the Historic Buildings Division of the Greater London Council (GLC), was completed in 1980. Covent Garden today is a centre for international tourism, a remarkable success story regularly cited as a model in plans for the regeneration of inner cities elsewhere, but more frequented

0.7 King's Cross Station, 1851–2; one of the pair of sheds, each spanning 105 feet (32 metres), whose timber arches were replaced in wrought iron in 1869 and 1887.

0.8 Midland Grand Hotel, St Pancras, 1868–74; the clock tower.

0.9 Covent Garden Market; interior view looking west.

0.10 Mansion House and No. 1 Poultry, from the east.

0.11 City Magistrate's Court, Queen Victoria Street, 1873–5.

by those in search of artfully tinted photographs and prints than those who might search in vain for a pint of milk and a packet of PG Tips (fig. 0.9).

At No. 1 Poultry, the outcome of a highly significant and long-running conservation battle was less clear-cut. Here the developer Peter (now Lord) Palumbo received permission in 1969 for the redevelopment of the area adjacent to George Dance's (Senior) eighteenth-century Mansion House at a key City intersection, subject to his acquiring thirteen freeholds and 348 leaseholds. This took him until 1981. A design for a tower by Mies van der Rohe, made in 1962–8, was rejected in 1985 following a public inquiry at which the forces of modernism were ranked against those of conservation. The proposal involved the demolition of nine listed buildings, including the Mappin and Webb building of 1870 on Queen Victoria Street by J. & J. Belcher. Palumbo then employed Stirling and Wilford to produce a new design with less demolition. A second inquiry followed in 1988, at which the Secretary of State approved the proposal. SAVE took the case to the Court of Appeal and won. Palumbo then went to the House of Lords, and the decision was overturned in his favour. Demolition and rebuilding on the corner site went ahead and was completed in 1998, six years after James Stirling's death (fig. 0.10). This second inquiry was less obviously modernists against conservationists, since Stirling's high-tech supporters did not favour his knowing postmodernism; the conservationists were more sympathetic to the design but opposed demolition of the Victorian buildings: the City Magistrate's Court, a potential victim in the first scheme, survived the second (fig. 0.11). Notwithstanding the demolition, there were positive results in this saga. SAVE was strengthened in defeat because of its courageous initiative; the Secretary of State was prompted to pronounce, Alice-like, that this potential precedent was not a precedent at all and that there should continue to be a general presumption in favour of preserving listed buildings and historic areas. In addition, we at last got a prominent building in the centre of London by one of the most eminent post-war architects, and the archaeological implications were profound: as the building rose on a concrete raft, investigation continued beneath to reveal much of the layout of Roman London (although archaeological potential is not a necessary and sufficient reason for demolition).

These individual cases of threatened and demolished buildings contribute towards an understanding of the breadth of London's built heritage and the efforts which have been made to preserve it. We have come some way nationally from the idea that traditionally monumental churches and palaces should be the objects to which we should give our sole attention. The notion of what is historic and what should be protected has broadened in recent years along with our notions of significant social relations. While buildings are still protected for historical or architectural reasons, the definition of what constitutes historical or architectural significance has been extended to include the monuments of everyday life, of industry and of the post-war period, the latter receiving an initially unexpected degree of public support. In fact, some of the post-war buildings now protected or old enough (at least thirty years old, with one or two outstanding exceptions), good enough and threatened enough to be proposed for protection come from the same period of alarming modernist reconstruction which helped to inspire the defensive end-of-century wave of heritage activity in the first place. The innovative Alexandra Road flats designed by Neave Brown, begun in 1972, were listed Grade II* in 1993, nine years before they would normally have been eligible, to protect them from insensitive repairs (fig. 0.12). As the government noted in the national *Planning Policy Guidance 15* (1994):

> *The physical survivals of our past are to be valued and protected for their own sake, as a central part of our cultural heritage and our sense of national identity. They are an irreplaceable record which contributes, through formal education and in many other ways, to our understanding of both the present and the past. Their presence adds to the quality of our lives, by enhancing the familiar and cherished local scene and sustaining the sense of local distinctiveness which is so important an aspect of the character and appearance of our towns, villages and countryside.*

The preservation and management of this irreplaceable record requires both vigilance and statutory procedures. The alteration or demolition of listed buildings requires 'listed building consent', a procedure which is designed to manage change, taking account of the need in many cases to accommodate new functions in older buildings. There were a little over 2,000 such applications nationally in 1979, rising rapidly and consistently during the 1980s and early 1990s to a peak of 8,033 in 1991. The figure at the time of writing in 2007 is about 5,000 per year, the great majority of which are for alteration rather than outright demolition. It certainly cannot be said, however, that the battle to save listed buildings has been won: unflagging awareness is still required, as readers of the Piloti column in the fortnightly *Private Eye* will recognise. Although there is now a better public understanding of the value of historic buildings as an economic as well as a social asset than pertained at the height of the ball-and-chain philistinism which the amenity societies did so much to counter, many developers and councils, in thrall to short-term economic gain, are still to be persuaded. It is not just listed buildings, moreover, which contribute to the quality of the environment. Conservation areas, part of 'the familiar and cherished local scene', designated by local authorities, are also at constant risk of erosion through small-scale interventions which have great cumulative impact. The replacement of wooden window frames in plastic and metal, and the paving of front gardens for car parking, both have a deleterious impact on the quality and aesthetics of urban life. So too does the eradication of the familiar and unprotected through the impact of gentrification and commerce: when all car repair and furniture workshops in railway arches have been replaced by wine bars and small shops driven out by supermarkets, vital constituents of the urban fabric will have been lost. The unintended negative consequences of desirable and necessary environmental improvements are potentially profound.

Thirty years after the Amsterdam Declaration, the Council of Europe continues to co-ordinate opinion and oversee strategies for the protection and promotion of the cultural heritage. In the Faro Convention of 2005, member states, invoking the idea of a collective responsibility, broke new ground in emphasising the social value of the cultural heritage, its role in the construction of peaceful and democratic societies and in the promotion of cultural diversity. A well-informed understanding of the evolution of the built environment is fundamental to the achievement of such social goals in helping us to define who we are and where we have been, without which understanding we move forward in a contextual void. This is a culturally defined route, basic to the idea and celebration of citizenship. Here, as Rebecca West put it in 1942, is the dream of London, Paris and New York, 'that there is no limit to the distance which man can travel from his base, the cabbage-patch, that there is no pleasure too delicate to be bought by all of us, if the world will but go on getting richer'. Writing in wartime London, she was sceptical about the realisation of the citizen's dream; we too may be sceptical, but we might still hope.

1.1 View south from Shakespeare Tower, Barbican, with London Wall and St Paul's Cathedral.

1.2 View east from Shakespeare Tower, Barbican, showing the Swiss Re Tower.

1.3 View south from Southwark Cathedral, with railway tracks (courtesy of Southwark Cathedral).

1.4 View north from Southwark Cathedral, with St Paul's Cathedral; Minerva House, 1979–83, is in the foreground (courtesy of Southwark Cathedral).

Chapter 1 PICTURING LONDON

From the thirty-sixth floor of Shakespeare Tower in the Barbican, London looks like the triumph of the accidental (fig. 1.1) (Walk 7). Something so large and so apparently amorphous could not possibly be planned: no one would do it like that, with an irregular river confounding ideas of north and south, and a random street pattern its apparent consequence. No one could imagine bringing this kind of vibrant sprawl into being. London has long ceased to be capable of being grasped visually or conceptually in its entirety. There have been plans and there is planning, but these are discrete events or finite activities; they leave their mark but they do not impose a lasting order or defined boundary. Fragmentation and growth consistently defy all attempts to confine or regulate a city which can no longer be visualised. On the ground, as V. S. Pritchett observed, we are 'surrounded by everything and see nothing'. From the thirty-sixth floor the views are thrilling, absorbing, hypnotic, but they are experienced in series and must be mentally reassembled in order to become fleetingly comprehensible (fig. 1.2). London is a modern archetype. In all its random, accidental grandeur, alongside the squalid and the commonplace, it is as potent as the city of Uruk, 'which no city on earth can equal', described for us over 3,000 years ago in *Gilgamesh*, the oldest story in the world.

If we go now to the top of the tower of Southwark Cathedral (Walk 5), it is the quotidian which prevails: the views are constrained. No. 1 London Bridge, part of the London Bridge City development, has interrupted the view to the east since 1986, and it is the free-form patterning of the competing railway tracks of south London which provides the lasting mental image (fig. 1.3). We can still see St Paul's Cathedral to the north, but like returning to the scenes of childhood it looks far smaller and further away than memory and imagination would allow (fig. 1.4). Old St Paul's looked bigger when Wenceslaus Hollar was here in the seventeenth century.

Between 1600 and 1666, 110 views of London to the north were published, taken as if from the top of the tower of the church of St Mary Overie, Southwark (Southwark Cathedral since 1905). Far from all of these were valuable, and almost all were copies of each other: possibly only two, by Norden (1600) and Hollar (1647), were based on direct observation. This was the period in which the creation of the panoramic view reached its full momentum. The trend had been begun in the mid-sixteenth century by the Antwerp artist Anthony van den Wyngaerde, who produced large pen and ink sketches of the royal palaces and of London between Westminster and Greenwich, which were fundamental to the development of landscape topography in Britain. His bird's-eye view from the south, made in 1544, placing the tower of St Mary Overie in the centre, was perhaps the originator of the view from Bankside.

The inspiration for the 110 views catalogued by Irene Scouloudi was Netherlandish, and more than a third of the London views were published in the Netherlands. Traders particularly needed to know how things looked (although John Gay in 1716 advised against relying on their directions: 'Ask the grave Tradesman to direct thee right / He ne'er deceives, but when he profits by't'). There was an ever-growing requirement for correct depictions of the surface of the earth. This graphic endeavour was intended to be descriptive rather than narrative, a world described rather than a world imagined as a stage for action – and often moreover a world, or at least landscape, which is owned: there was a powerful economic stimulus to this mode of depiction. Svetlana Alpers has contrasted this northern, descriptive picture-making with the rhetorical persuasion of Italian art, but in the desire to encapsulate form, to grasp a totality, north and south had much in common. A contrast has been drawn between the northern 'profile' approach in which a low viewpoint is taken at a distance, with a wide and open horizon, and the Italian search, noted by Lucia Nuti, for 'an all-embracing view, from an elevated vantage-point at a distance, such as surrounding hills, in order to grasp urban form and shape'. Behind such a strategy lies the idea of the town as a microcosm, embodying social and political identity as well as structure. The unavoidable presence of the River Thames, with St Mary's tower on its south bank, offered the panorama artist the best of both worlds, providing the opportunity for both horizontal expanse and an attempt at overall encapsulation.

But even in the seventeenth century, London was too large to be drawn and published in its entirety, and it was the wrong shape. It could be mapped, as Braun and Hogenberg had done in 1572, in the first surviving printed map of the whole of London and Westminster, and John Oliver did in c.1680 after the 'late dreadfull Fire', but the bend in the river severed the visual connection between the City and Westminster. The Thames flows approximately west to east as it passes the City and approximately south to north past Westminster. John Norden overcame the consequent problem of accurate topographical depiction in his panorama of 1600 by displaying Westminster as a separate view transplanted onto the empty marshes of Lambeth. Newcomers to London, unaware of this disposition of the river, may wonder why taxi drivers cross Westminster Bridge and drive along York Road and Stamford Street to Blackfriars Bridge in order to get to the City. In the seventeenth century, Samuel Pepys took the same route, using ferries to cross the river twice. The river is critical to orientation in London. Even Harry Beck's Underground map, first published in 1933, which places clarity above geographical accuracy, could not ignore the orientational significance of the Thames and the physical and psychological divide which it creates between its notional north and south banks. Basing his

1.5 Canaletto, *Greenwich: The Royal Naval Hospital*, *c*.1750 (© National Maritime Museum, London).

design on the electric circuit diagram, he placed the emphasis on connections, the process of travel, rather than on surface geography. But connections in London without an idea of their relationship to the river take place in a procedural void. The shift in the river flow from northwards to eastwards, and the relationship of Westminster to the City and Southwark, is well shown in Hollar's pre-Great Fire *Prospect of London and Westminster taken from Lambeth* (*c*.1643).

The emergence of Southwark, on the principal route to London from the south, as a viewpoint from which to contemplate and record the City – superseding earlier rare views from *c*.1480–1550 which showed the City as if from a raised viewpoint east of the Tower – inevitably brought the Thames into the foreground and gave it an artistic role which lasted well into the mid-eighteenth century. Although initially the river was subordinate to the City itself, it had become pre-eminent by the time of Canaletto's two lengthy stays in England between 1746 and 1755–6. He followed Antonio Joli in bringing a Venetian vision to bear on panoramic views taken from the terrace of Somerset House (Walk 3) which celebrated the wonders of modern London: St Paul's Cathedral to the east and Westminster Bridge to the west. In further views from Lambeth, from Richmond House, through an arch of Westminster Bridge, and, picturing Greenwich, from the Isle of Dogs, Canaletto celebrated space, vista and modernity (fig. 1.5). He was lucky with the weather. James Boswell in the winter of 1762–3 enjoyed the romantic frisson afforded by the frozen Thames: from London Bridge 'we viewed with a pleasing horror the rude and terrible appearance of the river, partly froze up, partly covered with enormous shoals of floating ice which often crashed against each other'. In the spring, this same viewpoint offered 'silver expanse and the springy bosom of the surrounding fields'. One month later Boswell conducted a 'strong, jolly young damsel' to Westminster Bridge: 'the whim of doing it there with the Thames rolling below us amused me much'. Where Boswell was amused, Blanchard Jerrold in 1872 found grandeur: 'It is from the bridges that London wears her noblest aspect – whether by night or by day ...' Even after the arrival of the London Eye in 2000, Thames-side still provides one of the best places for the public viewing of the city. As Paul Shepheard has noted, if you want to see London and do not have access to a tower, 'you go up on the hills around, five miles away; or you come down here to the Thames, where the open expanse of the river gives you wide, panoramic views'.

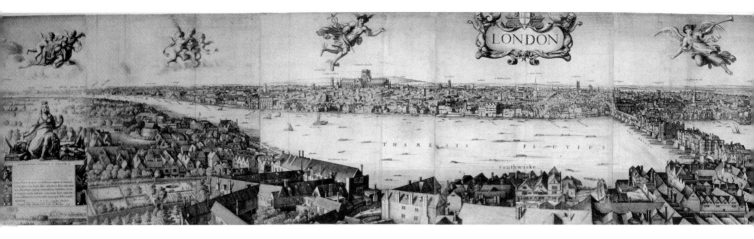

Hollar's masterpiece, his *Long View of London from Bankside*, was published in Antwerp in 1647, printed from six plates and based on drawings done in London in the early 1640s before the artist travelled to Antwerp in 1644 (fig. 1.6). This view had a predecessor in the panorama published by C. J. Visscher in 1616, which has been said to represent the City in c.1600 (fig. 1.7). Both Visscher and Hollar show the view from Whitehall to east of the Tower, and Hollar also shows a substantial amount of Southwark, although he excludes the tower of St Mary's from which the view north would have been taken. Visscher includes it, and this raises the question of perspective, the relationships between buildings, and the truth of appearances. Visscher clearly took his view from several different points, and scepticism was expressed by Scouloudi about his rather enthusiastic deployment of towers. Hollar's view is both more accurate and imbued with greater drama. For Malcolm Warner, his 'achievement lies not merely in his accuracy, however, but in the sense of power and glory that he imparts to the scene. Here the river no longer cuts a neat horizontal path across the city ...; it sweeps through on a Baroque curve, gradually swelling to reach a climactic breadth in the centre then dying away again to the right.' This is not merely the city depicted, but rather in the manner of the representation it imbues it with life.

Following his return to London in 1652, Hollar's greatest project, a map of London and Westminster with a perspective delineation of the buildings, would have measured 10 x 5 feet (3 x 1.5 metres), and would have covered about twenty-eight sheets. There seems to have been insufficient financial support for this venture, and after the Great Fire of 1666, most of his surveys and drawings would have become redundant in depicting a world which had gone rather than describing one which existed. Hollar and Francis Sandford were appointed by the king to survey the City after the fire. As well as a plan, within two and a half months Hollar had produced before and after views from Southwark based on the *Long View*. It is far easier to base a new illustration on an existing print than to resurvey entirely. Hollar's view from Lambeth was reissued in *c*.1707 with the City skyline updated to include Wren's St Paul's and numerous church towers.

These panoramas have a continuing popularity and charm, offering a prelapsarian view of a much-loved scene. But they were commercial endeavours, with the risks which are attendant upon such artistic translations. Scouloudi urges caution: notwithstanding the faith which we might place in Hollar, 'it cannot be overemphasised that it is useless to turn to the panoramic views in the hope of finding an accurate, detailed picture of the City. The general impression appears sound and the

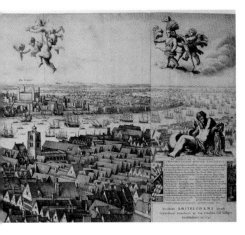

1.6 Wenceslaus Hollar,
Long View of London from Bankside, 1647
(Guildhall Library, City of London).

1.7 C. J. Visscher, panoramic view of
London, 1616, detail with St Mary Overie
(Southwark Cathedral) in the foreground
(Guildhall Library, City of London).

detail may be so, but it cannot be safely accepted without further evidence.' Some give greater confidence than others, but these are 'productions for a cheap and ready market. At the best, they can be relied upon to give a general picture, but not dependable detailed information.' Warner makes the same point: 'Historians of London are constantly disappointed by the failure of the visual documents to correspond to what they know, from more reliable sources, to have been fact.' But such historians ask too much: the making of choices militates against the idea of the absolute. These artful endeavours are distillations of reality, offering at their best a representation of a city inspired by imagination as much as by topography and built form but not tethered to either one.

All representation requires the making of choices. This is in fact implicit in the art of perspective, an art (as described by Andrea Pozzo) which 'does, with wonderful Pleasure, deceive the Eye': 'Since Perspective is but a Counterfeiting of the Truth, the Painter is not oblig'd to make it appear real when seen from *Any* part, but from *One* determinate Point only.' Pozzo's recommendation of single-point perspective, published in Rome in 1693, was 'Done into English' by John James in *c.*1707 as *Rules and Examples of Perspective Proper for Painters and Architects*, advertised as being 'after a new manner, wholly free from the confusion of occult lines'. The (relatively) new manner needed explanation, which James himself provided in his preface: 'Perspective is the Art of Delineating ... the Appearances of Objects, as seen from One determinate Point: For tho in Works of great Length, Two, Three, or more Points of Sight are sometimes made use of; yet such may more properly be said to be Several Views conjoin'd, than One Piece of Perspective.' Pozzo, the painter of the vault of Sant'Ignazio in Rome, was authoritative in his explanation of methods which were not new but had never been so clearly expressed. James's publication received the 'Approbation' of his Office of Works colleagues Wren, Vanbrugh and Hawksmoor, who judged it 'a Work that deserves Encouragement, and very proper for Instruction in that Art'.

The perspective drawing, as H. S. Goodhart-Rendel put it in 1951, has 'unrivalled powers of truth-telling [so] it can also magnificently lie'. Gavin Stamp quoted this remark and noted the need for both skill and honesty in the use of perspective by the architect presenting a design, but 'a perspective ... is never truly honest as there is no one dependable system for setting up the perspective view of a building from the plans and elevations; a convincing impression depends to a certain extent upon artist's licence ... A good perspective conforms to the way in which the spectator *thinks* a building looks.' This perception is as true for the perspective after the building as it is for the perspective based on the design: our view of buildings and topographical relationships is mediated by modes of depiction which dispel the notion of the innocent eye. Palladio's illustrations of his own buildings in the *Quattro libri dell'architettura* (1570) conditioned the eyes of a generation of British architects to perceive the flat white planes of an architecture of apparently great purity, which the robust appearance of the buildings themselves would surely have belied, yet even those who visited them in person tended to see them as if they were still flat on a page, lacking volume and divorced from context.

The Dutch School painting *London from Southwark* (Museum of London), which dates from the early 1630s, is the earliest surviving oil painting to have London (from Whitehall to the Tower) as its sole subject. It is closely related to the panoramas, showing the subject in *c*.1600, so is derived from received views and in turn influenced later prints. It also sits within the panoramic convention of compression, bringing into view buildings and riverscape to east and west which would fall outside the field of vision of an observer on top of the tower of St Mary's. It is notable that the format adopted in the painting is used for the first time, with a great expanse of sky, unlike the strip of sky in the panoramas accompanying the strip of buildings and the ribbon of river, emphasising the horizontal axis. An earlier (1620s) Flemish School *View of Greenwich* (Museum of London) shows the City on the horizon, a reference point which has remained a commonplace in views of Greenwich from the south since the seventeenth century (fig. 1.8).

1.8 View north from Greenwich Park with the National Maritime Museum, the former Royal Hospital for Seamen, and Docklands beyond; the City is visible to the west, the Millennium Dome to the east.

Outside the tradition of accurate topographical delineation but of great significance because of its maker, the *Landscape with St George and the Dragon*, painted in London by Rubens in 1629–30, was sent home by the artist into Flanders 'to remain as a monument of his abode and employment here'. It remained there for a very brief period, before being secured for the royal collection before 1635. It was hung in Whitehall Palace until the collections were dispersed after the execution of Charles I; it was subsequently reacquired for the royal collection by George IV in 1814. Rubens has given St George, the patron saint of England, the features of Charles I, and the Princess Cleodolinda, rescued from the jaws of the dragon, those of his queen, Henrietta Maria. The view of the city in the middle distance includes buildings which have been interpreted as Lambeth Palace and the tower of St Mary Overie, both of which Rubens would regularly have observed from his lodgings in York House on the north bank of the river.

The Great Fire of September 1666 fractured the contained settlement which hitherto had been visualised and depicted as the City within its walls and as much on either side of it as could be seen looking from the south. The burning of the City, a disaster beyond human control, taking on a life of its own, is an archetype as resonant as the Flood: 'Then the Lord rained upon Sodom and upon Gomorrah brimstone and fire from the Lord out of heaven' (Genesis 19:24). John Evelyn saw here 'a resemblance of Sodome, or the last day'. Pepys, in a boat on 2 September, found 'all over the Thames, with one's face in the wind you were almost burned with a shower of Firedrops'. Later, from Bankside, 'as far as we could see up the hill of the City, in a most horrid malicious bloody flame, not like the fine flame of an ordinary fire'. Two days later, 'now and then walking into the garden and saw how horridly the sky looks, all on a fire in the night, was enough to put us out of our wits; and endeed it was extremely dreadfull – for it looks just as if it was at us, and the whole heaven on fire'. Understanding fully the apocalyptic symbolism of the shocking event which he was witnessing, Pepys substituted 'heaven' for his initial 'sky' in this account. Painters made a comparable conflation, bringing together the traditions of panorama with those of apocalyptic conflagration painting, a combination given greater force in most cases by showing the fire by night; two such pictures, after Jan Griffier the Elder (Museum of London), underlined the idea by making Ludgate suggest the mouth of Hell. The consumption of the old City within the walls was significant politically as well as symbolically, representing the eradication of one of the two opposed factions (the City and Westminster) of the Civil War. In the immediate aftermath of the fire, the point of view from which London was depicted shifted, following the physical expansion westwards with the development of Lincoln's Inn Fields and Covent Garden (Walks 4 and 3) which had begun before the Fire, and its continuation afterwards with the development of St James's and Mayfair (Walk 6). From the terrace of Somerset House, artists looked east to the City or west to Westminster: the continuous panorama was fractured. The City was remade and Westminster developed. They separately presented the image of rational modernity which London was to retain for 250 years, even through the nineteenth century when its increasing labyrinthine vastness, dense atmosphere and social deprivation defied comprehension and inhibited exploration.

There was, however, at least one view which celebrated the modern London of the mid-eighteenth century with a seventeenth-century ambition of totality: *Panorama of London and Westminster from the Tower to Millbank* by Samuel and Nathaniel Buck. The river is straight, in the manner of Visscher, and bracketed by two bridges: London Bridge to the right is balanced by the new Westminster Bridge

1.9 View from the Monument with Tower Bridge (Sir John Wolfe Barry and Sir Horace Jones, 1886–94) and City Hall (Foster and Partners, 2002).

1.10 The Monument, 1671–6, with pedestal relief by C.G.Cibber, 1674.

to the left. Published in 1749, the print predates the opening in November 1750 of this new wonder of architecture and engineering. The view was taken from four points along the south bank of the river, including the tower of St Mary Overie, the height of which enabled the introduction of a perspectival element in the depiction of the scene east of London Bridge towards the Tower and beyond. Printed on five sheets, the panorama is about 13 feet (4 metres) in width and like an unrolling scroll invites a progressive reading. Nugent's smoky panorama of *London and Westminster from Millbank* (1819) by contrast has an apocalyptic sublimity, a world away in mood and artistic sensibility from the rationality of the Bucks.

The Monument (Walk 1), built to commemorate the fire and to celebrate recovery, was erected in 1671–6 to the designs of Christopher Wren and Robert Hooke close to where the fire had begun. A tall, fluted Doric column, it is surmounted by a flaming gilt urn (fig. 1.10). Details of the fire are provided in inscriptions on the pedestal, one of which, added in 1681, attributed it to 'the treachery and malice of the Popish faction … in order to the carrying on their horrid plot for extirpating the Protestant Religion and Old English Liberty and introducing Popery and Slavery'. The inscription was removed after the accession of James II in 1685, reinstated under William and Mary, and removed once more in 1830 following the passing of the law for Catholic emancipation in the previous year. François Colsoni transcribed the inscription and translated it into French in *Le Guide de Londres* (1693). He recommended climbing the spiral steps to the viewing platform, 'd'ou l'on peut voir (si le tems est bien claire) toute la Ville de Londres' (from where one can see (if the weather is clear) the whole City of London). So the point at which the fire had started, destroying the panoramic view from Southwark, became itself a viewing point. Boswell in 1763 was alarmed by both the climb and the viewpoint: 'It was horrid to find myself so monstrous a way up in the air, so far above London and all its spires. I durst not look round me. There is no real danger as there is a strong rail both on the stair and balcony. But I shuddered …' An iron cage was added to the railing around the platform in 1842 to discourage those who wished to make this their last prospect. For the more intrepid Karl Baedeker in 1900, this was the ideal spot from which to survey the traffic on the bridge and the river (fig. 1.9).

Colsoni was an observer. He noted in Edward Jerman's new Royal Exchange the four first-floor balconies facing the internal quadrangle from which the visitor could watch the crowd below. The commercial transactions on the trading floor of an exchange do not involve the display or transfer of objects – it is the interaction of the participants which provides a spectacle best described in another context by theatre

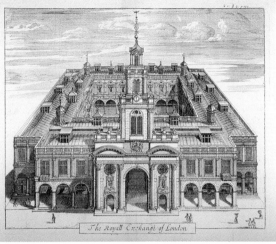

1.11 St Mary-le-Bow, Cheapside, 1670–80.

1.12 Royal Exchange, built 1667–71, burned down 1838; bird's eye view by an anonymous artist, engraving *c.*1720 (Guildhall Library, City of London).

1.13 Joseph Smith, *A Prospect of the City of London*, *c.*1710 (Guildhall Library, City of London).

director Peter Brook: 'A man walks across this empty space whilst someone else is watching him, and this is all that is needed for an act of theatre to be engaged.' The front of Jerman's Exchange was also designed with theatre in mind: two giant order aedicules with segmental pediments framed the central carriage arch, reminiscent of a stage set, above which a three-stage timber tower advertised Mammon and a resurgent post-fire City (fig. 1.12). Wren's stone tower at nearby St Mary-le-Bow (fig. 1.11) followed shortly after, to be accompanied during the closing years of the seventeenth century by a forest of towers and spires by Wren and his office, advertising God and Nation, to replace those lost in the fire (fig. 1.13) (Walk 1).

Both Wren and John Evelyn separately, within a few days of the fire (so quickly that they might have been thinking about it in theory in advance), had proposed rebuilding the City according to a new rational plan of north–south streets cut by radial routes and thoroughfares running roughly east–west. Time, political will, financing, and perhaps an entrenched view of how the City should look all militated against taking such radical steps, but some innovation was deemed necessary. It was determined that Fleet Street, Cheapside, Cornhill and 'all other eminent Streets' should be built wide enough to prevent flames spreading from one side to the other, but the most far-reaching of the post-fire rebuilding proposals was the uniformity imposed by the categorisation of houses according to site, with stipulations on height of storeys, depth of cellars and thickness of walls. Once the regulations were in place, rebuilding began in 1667, but the process was delayed by disputes in those cases where the new rules adversely affected owners of sites. Building speeded up thereafter, and in 1672 it was remarked that the handsomest part of the City

1.14 St Paul's Cathedral from Paternoster Square, with Wren's Chapter House of 1712–14, restored by Godfrey Allen, 1957, after wartime damage.

1.15 Painted Hall, former Royal Hospital for Seamen, Greenwich: the west wall of the Upper Hall, painted by Sir James Thornhill with the assistance of Dietrich Ernst Andreae, 1723–6.

had 'been rebuilt with greater magnificence since the terrible fire'. But much of this building was on the old street pattern, without the substantial vistas imagined by Evelyn and, to a still greater extent, by Wren. This was not baroque Rome: there were few long views. In these circumstances the towers of Wren's new churches were both ornaments and landmarks – practical necessities for navigating the densely built City.

The modern increase in scale in London's buildings reduces the impact of Wren's spires. We come upon them by chance and appreciate the sudden glimpse, the unexpected view. Close up, the same is true of St Paul's (fig. 1.14) (Walk 1). Rising above its surroundings until the twentieth century, this symbol of Church, State, Architecture and London was an icon from the moment of its completion. In the climax to his monumental painting in the Painted Hall at Greenwich, a celebration of constitutional monarchy, naval power and the global reach of imperial trade completed in 1726, James Thornhill depicts George I resting his arm proprietorially on a terrestrial globe as he receives the sceptre of sovereignty from Providence, and as a cornucopia of riches pours down. Behind, floating in ambiguous space, is the drum and dome of the recently completed St Paul's Cathedral (fig. 1.15). It appears again in countless later representations, as adornment to the skyline, as part of the imagery of empire or, as here, as architectural synecdoche.

St Paul's was designed to tower above its surroundings, to be seen from afar rather than from close up in its entirety. This was a heavily built-up area and the views therefore were distant. For Baedeker, 'the church is so hemmed in by streets and houses that it is difficult to find a point of view whence the colossal proportions of the building can be properly realised. The best idea of the majestic dome, allowed to be the finest known, is obtained from a distance': he recommends the view from

1.16 St Paul's Cathedral from the South Bank, with Faraday House and Baynard House.

Hampstead Heath. Two such views were to be among those later identified for special protection. Although the Heath had long been a place of resort, acknowledged by Daniel Defoe (1724–6) for its fine prospects, these had not been particularly exploited by artists. A rare view from the north, with St Paul's in the centre, was published by John Norden in c.1615, *The View of the Cittye of London from the North towards the Sowth*, but even in the nineteenth century most artists were more interested in the Heath itself than in the distant panorama. London was more frequently depicted in views from Greenwich and Blackheath, with St Paul's a distant incident in the vista. Now, as Kerry Downes has noted, 'zoning laws have set it in a kind of architectural saucer, in which heights are allowed to rise in proportion with remoteness'. Such considerations were prompted by the building of Faraday House in 1932–3, the first in the sequence of depressing telephone exchanges on Queen Victoria Street which culminated with Baynard House in 1972–9 (fig. 1.16). Faraday House, nine storeys high with square towers at each end, was allowed to go higher than the provisions of the London Building Act of the time normally permitted. Although this is not a high-rise building, it is high enough to break the cornice line between the drum and dome and the west towers of St Paul's in views from the South Bank, an aesthetic sin which now, following the regeneration of Thames-side Southwark as a place of popular recreation, is perhaps even more evident to more people than it was at the time of building.

Even though the Festival of Britain in 1951 obliged London to look south across the Thames, this was not a long view. A screen along York Road acted as a backdrop to the site while censoring the view of 'Darkest Lambeth' to the south. In fact, as Gavin Stamp has noted, the Festival of Britain looked north and east rather than south: 'back across the Thames towards Westminster and Charing Cross, as well as affording a fine prospect of the then unchallenged dome of St Paul's Cathedral to the east'. It was not the obstruction of views of the dome, but the severing by Faraday House of the connection between the component parts of the skyline of Wren's cathedral, that demonstrated the need for a comprehensible and comprehensive view of the building. The St Paul's Heights Code followed in 1937. This limits the height of developments 'so as to achieve the retention of views from certain selected viewpoints of the dome, the western towers and the main cornice line connecting them'. Without this connection we risk losing the sense of enormous scale which

Wren achieved (fig. 1.17). But although the Heights Code emphasises the cornice line, the Department of the Environment, when establishing in 1989–91 ten key views of London's most famous landmarks – St Paul's Cathedral and the Palace of Westminster, emblems of church and state – defined St Paul's as the drum, peristyle and dome, whereas Westminster was defined as the whole palace between the Clock Tower (Big Ben) and the Victoria Tower (fig. 1.18). (The ten key views for special protection are as follows: St Paul's from Primrose Hill, Parliament Hill, Kenwood, Alexandra Palace, Greenwich Park, Blackheath Point, Richmond Park (King Henry VIII's Mound) and Westminster Pier; the Palace of Westminster from Primrose Hill and Parliament Hill.)

In 1904 Niels Lund, looking west from the roof of the Royal Exchange, painted *The Heart of the Empire* (Guildhall Art Gallery) with the Mansion House in the foreground and St Paul's in the centre, the whole of the east-end cornice line and most of the upper storey visible through the smoky atmosphere (fig. 1.19). 'The Parish Church of the Empire' was celebrated in a souvenir issue of *The Times* in 1930 following the completion of restoration work made possible by the fundraising appeal conducted through the newspaper:

> *The number of small subscriptions ... is perhaps the most gratifying feature. They are practical proof that the fate of St Paul's is of heartfelt moment to thousands who cannot afford in these days to give large sums ... But we can all do something to promote the early and successful execution of what all English-speaking men and women must feel ... to be a necessary work.*

In his brilliant analysis of 'War's Greatest Picture', Brian Stater showed that Herbert Mason's heroic photograph of St Paul's in the Blitz on the night of 29 December 1940, published two days later (after some retouching) in the *Daily Mail*, did not create a new identity for the cathedral but reinforced one which already existed (fig. 1.20). The dome and west towers, standing proud above the smoke which engulfs the foreground warehouses, are depicted as features of a transient exceptional reality which is nevertheless rooted in the everyday: here is where people live, work and worship, and this is where they are being attacked. The burning warehouses constituted a further threat to the cathedral. As a building without a significant precinct, the neighbouring buildings were too close, as recorded in *Fire over London*:

1.17 St Paul's Cathedral from the South Bank.

1.18 The Palace of Westminster (Houses of Parliament) from the South Bank at Lambeth.

1.19 Niels Lund, *The Heart of the Empire*, 1904 (Guildhall Art Gallery, City of London).

1.20 St Paul's Cathedral in the Blitz, 29 December 1940, photographed by Herbert Mason, *Daily Mail*.

'flames reached out across the street, licking close to the venerable stone. Firemen on the ground and on ladders worked furiously. Hour after hour they slaved to hurl back that advancing wall of fire. But hurl it back they did, and ... St Paul's was saved.'

The St Paul's which 'stood as a symbol of the spirit of London', part of the image of England, was not an invention by Mason but a representation of an idea of safety and survival, set amidst the ordinary, which already existed and had done so since at least the First World War when it was used as an air-raid shelter. The large number of small subscriptions in 1925 to the restoration fund, and the number of people who served on the Watch during the Blitz of the Second World War, both testified to the need to protect a building which was not only the greatest work of architecture by England's greatest architect, but for which people had a warm and enduring attachment. It may seem surprising that the pragmatic, rational Wren should have produced such an emotional effect, but these sentiments are not mutually exclusive. As Wren himself wrote in his first *'Tract' on Architecture*: 'Architecture has its political Use; publick Buildings being the Ornament of a Country; it establishes a Nation, draws People and Commerce; makes the People love their native Country, which Passion is the Original of all great Actions in a Common-wealth.'

The Blitz at the end of December 1940 brought 'scenes unparalleled since the days of Pepys'. This was a new 'Great Fire of the City of London', intended to bring total destruction to a city which in the view of Hitler, according to W. G. Sebald, was so densely built that 'one fire alone would be enough to destroy the whole city'. Like the first Great Fire, the Blitz offered the possibility for renewal in the congested central areas, not just in London but in all those cities which had been bombed. In illustrating the damage that was done to significant buildings in 1940–1, J. M. Richards noted the peculiarly self-contained nature of the architecture of destruction, which 'not only possesses an aesthetic peculiar to itself, it contrives its effects out of its own range of raw materials'. It was this aesthetic which led artists to the depiction of the landscape of ruins in the Second World War. Cyril Farey, who was on St Paul's Watch duty in 1941, recorded the bombed City and the area around St Paul's in at least fourteen watercolour perspectives in 1942–4, which included a proposal for a new post-war western approach to the cathedral. He waited until the sites had been cleared of rubble in order to present rational views of the consequences of irrational actions. David Bomberg was altogether more dramatic in approach. His magnificent

Evening in the City of London (Museum of London), painted from the tower of St Mary-le-Bow in 1944, has St Paul's as the dominant centrepiece of a blasted panorama of burned-out buildings, still glowing, running from the river to Cheapside and beyond. If the artist's dreams had been fulfilled, this would have been just one part of a huge painted panorama of the whole of blitzed London, rivalling Cecil Brown's bird's-eye *A Prospect of the City of London from the South East* (1945) and Lawrence Wright's 360-degree panorama from the dome of St Paul's (1948).

Bird's-eye views, a commonplace imaginative conceit of early panoramas, were to gain a more tangible reality through the advent of depiction from balloons, a particularly popular technique in nineteenth-century France where Nadar's photography of Paris from a balloon, 'elevating photography to the height of art', was celebrated in a lithograph by Honoré Daumier in 1862. In 1811, Mr Sadler had piloted a balloon from Hackney to Tilbury, an exceptional event inspiring a commemorative print. Such excursions were to become more purposeful. An 1830s 'Aeronautical View' of London published by Robert Havell appears to have been taken from a position above the present Tower Bridge. This print perhaps was a reworking of the so-called 'Rhinebeck' panorama of *c.*1810 (Museum of London), which it has been suggested was the design for an entertainment panorama that, colossally enlarged, would have given the viewer the illusion of being in the scene. Louis-Jules Arnout's *Excursions aériennes*, made in *c.*1850–60, included a view centred on Trafalgar Square and one which took an elevated view from Greenwich Park looking towards London (fig. 1.21). W. L. Wyllie and H. W. Brewer's balloon view of London and Westminster in 1884 showed Westminster Abbey and the Houses of Parliament in the foreground, with the river and docklands stretching hazily towards the skyline. Like the seventeenth-century panoramas, such views used earlier depictions to enhance observation from nature.

The 'Rhinebeck' panorama gave prominence to working London, with shipping filling the Pool of London (between London Bridge and Tower Bridge). This commercial activity was to become one of the attractions of a visit to the capital, with guidebooks, including Baedeker, recommending a visit to St Katherine's and London Docks: 'Nothing will convey to the stranger a better idea of the vast activity and stupendous wealth of London than a visit to these warehouses, filled to overflowing with interminable stores of every kind of foreign and colonial products; to these enormous vaults, with their apparently inexhaustible quantities of wine; and to these extensive quays and landing-stages, cumbered with huge stacks of hides, heaps of bales, and long rows of casks' (fig. 1.22).

1.21 Louis-Jules Arnout, view of Greenwich Park and the River Thames, drawn after nature from a balloon and published *c.*1850–60 (English Heritage, National Monuments Record).

1.22 The West India Docks, engraved 1815 after a drawing by J. Neale and published in J. Norris Brewer, *London and Middlesex*, vol. IV, London 1816.

The nineteenth-century emphasis on working London and its worldwide trade, emphasised by Jerrold in *London: A Pilgrimage* (1872), gradually became one of the features by which the city was internationally known and depicted: 'London wears a dismal exterior to the eye of the foreigner, because all London is hard at work.' Certainly by 1906–7, when André Derain made three visits in the space of ten months, it was to the Pool of London that he was drawn, together with such other sites of modernity as the Victoria Embankment (a new road built in the 1860s with modern sewage and drainage systems beneath and therefore the acme of speed and modernity), the Hungerford Bridge (completed in 1864 to bring trains into Charing Cross), and the Palace of Westminster. Here he competed with Monet, who had exhibited thirty-seven canvases in Paris in 1904. These comprised groups of paintings of three views across the Thames in different conditions of light and weather: two sequences from the Savoy Hotel, looking downstream over Waterloo Bridge and upstream over Hungerford Bridge to the Palace of Westminster, and one from St Thomas's Hospital towards the Palace of Westminster. Derain admired Monet but wanted to go beyond the 'impression' to what is 'fixed, eternal, complex'. In approaching sites which were by this time part of London's stock imagery, but bringing to the subject a style described by John House as 'aggressively experimental', Derain produced twenty-nine canvases which are among the greatest of London paintings. These include views of both banks of the river, with 'no differentiation in colour or technique between the old and the new, the ramshackle and the monumental; all are seemingly treated with the same visual engagement and relish'. Derain's output from the London visits included at least six paintings of the Palace of Westminster, two of Hungerford Bridge, and two of the Victoria Embankment. Other Thames-side views included Waterloo, Blackfriars and London Bridges; the Pool of London looking east towards Tower Bridge; and one of St Paul's Cathedral from the South Bank, a brilliant evocation in non-naturalistic colour on the only canvas to use a vertical format (fig. 1.23). In these London paintings, Derain fulfilled his aim of going beyond Monet towards something fixed and eternal, and also to make something other than coloured photographs. The tension achieved in these superb paintings between the topographical and the pictorial is made all the more valuable by the brief duration of the fleeting 'Fauve moment' and the small number of major works which were produced at its high point.

Derain's St Paul's has an imminence and scale which would be denied to the photographer. Taking an elevated viewpoint, he has narrowed the River Thames to the width of the River Seine, reduced the sky and created a powerful image of a scene which we recognise instantly but could never see in precisely the same way. For Derain, just as for Hollar, the artistic conventions allow scope for adjustments of scale in response to significance. Derain's arrangement of vertically stacked horizontals appears to bring the cathedral nearer to our viewpoint. It is in this pressing imminence of his images, bringing the components to the surface of the picture plane, that Derain differs from those previous artists who imposed distance and perspective, and indeed exaggerated them in the interests of imparting a sense of scale and extent to views of a city which is for the most part constrained by the absence of long views. When Thomas Shotter Boys published his *Original Views of London As It Is* in 1842, he followed the conventions established by earlier view-makers in taking a wide-angle view of the foreground, putting distance between the point of depiction and the scene depicted which often, like a Renaissance stage set, extended back into improbably deep space. This method translated readily in the mid-nine-

1.23 André Derain, *St Paul's Cathedral seen from the Thames*, 1906–7 (The Minneapolis Institute of Arts, Bequest of Putnam Dana McMillan).

teenth century into the new technique of photography. Commercial photographers sought to produce recognisable, and therefore saleable, images which were bound by the existing conventions and expectations of topographical depiction, designed to satisfy a market that saw what it expected to see. Derain's paintings, particularly his St Paul's, triumphantly subverted such expectations.

Our mode of seeing is now predominantly established by the photographic image, although from the early days of photography doubts have been raised about its veracity, particularly in relation to the hand-drawn image. John Ruskin's view, expressed in 1870 and quoted by Aaron Scharf, that 'photographs supersede no single quality nor use of fine art', was followed in 1891 by Joseph Pennell's comparison of drawings and photographs of English cathedrals: 'I do not mean to say decidedly that this photographic view is incorrect. It is quite possible that it is literally correct. But artistically it is absurd. At any rate, if it is correct, it destroys all feeling of size, impressiveness and dignity.' Aside from any potential artistic shortcomings in the failure of photography to capture grandeur, for Susan Sontag 'a photograph passes for incontrovertible proof that a given thing happened'; there is a 'presumption of veracity' that gives authority. Since 'reality has always been interpreted through the reports given by images', we are habituated towards the acceptance of the photographic image as a truthful transcription of objects and events – notwithstanding the evidence to the contrary which digital manipulation now more readily allows, and disregarding our knowledge of the medium as a tool of politics, propaganda and surveillance capable of malign application and presentation.

Despite doubts which we might harbour about the veracity of the image, our knowledge of buildings around the world now comes to us through photography, just as for the stay-at-home British architects in the seventeenth and eighteenth centuries it came through engravings of things too remote or politically inaccessible to visit. Two-dimensional images have been eloquently characterised by Robin Evans as the familiar 'flat versions of embodied events', 'postcards from reality' which 'elicit the idea of an object which could stand in their place'. This is not to say that they substitute for the object itself – no amount of photography prepares us for the shock of seeing Michelangelo's David for the first time – but that they provide a way of thinking about an object which is out of reach spatially or temporally. The enormous proliferation of images in the years since the development of an international print culture in the sixteenth and seventeenth centuries, and the exponential increase in the availability and dissemination of images through the media explosion of the later twentieth century, serve not just to report phenomena but inspire their creation and profoundly influence the ways in which we view them, to the extent that the innocent eye, if ever it existed, certainly no longer does so. Just as the panorama producers of the seventeenth century relied substantially on previous images rather than on direct observation, so do we have a world view which is mediated by photography to the extent that when we confront the view head-on, we often think of it in terms determined by the hegemony of photographic conventions and image-framing. It was this tyranny of the established mode of viewing which Cubism sought to overturn in the early twentieth century. But outside dreams and hallucinogens, and notwithstanding the work of Robert Delaunay, we do not generally take a cubist view of the topography of the city.

Our view of the city in the twentieth century has been given a further dimension by the aeroplane, by direct views from it and by aerial photography. Flight not only presents sensory possibilities but as an idea acts as a spur to the imagination.

John Summerson invited readers of *Georgian London* to take the view of the evolving landscape from the air: 'I ask you to imagine yourself suspended a mile above London; and to imagine yourself staying up there for a period of time proportional to two centuries, with the years speeding past at one a second.' The ancient dream of flying above the earth and enjoying a view hitherto attained only by God, or by Satan on his high mountain from which he 'shewed unto him all the kingdoms of the world in a moment of time' (Luke 4:5), initially was reflected in the notional bird's-eye view – a feat of the imagination – and then by the balloon, the preserve of the intrepid few. The aeroplane made such views commonplace, and the idea of the total vision became a seductive possibility. The aeroplane became a ubiquitous signifier of modernity, making an appearance in Le Corbusier's drawing of *A Contemporary City for Three Million Inhabitants* (1922), which included a railway station below and an aircraft runway on top, and in Fritz Lang's film *Metropolis* (1926–7), flying between the railway tracks and roads in the sky between the towers of the dystopian futuristic city. Those who followed the Futurists in celebrating the beauty of speed in a racing car 'more beautiful than the Victory of Samothrace' could, by the 1930s, transfer their allegiance to something even faster. Le Corbusier recognised that the aeroplane allowed us to see that which previously could only be imagined: 'The eye now sees in substance what the mind formerly could only subjectively conceive.' As a result, it is tempting to visualise from the air the need for change and rebuilding, 'for the bird's-eye view has enabled us to see our cities ... and the sight is not good ... we now have proof, recorded on the photographic plate, of the rightness of our desire to alter methods of architecture and town-planning.' In the same year as Le Corbusier's publication of *Aircraft*, 1935, Walter Gropius made a more modest observation: 'With the development of air transport the architect will have to pay as much attention to the bird's eye perspective of his houses as to their elevations ... Seen from the skies, the [flat-roofed] leafy house-tops of the cities of the future will look like endless chains of hanging gardens.'

The call to order of early modernism, explicit in Le Corbusier and implicit in Gropius, has had a significant effect on how professional viewers and planners see the city, encouraging the arrogance of technological man. For Melville Branch, 'aerial photography provides the visualization of the three-dimensional reality of the city which can be acquired in no other way ... and which is essential for urban analysis ... Even when one examines a city in perspective from a tall building or nearby hilltop, most of the street pattern and many other features are hidden from view by intervening structures and terrain.' Branch is arguing for the use of vertical air photographs taken from directly above the object. These tend to be incomprehensible to the uninitiated, providing pattern without meaning. Even vertical photographs of those buildings with which we count ourselves most familiar – our house, our place of work – are very difficult to recognise on Google Earth, because the vertical view, unlike the oblique, is devoid of the recognisable context with which we are familiar as pedestrians. Branch acknowledges that oblique photographs are more readily understood, but such perspectives 'cannot be assembled to form the continuous representation readily accomplished with vertical photographs'. This is a plea to leave planning to the professionals, trained in photographic analysis, distanced from the everyday reality of the streets and not distracted by the changes in scale from foreground to middleground to background – those changes which the panorama makers used to make views that made up in apparent realism what they might have lacked in reality. The problem in viewing London is one of size; for Patrick Geddes in 1915 it had become polypus rather than octopus, 'a vast irregular

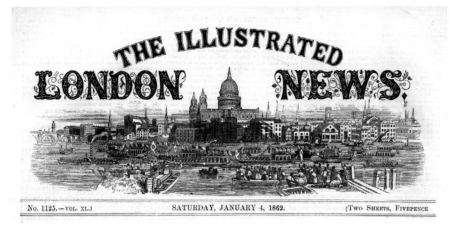

1.24 *The Illustrated London News*, masthead, 4 January 1862.

growth without previous parallel in the world of life'. Following Aristotle in the desire for a synoptic vision, he urged a seeing of the city dependent upon large views both abstract and concrete.

The view from the air is seductive because we believe that it will offer the possibility of the synoptic all-powerful vision favoured by an omniscient God, city planners and the wagers of war. Implicit in the view from the air is the prospect of totalitarianism. But from the window seat, even in the privileged purlieus of business class, it is fragments we see rather than the whole. As the plane circles above central London to align itself for the landing into the wind at Heathrow, we identify the frustrated ox-bow lake of the River Thames as it flows round the Isle of Dogs. We recognise this, and very little else, since it has both of the required elements for recognition of London combined, the river and a comprehensible pattern. The extraordinary importance of the river in the identification of London in the view from the air emphasises its centrality to the Londoner in perceiving and imagining the city. This centrality had been lost through years of neglect of both the river and its banks until recent regeneration began to see it as a venue rather than a barrier. We might wonder whether a more comprehensive image of the city in its entirety is available to those with a better view – from the flight deck. It is, but although pilots recognise the river, they do not use it for purposes of navigation, for which it is incidental. It is a subliminal view for contemporary pilots who, just like Antoine de Saint-Exupéry in 1939, 'are shut up in what might be a laboratory. They are obedient to the play of dial-hands, not to the unrolling of the landscape.' Pilots coming into London Heathrow follow flight maps with prescribed routes determined long in advance and follow instructions from air traffic control concerning distance and height as they circle around the four stacking points waiting for the instruction to break out of the circle and come in to land. Visual cues are not generally required in this process – pilots will only inform passengers of what is on the ground if they have nothing else to do – although Wayne Attoe relays an alarming comment from a pilot landing at Chicago O'Hare on a cloudy day who was able to orientate himself on sighting the Sears Tower.

Although modes of depiction and vantage points for that depiction have changed considerably since Wenceslaus Hollar stood on top of a church tower and drew the panorama of London in front of him, it is doubtful whether a better method of making an accurate impression has been developed in the subsequent three and a half centuries: we need look no further than the masthead of the *Illustrated London News* (first published in 1842) to grasp its emblematic significance (fig. 1.24). In order to understand what we see, we need context. In the case

1.25 View west from Shakespeare Tower, Barbican, showing Lauderdale Tower.

of London we need the river or the skyline: Hollar had both. It is from an elevated position that we can recognise the relationships between buildings, but the elevation must not be so high that we cease to understand the context. Our view of London, which has long been far too big to be comprehensible, will necessarily be an agglomeration of fragments. It was perhaps perceived as such even as early as 1666 when the formal replanning of the City was mooted and rejected after the Great Fire. Certainly Boswell, a century later, had difficulty in apprehending the whole when, rather than viewing St Paul's from a distance, he attempted the reverse. From the leads of the cathedral, he 'had the immense prospect of London and its environs'. But, 'London gave me no great idea. I just saw a prodigious group of tiled roofs and narrow lanes operating here and there, for the streets and beauty of the buildings cannot be observed on account of the distance', although the Thames and the hills of Hampstead and Highgate 'looked very fine'.

No user of London can possibly have a comprehensive overview of an essentially amorphous growth, but everyone has reference points as they navigate, so how we picture London becomes a portmanteau of images and impressions enabling the making of a mental map of landmarks. Taxi drivers do not imagine the whole, but drive from point to point as if joining up the dots. However, the cityscape is not just buildings and spaces; it is also the expression of collective activities and attainments. Comprehensive replanning destroys such spatial relationships and buries collective memory. It is paradoxical perhaps that it was the comprehensive rebuilding of the Barbican after the destruction of the Second World War which enables us now to enjoy the views from the thirty-sixth floor of Shakespeare Tower and assemble the fragments into a recognisable image of how London looks (fig. 1.25 and p. 18). The image we make will have a great deal in common with that of the panorama makers of the seventeenth century who came close to replicating the optical experience in perspectival terms, developing both impetus and method for viewing the city and in so doing providing the key to satisfying the physiological and psychological needs of our eyes.

Chapter 2 THE LONDON HOUSE

London house building since the seventeenth century has come in waves according to the demand and the financial resources available. The periods of most prolific house building resulted in two types which came at different times to dominate London's residential building: the 'Georgian' terrace and the suburban semi-detached house. Both these types came about because they satisfied all the players in the housing market of their day, and except for blocks of flats – to be considered in the next chapter – these two housing types continue to dominate the London domestic experience.

Medieval London was largely a timber-framed city, with nonetheless a number of substantial stone buildings, usually of ecclesiastical origin. Timber houses were very easily extended either out to the side or up through the roof, and one of the characteristics of the more densely inhabited areas of the City of London was the plethora of courts behind the street fronts, where house extensions gradually absorbed nearly all the available space, creating a labyrinth of passages. Extensions to the fronts of the houses appeared in the form of jettied floors beyond the ground-floor building line, which brought the houses closer together across the street as the number of floors increased (fig. 2.1).

London in the seventeenth century was still a medieval city clustered around its cathedral. Such 'modern' developments as there were occurred outside the city walls to the west, between the Cities of London and Westminster. The Strand, linking the two, had been the location since the Middle Ages of grand houses such as Arundel and Somerset Houses, but now new developments were making an appearance close to these ambitious properties, just at the time that their influence was fading. One of the first new schemes was the square in Covent Garden (from 1629) developed by the Earl of Bedford to designs by Inigo Jones (Walk 3). The model adopted was reminiscent of Continental custom where a continuous brick façade was regularly arranged with an arcaded loggia at ground level, while each house had its own flexible distribution of rooms. The houses were intended for a wealthy clientele, and the square continued to attract wealth until the area became the locale of theatres and coffee houses in the eighteenth century, when a more dubious population moved in. What remains of this influential development is a nineteenth-century rebuilding of the north side of the square, which nonetheless gives an idea of the classical discipline applied to the domestic façade.

Before housing could be built in the West End on a large scale, there had to develop a system of finance which would ensure sufficient profit for landowners and developers. The large landowners, such as the Earl of Bedford, depended on rents for their wealth, much of it from agricultural land, but it was indifferent to them whether their rent came in respect of agriculture or houses. The leasing systems whereby the owner gave someone else the use of the land for a given period on receipt of a sum of money were based on an agricultural model. This model needed only slight adjustments to turn it into a useful tool for the housing developer. In most cases the leases were extended to 60 or 99 years, and the ground rent was payable annually in small amounts. The builder would take a lease on building plots, erect the houses, and sell these on together with the lease. At the end of the lease, whoever was the leaseholder would surrender the property to the ground landlord, together with any buildings. The landowner could then decide what to do with the buildings: renew the lease or redevelop the property. Whatever he did, he could not lose. The builder, on the other hand, could begin building his houses without having to acquire the land, a substantial cost for any development. He could also use the building lease of the land to borrow the necessary cash to start building. Once the house was up, the builder sold it, often to someone who would let it as an investment. Finally, there was the occupier, who would usually rent the house, even if wealthy.

During the seventeenth century, West End development was linked with a number of developers such as Lord St Albans at St James's Square (1665) and Nicholas Barbon, who worked on houses in the Strand, the Temple, and Red Lion and Queen Squares (fig. 2.2). Each of Barbon's houses was allotted a plot with a narrow fixed frontage of no more than 20 feet (6 metres) to the street or square; the houses shared a party wall, and the shell was built of brick, although much of the interior continued to be constructed in wood. These were substantial houses, consisting of a basement and three or four upper floors, often with an attic. However, since the house was confined within brick party walls on a narrow site, it tended to consist of just two rooms per floor, with an entrance passage and staircase leading to the upper rooms. On the first floor there would be at least one room of some elegance, with the ground floor used for a parlour, while the bedrooms were found on the upper floors. Even if these houses originally were intended for the occupation of one household, they were flexible enough to be let as apartments, or even single rooms if necessary.

Externally the houses were generally built in dark red or purple brick, with fine red bricks around the windows, whose wooden frames were still flush with the walls. A heavy wooden cornice topped the wall, and, above, the roof still retained a steep pitch (fig. 2.3). Decoration was reserved for the door-case, which was often elaborately carved with a hood, sometimes in the form of a shell as found in Nos 11 and 12 Kensington Square, 1700 (Walk 9). Although the façades were much more uniform than the timber-framed houses of the immediate past, they still retained a variety of individual characteristics.

It took some time before the leasehold system was mature enough to attract others than the pioneers, such as Barbon, and guarantee a profit. In the meantime, the event occurred which is often seen as the launch of 'modern' London, the Great Fire of 1666. As a result of the fire which burned for four days in September 1666, much of the City of London had to be rebuilt. While the City merchants tended to be conservative in their reconstruction, the fire ensured that speculative building carried on at an even brisker rate in the West End, and layouts assumed a more regular street pattern.

In his *Autobiography* (1887), Roger North, the seventeenth-century lawyer and architectural critic, commented that Barbon's houses were intended for families and were not the houses of the great. There were palatial houses built along Piccadilly such as Clarendon, Burlington and Devonshire Houses, but what was distinctive about the West End developments was their homogeneous character, especially as the eighteenth century progressed and the fashion for unified streets and squares took hold (fig. 2.4). Grosvenor Square (1727) (Walk 6) introduced a terrace of individual houses pulled together into one façade by a central colonnade and pediment. While the houses continued the basic interior arrangement developed by the likes of Barbon, the exterior was made to adhere to an overall aesthetic, which was reinforced by the introduction of the Palladian schema. London stock bricks of a greyish yellow were favoured over the previous reddish brown, and rusticated plaster work on the ground floor represented the basement of the Palladian villa. This emphasised the *piano nobile* or first floor with its elongated windows, while smaller windows in the upper floors, and a parapet hiding any pitch to the roof, completed the ensemble. In order to ensure these external characteristics it was necessary that there be some overall control over the building, and this usually came about when there was one landlord of an extensive estate who employed someone to oversee the building, as was the case in Bedford Square, 1775–86 (see p.13) (Walk 3). Here the Bedford estate seems to have entrusted the overall control of the development to the builders Robert Grews and William Scott, and they were able to ensure that the façades followed a uniform scheme. Rendered and pedimented central sections on each of the four sides of the square lent a palatial scale to the whole, but each door was provided with an identical surround of vermiculated blocking and keystone bearing a head in Coade stone. Bedford Square was occupied from the 1780s by the new professional middle class, composed of lawyers in government employ, members of the newly respected medical profession, and successful merchants and bankers. Although there was nothing about these houses to indicate excessive consumption, they were large and all would require significant resources to equip and run.

Robert Adam, the eminent classical architect, contributed to the sophistication of London domestic architecture through his designs for elegant town houses for individual clients, such as Chandos House (1769–71) for the third duke (fig. 2.6) (Walk 6). Adam and his brothers also engaged in housing developments in nearby Portland Place (1776) and the Adelphi (1768–72). The latter, built on the river side of the Strand, was especially ambitious, combining superior housing with commerce, by attempting to persuade the government's Ordnance Department to rent the vaults giving onto the river. However, that part of the scheme fell through, and the location between the river and the Strand could not compete with more open sites further west for desirable residential property. In the nineteenth century the Adelphi became a favourite location for chambers of professionals such as lawyers and architects, and could be said to have been more successful as office develop-

ment than housing, although this made it vulnerable in the twentieth century when much of it was replaced by new office buildings.

The sober exterior of the London house of this period, as exemplified by Lichfield House (1764–6) (fig. 2.7) in St James's Square, often belied the rich rococo style within. The rococo music room from nearby Norfolk House (1748–56), now demolished, is a fine example of such interiors and is preserved in the Victoria and Albert Museum. The art of plaster replaced wood carving as the main element of decoration, and examples are still to be found in Portland Place and Bedford Square. The Adam brothers evolved a neoclassical decorative schema and a mode of production which they employed in their bespoke houses such as Home House in Portman Square (1773–6) and in their speculative ventures (fig. 2.5) (Walk 6). Greater sophistication in interior decoration coincided with a growth in domestic consumer goods. Fine furniture, linen, china and silver were increasingly in demand, not just among the rich but also among the middle classes. The increased consumption of material goods drove the economy as much as did the agricultural revolution and the improvements in manufacture for export, and the location for most of these goods was to be found in the house.

The production of consumer goods had a direct influence on house production in other parts of the capital, since the consumption of the wealthy stimulated many types of manufacture, and these migrated to specific areas of the city. To the north-

2.8 King's Bench Walk, Temple, *c.*1670.

2.9 Fournier Street, Spitalfields, *c.*1725.

2.10 Church Row, Hampstead, 1713–30.

2.11 Cumberland Terrace, Regent's Park, John Nash, 1826–7.

east around Spitalfields there grew up a very active silk weaving trade, especially when the Huguenots arrived from France after 1685. Immediately to the north of the City in Clerkenwell, metal trades were to be found, while along the river wharves, warehouses and boat-building ensured a movement ever east. House building took place along with the expansion of manufacture and trade, but on a more modest scale to that which was going on in the western suburbs.

London grew without an overall plan, and it was the conjunction of interests among landowners, developers, builders and householders which directed housing production in the capital. The dispersal of housing of this period can be frustrating when looking for still existing examples, of which there are a surprising number. Understandably, little remains in the City of London where successive rebuildings have carried most domestic examples away, although Wardrobe Place (*c.*1714) close to St Paul's is an instructive hybrid type of domestic and commercial architecture (see p. 97). There are still West End examples around St James's and Piccadilly as

well as in Soho and Mayfair, and the Inns of Court retain some good examples
(fig. 2.8). Queen Anne's Gate (1704–5) in Victoria is an exceptional remnant. To the
east, Spitalfields is probably the most satisfying location for complete streets of eighteenth-century houses, for example Elder, Fournier and Princelet Streets from the
1720s (fig. 2.9) (Walk 7), while some remain in Mile End and Deptford, especially
Albury Street (1706). But there are also examples in what we would still consider
outer areas, where the urbane terrace would have seemed to be an export from the
modernising city. Church Row, Hampstead (1713–30) (Walk 10), Maids of Honour
Row, Richmond (1724), and Croom's Hill, Greenwich (1721) (Walk 12), are all fine
examples (fig. 2.10). These scattered but complete residential terraces, which were
separated by still existing countryside, emphasise the extent of Greater London even
in the eighteenth century.

An exception to the haphazard building of much of London's housing was the
development of Regent's Park (1811 onwards) and the processional route from
there to Carlton House Terrace on the edge of St James's Park, laid out by the ever
inventive John Nash. The Adams' development in Portland Place formed a part of
the processional route, but the most striking element in the development of Regent's
Park was the building of high-class housing within its borders. James Burton produced a scheme which would entail building picturesque villas throughout the park
as well as the terraces along its edge. In the end the villas were largely dropped from
the scheme, but the terraces remained, and they were unlike any terraces yet seen
in London. Instead of the rather discreet Palladian proportions, the Regent's Park
terraces replicated a vision of Roman splendour executed in London stock brick and
plaster (fig. 2.11). Yet despite the palatial proportions of the terraces and the monumental plaster details, they consisted of individual terraced houses, each with its
own front door and shared party walls.

The nineteenth century saw the great rebuilding of the City of London, so that
by the end of the century it was almost entirely commercial in character, and the
expansion of the rest of the capital was far beyond anything anyone could have
imagined a century before. The financial systems devised to build swiftly at a profit

had become established as accepted practice, with the result that large tracts of land could be taken in hand and developed with new terraces in a very short space of time. The London house retained its basic arrangement, and this led to a greater degree of standardisation, which in turn brought down prices and rates of time for building. The wealth generated by the City through the movement of goods in and out of the country and the movement of money around the world provided the basis for a growing middle class with aspirations beyond their parents. A house with its own front door was preferable to rooms above a shop or office (fig. 2.12).

During the 1840s there was still a shortage of moderate sized houses, but this was to change with the introduction of the omnibus. Cheap and convenient, the omnibus opened up a hinterland beyond the central districts of the city for residential purposes. London had long been surrounded by functional suburbs where much of its food was produced. This agricultural land was cheaper than inner areas near to the commercial centre, but it was just too far to make commuting by foot really practical, despite the distances habitually walked by people in the nineteenth century. The introduction of the omnibus around 1830 meant that cheap agricultural land on the edge of the city could be turned into houses for which there was a ready market. Parishes such as Hackney, Islington and St Pancras in the north and Camberwell in the south were quickly in the throes of a house-building boom. Houses came to be considered a good investment – 'safe as houses', as the saying goes – and this led to money being available for building and buying houses.

Bricks were frequently made on the site and sold by the developer to the prospective builders, leading to London's terraces being built of the same clay as lay beneath their foundations. The excess ground from the foundations was also used to build up the roads between the houses, so that at the front the basements were below street level behind a small area, while at the rear they opened directly onto the garden or yard. In any development of a number of streets, local builders would undertake a few houses, which they might build to carcass stage, leaving the buyer then to complete the fitting out of the houses (fig. 2.13). Houses were bought for the most part by rentiers intent on an income from rents, which was the main type of tenancy. In the better parts of town, tenants would take a house on a yearly lease, while others were taken for periods of a quarter, month or week. The rents were often collected by an agent managing the property for absentee landlords, who might be anyone from a large property holder to spinsters living in modest retirement on the south coast. Houses were often seen as a good investment by trustees of widows and orphans. This worked well when the houses were new, but as time went on and the properties needed upgrading, the capital was often not available, with the result that they lost value.

During much of the nineteenth century, the London terrace continued to dominate as the preferred housing type, satisfying householders by its flexible form. Although the terraced house in plan was similar throughout London, it came in a variety of sizes from the very large Kensington house (fig. 2.14) (Walk 9) to the very modest two- or three-storey houses in the northern and eastern suburbs (fig. 2.15) (Walk 11). Despite the small dimensions of a three-storey house, it was still possible for a middle-class family to maintain separate living, eating and sleeping spaces, and to ensure that a live-in servant was accommodated somewhere on the premises. On the other hand, if times were hard, the house allowed middle-class families to take in lodgers, since all the rooms opened off the stair, enabling the family to maintain its privacy.

Multi-occupation is often seen as a failure of a house to maintain its status as a single household dwelling, but it is likely that many London terraces were multi-occupied either from the beginning or very soon after building. Again, the form of the house lent itself to multi-occupation since each floor could be more or less self-contained, and because all the rooms had a door to the corridor or stair, it was possible to rent out the house room by room. For example, in Barnsbury, a new suburb in Islington built from the 1830s, a study of the census returns from 1841 to 1891 demonstrates that the smaller houses in the south of Barnsbury quickly

became overcrowded. In five houses in Edward Street, the average number of persons per house increased from 6 to 15 over the fifty years. On the other hand, in Barnsbury Park (Walk 8) with a low incidence of multi-occupation, the average number of inhabitants per house went down over the same period from 8 to 7. Once an area gained the reputation for multi-occupation, this was difficult to shift, as the houses attracted people who needed to share. However, in contrast, Barnsbury Park continued to demonstrate middle-class characteristics with a low level of sharing and a relatively high number of servants.

Since the London terrace was such a homogeneous type wherever it was found, status depended on size and location. The large houses erected by the nineteenth-century builder Thomas Cubitt in Bloomsbury, Belgravia and Pimlico continued to provide the wealthy with appropriate accommodation, whether they came to London just for the social season or remained all the year round. But whereas Mayfair and the West End continued to maintain status, other areas that had started off as high-class housing were subject to changes in fashion. One change in taste that became more evident as the nineteenth century progressed was the preference for houses of 'character' (fig. 2.16).

During the nineteenth century, architectural taste widened to include many more historical styles besides the classical. Premium was placed on the picturesque and the idiosyncratic, particularly in private building where the householder increasingly wanted to mark his individuality. As residential London spread, it became more difficult to determine status through location, and people looked to the surface decoration of their houses to signal their wealth and personal taste. Gloucester Crescent, Camden Town (c.1845–50), is an example of the picturesque where, although built in London stock bricks, the composition sports belvederes of the Italianate style, supposedly reminiscent of the vernacular of the Italian Lakes (fig. 2.17). The most successful break with the standard London terrace emerged in the work of architects exploring the 'English freestyle' in the last quarter of the century. After an obsession with historical styles, architects increasingly turned their attention to what was identified as vernacular architecture, and developed for

2.16 Charles Street, Mayfair, eighteenth and nineteenth centuries.

2.17 Gloucester Crescent, Camden, c.1845–50.

2.18 No 35 Glebe Place, Chelsea, Philip Webb, 1868–71.

2.19 Swan House, 17 Chelsea Embankment, R. Norman Shaw, 1875–7.

2.20 Collingham Gardens, Ernest George and Harold Peto, 1883–8.

themselves a style based on an eclectic collection of elements from domestic English building of the previous two hundred years. Richard Norman Shaw is considered as one of the most innovative of these architects, and was responsible for some distinguished examples of town houses in Queen's Gate, Chelsea Embankment and Cadogan Square (fig. 2.19). As well as inventive interior planning, Shaw employed asymmetrical façades using materials not seen since the eighteenth century: that is, red brick, exposed wooden window frames, small-paned sash windows and distinctive Dutch gables. The new style was referred to rather arbitrarily as 'Queen Anne', but it could be said to refer to a period around 1700 when classical details from the Continent were being assimilated into traditional building materials.

Contemporary architects engaged in similar work in London were R. W. Edis and E. W. Godwin in Tite Street, Philip Webb in Palace Green and Glebe Place, Chelsea (fig. 2.18) (Walk 9), and J. J. Stevenson, who designed the Red House in Bayswater (demolished) and also speculative terraces in Cadogan Square and Kensington Court (Walk 9), using the new picturesque Queen Anne style. Some of the most extreme houses in the eclectic style are to be found in Collingham and Harrington Gardens (1880–8), where Ernest George and Harold Peto produced very large town houses employing the imaginative use of Flemish and Renaissance detail, including a heady mix of red brick and terracotta (fig. 2.20) (Walk 9).

The change in taste in house design accompanied a corresponding change in the taste for interior design, which became much more personal and dependent on handcrafted objects from firms such as Marshall, Morris and Company, set up by William Morris to produce household furnishings emphasising craftsmanship over historical style. One group of clients who supported both the architects in their fanciful façades and the designers of the more aesthetic furnishings was that comprising numerous wealthy artists who had houses built for themselves in Kensington and Chelsea. James McNeill Whistler and John Singer Sargent both had houses in Tite Street, Chelsea (fig. 2.21) (Walk 9), while Lord Leighton and Luke Fildes joined a colony of artists around Holland House, off Kensington High Street.

The artists commissioned their own detached houses, while the new styles found their way into the speculative terraces intended for the middle classes in the more far flung suburbs. However, the type where individuality could be expressed more satisfactorily was the detached or semi-detached house. For many years 'villas', in imitation of the Roman retreat, had been built in the suburban villages of London. In his *A Tour through the Whole Island of Great Britain* (1724–6), Daniel Defoe makes note of a number of these along the upper reaches of the Thames in the early eighteenth century, where the houses were set in pleasure grounds and paddocks to be enjoyed rather than exploited for profit. The source of their owners' wealth lay elsewhere, with many of them being bankers or the new-style entrepreneurs, and it was the ambition of even the middle class to retire in mid-life to the suburban villages beyond urban sprawl. If successful, a merchant or manufacturer could afford to exercise his individuality in the design of his own villa, and to help with this desire a great number of publications appeared from the late eighteenth century dedicated to providing examples of villas and cottages in every conceivable style, and quite often during the nineteenth century with an estimate of the cost appended. In his 1838 publication, *Suburban Gardener and Villa Companion*, J. C. Loudon expanded on the virtues of the suburban house and garden, and the opportunity this gave its owner to develop and express his individual taste. Numerous examples of these houses appeared starting from the late eighteenth century, some of which have survived, such as the wildly eccentric The Logs (now Lion House) in Hampstead (1867–8) by J. S. Nightingale for the engineer Edward Gotto (fig. 2.22) (Walk 10).

The relentless spread of residential London made these detached houses and their gardens vulnerable almost as soon as they were built. The detached house came into its own, however, when developers began to combine the form with the mode of development usually employed in terrace building. The inspiration for this could have come from the two Regent's Park Villages, small enclaves of detached houses on the eastern periphery of Regent's Park, begun by Nash in 1824 and later finished by James Pennethorne (fig. 2.25). The developments were fragments of a suburban layout of small villas of different styles, set within their own gardens, and arranged in a relaxed fashion for maximum picturesque effect. The novelty was the subdivision of the building land into limited plots which were nonetheless large enough for a modest house and garden, and well-planted curving roads so that the layout produced its own semi-rural scene. Once developers recognised the advantages of marrying the small detached house to the minimum lot, London saw a rash of 'villa estates' cropping up in its suburbs. An early example in Islington was Canonbury Park North and South from 1837 by Charles Hamor Hill. A more elaborate example, just to the north, was Highbury New Park, planned by Henry Rydon in 1851 to coincide with the opening of the North London Railway at the south end

2.21 No 31 Tite Street, R. W. Edis for John Singer Sargent, 1878–9.

2.22 The Logs (Lion House), Hampstead, J.S.Nightingale, 1867–8.

2.23 Highbury New Park, Islington, Charles Hambridge, *The Building News*, vol.3, 25 September 1857, p.1008.

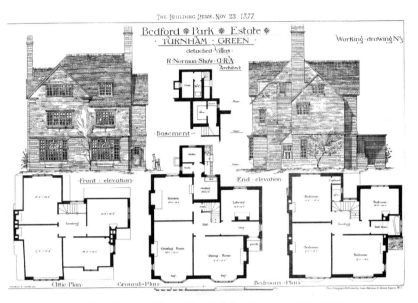

2.24 Bedford Park, R.Norman Shaw, *The Building News*, vol. 33, 23 November 1877, p. 508.

2.25 Park Village West, Regent's Park, John Nash and James Pennethorne, begun 1824.

of the estate (fig. 2.23). Rydon himself lived on the estate and kept a close eye on what was built, along with his architect, Charles Hambridge. For the most part the houses are detached or semi-detached, but some terraces, with the distinctive raised basements of the later nineteenth century, finished off the estate in the 1880s. These are large houses with leafy front and back gardens, and a generous range of rooms for different functions. They come in an eclectic variety of styles, and identical houses could be had in a red brick 'Lombardic' style or rendered with Greek details. What distinguishes this and similar estates is the generosity of the road layout, along with the mature plane trees which now give a monumental sweep to the main thoroughfare.

Attention is drawn to the landscape of these villa estates by the inclusion of the word 'park' in many of their names. Bedford Park on the edge of Chiswick in west London is the best known, because it incorporated not just the generous gardens and tree-lined streets of the suburban estates, but also the new style of English house design initiated by R. Norman Shaw (fig. 2.24). Just as in his town houses, Shaw drew on details found in houses of the Sussex and Kent countryside and in the small country towns, but the suburban setting, while limiting the size of the houses, gave greater scope for picturesque compositions than he could manage in Kensington, or even in his own house, No. 6 Ellerdale Road in Hampstead (see p.219). The estate was begun by Jonathan T. Carr when he bought twenty-four acres with mature trees at Turnham Green in 1875. His first architect was E. W. Godwin, who designed two houses in The Avenue, but Carr soon turned to Shaw in 1877. The house designs included details such as sharply pitched roofs, large red-brick chimneys, tile-hung walls, turned wooden balusters in front porches and on balconies, and large windows with small panes, which were carefully assembled to convey the impression of houses in a village street.

Nevertheless, the architects – Shaw, E. J. May and Maurice Adams – endeavoured to provide as much space and light inside as compatible with the compact, suburban houses. Community life was encouraged on the estate, and to further this, amenities were included in the final scheme such as a church, village stores, a public house and clubhouse, all designed by Shaw.

Although comfort and convenience became of ever more concern to the middle classes, everyone was intent on making houses healthier as the nineteenth century drew to a close. The century had witnessed the terrible cholera epidemics and periodic visitations of smallpox, but tuberculosis was probably of most concern in the later years. While curative drugs were lacking, anyone was vulnerable, no matter what their place in society, and the disease was particularly cruel because it often seemed to attack the young. In 1884 two events occurred which reflected the connection being made between housing and health. One was a Royal Commission set up to investigate the housing conditions among the working classes, and the other was the International Health Exhibition at South Kensington. The Public Health Act of 1875 had required local authorities to establish bye-laws within their jurisdiction to ensure that new houses were of sound construction and with ample space around them. The model bye-laws issued in 1877 stipulated a 36-foot (11-metre) width for a street length of 100 feet (30.5 metres), all in the interest of providing a healthy supply of light and air to each house. The result was row upon row of identical houses in soul-destroying repetition, as can be found, for example, in large areas of suburban south London. Nonetheless, small houses were preferred to blocks of flats even for the working classes, and to further their building some philanthropic endeavours devoted themselves to this cause.

The thinking behind the philanthropic involvement in suburban cottage estates was that cottages were better on health and moral grounds than blocks of flats. The Artizans', Labourers', and General Dwellings Company managed to build a number of cottage estates around London, including Shaftesbury Park in Battersea from 1873, Queen's Park, Harrow Road from 1875, and Noel Park, Wood Green from 1883 onwards (fig. 2.26). Some variety was attempted in the façades through the use of turrets and porches, and a variety of house size ensured that the dwellings were let at a range of rents. Nevertheless, these estates were still beyond the means of most of the working poor, who were able to afford neither the rents nor the transport costs that suburban living entailed.

A healthy environment and affordable housing were principles lying behind the foundation of Hampstead Garden Suburb. The project was the brainchild of Henrietta Barnett, the wife of the Reverend Samuel Barnett, vicar of St Jude Whitechapel and founder of the Toynbee Hall settlement there; the occasion was the proposed extension of the Northern Line from Hampstead to Golders Green. The land in the immediate area of the proposed railway extension was owned by Eton College, who wished to develop their 323 acres, and this led Henrietta Barnett to campaign in 1903 to ensure that at least 80 acres of the land would remain free of houses for recreational purposes. From this emerged the idea of building on the edge of the Heath extension a garden suburb dedicated to well-designed houses for all classes. The project was directed by a trust that worked together with co-partnership companies to organise the finances of the suburb, while the Garden Suburb Development Company (Hampstead) Ltd oversaw what was built. The architect to the trust responsible for the layout was Raymond Unwin, already known for his work with his partner Barry Parker on the model village of New Earswick outside York and on Letchworth, the first garden city. The architectural consultant was Edwin

2.26 Vincent Road, Noel Park, Roland Plumbe, from 1883.

2.27 Nos 6–10 Meadway, Hampstead Garden Suburb, M.H.Baillie Scott, 1909.

Lutyens, who was entrusted with the Central Square and its two large churches. A number of other architects, among them M. H. Baillie Scott, Michael Bunney and Courtenay Crickmer, designed many of the houses, but always in a variation of the cottage style, now less elaborate than that of Shaw but still tied to English rural traditions (fig. 2.27). Steeply pitched roofs, lightly coloured rendered walls, small-paned windows and plenty of garden space gave the suburb a more expansive and progressive feel compared to much contemporary house building. But despite the intention to include a generous amount of working-class accommodation, in the end it accounted for only about one-tenth of the total houses and is found to the north of Central Square. The suburb also suffers from a lack of accessible shops despite numerous plans, although those shops that were built on Finchley Road to designs by A. J. Penty provide a monumental entrance to the suburb, with their arcades and turrets reminiscent of a medieval German town.

Hampstead Garden Suburb proved a success, as did other co-partnership ventures, such as the smaller Brentham Garden Estate in Ealing (1901–15). However, around 1912 the housing market suffered a general collapse, and even before the First World War the rate of house building dropped significantly. This did not mean that there was not a shortage of houses, especially for the working poor, rather that investors and builders were not interested in or were unable to undertake housing schemes that failed to give them a secure return. The result was overprovision for some sections of society and underprovision for others, forcing families into shared housing in old property near the centres of work, such as the docks and the markets. This was not a new situation, of course, but the extension of the franchise in 1867 gave working men a greater stake in the political process, with the result that working-class housing became firmly established as a political issue. The housing difficulties of working people were illustrated during the First World War when munitions workers were drafted into communities to work in local munitions factories. They soon discovered a lack of suitable accommodation, with unscrupulous landlords ready to take advantage. In some instances the government built houses, as at the Well Hall Estate in Woolwich in 1915, designed by the Office of Works

under Frank Baines and clearly inspired by Hampstead Garden Suburb. Many workers around the country were less fortunate, and the strains of wartime and the resulting social discontent tended to be expressed through complaints about housing. The fear of social unrest led the government to become engaged in the housing market, first by the Rent Restrictions Acts and second by subsidised post-war house building, the 'homes for heroes' programmes.

The first Rent Restrictions Act 1915 was intended to stop landlords profiteering, by ensuring that a working-class tenant's rent would not rise while he remained in occupation of his dwelling. Only when the property fell vacant could the landlord raise the rent. Although this was a wartime measure, the restrictions continued even at the end of the war, and as a consequence working-class housing production failed to attract new private investment. Those owning such property found they could neither depend on a return nor dispose of the property profitably, with the result that many older houses in the inner suburbs of London were left to deteriorate. Because houses had been seen as a safe investment in the nineteenth century, many, as noted above, were owned by family trusts and provided pensions for spinsters and widows, just the people who were unable to spend money on repairs and improved amenities.

Under the Housing Act 1919, the government undertook to pay from the Treasury a subsidy to local authorities who built and managed housing for the working class in their jurisdiction. In London, the London County Council was the overall administrator of the subsidy, but the metropolitan boroughs were encouraged to build in their own areas. As we shall see in the next chapter, the LCC undertook slum clearance in London with a programme of flat building, but it also engaged in a vast house-building scheme, the Becontree Estate at Dagenham in Essex, where the plan was to build 24,000 terraced cottages for a population of 120,000. The LCC had engaged in some cottage building before the war in small estates at, for example, Totterdown Fields, Tooting Bec and at White Hart Lane in north London, where architects experimented with plans and materials to produce a viable form of working-class housing (fig. 2.28). Thus, before the end of the war, the LCC was able to contribute to a Royal Commission set up to consider what sort of housing would be appropriately built with government funds, the result of which was the Tudor Walters Report, 1918. One of the prominent contributors was Raymond Unwin,

the designer of the layout for Hampstead Garden Suburb and a great advocate of cottage estates with low housing densities. The report looked carefully at the planning and detailing of working-class housing, and the consensus was that the simple semi-detached or terraced cottage with basic amenities, such as indoor lavatory and self-contained bathroom, was the preferred housing type. When the LCC came to build cottage estates at Becontree, Roehampton, Bellingham and later at St Helier and the Watling Estate, the cottage predominated, but whereas the garden suburb endeavoured to provide a picturesque evocation of the English village, the sheer size of these developments tended to swamp any notion of the rural village (fig. 2.29).

With each subsequent housing Act, the subsidy tended to be cut from the very generous arrangement of 1919, when it was agreed that local authorities would receive back from the government anything over a penny rate they spent on their housing provision. Nevertheless, over the decades, council housing became a popular form of tenure among working-class families, and this coincided with a corresponding decline in the quality of provision in the privately rented sector. Private house builders and landlords deplored the involvement of government in housing provision, despite the work put in the way of private contractors, but post-war conditions opened up a new area for house builders, that of home ownership.

Just before the First World War about 10 per cent of households in England and Wales owned their dwelling, while the others rented. After the war the Rent Restrictions Acts noted above made rented houses less attractive as a direct investment, but building societies, which lent their funds for the purpose of buying houses, provided a better and more trouble-free return. Changes in the regulations allowed building societies to lend for a much longer term on a much smaller initial deposit, so that in the immediate post-war period many middle-class families could afford to buy their house. This coincided with a release of extensive stretches of agricultural land for building purposes and the extension of public transport even further out beyond the accepted borders of London. In addition, after the initial post-war inflation, prices of materials and labour remained low throughout the 1920s, falling even further as a result of the 1929 stock market crash and subsequent depression. Private builders were quick to take advantage of these favourable conditions, and a building boom began in the outer suburbs of London comparable to that of the nineteenth century in the inner suburbs.

The greatest period of house building was during the mid-1930s when the low cost of labour and materials made houses relatively cheap. Those in work, particularly those with jobs in the new industries such as electronics and car manufacture, found that their weekly mortgage payments were no more than they would have had to pay in rent for much less desirable accommodation in the inner suburbs. Higher fares and dearer food were drawbacks, but these were offset by new schools, better recreational facilities, and something not to be belittled: a sense of respectability and of 'getting on'.

The layout of the new estates owed much to the villa estates of the nineteenth century and something as well to the garden suburb, with densities depending on the social group to which the builder sought to appeal. Curving roads and picturesque massing was feasible at low densities, but when it was important to get the maximum profit from the scheme, roads were straight and houses tightly packed. For the most part the houses were either detached or semi-detached, and the preferred decorative details referred to the Tudor style, with half-timbering intimated on many houses by a few upright battens embedded in the gables (fig. 2.30). Roughcast render on the first storey and a stylised band of hung tiles, usually on the ubiquitous projecting bay, were further favourite details.

The typical detached or semi-detached suburban house of the 1920s and 1930s tended to have a wider frontage than the London terraced house. This gave a greater opportunity to bring light into the living rooms and kitchen on the ground floor. The houses were without basements, so access to the garden was easy, an encouragement to children to play out of doors and for the family to enjoy the garden as an additional living space. All this hinged on the supposition that there was a garden to enjoy, and gardening along with DIY became accepted lower-middle-class activities in London as elsewhere. The house itself tended to be of a standard form, and standardised details such as factory-made metal window frames soon made their appearance. However, they never wholly lost their references to notions of the vernacular house, particularly the Tudor cottage, as can be appreciated in the vast estates put up by mass builders, such as Laings in north London and Wates south of the Thames.

Although today the references to the Tudor might appear nostalgic and reactionary, at the time the Tudor reigns of Henry VIII and Elizabeth I represented a period when England stood optimistically at the start of its imperial ambitions. Somehow within the one style, stability and progress were united: the aspirations of the modest suburban house. The house itself became the location for public education through radio and the press in how to educate and to keep a family healthy, and how to consume contemporary material goods.

There were some efforts at introducing a modernist agenda into London houses. For Frognal Way, Hampstead, Maxwell Fry designed the Sun House in 1934–5, a flat-roofed, white rendered house of impressive voids and solids (fig. 2.31) (Walk 10). Further down the hill, Connell, Ward and Lucas produced another modernist house in 1937, and took satisfaction in disturbing the conservative sensibilities of the neighbours, such as those of the eminent architect and historian Reginald Blomfield (see p. 219). The previous year Connell, Ward and Lucas were thwarted in their attempt to introduce modernism at a greater scale in Ruislip, where they did nonetheless manage to build three houses, 97–101 Park Avenue, in the modernist idiom.

On the other side of London at Gidea Park, Romford, a further attempt was made to introduce a more progressive style of house building to the London suburbs. Gidea Park was laid out in 1910 as a garden suburb, and many houses were designed at that time by prominent Arts and Crafts architects. In 1934 a 'Modern Homes' exhibition was intended to produce built examples of good modern house design on the remaining building land, but the results were rather disappointing except for the winner, 64 Heath Drive by Francis Skinner and Tecton, the firm established by Berthold Lubetkin. In the same year, a competition was held under the auspices of the Architectural Association and the house builders Laing to encourage young architects to experiment in house design, with the incentive that the winning schemes would be built. A street in Mill Hill, Sunnyfields, was laid out by T. Alwyn Lloyd, and the houses demonstrate a number of alternatives to the typical suburban house with their pantile roofs and wrap-around windows. But the houses did not sell well, and the street is now an intriguing anomaly amongst the surrounding suburbs.

Another modernist experiment, somewhat different from the attempt to recast the suburban house, was Erno Goldfinger's version of the London terrace, 1–3 Willow

Road in Hampstead (1937–9) (see p. 221). The planning within the constraints of the terrace is extraordinarily inventive, and is aided by the circular staircase in each of the three houses, which frees extra space. Although the houses have flat roofs, the walls are unrendered brick, and like the Georgian terraced house the virtues are almost all inside.

The preceding examples are exceptions to the general run of suburban houses in London, but for most people homeownership was the overriding consideration. That many householders 'owned' their houses , however much they were indebted to the building societies, made a difference to how they felt about their house and domestic life, and may have contributed to the stability we have come to associate with suburban life (fig. 2.32). Owner occupation probably ranks with the invention of the leasehold house market as among the most influential elements in London's housing history. It also ultimately fragmented the London housing market into very separate categories: owner occupation, private renting and council housing.

House building slowed towards the end of the 1930s with the rise of inflation and rearmament, and during the Second World War it came to a complete halt. After the war the state once more took a leading role in house production, not just with subsidies, but also with a number of measures to control where new areas of houses were built. Architects and planners had been appalled by the inter-war urban sprawl over good farmland and the most picturesque areas of London's near countryside. Partly in order to eliminate the worst excesses of house building around cities, the government introduced the Town and Country Planning Act 1947 and the green belt in 1955. The result was to remove much new house building, as opposed to flat building, beyond London's borders to towns and villages within commuting distance of the capital and to the new towns, such as Harlow and Stevenage.

Most new post-war domestic building in London was in the form of flats, although houses were built on the London County Council mixed development estates, such as the Alton East Estate in Roehampton, west London in 1951. Private money in the meantime was going into a different form of housing stock, the refurbishment of London's already existing houses. The population of inner London had declined markedly over the first half of the twentieth century. By the 1950s, the population of an inner suburb such as Islington had declined from a high of 327,403 in 1911 to 193,000 in 1961. There were a number of reasons for this, including the attraction of the outer suburbs for those able to afford the additional expense, wartime bomb damage of the existing housing stock, and the government policy of rehousing as many people as they could manage outside London in the new towns. Those remaining in London were accommodated in new council estates wherever the LCC was able to obtain sites. Another reason why working people wanted to get out of their private-rented accommodation was the poor quality of much of it. Boroughs such as Islington, St Pancras, Paddington and Camberwell had a generous supply of large and well-built nineteenth-century houses, but over the years they had suffered neglect. Again the reasons for this neglect are varied, but the Rent Restrictions Acts, maintained for economic reasons after the wars, kept rents artificially low and the financial return on working-class rents a poor investment. The effect of this was to prevent small landlords from selling up and moving their money into more profitable investments, perpetuating what the government considered an old-fashioned form of tenure. Many nineteenth-century leases were on the point of falling in, the downside of the leasehold system, and another reason for a fall in house value. Low returns led to low maintenance, and many properties, while look-

2.32 Village Way, Rayners Lane.

2.33 Lonsdale Square, Islington, R.C.Carpenter, 1838–45.

ing substantial on the exterior, were shocking within, with poor amenities such as outdoor WCs, no fixed baths, and shared cooking facilities.

While working-class families were desperate to move out of poor quality, privately owned housing into council accommodation, the worn-out terraces were going cheap. The owners were perhaps expecting that entrepreneurs would buy them for redevelopment as middle-class flats, but what happened in certain areas of London was that a developer would indeed buy houses cheaply, but with the intention of selling them on to people prepared to renovate them for their own use or for sale. The movement started in Kensington and Chelsea where many small mews cottages became available for transformation into acceptable modern houses, and this created a new market in gentrified houses in former working-class areas. With only one household inhabiting the London terraced house, it lent itself admirably to modern living. Modest investment in new technology brought plumbing and central heating to houses bereft of both when occupied by private tenants, and this investment came in the form of improvement grants and generous mortgages. Not all gentrifiers were middle class, since refurbishment was one route to owner occupation for many working-class families, but the end result for areas with appropriate houses was a gradual shift in balance from a predominant working-class population to a middle-class one (fig. 2.33). The Barnsbury area of Islington, around Gibson and Thornhill Squares (Walk 8), is a very good example, where a mixture of new-built redevelopment exists alongside refurbished terraces now housing single families engaged in the middle-class professions and finance.

There were a few post-war attempts to introduce new types of housing in London based on novel methods of production and development. The Span Estates (1950s–70s) were designed by Eric Lyons with Geoffrey Townsend, and consisted of flats and houses in Twickenham, Richmond and Blackheath. The interiors were open plan, and the houses themselves built at relatively high densities on secluded sites with generous landscaping. Materials consist of stock brick, tile-hanging and weatherboarding, but the overall thrust of the design is of progressive, modern houses. For some people self-build was a popular concept during the 1980s, although it usually required sophisticated building skills. The architect Walter Segal devised a system of house building which enabled unskilled people to build their own lightweight, timber-framed houses. Segal Close off Brockley Rise in south London is an example, but the number of these schemes was limited and they remain isolated experiments in the mass of London's houses.

Since the Second World War, the most important development has been the refurbishment of the existing housing stock, so that the many terraces of the eighteenth and nineteenth centuries have been given a new life as single household dwellings. Just as important has been the conversion of many older houses into flats, which have then been transferred out of the rented sector into private ownership. This has been part of the process by which Londoners have gradually come to be a flat-dwelling population. Much of the flat dwelling goes on in purpose-built buildings, a type which was viewed with distaste during the nineteenth century as alien to the English temperament, and in the next chapter we will consider how the flat came to be built in ever increasing numbers despite this antipathy.

Chapter 3 THE LONDON FLAT

The built fabric of London does feel different from that of other European cities. There is the absence of the near uniform apartment blocks and wide pavements found in Paris and many other cities in imitation of the French capital. Reasons why this is so are many. For one, the rebuilding of London occurred before the evolution of the type of apartment building that emerged in Paris after the French Revolution. Conditions obtaining around 1700 set the pattern for the London house type, and these depended on patterns of landholding, availability of funds, organisation of the building trades, and desires of the tenants. As we have seen in the previous chapter, the terraced house satisfied to a large extent the demands of all these players.

From the prevailing house type at the beginning of the nineteenth century emerged the preference for a dwelling whose outside door opened directly onto the street and not onto a shared stairway, as was the case in the Paris apartment block. Despite many examples where houses were shared, and by necessity the access to individual rooms, the English middle class developed a preference for the separation of individual families. This reflects a general desire to categorise and to segregate, so we find neighbours separated by party walls and front doors, classes separated into different streets, neighbourhoods designated for one group or another, east London a world away from west London. Within the house, increasingly every function of domestic life occupied its own space, however small. Children inhabited the nursery and servants their own quarters below stairs (or in the attics).

"MODEL" TOWN HOUSES FOR THE MIDDLE CLASSES.

VIEW SHOWING PUBLIC STAIRCASES AND GENERAL ARRANGEMENT OF THE STREETS AND SQUARES.

3.1 '"Model" town houses for the middle classes', *The Builder*, vol. 7, 1 December 1849, p. 567.

3.2 Cromwell Buildings, Redcross Way, Southwark, Improved Industrial Dwellings Company, 1864.

Martin Daunton in *House and Home* has demonstrated how the idea of 'encapsulation' spread through the middle classes and came to be thought desirable for all classes. We can see the ideology of the family gradually evolving through the first half of the nineteenth century, so that by the time John Ruskin wrote *Sesame and Lilies* in 1864–5, he was able to depict a particular form of the family familiar enough to us today, where the male householder went forth from the house to encounter the evils of the world, while the woman waited at home, making it secure and peaceful for his return. Strangers hanging about shared front doors, chance encounters on the stairs, and altercations with near neighbours were not conducive to the sort of secure privacy Ruskin was demanding for the family home. This could only be achieved through the physical separation of each family so that the individual could be responsible for and in control of his own domestic happiness.

Promiscuous living was thought detrimental to morals and to the responsibility of the individual, but many of the houses of the working classes were shared, as we have seen, and many too were built behind the main thoroughfares in courts and alleys. The courts lay outside public scrutiny, but at the same time the houses in the courts were permeable by strangers as their front doors remained open for the convenience of the many tenants of the house. When middle-class philanthropists ventured into areas of poor housing to investigate the conditions there, they were disturbed by the number of front doors left open. How were the poor to maintain their respectability if they were not able to control access to the home? One solution seemed to reside in getting the poor out of their sequestered courts, and into exposed dwellings which had their own front doors.

At mid-century, however, the poor working population had few choices when it came to accommodation. The sheer wealth of London was attracting an army of working people to the city, and there was a severe shortage of housing they could afford. This shortage was made worse by the demolition of many working-class districts for the erection of the new railway stations and their adjacent rail yards. Further public works such as the construction of the docks reduced the amount of accommodation, at the same time drawing more people into work. A middle-class housing crisis had occurred in the 1840s, and at this time there were suggestions that this section of the population could be housed in blocks of flats, which would have balcony access so that each family could have its own front door (fig. 3.1). The appearance of cheap transport meant that the middle-class flat in central London proved unnecessary as many more houses were built in the surrounding suburbs. But transport cheap enough for the workers was a long way off, and in the meantime their housing situation was worsening.

Part of the housing crisis resulted from the lack of interest on the part of investors and builders in constructing houses cheap enough for working people, particularly in central London where they were needed most. A mixture of motives, including sympathy with the plight of the poor and a desire to reform their behaviour, led some among the middle classes to intervene directly in the housing market by investing in dwellings built specifically for working people, with the expectation of only a small return. The accommodation was termed 'model' dwellings, since they were intended to show how the workers should be housed in future, and the type of building prescribed was almost invariably the block of flats (fig. 3.2).

Model dwellings were familiar in the countryside where conscientious landowners were expected to provide decent accommodation for their workers. We need only remember Dorothea Brooke's interest in the workers' cottages in George Eliot's novel, *Middlemarch* (1871–2). In the city, model dwellings required certain characteristics: they needed to provide encapsulation so that every family could have its own front door; the tenants needed access at least to adequate supplies of clean water; and surveillance of tenants and anyone else in the area continued to be important. Added to this, the dwellings were still required to make a profit, however small, and with the high cost of land in the city, the block of flats became the obvious answer, despite the preference among reformers for cottages for working people.

The outcome of deliberations on the housing requirements of the workers was the emergence of philanthropic trusts whose purpose was to invest money at low interest into housing schemes which they would then manage. Management was an important aspect of the schemes because the purpose of the dwellings was not just to provide adequate housing, but also to change behaviour and to contribute to a sober and industrious working population. An early example of these trusts was the Metropolitan Association for Improving the Dwellings of the Industrious Classes founded in 1841, and active in St Pancras and Spitalfields during the 1840s and

1850s. The earliest extant example of what became referred to as philanthropic housing is Parnell House, Streatham Street, erected by the Society for Improving the Condition of the Labouring Classes and designed by Henry Roberts in 1849. At the request of the Prince Consort, Roberts designed a small model building in conjunction with the Great Exhibition of 1851, which was intended to demonstrate an acceptable form for working-class dwellings, and this example still remains, though altered, in Kennington Park, south London. A distinguishing feature of the design is the open staircase in the centre of the building, a characteristic of many later blocks of flats, particularly those facing the street. This ensured that people coming and going were observed, thus discouraging clandestine activities. A similar idea lay behind the introduction of balcony access in many philanthropic buildings, such as Streatham Street, where whoever mounted to the flats was clearly visible.

Another possible arrangement of the philanthropic blocks was as associated flats. This meant that amenities such as scullery sinks and WCs were shared on the landings among a number of tenants. The Peabody Trust, established in 1862 by the wealthy American steel magnate George Peabody, provided associated flats in their early schemes, although they were accessed not by open balconies but by enclosed stairs (fig. 3.3). H. A. Darbishire was the architect for the distinctive stock brick Italianate design of their four- and five-storey blocks, which tended to be built at high density on sites right across central London, including Clerkenwell, Blackfriars Road, Islington, Victoria and Chelsea.

Another example of the philanthropic housing company was the Improved Industrial Dwellings Company founded by Sir Sydney Waterlow. They built a number of schemes throughout London, but some of their largest projects are in the East End. Still extant is part of an ambitious group of flats in Corfield and Wilmot Streets in Bethnal Green, 1868–80 (fig. 3.4) (Walk 11). The buildings demonstrate the company's Jacobean-Italianate style, but with partially enclosed stairs. More typical of the company's housing type is Leopold Buildings in Columbia Road (1872), which follows the type developed by their architect, Matthew Allen, during the 1860s with open stairs and balcony access (fig. 3.5) (Walk 11).

The accommodation in the philanthropic flats was often cramped, but effort was made to ensure that every family had a living room separate from the sleeping spaces. Efforts, too, were made to provide enough sleeping accommodation so that the sexes within the family could be segregated at night. For the streetwise London family the restrictions placed on tenants of the philanthropic flats might be too

3.3 Peabody Estate, Lawrence Street, Chelsea, H. A. Darbishire, c.1880.

3.4 Corfield Street, Bethnal Green, Improved Industrial Dwellings Company, 1868–80.

3.5 Leopold Buildings, Bethnal Green, Improved Industrial Dwellings Company, 1872.

3.6 Boundary Street Estate, Bethnal Green, London County Council, 1895–1900.

stringent, and the requirement to take on a whole flat with a weekly rent paid in advance was too much for the fragile finances of many families. Witnesses to the Royal Commission on Housing of the Working Classes (1884) claimed that the philanthropic flats were favoured by people coming into London, who had little experience of local housing markets. They also attracted people in occupations such as the police, for whom it was important to maintain respectability. However, the blocks remained generally unpopular for their dreary, utilitarian appearance – which led them to be compared to barracks by all classes – and set particularly the working classes against the flat as an acceptable housing type.

The Royal Commission on Housing of the Working Classes was formed largely in response to the perceived crisis in London's housing provision. The labour market in London depended on much casual work, and this needed people to be on the spot when the work became available. For these people, as reported to the Commission, working-class suburbs were not appropriate, especially since the relatively high fares of omnibuses and trains put them out of reach of the poor. Workers had to be near their work, and that meant living in areas of highly valued urban land, which led to high rents, overcrowding and the associated social problems. Philanthropic housing was one solution, but there seemed to be the need for a more official response. This was made possible by the formation of the London County Council in 1888 and the Housing of the Working Classes Act 1890, which allowed the LCC to engage in slum clearance and the building and management of working-class dwellings.

In the previous chapter, we came across the LCC engaged in building suburban cottage estates along garden suburb lines, but it also engaged in flat building in conjunction with slum clearance programmes. One of its early estates of flats was undertaken in Bethnal Green in an area off Commercial Road called the Old Nichol, the Jago of Arthur Morrison's *Child of the Jago* (1896). This was a notorious area of tightly packed dwellings in a maze of alleys where villains could easily escape from the police, who refused to venture into the precinct. The LCC demolished the entire Old Nichol and replaced it with twenty blocks of flats, arranged around a green with a bandstand, and enhanced with a laundry and schools. The flats were designed by the new Housing of the Working Classes branch of the LCC under the direction of Thomas Blashill and Owen Fleming, and under the influence of the architect W. R. Lethaby. What is immediately apparent on the Boundary Street Estate is the variety of form and detail of the blocks (fig. 3.6) (Walk 7). The flats are arranged off the staircase, two per floor, the amenities enclosed within the flats and

not on the landings as in the associated type. Although the blocks are substantial and of five storeys, each block has its own character derived from the distinctive arrangement of gables, projecting bays, multi-coloured bricks and tiles. The generous width of the streets allows light and air into the estate, thus avoiding the oppressive atmosphere of many of the philanthropic schemes.

   As the LCC was feeling its way with this new estate, there were many complaints about the expense which the architects seemed to be incurring, and there were misgivings in the press that Boundary Street resembled too closely middle-class flats in the West End, built under the influence of the prevailing Queen Anne style. This was also the complaint made of the Islington estate built by the Samuel Lewis Trust in 1910 in Liverpool Road, where the same comparison with West End flats was made (fig. 3.7) (Walk 8). The next large estate undertaken by the LCC at Millbank from 1897 demonstrated more symmetry and a greater homogeneity of style than Boundary Street, while still keeping the careful detailing and variety of materials, including red bricks, tiles, white painted render and window frames (fig. 3.8) (Walk 2). More standardisation still can be found on the Bourne Estate, Clerkenwell Road (1901–7), where six parallel blocks are arranged around small gardens, and where, like the Caledonian Estate in Islington built 1904–7, access is from open balconies. In the face of the housing problems faced by London's poor, the efforts of the LCC might appear scant, but it continued to build blocks of flats and hostels, and of course the cottage estates on the fringes of London, so that after the First World War it was well placed to take an active role in slum clearance under the 1919 Housing Act considered below.

   Private West End flats have been referred to in comparison with those on the Boundary Street Estate, and by 1900 the middle-class flat had, de-

3.7 Samuel Lewis Trust Estate, Liverpool Road, Islington, C.S.Joseph and Smithem, 1909–10.

3.8 Millbank Estate, Westminster, London County Council, 1897–1902.

3.9 Athenaeum, Waterloo Place, Decimus Burton, 1827–30.

3.10 Albert Hall Mansions, Kensington Gore, R. Norman Shaw, 1879.

3.11 Mount Street, Mayfair, 1880–97.

spite the apparent antipathy to flats, become established as one of London's dwelling types, if not the most prevalent. As we have seen, the terraced house lent itself to flat living by virtue of the fact that each floor could be inhabited in isolation, and in recent times many houses have been divided in this way. Another type of dwelling similar to the block of flats was the block of chambers, a type favoured by single men, usually in the professions. The accommodation would consist like the college 'set' of separate sitting rooms and bedrooms, with the expectation that meals would be prepared somewhere on the premises by a servant or would be taken out at a chop-house. A superior example of chambers was Albany in Piccadilly, but the type was common around the Inns of Court. The West End clubs also provided accommodation for wealthy single men and those who required a pied-à-terre in London (fig. 3.9).

The reluctance of Londoners to embrace the flat was deplored by the Francophile W. H. White, who campaigned during the 1870s in the press for the flat. There were, however, some early instances of flat building, one of the first being a block in the newly laid out Victoria Street by H. Ashton in 1853, which suggests that the flat had associations with new initiatives in London's infrastructure. Albert Hall Mansions in Kensington Gore by R. Norman Shaw in 1879 saw many imitations, and launched the wider acceptance of the flat as an alternative to the West End house (fig. 3.10). As might be expected at this date, Shaw's design included Queen Anne details such as oriels high up on the building and tall windows with small panes delineated by thin glazing bars, and the main material was typically red brick. The flats themselves were ingeniously arranged across the building, giving aspects to opposite sides of the block.

Some quite large blocks of flats made their appearances in the West End, such as those in Mount Street, and indeed when new roads were laid out flats were often the preferred building form, sometimes with shops at ground floor (fig. 3.11) (Walk 6). Flats over the shop were built in many middle-class high streets, especially in the new suburbs, where the parade of shops began to make an appearance. In the suburbs, too, are found some odd hybrids. In Bethune Road, Hackney, there is a unique estate of middle-class flats from 1874. The blocks of three-storey self-contained flats were designed by Matthew Allen, the architect associated with Sydney Waterlow's Improved Industrial Dwellings Company. A decade later, cottage flats were developed by Courtenay Warner in Walthamstow. These were designed to look like two-storey houses, but they were already divided into two self-contained flats, for example in Leucha Road (1895).

Edwardian London saw the building of flats become more common. Some were the result of redevelopment after house leases expired, or where new roads were laid out as, for example, Chiltern Street just behind Baker Street or Kensington Court (fig. 3.12) (Walk 9). Flats were also built in the suburbs, such as a purpose-built block in Aberdeen Park in Islington, where at the time there was ample building land. It would seem, then, that the reluctance of Londoners to take to the flat had been overcome, although the perceived reluctance might have had more to do with the evolution of middle-class ideas about family life and respectability than about general preferences. Certainly after the First World War purpose-built blocks of flats formed a significant amount of new building in the capital.

In their study of the market in flats, Chris Hamnett and Bill Randolph give a number of reasons why flat building had a resurgence between the wars. First, in the older suburbs the redundancy of the larger houses and their gardens made available sites extensive enough to build sufficient flats for a good return. This was the case in districts such as Tufnell Park and Highbury New Park in Islington, where objections were raised when the London County Council wanted to buy up houses through compulsory purchase for redevelopment as council flats, while the house owners were hoping to sell their houses on the open market to the private sector for redevelopment as flats.

Second, the 1930s saw the establishment of property investment companies which built flats and managed them as an investment. This was an alternative method to the mortgage for bringing new money into the production of residential property. Property companies had the resources to build and manage residential property, whereas individuals, who had put their capital into this area in the past, found that they could no longer compete in the market. It was not just a question of marshalling together the funds required for the investment; it was also necessary to piece together the sites, and to benefit from magnitude of scale in building and managing the flats.

Third, even while the market for suburban family houses seemed insatiable, there was still a residue of single people and couples with or without children who wanted smaller, well-serviced properties to rent. Renting was after all the accepted type of tenancy, and although houses were still being built for rent, for many the flat suited them at specific moments in their lives. For the newly married, the retired and the single, the purpose-built flat – whether in the city centre or in the suburbs – could be preferred to a house.

Besides these important reasons, there were two further aspects to flat living which appealed to the professional planners and architects, who sought to promote them in preference to the suburban house. The first of these was concern over suburban sprawl and the defacement of the countryside. As we saw in the previous chapter, the expansion of transport facilities to the outer reaches of London encouraged suburban development into areas recently rural. By 1935 there was general alarm that the countryside was disappearing under the march of building, as expressed by modernist engineer and journalist Geoffrey Boumphrey in a BBC debate with Sir Ernest Simon of Wythenshawe, which was reported in *The Architects' Journal*:

3.12 Roxburghe Mansions, 32 Kensington Court, Kensington, Paul Hoffmann, *c*.1896.

We are spoiling the countryside. The English landscape that many people, even foreigners, think the most beautiful in the world in its own way, is being ruined. Thousands of acres of good agricultural land, and especially valuable land for market gardening, lying on the outskirts of towns, is being ruined for agricultural purposes almost for centuries.

It might appear strange to us that the modernists were so attached to the English countryside, but they are distinguished from their more conservative contemporaries who were also aghast at the untrammelled spread of suburbia by their solution. This was to build blocks of flats in the landscape, as F. R. S. Yorke and Frederick Gibberd proposed in their publication, *The Modern Flat*, in 1937:

A few tall buildings rising up to the light and air, spaced well apart, properly served with communications, would keep the dwellings away from through traffic roads, and their noise and danger, and would house all the people whose individual villa-homes now make congested areas that stretch for miles.

Far from creating corridors of concrete, the English modernists wished to bring city and country into harmony by concentrating living space in flats, but within a green landscape.

The second consideration – of the design professionals at least – was that the flat seemed to offer opportunities for truly modern living far more than the suburban house. Yorke and Gibberd associated the comfort of the modern flat with design 'on scientific lines', a direct appeal to an increasing section of the population which identified with 'modernity' and 'science'. According to Ross McKibbin in *Classes and Cultures* (1998), the 1930s saw a great increase in the numbers of the middle classes engaged in science and technology, and an increase in the prestige that such work acquired. The appeal to scientific principles in planning and design reflected this broader change in society, but also signalled that the middle classes were prepared to absorb the 'scientific' suggestions of the experts – and by association the aesthetic to which they subscribed.

The plan of the modern flat evolved rapidly from the rather linear arrangements of the late 1920s at Chiltern Court over Baker Street Underground Station. Here, although the plan of the flats was not very imaginative, the amenities included in

the scheme offered an in-house dining room and ballroom for a sophisticated lifestyle. Dolphin Square of ten years later carried the idea of a total environment further (fig. 3.13). For a supposedly flat-hating nation, this development of over 1,300 flats for a population of 3,000 seems rather excessive even today. But the range of amenities and variety of flat types, from the pied-à-terre to the comfortable main residence, presented a new concept in living. In addition to the flats were open gardens, a recreational centre with squash courts, a swimming pool and gymnasium, and public areas including restaurant, winter garden and palm court. There was also accommodation for 300 cars in the garage at basement level, and the car became increasingly an essential part of flat living, especially in central London, because it gave access to life beyond the city. Russell Court in Upper Woburn Place included garage spaces for the tenants' cars and a service station, but the flat accommodation consisted almost entirely of bedsitting rooms.

Most of the flats, however modern the ideas lying behind their design, were given Georgian garb, and even those of frame construction displayed load-bearing brick exterior walls. There were a few exceptions. The development of Lawn Road flats near Belsize Park was designed by Wells Coates to exemplify modern, mobile living, and its white, rectangular form did nothing to compromise its modernist intentions (fig. 3.14) (Walk 10). The individual flats were small but cleverly arranged, and the concept included communal dining in the ground-floor club room. The flats attracted artists and people wanting a degree of flexibility in their living arrangements. Another attempt to bring modernist principles into flat design occurred at Highgate where Berthold Lubetkin designed two very distinctive buildings, Highpoints One and Two (fig. 3.15). The flats here were generous in size, and the result was to bring ample light and air into the interiors. The aspect of the flats overlooking

3.14 Isokon Flats, Lawn Road, Hampstead, Wells Coates, 1934.

3.15 Highpoint One, North Hill, Highgate, Berthold Lubetkin, 1933–5.

3.16 Barnhill Estate, Wembley Park, Welch, Cachemaille-Day and Lander, 1935.

3.17 Lichfield Court, Richmond, Bertram Carter and Sloot, 1935, rear elevation.

3.18 Pinner Court, Pinner Road, H.J.Mark, 1935.

Highgate and the sweep of land down to Hampstead Heath contributed to the exhilaration of these buildings.

Most private blocks built during the 1930s were not so blatantly modernist, although it is not unusual to come across striking compositions such as the flats at Wembley Park by Welch, Cachemaille-Day and Lander, where white render has been used to good effect on three-storey blocks with flat roofs (fig. 3.16). Although these flats are distinctive in appearance, it was not always open to the architect to decide the external finish of the flats. Frederick Gibberd was required by the local authority to provide Georgian façades at Ellington Court, Southgate. His Pullman Court at Crystal Palace, however, still retains the smooth surface and light render of his original design. In another example, Lichfield Court in Richmond, the height of the buildings was reduced to seven storeys from ten so as not to offend local sensibilities, but in the interior of the courtyards a striking sculptural quality is maintained by the dramatic abstraction of the access galleries (fig. 3.17).

It might be thought that flats were ideal in densely built areas, but many in the suburbs occupied sites along roads, newly widened for the increase in car traffic (fig. 3.18). The space around these flats was often generous, or they were sited near open space, as was Fairacres by Minoprio and Spencely, which backs onto the Roehampton Golf Club, or Gibberd's Ellington Court, which is flanked by playing fields. Many of the flats in Hillbrow on Richmond Hill enjoy spectacular views over the Thames Valley.

The communal efficiency of the flats and shared amenities were highly valued, in comparison to the independence and individuality of the owner occupiers of the suburban house. Central heating and hot water were for the most part provided centrally. In order to tempt tenants they were offered open fires in the sitting room but electric fires in the bedrooms; refrigerators in the kitchen, which inevitably had fitted cupboards; telephones and even an electric clock over the mantelpiece. Besides these tangible amenities, the greatest concern was that the flats be generous in size and light and open in aspect. Balconies, at least in the suburbs, were almost a necessity, and the entrance hall of each flat occupied a substantial amount of space.

Although the inter-war flats proved popular among a constituency of the middle classes, they by no means appealed to everyone, nor could everyone afford them. The rent of a well-appointed, spacious flat would have been beyond the means of most purchasers of the small suburban house. A salary of £250 per year has been given as the cut-off point between working class and middle class, though £500 was the minimum for a 'comfortable' middle-class lifestyle. But for the cheapest flat in Hillbrow, Richmond

Hill, the tenant would have had to spend 40 per cent of his £500 per year (fig. 3.19). By comparison, the rent for a one-room flat in Lichfield Court would cover the rent of a five-room council flat in Islington.

We have seen how the London County Council built houses and flats before the First World War and how it continued after the war to build large out of county cottage estates. It also continued to assume responsibility for slum clearance under a series of Housing Acts from 1919, while the metropolitan boroughs, to varying degrees, built for general housing need. By their nature, the slums consisted of worn-out terraces in parts of the city where the quality of building had often been poor, and where the density of the population had become great. In order to rehouse the same number of people on the vacant sites but with modern amenities, it seemed necessary to build large estates of flats. During the inter-war years the LCC developed a type of block which is now as recognisable as the board schools of the late nineteenth century (fig. 3.20) (Walk 8). The blocks were five storeys and consisted of three floors of flats topped by two-storey maisonettes. Despite the size of many of the buildings, stylistic references were to Georgian houses. Construction was load-bearing brick, and façades were composed with facing brick and rows of symmetrically placed sash windows, while the tiled pitched roof rose above a parapet. Access balconies at the rear of the building overlooked a courtyard, and the front faced narrow stretches of railed-in grass. The head of the house-building programme at the LCC, G. Topham Forrest, described the blocks as cottages stacked one on the other, and saw them as an interim solution until every family could have its own cottage.

Some of the very large inter-war estates in London have disappeared, but many examples still remain such as the Whitmore Estate, Hoxton Street (1924–37), and the Northwold Estate, Hackney (1934). Although the buildings were substantial, the flats were often minimal in their amenities. Despite the desire for a separate kitchen, most flats were supplied with a cooking range in the living room and a small scullery for wet chores. There was an attempt to keep the bedrooms opening off a corridor within the flat, but there were instances where at least one bedroom opened directly off the living room. Still, for most of the tenants, possession of their own cooking facilities and their own bathroom and WC was an improvement only dreamed of in their previous private rented accommodation.

One estate where the LCC tried to implement innovation was at Ossulston Street, with mixed results. Early

3.19 Hillbrow, Richmond, C.Beresford Marshal and Partners, 1937.

3.20 Barnsbury Estate, London County Council, from 1935.

3.21 Manchester Mansions, Islington, E.C.P. Monson, 1920.

3.22 Grosvenor Estate, Page Street, Westminster, Edwin Lutyens, 1929–35.

on in the LCC's post-war building programme it considered a type of housing derived from American cities where there were apartment blocks of up to eleven storeys with shops at ground level. Such a height demanded a lift, and this was fitted as a matter of necessity. The site the LCC was proposing for a similar scheme in London was Somers Town, a notorious slum close to Euston Station. The 1925 scheme was to be nine storeys with lifts and some private flats on the upper floors. This scheme was refused on two counts, the lifts and the private flats, since neither was considered appropriate for flats subsidised under the Housing Acts. Instead, the inspiration for the existing estate (1927–31) came from Viennese housing of the period such as Karl Marx Hof. The construction of the blocks was steel frame and the walls of distinctive roughcast. Levita House of 1930–1 rises to seven storeys, and in the courtyard the access balconies are masked by tall arches. The Ossulston Estate proved to be a one-off, with no further attempts by the LCC at this time radically to break the mould of its blocks of flats.

The metropolitan boroughs were also charged under the Housing Acts to provide accommodation where appropriate for their working-class populations. Under the 1919 Act the boroughs were subsidised to build general-need housing, while it was the responsibility of the LCC to rehouse those from slum clearance sites. Each borough evaluated its own housing needs, and some were more active than others. Islington, for example, provided three estates of working-class flats, all designed by E. C. P. Monson, an architect previously engaged with the building of flats for the Sutton Trust in various areas of London. Addington Mansions in Highbury consisted of substantial red brick blocks, with some of the flats including parlours in their layout. This was also the case at Manchester Mansions at the north end of the borough near Hornsey Lane (fig. 3.21). The other estate, Halton Mansions, behind the new town hall in Upper Street, was less generous in its provision, and its flats were let at a lower rent. Although all the tenants of the council's flats were 'working class', some of the earliest tenants verged on the lower middle class and included a bank clerk and a clergyman. The tenants were also demanding, asking the council to make changes to their flats, and requesting permission to install telephones and keep cars, as they did at Addington Mansions.

In 1930, the Housing Act of that year specified that housing subsidies were to be used to rehouse tenants from specific slum clearance areas, and this drew the boroughs into slum clearance along with the LCC (fig. 3.22). Five years later, the Housing Act made the local authorities responsible for alleviating overcrowding within their borders. Both these Acts set strict limits on the amount the boroughs could spend on their estates, and specified the type of tenants for whom the flats were intended. Islington, for example, found that the population who most needed the housing lived in the overcrowded south of the borough, but the sites available for the new estates were located in the north of the borough where there still remained the largest of the old suburban villas. It proved difficult to entice many north, since that would take them away from their work and any credit they had been able to establish in their area. Islington also found that the management of their new estates was more demanding, as the tenants had problems paying their rent and accommodating themselves to living in self-contained flats.

Most of the flats built by the metropolitan boroughs were conventional enough, such as the flats designed by E. C. P. Monson for Bethnal Green (fig. 3.23) (Walk 11). Finsbury (now part of Islington) proved an exception when they called upon Tecton in 1937 to design new housing on a site between Rosebery Avenue and St John Street. The Second World War intervened and the flats were not built

until 1946–50 (see below). Innovation in design was more likely in the flats built in the inter-war period by housing associations and other agents engaged in working-class housing. The modernist architect Maxwell Fry designed Sassoon House, Southwark (1932) and, in collaboration with Elizabeth Denby, Kensal House in North Kensington for the Gas Light and Coke Company (1936–7). The latter consisted of two slab blocks of reinforced concrete construction, curved around the site of a former gasometer. The blocks are flat-roofed and rendered, and were intended to demonstrate the efficiency of gas fuel. Another scheme of modernist appearance is Evelyn Court (1934–5) in Amhurst Road, Hackney for the Four Per Cent Industrial Dwellings Company by Burnet, Tait and Lorne. The ten five-storey blocks are built of standardised reinforced concrete and have flat roofs and smooth rendered walls, and still cause surprise in the passer-by with their uncompromising appearance.

The Second World War interrupted a number of housing projects. The LCC's vast White City Estate was designed in 1934–6 and begun in 1938–9, but completed only after the war. In 1936 the LCC acquired the site for the Woodberry Down Estate at Manor House. The original scheme dates from 1938, but the layout was revised in 1943 under the influence of the County of London Plan of the same year, and construction took place between 1946 and 1952. At Woodberry Down, J. H. Forshaw, co-author with Patrick Abercrombie of the London Plan, insisted on four eight-storey concrete blocks with lifts, the first tall blocks of flats to be built by the London County Council. In Finsbury the Spa Green Estate was finally built to revised plans by Tecton for Finsbury Local Authority (fig. 3.24) (Walk 8). Here two blocks were of eight storeys and one of four, in reinforced concrete, box-frame construction. Visually what distinguishes these flats is the abstract arrangement of window openings and balconies, and the extensive use of colour and texture, to produce an overall effect of rich design. The result has affinities with modernist Continental flats, and leaves behind the 'stacked cottage' concept of the inter-war LCC blocks.

Just as after the First World War, housing provision was an important political issue, and it was perceived as having a role in the hoped-for social changes in post-war Britain. To help illustrate the potential benefits of new housing to the population of London, a bombed area of Poplar in east London was designated as a Live

3.23 Claredale House, Bethnal Green, E.C.P. Monson, 1931–2.

3.24 Spa Green Estate, Finsbury, Tecton, 1937, 1946–50.

3.25 Churchill Gardens Estate, Pimlico, Powell and Moya, 1947–62.

3.26 Slab blocks, Alton West Estate, Roehampton, London County Council, 1954–8.

Architecture exhibit in conjunction with the Festival of Britain of 1951. The Lansbury Estate, named for the local radical MP George Lansbury, consisted of flats and houses of stock brick arranged around generous open greens. What distinguished the estate was the inclusion of schools, churches and a pedestrianised market square, with the anticipation that the area would coalesce into a neighbourhood. The generous layout and dwelling size contrasted with the tightly built, overcrowded conditions of adjacent streets, but the design, while pleasant, was not as 'progressive' as some younger architects would have liked.

In 1946 the young practice of Powell and Moya won the competition to build the large Pimlico estate, Churchill Gardens, for Westminster City Council (fig. 3.25). They introduced a number of innovations, including district heating derived from the hot water expelled by Battersea Power Station across the Thames. The estate is an early example of what is known as 'mixed development', whereby tall slabs of nine to eleven storeys are mixed with three- and four-storey terraces of houses, flats and maisonettes. The blocks are set out in parallel rows according to the prevailing *Zeilenbau* theory of block layout, which gave equal exposure to light and air for the living rooms in all flats. The generous space between the blocks, the abstract arrangement of windows and balconies, and the flat roofs contribute to a progressive appearance while still retaining a sense of scale.

The newly formed London County Council Architect's Department undertook the Alton Estates in Roehampton, west London, in a similar spirit of innovation. Alton East and West were planned as mixed development estates, but their main advantage was their sites, which allowed generous layout and good landscaping. The estates were planned from 1951, and Alton East built from 1952 to 1955. This section consists of ten eleven-storey point blocks and lower terraces of houses and maisonettes, set at right angles to the winding roads where some of the mature planting remained. Alton West from 1954 is more urban and less bosky at the entrance to the estate, but further on it opens out into a sweep of parkland on which are dramatically placed five slab blocks on pilotis (fig. 3.26). The reference is to Le Corbusier's Unité d'Habitation in Marseilles, and the siting of the blocks originates in the concept of the 'towers in the park' so favoured by the likes of Thomas Sharp and Frederick Gibberd before the war.

It was very difficult for local authorities to find such favourable sites, although bomb damage and slum clearance provided much-needed locations for new housing. The County of London Plan 1943 divided London into three density zones, and laid down accepted density levels for the three: 200 persons per acre of housing area in the central locations; 136 persons per acre in the middle ring; and 100 persons per acre in the outer or suburban ring. Central sites were expensive, and it was not always easy to acquire enough land to make an estate viable, but where it was possible the temptation was to fill the sites with as many flats as were permissible. A typical LCC estate is St George's in Tower Hamlets, which was built in an area of small houses damaged by bombing, but also the sort of area the planners wanted to see cleared and opened up. The estate demonstrates mixed development and combines point blocks with smaller houses.

As in other parts of the country, many local authorities turned to the new building systems which promised rapid construction and a quick solution to the housing problem. The systems depended on frame construction and prefabricated panels of concrete or plastic, which in turn depended on standardisation and economies of scale, two characteristics which led inevitably to monumental estates of identical dwelling units. The Aylesbury Estate built by Southwark Council from 1967 to 1977 is one of the largest of these estates. The 2,434 dwellings are contained in slab blocks of from four to fourteen storeys, which were constructed by Laings with the Jespersen industrialised building system. Such mammoth estates greatly contributed to the housing stock and helped to alleviate the housing shortage, but their enormous size and impersonality began to give flats a bad name among council tenants, especially during the 1970s when the high cost of maintenance and management became apparent.

3.27 Keeling House, Bethnal Green, Denys Lasdun, 1955–9.

During this period there were, however, some examples of architects engaging in the design issues of blocks of flats with some distinguished results. Denys Lasdun's Keeling House in Claredale Street, Bethnal Green (1955–9) is a cluster block of sixteen storeys, which consists of two-storey maisonettes in four wings linked by bridges to service lobbies (fig. 3.27) (Walk 11). Lasdun hoped that the lobbies and the individual balconies would foster neighbourliness among the tenants, and reproduce something of the closeness of the East End street. The block was threatened by demolition after Tower Hamlets emptied it in 1993, but refurbishment by private owners has ensured that it now has an extended life.

In 1952 Chamberlin, Powell and Bon won the competition for the Golden Lane Estate. It is on the edge of the City, and forms the first initiative in the rebuilding of the London Wall and Barbican areas which had been so badly damaged in the war. The ten blocks were intended for single people and couples working in the City, and the architects consciously provided an urban environment, which is nonetheless made colourful by the use of yellow, red and blue glass cladding. Included in the scheme are amenities such as a swimming pool, nursery school and what is now a tennis court, but although this estate was built by the City Corporation, it was still social housing.

One of the entries in the 1952 competition for Golden Lane was by Alison and Peter Smithson. Although they did not win the competition, their entry had a great influence on the design of the large monumental estates in London and elsewhere. By the time they built their own estate, Robin Hood Gardens (1966–72), the energy was beginning to go out of their ideas, such as 'streets in the air' and the rough precast concrete of what was known as the New Brutalism. The estate is not helped by the site, which is on the edge of the Blackwall Tunnel Approach and surrounded by main roads. Quite near Robin Hood Gardens is Balfron Tower, part of the Brownfield

3.28 Modling House, Cranbrook Estate, Bethnal Green, Skinner Bailey and Lubetkin, 1961–8.

Estate. This was Erno Goldfinger's first venture into public housing for the Greater London Council (1965–7), and it demonstrates some of the same features he incorporated later into Trellick Tower in west London. The block is twenty-six storeys and distinguished by the adjacent lift and services tower, which is connected to the main block by a bridge at every third floor.

Trellick Tower on the Cheltenham Estate in North Kensington (1966–72) is thirty storeys. Here there is the same arrangement with the stair and lift tower separated from the main block and joined at every third floor. The balconies are generous in size, and the flats are arranged across the block, so that light comes in from two sides rather than the usual one in other GLC blocks. The bush-hammered concrete finish contrasts with the wood of the balconies on a façade which is vast but well proportioned. Despite the design features, the block fell into disrepute along with other tall blocks of flats, and the partial collapse in 1968 of the point block, Ronan Point, after a gas explosion did nothing to reconcile the public to high-rise living.

Across London there are many mixed development estates which were built either by the GLC or the individual boroughs during the 1960s and 1970s (fig. 3.28). Although most remain, some have been reconfigured as they have become more and more difficult to maintain. The Holly Street Estate in Hackney is an example where two of the four system-built tower blocks have been demolished and replaced with low-rise rebuilding and individual houses. The consensus has emerged that tall flats are inappropriate for families, and especially families on low income who are the ones usually occupying public housing. During the 1970s, before the political climate militated against government involvement in housing provision, attempts were made to build high-density, low-rise estates with varying success. Darbourne and Darke designed Lillington Gardens on a site off Vauxhall Bridge Road in Victoria which has prospered, especially after the 'right to buy' in the 1980s put much of it into the private sector. Not so successful was the same architects' Marquess Road Estate in Islington. Although it was designed on the same lines, the density combined with the layout of cul de sacs and covered passages had unfortunate social results, and the estate is now being reconfigured along more traditional lines with the reintroduction of streets.

The experiment with post-war flat building by local government might have confirmed the cultural prejudice against flat living among Londoners, and others across the country, if it were not for the Barbican (Walk 7). This development was a joint scheme between the City of London and the LCC to rebuild part of the war-devastated area on the north side of the City. Chamberlin, Powell and Bon, the architects of the Golden Lane Estate, were asked to provide a mixed-use scheme to include residences, schools and an arts centre. Plans for the 35-acre site evolved from 1956 to the mid-1960s when work began on the present scheme. There are three tower blocks, the tallest residential blocks in Europe, of forty-three and forty-four storeys above the podium. In addition, there are terraces of up to eleven storeys, linked by pedestrian walkways and overlooking internal courtyards and a lake (fig. 3.29). The bush-hammered finish of the towers marks them out as brutalist, while the terraces impress through their sheer length, some of 600 feet (183 metres). Although the podium is a public space and provides access to the arts centre and the Guildhall School of Music and Drama, security is an important consideration, with residents paying a substantial service charge for security and maintenance. Flat size and design are varied, ranging from large penthouses to one-room studios, and although intended for rent are now mostly owner occupied. Flats in the Barbican continue to be in demand, but it is an open question how many similar schemes

3.29 Barbican, City of London, Chamberlin, Powell and Bon, 1956–81.

London could sustain, since nothing on this scale for a middle-class clientele has been attempted elsewhere in the city.

Blocks of purpose-built flats continue to form an essential part of London's residential stock, and many Londoners, of whatever economic level, live in such buildings. But flat living is not confined to purpose-built blocks. We have seen in the previous chapter that the London house proved flexible enough to provide accommodation for single or multiple households, depending on the area and the conditions of the time. After the First World War, it became increasingly common for the informal division of houses to be made more formal by conversion into self-contained flats. In 1919 a government initiative attempted to encourage the private sector to engage with flat conversions by urging local authorities in London to buy up empty houses and carry out the conversions themselves. Despite the accepted belief that many houses were standing empty, only a fraction of the expected flats were produced in this way.

After the Second World War, however, the division of houses into self-contained flats rapidly became the new investment opportunity in areas of mature housing. Conversions became easier with the new domestic technology, so that kitchens and bathrooms could be fitted into awkward spaces within the house and at every level. Amenities such as central heating and individual hot water heating gave the same advantages to the conversions as were to be found in new purpose-built flats. The process also meant that houses which had reduced in value could be brought back into the market at a greatly enhanced value.

The situation changed again when it became common practice to buy converted flats. Chris Hamnett in *Cities, Housing and Profits* (1988) has charted the rise of flat owner occupation, and how it radically changed the nature of the housing market

3.30 Cornwall Gardens, Kensington, south side, Thomas Cundy III, 1866–79.

3.31 Brunswick Centre, Bloomsbury, Patrick Hodgkinson, 1968–72, refurbished 2006.

in London. At one time a whole swathe of housing disappeared from the rented sector, and people were more or less forced to buy their flat, whether this suited them or not. This depended on changes in the regulations governing mortgages, but it also relied on sufficient numbers of small rentiers willing to sell up once the increased value of their house transformed it into an asset.

Georgian terraces were relatively easy to convert, since once the staircase was boxed in, one flat per floor could be provided without difficulty. Houses dating from later periods, when the detached and semi-detached house had become preferred to the terrace, were more problematic and required more ingenious planning to fit in viable flats. The result was that many areas of London which might have been demolished, or become commercial in character, retained their old residential function, even though they were very close to the centre. Islington, Camden and Kensington are all boroughs where many of the houses have been converted, and their populations are for the most part flat dwellers (fig. 3.30) (Walk 9).

Another more recent development has been the conversion of buildings never intended for residential purposes into flats. The concept of the loft, developed in cities such as New York, hit London in the 1980s when redundant warehouses and factories offered space in unexpected places. The revitalisation of the City of London made areas such as Wapping attractive, and the nineteenth-century warehouses along the river were ready-made structures with stretches of undifferentiated interior space ripe for conversion. Once again domestic technology made it possible to transform these buildings into desirable flats, with modern amenities plus views of the Thames and proximity to the financial centres of London. The result was a new kind of gentrification, whereby the redundant workplaces of the local inhabitants became the dwellings of much wealthier workers.

Even if London does not have the perimeter blocks found in most European cities, Londoners are for the most part a flat-dwelling population (fig. 3.31). This is partly due to the ideas put forward in the inter-war period, when flats were seen as progressive and a means to achieve modernity in domestic life. These ideas lay behind the government-sponsored house building after the Second World War, and ensured that much of the public housing came in the form of flats, some of which occurred in tower blocks. However, despite some private flat building, many flat dwellers occupy converted houses, especially in the last thirty years. This movement has been closely related to the transfer from private renting to owner occupation as the chief form of housing tenure.

Chapter 4 SERVICING LONDON
Transport, shops, pubs and schools

There was an enormous growth in population in London during the nineteenth century, from 1.5 million in the 1820s to 4.5 million in the county of London and another 2 million in Greater London (beyond the jurisdiction of the LCC) by 1900. By 1911 it had risen to over 7 million and by 1939 to 8.6 million, falling to 7.1 million in 2001. During this period of growth, terraces and streets of speculative housing inexorably swallowed up villages and open spaces on all sides of the capital. This unregulated increase, often painful and variously pathologised as a cancerous growth or as evidence of the head's growing too large for the body, excited concern for health, morality, order and provision. Anthropomorphic images of impending disaster reflected surprise, wonder and horror in the confrontation of excess: we know what the body is supposed to look like and it should not look like this. Growth itself was not new (John Evelyn in 1680 urged bringing 'this monstrous body into shape'), but this exponential expansion, to which the urban world has now become habituated, appeared to be a new phenomenon. It carried with it the corollary of extremes of human triumph and disaster as participants scrabbled for footholds in a shifting landscape of new building and roads, demolition and physical displacement. Here was opportunity but also the possibility of failure, as noted by Jerrold: 'Hard solid work: work that makes millionaires and leaves the worn-out fingers of the heroic honest man cold upon a pallet ...' Those who survived long enough during this period of intense and startling upheaval – with its attendant enormous increase in manufacturing and commerce – witnessed the emergence of a recognisably modern, industrialised, serviced city. We are still living with its legacy and with many of its original and more enduring manifestations.

Getting there: the Underground
There were horse-drawn omnibuses in London from 1829. The first suburban railway line – from London Bridge to Greenwich in 1836 – was followed by separate companies pushing railway lines as far into the centre of the city as possible, displacing the poorest who were the most easily bought out, and stopping short of the great estates owned by the aristocracy. This is why the north London mainline stations stop at the Marylebone and Euston Roads, unable to go further without unfeasible expense and prohibitively lengthy Acts of Parliament, a procedural restriction supported by government-decreed limits on expansion into the centre. Those who were displaced did not immediately benefit from the arrival of stations at Euston (London-Birmingham 1837), King's Cross (Great Northern 1851–2), St Pancras (Midland 1866–8) and Marylebone (Great Central 1899). From the 1860s some of the individual railway companies were required to provide cheap tickets through 'workmen's fares', but it was not until the Cheap Trains Act of 1883 that the displaced were able to take full advantage of the new services. By 1911, 390,000 passengers per day were coming into London from stations between four and thirty miles away, 105,000 of them on workmen's tickets.

From the 1860s there was the beginning of the London Underground system. Consideration had been given earlier in 1855 to a 'crystal way', proposed by William Moseley, with a railway 12 feet (3.6 metres) below street level and a glazed, arcaded walkway above, with shops, houses and hotels on either side. A similar scheme, put

4.1 Gillespie Road Underground Station, opened 1906, renamed Arsenal 1932 (English Heritage, National Monuments Record).

forward by Joseph Paxton, designed with the intention of linking all London's railway termini, placed the trains at an upper level above arcaded walkways which ran alongside the road. Atmospheric pressure was proposed for drawing the trains along in both these schemes, but experiments showed that the joints tended to fail.

The first underground line, built by the cut-and-cover method just below the surface of the road, provided steam trains from Paddington to Farringdon, via Baker Street and King's Cross, from 1863, with continuations westward to Ladbroke Grove and Kensington in 1864 and eastward to Moorgate in 1865. There had long been a need to effect such a link between Brunel's terminus at Paddington, which had opened in 1838 on the edge of the built-up area, and the City. There were initially two tracks on the Paddington to Farringdon route to accommodate the two types of gauge in use, in order to allow Great Western Trains to progress beyond the terminus. The trains had smoke compartments which enabled them to store smoke before releasing it at appropriate open-air moments. They also had water tanks underneath in order to absorb the steam, but the tunnels nevertheless were full of smoke and passengers feared asphyxiation. Chemist shops in the vicinity of stations enjoyed good business. In addition to the underground trains, there were trams from the 1870s, and on the river there had been steamboats since the 1830s. All of this travelling was relatively unregulated, with private companies in competition trying to limit each other's growth in order to protect a monopoly on an area or route. The absence of an overall planning authority for transport did not necessarily work in the interest of the consumer.

The development of the underground network on deeper lines was made possible by the tunnelling shield, allowing deep-level tunnels to be dug and consolidated in one operation, and by electrification for the trains and the passenger lifts required to get down to the new lines: the Northern 1890–1907, Waterloo and City 1898, Central 1900, Bakerloo and Piccadilly 1906. Built with American investment, most notably through the entrepreneurial efforts of Charles Tyson Yerkes, a Philadelphian weaver of financial webs, and administered by separate companies, the stations on these lines nevertheless achieved a robust house style although each was adapted to its site, with no two wholly alike (fig. 4.1). The architects Leslie Green and Stanley Heaps provided stations designed to give confidence to passengers who were invited to go where only coalminers had been before. To go voluntarily several hundred feet into the earth in order to be transported rapidly along a tubeline, with no external orientation, surely required an act of faith. The Edwardian classical style adopted for the stations at ground level presented an image of confidence and capability to counter the inherently bizarre undertaking orchestrated by the tunnelling engineers: moulded terracotta oxblood blocks, bottle-green tiling, heavy glazing, arcaded booking halls and Otis lifts. This was the first great period of underground railway construction, and it is greatly to be regretted that so many of these confident creations have been lost or defaced.

Yerkes, who died in 1905, was the first chairman of the Underground Electric Railways Company of London (UERL), a holding company which attempted to consolidate and co-ordinate other competing businesses through merger. Under the direction of Albert Stanley, appointed in 1907, the UERL by 1913 had successfully merged with most of the other underground enterprises and had bought up the London General Omnibus Company. The first symbol of the growing group, in 1907, depicted lines burrowing under a silhouetted prospect of the City, with a prominent St Paul's and a rising sun above. This pictorial marriage of the new and the familiar was the first attempt at corporate branding for the system. Further acquisitions were made by the UERL in the 1920s, but the growth in the number of competing bus companies, the continuing independence of the Metropolitan Railway and the local authority-administered tramways prevented a monopoly. This eventually was created by the government action which established London Transport in 1933, under the control of the London Passenger Transport Board; it amalgamated 165 companies, of which 73 had been part of the UERL group.

The second major underground construction phase began in the 1920s and continued through the 1930s under the direction of Frank Pick, who with the architect Charles Holden extended the system into the new suburbs. London Transport, in continuation of this programme, with Pick as vice chairman and chief executive, has become a key exemplar in the history of the establishment of corporate identity. Edward Johnston's typeface, created for the UERL in 1916, and his design for the bar and circle motif two years later were in due course extended throughout the system to identify all its property and publicity. This imposition of a coherent image, reinforced by improvements in rolling stock, the installation of unified station furniture, the commissioning of stylish, high-quality poster art, and most memorably the building of new stations of international quality, was a strategy based on a precise vision, enunciated by Pick: 'Every element should bear a visual relation to everything else.' A system formed through the merging of 165 companies demanded this apparent coherence in order to continue to inspire the public confidence which would ensure financial viability. Pick's strategy was based in politics and economics as much as it was based on the moral imperative of providing a safe, secure and attractive mode of transport for millions of passengers. As the dilapidated system creaks towards recovery in the early twenty-first century, it is easy to lose sight of the initial vision, not only of contented commuters, but of those who were persuaded by such notable graphic artists as McKnight Kauffer, Edward Bawden and others to make journeys it had not occurred to them to make. Harry Beck's diagrammatic map of 1933, which has become a key mental image of the city, stressed connections, obscuring the difficulties of interchange at stations with separate lines far apart, once run by different companies, and distorted scale by compressing the suburbs so that distance appeared to be no object.

This 1920s–30s phase was able to capitalise on the introduction of the escalator. It was first tested at Holloway Road in 1906 but not put into service, then tested again at Earl's Court in 1911 and Paddington in 1913 before coming into common use in the 1920s, when the extension of the Piccadilly Line in particular prompted the building of a number of stations of significant architectural merit (fig. 4.2). A stripped north European modernism was favoured, with two-storey booking halls with large windows, naturally lit by day and appearing as electrically lit beacons by

4.2 Arnos Grove Underground Station, opened 1932.

night. Uplighters on the escalators provided a reflected light, minimising glare, with directions clearly indicated in Johnston's stylish typography. The spacious and airy quality of these new stations encouraged an idea of healthy, efficient and reliable transport, no mean feat for a system which goes underground, into the unknown where spiritual vacancy and archetypal fears are but one malfunction away. The escalator was fundamental to the success of this proposition, and it is the loss of the escalator – and the airy ease and flow that it enables – which most undermines confidence in the system when repair or replacement is required. This takes a long time: as Peter Campbell has explained, these are 'big, complicated machines packed into tight shafts and there aren't many hours when you can work on them'.

The Pick–Holden period brought the number of stations to 270, with only twenty-nine south of the river, an absence partly for reasons of tunnelling difficulties in the marshier ground and also because of the great number of competing suburban railway lines. Funding for the extension to the system was by a mixture of public and private finance, much of it deployed in order to encourage the unemployed back into work. Population expansion and movement accompanied the construction of the lines. 450,000 people moved out of central London in the 1920s and 1930s into the suburbs, which were perceived as healthier, to be joined by large numbers who came into suburban London from outside, looking for the work that the suburbs provided: light industry, electrical engineering, food processing, armaments and motor car manufacture. However, to state baldly as an example that the Piccadilly Line was extended northwards from Finsbury Park to Cockfosters in 1932–3 to serve the growing population suggests a straightforward and rational process. It was not. The Finsbury Park station site was owned by the Great Northern Railway, which operated its own suburban services. The Underground had been compelled to agree not to build any line to the north following the termination of the Piccadilly Line in 1906. It soon became clear that this was highly problematic: travellers to the north could get onto trains, but those going to the north-east had to take buses or trams. In the later 1920s it was reported that over 30,000 people made the transfer in peak periods – there were frequent reports of women fainting and men fighting to get onto buses. It took an inquiry, several reports, innumerable photographs demonstrating congestion, government intervention, the Treasury underwriting the capital costs, and the House of Lords rejecting the appeals of the railway company before the line and stations could be constructed. By the same enabling legislation, the line west from Hammersmith was built to ease the traffic from the growing suburbs of Hounslow, Harrow and Ealing.

These stations are among the highpoints of English civic architecture, prompting Nikolaus Pevsner to compare the enlightened patronage of Frank Pick and London Transport to that of the Medici and Louis XIV. For Pevsner, these buildings paved the way for the twentieth-century style in England. They are still arresting, still demonstrating both clarity of design and care for their users (fig. 4.4). The new headquarters building for the Underground at 55 Broadway, above St James's Park station, at the time of opening in 1929 the tallest office building in London, was a similarly distinguished design by Holden, built on a cruciform plan with set-backs at the seventh, ninth and tenth floors culminating in a central clock tower (fig. 4.3). Sculpture by a team including Jacob Epstein and Eric Gill – notwithstanding the latter's misgivings about the redundancy of such work on a 'good and plain' building – further extended the enlightened patronage of Pick's institution, and manifested, as Terry Friedman notes, a 'progressive attempt ... to experiment with the alliance of architecture and sculpture', although the proportional relationship of building and sculpture inhibits close appreciation.

Frank Pick retired in 1940 and died only one year later. He had made an enormous impact, but he had not achieved all he might have wished. Writing to Holden in May 1940, he reflected (as quoted by David Lawrence):

> It is indeed strange how the idea of a railway station still germinates to bring forth fresh flower and fruit. Just as you suppose you have analysed its functions and purposes completely and given them just expression, so something new springs into view and a fresh rationalisation of the elements in an architectural unity is demanded. We have not yet solved for example interchange in comfort and convenience between road and rail vehicles ... So I can wish you joy as soon as this war is over in another attempt to catch up with requirements and add to the monuments of London suited to this industrial age.

In fact, in the immediate post-war period, only the extension of the Central Line, both east and west, was achieved. The Victoria Line, following a route first considered in

4.3 London Underground Headquarters, 55 Broadway, Westminster, 1927–9.

4.4 Arnos Grove Underground Station, booking hall.

4.5 Southwark Underground Station, opened 1999.

the 1930s, eventually was opened in stages between 1968 and 1972. As the first new deep-level line for over half a century, linking four mainline rail termini with the West End of London and suburbs to south and north-east, this was a highly effective piece of infrastructure, although hardly monumental and mainly requiring interchange facilities at existing stations rather than the construction of striking new buildings.

For these, we had to wait until the extension of the Jubilee Line south-east from Green Park to link hitherto neglected parts south of the river with Docklands and points east as far as Stratford. This was an act of regeneration both literal and symbolic conceived only three years after the fire at King's Cross in 1987 killed thirty-one and dealt a massive blow to public confidence. Nine new stations were built together with greatly expanded interchanges at Green Park, Waterloo and London Bridge. Revealed in 1999 rather as Wren had revealed his previously obscured St Paul's after completion, these stations were similarly revelatory. St Paul's was perhaps less of a surprise than the Jubilee Line stations. After twenty years of political and economic erosion of the concept of high-quality, publicly funded civic architecture, with a market-led approach designed to convince the lowest common denominator of bankers, planners and politicians of a 'cost-effectiveness' which entirely fails to acknowledge the spiritual uplift good architecture can provide, superb buildings suddenly appeared in the most unexpected of contexts. The overall planning for the line was by the architect Roland Paoletti, invited to London by the accountant Sir Wilfred Newton, with whom he had worked on the Hong Kong Rapid Transit System. With 'ring-fenced' public funding and management of the project separated from London Transport – both elements vital to success being secured by Newton and maintained by his successor Dennis Tunnicliffe – Paoletti (quoted by J. Bumpus) aimed for a style which is 'jazz, not chamber music': varying upon and returning to a theme. The architecture of the stations is unified only by its high quality and the fact that the architecture and engineering work together and both go right down to the tracks, to which natural light has been brought as closely as possible. The Jubilee Line stations, designed by a number of different architectural practices, revel in the spatial possibilities of the light-filled excavated box, criss-crossed by supporting trusses. Although directional signage has been added to the buildings, it is not always required since the architecture itself leads the eye and directs the traveller, often with impressive theatricality: the crisply elegant Southwark (fig. 4.5), with the exit defined by a blue-glazed wall (MacCormac, Jamieson, Prichard; the glass designed with Alexander Beleschenko); the glass-roofed

bank of escalators at Bermondsey, with light spilling onto the platforms (fig. 4.8) (Ian Ritchie Architects); and the quasi-sacral space of the reused West India Dock basin at Canary Wharf (fig. 4.6) (Foster and Partners) all attest to a civic ambition which users of the system had not expected to see recurring so long after the great days of Pick and Holden.

Although the stations are not imitative, they do look back in some cases to the best work of those innovators, quoting elements and forms from the suburban stations of the 1930s and harking back, beyond those predecessors, to the great age of overground railway architecture in which the drama of transit was celebrated in the monumental train-sheds of King's Cross (Lewis Cubitt, 1851–2, with the adjacent Great Northern Hotel, 1854), St Pancras (W. H. Barlow, 1866–8, behind G. G. Scott's Midland Grand Hotel of 1868–74), and Paddington (I. K. Brunel, M. D. Wyatt and Owen Jones, 1850–4, with the Great Western Hotel by P .C. Hardwick, 1851–4). This theme was revived more recently above-ground by Nicholas Grimshaw and Partners and YRM Anthony Hunt Associates at the serpentine Eurostar terminal at Waterloo, completed in 1993 and constructed as a series of intersecting arches to accommodate the curve of the track (fig. 4.7) (Walk 5). Although, as Andrew Saint noted shortly after the Jubilee Line stations were unveiled, it is too soon for mature judgement, nevertheless 'there can have been few occasions when London has seen so many aspiring works of architecture on the same theme opened simultaneously; a parallel with the City churches built after the Great Fire is not out of place'.

4.6 Canary Wharf Underground Station, opened 1999.

4.7 Waterloo International Station, completed 1993.

4.8 Bermondsey Underground Station, opened 1999.

Destination: shopping

For Stuart Rose, chief executive in 2006 of Marks and Spencer, the omnipresent store which began as a market stall in Leeds in 1886, 'retail is a simple business made complicated by management ... we must never forget we're barrow boys'. Like many simple things, however, and as Marks and Spencer have themselves shown in the recent past, it is easy to get it wrong.

4.9 Fox umbrella shop, London Wall, 1937; one of the best surviving shopfronts of the period.

4.10 Burlington Arcade, Piccadilly, 1818–19; a speculative development next to Burlington House, designed by Samuel Ware.

Buying and selling can and do take place anywhere: informally in the street and more formally in markets, warehouses, shops (fig. 4.9), bazaars and arcades (fig. 4.10), department stores, malls and as adjuncts to waiting for a train or an aeroplane. Such ostensibly primary activities as catching a train or taking a plane often appear to be given a lower priority than the exchange of commodities in these new emporia. It seems easier to buy a tie at Liverpool Street Station than it does to buy a ticket and find the train. The British Airports Authority issues guides to its terminals at Gatwick and Heathrow which include location plans of shops and bars, but not the tortuous routes to departure gates. So shopping is no longer necessarily an action requiring travel to a destination, but has become an incident on the way to a destination, exploiting a captive audience.

Retailing has an evolutionary quality, with perpetual reinvention and reconfiguring of its underlying concepts required in order to attract and maintain the attention of the consumer. Although buying and selling remain fundamental impulses, their mechanisms are subject to change. The trajectory of growth and decline in the London department store in the post-Second World War period, in reaction to changes in patterns of consumption as well as in response to the strategies of property developers, has been well described by Sonia Ashmore. Although a consideration of retailers' own analyses of shopping trends might confirm this as a simple business, it is also apparent that it is fluctuating and inherently unstable. The great size of department stores, necessary to accommodate the range of commodities required to seduce and then fulfil the aspirations of ever more sophisticated consumers, militates against the flexibility required for rapid response in changing circumstances. The ocean liner – vast and populous with an enormous turning circle – provides an obvious trope: for *The Times*, the closure of Gamages in 1972 was 'as majestic a sight as a ship sinking'. More recently, Dickins and Jones closed in 2006. Beginning as a draper's shop on Oxford Street, the business had steadily expanded on Regent Street from the mid-nineteenth century before occupying a whole block in a building of 1920–2 by Henry Tanner. Redevelopment as smaller and therefore more flexible retail units is proceeding (in 2007), with flats and offices above.

Historically, retailing has been carried out in settings of differing size and type, well described by Harwood and Saint:

> it cleaves to two distinctive species of London building, the party-walled house and the warehouse. Houses, infinitely adaptable, need little alteration to fit them up for exchange; the front parlour on the ground floor simply becomes the shop. If you want to expand, you knock through to the back and make the shop deeper, or take in the house next door and demolish the party wall. If you want to display your wares, as begins to be the fashion after about 1700, you hack away the ground floor front wall and put in an arresting shop window … Such premises were enough for even the largest London shopkeepers down to about 1875.

One of Charles Booth's investigators in the late nineteenth century (in the course of the enormous work of investigation, analysis and classification, published in 1892–7 as *Life and Labour of the People in London*) commented on the evolution of the shop: the first stage was the house, with a garden in front; onto this a single-storey shop could be built; success would then involve demolition and rebuilding as a larger shop with workrooms and/or flats above, the latter often for the use of the sales staff. This is how Harrods began in 1853. The introduction of plate glass and gas lighting, which for Dickens in 1835 were 'the primary symptoms' of an epidemic that had first attacked linen-drapers and haberdashers 'six or eight years ago', was fundamental to the evolving process of display and temptation he pathologised: 'Quiet dusty old shops in different parts of town were pulled down; spacious premises with stuccoed fronts and gold letters, were erected instead; floors were covered with Turkey carpets; roofs supported by massive pillars; doors knocked into windows, a dozen squares of glass into one; one shopman into a dozen ...' Some were driven into bankruptcy by the excess of their ambition and 'the disease abated', only to 'burst out again among the chemists; the symptoms were the same, with the addition of a strong desire to stick the royal arms over the shop-door, and a great rage for mahogany, varnish, and expensive floor-cloth. Then the hosiers were infected,' and after them the publicans. Dickens was no longer available later in the century to satirise the growth of the department store.

The great department stores of the turn of the nineteenth and twentieth centuries in both the centre and the suburbs of London were all-embracing in terms of product and were geared up to a new concept of shopping as a leisure activity, made possible in part by the availability of reliable public transport. Shoppers were exhorted in poster campaigns from the first decade of the century and through the 1920s and 1930s to travel by Underground into the heart of the shopping centres, women being encouraged particularly to do so during 'the quiet hours' between 10 and 4. This was presented with often considerable graphic bravura as the summit of aspirational, stylish modernity. As London Transport's Annual Report for 1938 (quoted by J. Riddell) sagely observed: 'Shopping must be reckoned among the pleasures. Certainly so far as the principal shops and stores of the West End are concerned.'

Such stores had since the later nineteenth century represented an evolutionary change in which shopping had been transformed in a manner informed by the experience of Paris, New York and Chicago. The passion and excitement of this new mode of retailing, as well as the physical and social upheaval which attended its birth, were wonderfully captured by Émile Zola in *Au Bonheur des Dames* (1883, translated into English as *The Ladies' Paradise*). Modelling his saga on that of the Bon Marché, Paris's first department store, which opened in 1855 and was the biggest in the world until 1914, occupying a whole city block, Zola chronicled the new mechanisms of seduction. These included advertising; free entry (browsing in a safe environment without any obligation to buy); fixed prices rather than bargaining, fostering speed and impersonality; the system of returns (exchangeability); the manipulation of space – the creation of disorder and disconnection, compelling the shopper to travel through the store in order to be exposed to the unexpected. Here, in Brian Nelson's analysis, was 'the seduction of pure spectacle' – an orgiastic display of visual pleasures, indicated from the outside by sheet glass through which the window-shopper could gaze at electrically lit displays, and consummated within in the welter of commodities signalling the triumph of capitalism, the celebration of the buying power of the middle-class woman, aided and abetted by the middle-class man, and at the same time the commodification of women themselves. In this reading, everything for sale is an object of desire:

> The crowd had reached the silk department ... At the far end of the hall,
> around one of the small cast iron columns which supported the glass roof,
> material was streaming down like a bubbling sheet of water ... Women
> pale with desire were leaning over as if to look at themselves. Faced with this
> wild cataract, they all remained standing there, filled with the secret fear of
> being caught in the overflow of all this luxury and with an irresistible desire
> to throw themselves into it and be lost.

4.11 Selfridge's department store, Oxford Street, from the east.

Zola here describes the modern world of consumption and display – products from all over the globe brought by new transport systems to be sold to the consumers who themselves are there because the transit systems are in place. The completion of the grandiloquent façade of Harrods in 1905 took place just one year before the arrival of the new Piccadilly Line with stations at Brompton Road and Knightsbridge.

The advertisement announcing the opening of Selfridge's (fig. 4.11) in 1909 showed a herald on a horse riding into the countryside to summon potential shoppers from afar: 'We wish it to be clearly understood that our invitation [to the opening] is to the whole British public and to visitors from overseas – that no cards of admission are required – that all are welcome – and that the pleasures of shopping as well as those of sight-seeing begin from the opening hour.' In promoting the idea of shopping as a leisure activity with places for women particularly to meet, eat or rest as well as shop, Selfridge's was not doing anything that other stores in both the centre and the suburbs of London had ignored: Dickins and Jones, for example, had introduced an afternoon tea room in 1895. But Harry Gordon Selfridge was particularly good at cultivating a modern impression – he was an outspoken champion of women's suffrage and a strong believer in the involvement of women in the masculine world of business. Architecturally, his store was urban and inviting; within, it was modern and progressive.

When Selfridge came to London from Chicago after a successful career at the Marshall Field wholesale store, he was taking a risk because the normal pattern of development was to start small and grow, as Jones the draper did in Holloway Road on his way to creating the large Jones Brothers store in 1892, once one of north London's biggest department stores, now a branch of Waitrose. William Jones had come to London from Wales and established his drapery store in a small shop with brother John in 1867. Harrods, in a more prosperous suburban location, grew in a similar way. Charles Henry Harrod was a wholesale grocer and tea dealer from the East End who opened his grocery shop on Brompton Road in 1853, expanding in the 1870s into adjacent premises; it was rebuilt after a fire in 1884, following the established pattern of expansion with a single-storey projection on the site of the original front gardens. The arrival of Richard Burbidge, formerly of Army and Navy Stores and Whiteleys, as managing director in 1891 prompted the expansion (adding drapery) and rebuilding which began in the mid-1890s and continued until 1912. This was an accretive building – a series of interconnected showrooms built over a period of eighteen years. From the start, the new building included flats on the upper floors, as did Barkers on Kensington High Street: these were areas where exclusive suburban mansion blocks and commerce could co-exist. It is appropriate that the large depository on the other side of the road from Harrods, linked by underground tunnel with the store, should now be mansion flats. In 1898, Burbidge installed a French contraption, the first escalator in England, a continuous belt – an assistant at the top was ready with smelling salts and cognac – but escalators in stores did not come into general usage until the 1930s. Electric light, replacing gas, was another innovation of the late nineteenth century. Harrods has also festively lit up the outside of the store with strings of electric lights since 1959.

Selfridge's was different (Walk 6). Starting big was risky, but the grandeur of Selfridge's architecture – colonnaded magnificence punctuated by bronze and glass, slung from a steel frame, supported by Gordon Selfridge's consummate command of advertising and publicity stunts – eventually assured success. Albert Millar from the Burnham office in Chicago produced the design for the building of 1907–9, working closely with the local architect, Frank Atkinson. Expansion under Sir John

Burnet and Partners followed in 1920–8. Atkinson's specialist knowledge was needed in order to effect the modification to the open and unimpeded American style in order to satisfy the London fire regulations. These necessitated the construction of party walls in order to create divisions between departments, a requirement which pertained until the regulations changed in the 1930s and the unrestricted openness with which we are now familiar became the norm. Peter Jones (fig. 4.12) (Walk 9), part of the John Lewis Partnership, one of the most admired modern buildings as well as one of the first examples of the use of the curtain wall in England, and John Lewis itself on Oxford Street, both completed in 1939 (although John Lewis was bombed in 1940 and rebuilding was eventually completed in 1960), were among the first to have large open floors. Walter Gropius (quoted by Edwards) recommended cantilever construction for new stores in 1939, obviating the need for piers, beams and supporting walls and permitting unrestricted daylight and fresh air. Peter Jones also had light wells to provide greater openness and natural light, so that visitors could enjoy the spectacle of commerce in much the same way as they had done at the Royal Exchange, at the nineteenth-century Pantheon Bazaar on Oxford Street, and more recently at Lloyds before security concerns prohibited public access.

This openness is the preserve not just of the department store but also of the big shed-style supermarket and, with a good architect, the small boutique as well. Built on the traditional leasehold London house plot, narrow and deep, these require particular architectural inventiveness if they are to overcome the constraints of site. Eva Jiricna, for example, at the Joseph shops on Fulham Road and Sloane Street, rather than placing staircases in the overcrowded areas at the back, inhibiting the movement of shoppers already constrained by carrying bags, made them into a prominent feature. These minimalist steel and glass staircases annihilate distance and invite ascent and descent by offering glimpses of a promised land of commodities. This strategy had earlier been employed by the architect William Crabtree at Peter Jones, where his steel spiral staircase – perhaps inspired by Erich Mendelsohn's stair at the De La Warr Pavilion, the modernist masterpiece at Bexhill on Sea – was described in *The Architectural Review* in 1939 (quoted by Calladine) as 'a new departure in customer temptation [which] attracts by its openness': gratification is only temporarily deferred. Since these shops are selling desirable rather than necessary commodities, browsing and purchasing must be made as attractive and stress-free a proposition as possible.

Pleasure and leisure are again at the forefront of thinking in the design of the shopping mall, in which the intention of the developer is to keep people there as long as possible and to make the experience such that they will want to come back. In order to achieve this, a feeling of unthreatened relaxation has to be encouraged. There needs to be enough to engage attention, and it needs to be easier to stay than to go. The out-of-town shopping mall already has the advantage of being a destination. The shopper, having driven to it with one purpose in mind, is predisposed to spend more time than would be spent in a single department store: three hours is not unusual.

Historically the mall began with the 1950s dumb-bell design in America comprising 'anchor stores' at each end with a string of smaller shops between and unlimited car parking. The first enclosed mall, designed by Victor Gruen in 1956 in Southdale, Minneapolis, provided recreational shopping with a fantasy urbanism: safe, warm, dry, no traffic, no poor people. This was a supervised, surveillance-intensive private zone with two levels and a central court with events and eating areas. This is now the worldwide model, standing independently or conjoined with offices, hotels, cultural centres and airports, and like airports intended to be recognisable to all, regardless of cultural background or language: you know where to go; you know what to do.

Malls, like airports, have their own logic. They are internalised. There are no external reference points. People tend to walk on the right, directed by signs and by what they see within controlled lines of vision: you do not navigate by seeing the outside. You do not see aeroplanes at airports until it is time to get onto one; you do not see the outside of a mall until you are fortunate enough to locate the door. This is not easy because they tend to be rather suggestively marked 'To the car park', on much the same level of hinting at options as 'To the food court' – nothing so bald, blunt and uncompromising as 'Exit', which is a word to avoid.

The pursuit of pleasure through shopping was recognised through its absence in a government report in 1971, 'The Future Pattern of Shopping', in which it was noted that satisfaction lay in the enjoyment of the goods purchased rather than in the manner of their acquisition: 'There seems to be relatively little "enjoyment" of shopping as a social activity. This surely represents a challenge to retailers, developers and planners alike.' This challenge eventually was met by the mall, but as with department stores the French got there first with a great boom in out-of-town shopping centres in 1970–5. The first in England, at Brent Cross in north London, opened in 1976. As an alternative to the West End it was successful right from the start: a two-levels mall covering one million square feet (93,000 square metres), with three-storey anchor stores, including John Lewis, and 3,550 car parking spaces. Superseded in 1990 by Lakeside, it was revamped in 1994–6 to incorporate amenities which were felt to be lacking – natural light, a soothing 'water feature' and a 'food court'. Further competition has been presented by Bluewater (1999).

'Bluewater' the product is the substance put into mall fountains to counteract the unpleasant colour caused by throwing in pennies. Bluewater the place has been presented by its architect Eric Kuhne and the Australian developers Lend Lease as a revolution in retailing. Rather like Selfridge's, it is not so much that it is doing things which are wholly new, but that it is doing them slightly differently in presentational terms or doing them better. A bald comparison between Bluewater and its nearest rival Lakeside, both built in former chalk pits on opposite sides of the River Thames next to the M25, reveals how similar they are to each other and how closely they adhere to the well-established American model. Both have 320 shops and multi-screen cinemas; both have over 10,000 car parking spaces; both have ten million potential customers within one hour's drive. Lakeside has four department stores and Bluewater three, at each corner of its triangular plan.

4.13 Thames Walk, Bluewater, Ebbsfleet, Kent, opened 1999.

Simple comparisons, however, can mislead. The shops may be the same, but the content may vary according to retailers' expectations of their customers. Kentish Bluewater has presented itself as being rather higher class, more Middle England than Essex's Lakeside. Certainly, Bluewater is semiologically more ambitious with its poetry, its visual references to Kentish crafts and trades, its plan of the River Thames inscribed on the ground, its 'break-out' areas disguised as archaeological sites, its food areas with natural light and running water mimicking the country picnic. Bluewater is a brand new constructed heritage which follows the basic retailing rules for this kind of complex: the sight lines are broken by the curve of the building (fig. 4.13), so nothing looks too far away; there are familiar stores, regular 'break-out' areas and no external reference points. The 'guests' are safe and sound, looked after by 'hosts' under the watchful eyes of 400 CCTV cameras and Bluewater's own branch of the Kent Police Force, which can close the single gateway into or out of the chalk pit within seconds of the occurrence of a crime or even the appearance of a youth in a hoodie.

Markets

As the traders and residents in Brick Lane (Walk 7) contest the desirability and accuracy of their depiction in recent novels, the role of the market in the community and the nature of that community are in question. Here and at nearby

Spitalfields Market the community of stall-holders is seldom as fixed as appearances would suggest or the tenants would aver. The Bangladeshi community of Brick Lane and its environs follows the Huguenot silk weavers of the late seventeenth and eighteenth centuries, established here in this bastion of Nonconformity after the revocation of the Edict of Nantes in 1685 forced non-Catholics to convert or to leave France. The Huguenots in their turn were followed by a Jewish population which was augmented in the later nineteenth century by waves of Jewish immigrants from eastern and central Europe. So the Nonconformist chapel on the corner of Brick Lane and Fournier Street later served as a synagogue and is now a mosque. The vaults below were leased to brewery and wine merchants through the eighteenth and nineteenth centuries. This is a place where successive generations have contributed to a rich cultural, commercial and architectural history.

Spitalfields Market, licensed in 1682 for the sale of fruit and vegetables, flourished with the influx of new business. Initially in private ownership, the Balch family, the original licensees, sold it to the Goldschmidts, who in turn sold it to Robert Horner, a former market porter who rebuilt it in 1883–93. The Corporation of London expanded the market in 1926–9, and it continued to trade in fruit and vegetables – with heated cellars for ripening bananas – until 1986. Now reduced in size by banal commercial development to the west, as corporate capital has crossed Bishopsgate from the Broadgate development and begun its contested colonisation of Brushfield Street, the market is mixed use with stall-holders selling the full range of aromatic candles, African carvings, bread, bags, books, CDs and pashminas. This new use is comparable with developments elsewhere in London, most notably at Covent Garden and to a lesser extent at Greenwich, where the original provision of foodstuffs for a local population has been driven out by difficulties of access, to and from, on overcrowded roads, together with the ready provision of big sheds on sites outside the central area. The New Spitalfields Market is sited on former railway land near Hackney Marshes in Leyton.

Covent Garden Market had earlier set this pattern of redevelopment (Walk 3). Always the most picturesque of London's markets, it began informally before being chartered in 1670 on the site of Inigo Jones's piazza of 1639 for the sale of flowers, fruit, roots and herbs. The first records of the square, by Hollar in 1647 and by an unidentified artist two years later, predated the market. Eighteenth-century paintings by Van Aken, Balthasar Nebot, Samuel Scott and John Collet exploited the picturesque possibilities offered by stalls, stall-holders, high- and low-life passers-by,

4.15 Nelson Road (formerly Street), Greenwich, laid out from 1827 to the design of Joseph Kay.

pickpockets and bare-knuckle boxers. By this time, as John Brewer notes, the Earl of Bedford's sophisticated speculation had also become 'the greatest square of Venus, ... its purlieus ... crowded with the votaries of this goddess'.

The market buildings erected to the design of Charles Fowler in 1828–30 were roofed in the later nineteenth century, by which time, according to Jerrold, this was 'the most famous place of barter in England' (fig. 4.14). They were threatened by re-development when the decision was taken to re-site the market in 1964. Ten years later, trading in flowers, fruit and vegetables was transferred to new buildings on disused railway and industrial land at Nine Elms, Vauxhall. By this time, wide-ranging plans for the redevelopment of the Covent Garden area with new buildings, a conference centre, elevated pedestrian decks and new roads had been defeated. With the removal of the wholesale trade and the redevelopment of the buildings, Covent Garden's emphasis has shifted successfully towards the tourist and gift-buying market rather than fulfilling the everyday needs of a local clientele.

There is a concern among the antiques traders at Greenwich Market that a similar gentrification of the retailing trade will take place if Greenwich Hospital, the landlord, redevelops the site (Walk 12). But it appears to be fundamental in the retailing trade that change cannot be wholly managed. At some stage, the accidental or the unforeseen will intrude. It is also apparent, notwithstanding the desires of those who have lived or worked in Brick Lane, Covent Garden or Greenwich, that many things which appear to be the same as they have always been have, in fact, been subject to significant alteration in the past, but distance is required in order to bring the changes into focus. There has been a market at Greenwich since the fourteenth century, but the history of the present market began in 1700 when a charter to run markets on Wednesdays and Saturdays was granted to the Commissioners of Greenwich Hospital. The first building, as opposed to stalls, was proposed in 1737, but it was not until 1810 that a new colonnaded Market House was built. This was superseded in 1827–33 by a significant new complex designed by Joseph Kay: new streets of terraced houses, some with ground-floor shops, were built around an island site with a covered market in the middle (fig. 4.15). Selling meat, vegetables, fish, poultry and eggs, this survived until the condition of the building and the changing nature of retailing and transport prompted redevelopment. The market was rebuilt in 1902–8 as a steel-framed, glass-roofed building which substantially survives (fig. 4.16). New warehouses were built around the central space, with offices above, in 1958–60, and the wholesale trade continued for another twenty years, gradually to be superseded by retail shops and, in the 1980s, a weekend antiques market. The desire of the local authority, expressed in the 1990s, that Greenwich might become a mini-Covent Garden has yet to be fulfilled.

4.16 Greenwich Market, from the entrance on College Approach (formerly Clarence Street).

Of London's major markets, only Smithfield retains its original position and function. There has been a livestock market here, just outside the original City walls, since the tenth century. The City Corporation was granted the tolls from the market in 1400. The animals were driven to the site and slaughtered nearby in what was also a place for criminal execution, a venue for duelling and the site of Bartholomew Fair, held annually from 1123 until its suppression in 1855. There had been complaints since the mid-eighteenth century about the practice of holding a live meat market so close to the centre of London, with all the attendant dangers and barbaric scenes, but it was not until 1851 that the government was moved to enact a bill to remove the live meat trade. This moved north to Bunning's new Metropolitan Cattle Market, near Caledonian Road at Copenhagen Fields, Islington, in 1855, where a cattle market remained until 1963: the Italianate clock tower survives. Smithfield was redeveloped as a dead meat market, served by a railway station constructed below in 1862–5. The design by the City's architect Horace Jones, realised in 1866–8, comprises four rectangles formed by dividing the area into quarters with a central east–west avenue and a central north–south roadway. The building is uncomfortably proportioned, long and low with a central roadway of unusual width with cast-iron beams supporting a wooden roof. The corner towers also lack the weight to delimit so large an expanse of building. The entrance arches are crowned by allegorical figures: London, Edinburgh, Dublin and Liverpool, accompanied by post-war griffins, emblematic of the City, writhing in the spandrels. The narrower roadway with trussed timber roof and shops below, refurbished in the 1980s, has a

more successful ratio of height to width (fig. 4.17). Later work included the shell-concrete-roofed Poultry Market of 1961–3 by T. P. Bennett and Sons. There are also notable associated buildings on Charterhouse Street, ancillary to the market: the Central Cold Storage building of 1899; the Port of London Authority Cold Store of 1914; and the Meat Inspection Offices, by the Corporation of London Engineers' department of 1930. Following its refurbishment, Smithfield should be secure as a rare survival from the great age of market building, fulfilling its original function. However, some of its later unprotected parts are at risk of redevelopment, and the rapaciousness of corporate finance is such that its long-term future may not be guaranteed.

Horace Jones was responsible also for the design of the cruciform Leadenhall Market of 1880–1 (Walk 1), its form influenced by Giuseppe Mengoni's Galleria in Milan of 1865–77. Leadenhall, centrally placed in the City, occupies a position where a poultry market had been established in 1345 on the site of the original Roman forum. The tall open-ended glass-roofed alleys, flanked by shops with offices above, are ventilated by louvres in the roof. Following refurbishment in 1990–1, this is a flourishing retail centre (fig. 4.18). Jones's other significant market building, the handsome, arcaded Billingsgate Fish Market sited on the north bank of the river and built in 1874–8, remained in use until 1982, and was converted into offices in 1985–9 by the Richard Rogers Partnership. The New Billingsgate Market of 1980–2, shiny sheds next to the former West India Docks on the Isle of Dogs by Newman Levinson and Partners, looks strangely dated by comparison.

Pubs

From the 1830s, the public house was established as the brightest, most splendidly appointed and handsome building in areas of poverty and deprivation. It took full advantage of the plate glass, gas lighting, mahogany and rosewood which had revolutionised the appearance of shops. It was there to tempt the customer with otherwise unavailable pleasures, at a price, and in so doing served to dull the pain of living in areas of filth and misery, as Jerrold noted in 1872: 'At the corner of every tumbledown street is the flaring public house lamp – hateful as the fabled jewel in the loathsome toad's head.' Dickens had earlier found the 'numerous and splendid'

4.19 King's Head public house, c.1860, with the Whitbread Brewery Partners' House of c.1700 next door on Chiswell Street, City.

4.20 Royal Oak public house, Columbia Road, Bethnal Green, 1923.

gin shops in Covent Garden, St Giles's and Holborn to be 'in precise proportion to the dirt and poverty of their surrounding neighbourhood'. Here lived 'men and women, in every variety of scanty and dirty apparel, lounging, scolding, drinking, smoking, squabling, fighting, and swearing', but on turning the corner, 'all is light and brilliancy. The hum of many voices, issues from that splendid gin-shop ... with the fantastically ornamented parapet, the illuminated clock, the plate-glass windows surrounded by stucco rosettes, and its profusion of gas-lights in richly-gilt burners', all 'perfectly dazzling when contrasted with the darkness and dirt we have just left', and the interior is 'even gayer than the exterior'. Much is drunk and as the evening reaches its sorry climax, the 'knot of Irish labourers ... who have been alternately shaking hands with, and threatening the life of, each other for the last hour, become furious in their disputes, and finding it impossible to silence one man ... resort to the infallible expedient of knocking him down and jumping on him afterwards ... a scene of riot and confusion ensues ... the landlord hits everybody and everybody hits the landlord, the barmaids scream, the police come in ...' 'Gin-drinking', Dickens concludes, 'is a great vice in England, but poverty is a greater; and until you can cure it, or persuade a half-famished wretch not to seek relief in the temporary oblivion of his own misery ... gin-shops will increase in number and splendour.'

For this expansion in gin houses, the poor were indebted to free trade. Gin sales had been rising and beer declining because gin was cheaper, so in 1830, in the culmination of a series of deregulatory drinking acts, the government abolished the duty on beer, enabling any ratepayer to sell beer for on or off consumption in his own house for the price of a two-guinea licence. This measure was intended to throw open the trade and give the poor and working classes a chance to drink a better, cheaper and more wholesome beverage. Beer prices were halved, from 4d. to 2d. per quart, and an enormous number of new beer houses, often very simple, were opened. An unintended consequence of the legislation was the invention by the distillers of the tempting, palatial gin house. The anti-spirits movement in 1831

found its voice through the worthy benevolence of the London Temperance Society, later to increase in ambition to become the British and Foreign Temperance Society. This was interdenominational but run by Anglican clergymen, funded by philanthropists and pledged to moral persuasion and moderate reforms. Others pressed for total abstinence. Knowing what is best for other people is a besetting human sin; acting on such beliefs and meddling in matters of personal behaviour can be even worse. As Dickens noted, these were attacks on symptoms rather than on causes.

It was regulation which changed the situation once more when an Act of 1869 restored jurisdiction to magistrates after thirty-nine years of free trade. The granting of these regulatory powers inevitably resulted in a greatly reduced number of beer houses. The market value of the survivors thus rose, and brewers competed to lend money to pub landlords at cheap rates for refitting and expansion. As prices continued to rise, they further inflated property values by buying up the freeholds themselves. Prominent sites were favoured, with the lavish decoration made possible by new technologies, particularly the manufacture of larger and thicker sheets of glass enabling etching, cutting, embossing, gilding and back-painting (figs 4.19 and 4.20). Tile painting, oak panelling and the new embossed wallpapers simulating plaster – Tynecastle and Lincrusta in the 1870s and Anaglypta from 1887 – all contributed to the qualities which J. M. Richards (quoted by Spiller) identified in 1957 as essential to real pub character: 'dark, rich colours to give an effect of warmth and cosiness; the breaking-up of the plan into small distinct areas to give an effect of intimacy and enclosure and richness of texture to give a sense of plenty and well-being'. These attributes now are hard to find. The desire of both magistrates and publicans for overall surveillance in order to inhibit licentious behaviour and exuberant misdemeanour has resulted in the opening up of the plan of most pubs, and the removal of snob-screens has reduced the possibilities for intimacy and seclusion even further. Even class distinction, the great bastion of Englishness in this most English of institutions, enshrined in the separation of saloon and public bars, has been eroded.

The identification of authenticity in pubs is problematic. The dating of decorative features is notoriously difficult, and besides, as Harwood and Saint observe, 'where drinking takes place, nothing ornamental lasts very long'. There are, however, some notable survivors of the great building boom of the 1880s and 1890s, in part if not in whole, in both the centre and the late nineteenth-century suburbs. Baedeker (1900) might recognise some of them: 'The traveller's thirst can at all times be conveniently quenched at a Public House, where a glass [half pint] of bitter beer, ale, stout or "half-and-half" ... is to be had for 1½ – 2d.'

Board schools

There was a great national proliferation of schools in the nineteenth century – elementary and advanced, religious and secular. In the 1860s there were 860 public day schools and 1,700 private schools in London, but there were only 40 grammar schools for boys and 12 for girls. Girls' education was improved in 1851 when Miss Frances Buss set up her first school in Camden Street. She followed this twenty years later with the highly successful and well-regarded Camden School for Girls for the daughters of copy clerks, tailors, civil servants, builders and grocers, whose ignorance of general knowledge she found beyond belief.

Education of the poor lagged even further behind. The establishment of the Ragged School Union in 1844 provided some education, but there might be one

4.21 Gillespie Road Primary School, Highbury, 1878.

4.22 New End Primary School, Hampstead, T.J.Bailey for the LCC, 1905–6.

master in charge of 200 boys, and because of the demand for child labour, the average age for leaving school in east London in 1845 was ten.

It was the Education Act of 1870, the Forster Act, which laid the foundations for elementary education in England with local, directly elected, secular boards running the schools. As a result, fifty members, including women, were elected by all ratepayers to run the London School Board, the first directly elected, London-wide body. Elementary education was to be provided for all children between 5 and 12 years old, later raised to 14. School attendance initially was voluntary, and after it became compulsory there were difficulties with enforcing attendance. The new schools supplemented the voluntary religious schools rather than replacing them, a circumstance as distressing for radicals at the time as the support of 'faith schools' by the government is today.

The London School Board carried out a crash programme of building in the poorer areas, and between 1870 and 1904 built 469 schools with 554,198 places (there were 217,088 in voluntary schools), about 14 per year. The 1902 Education Act transferred responsibility nationally from the school boards to the local authorities, paid for from a 2d. rate; the LCC took over responsibility in London in 1904.

The board schools were built high and imposing, colonies of health and enlightenment, but without the symbols of religion (fig. 4.21). Religious teaching was admitted so long as it involved no dogma – as Mark Girouard describes (in *Sweetness and Light*), William Cowper-Temple had managed to add a clause to the Bill: 'no religious catechism or religious formulary of any particular denomination shall be taught in the schools'. This affected the style so the initial churchy Gothic gave way to Queen Anne: tall gables, red brick, big windows with small panes of glass. These were formidable oases of civilisation in crowded areas of need, with walled playgrounds, sometimes on the roof, and separate entrances for boys, girls and infants. There were three architectural phases, beginning with work by individual architects selected through competition, then E. R. Robson and a team, and lastly T. J. Bailey from 1884. It was during this last period that the buildings grew bigger and the rooflines more ebullient (fig. 4.22) (Walk 10). Roy Porter quotes Conan-Doyle's Sherlock Holmes on the board schools: 'isolated clumps of buildings rising up above the slates like brick islands in a lead-coloured sea ... Lighthouses ... Beacons of the future! Capsules with hundreds of bright little seeds in each, out of which will spring the wiser, better England of the future.'

This was a remarkable achievement. The attendance level rose from 65 per cent in 1872 to 88 per cent in 1904, above the national average. Fees were 2d. or 3d. per week until free education was introduced in 1891. Charles Booth (1892) recognised their significance:

> In every quarter the eye is arrested by their distinctive architecture, as they stand, closest where the need is greatest, each one 'like a tall sentinel at his post', keeping watch and ward over the interests of the generation that is to replace our own ... Taken as a whole, they may be said fairly to represent the high-water mark of the public conscience in this country in its relation to the education of the children of the people.

Girouard discusses the architectural success of the board schools: cheap, convenient, attractive and easily recognisable, built with small budgets on constricted sites. There was separation of boys from girls (crafts for boys, domestic work for girls) and separate co-educational infants' schools. All three divisions had to have their own big schoolroom, in which all members could be seated, as well as large separate classrooms. They were as transparent as possible within, with views from schoolroom to classrooms, and they were well provided with services: lavatories, cloakrooms, teachers' rooms, outdoor playgrounds and covered space for play in wet weather. There were openings on each side of the classroom for cross-ventilation – vital for health but potentially cold in winter – 30 square inches (0.58 square metres) of glass to each square foot (0.09 square metres) of floor, a ceiling height of at least 14 feet (4 metres) for classrooms and schoolrooms, no corridors. The ideal plan was a central schoolroom between pairs of classrooms for easy supervision of both pupils and the numerous pupil-teachers. If space allowed, the infants would be in a separate single-storey building.

The adoption of the Queen Anne style was political as well as secular. It was associated with middle-class values, the antithesis of the urban slum. Board schools were safe and secure, designed to inspire confidence as temporary alternatives to home, bridging social divisions and instilling habits of cleanliness, order and industry in the working class. This was the message implicit in the bold, light-filled architecture.

They have proved to be impressively durable: instantly recognisable, well built, imposing, and essentially humane in appearance. Subdivided internally by transparent partitions rather than by load-bearing walls, the schools may be readily converted to new uses, but the best contemporary use for them is the original one, since in giving a secular focus to their areas they can still offer much-needed lessons in the image of non-sectarian equality and democracy. This great late nineteenth- and early twentieth-century age of school building, through the coincidence of legislative timing, ran concurrently with the great age of public-house building. Both building types have left an indelible and often handsome mark on the London landscape. In their different ways they have provided enduring lessons in the sociability of city life and the contribution of good, plain, functional architecture to the maintenance of the civility of the public realm.

Chapter 5 COMMERCIAL LONDON

Commercial London is perpetually reinventing itself. Commerce requires the appearance of stability in order to engender trust, but it also thrives on speculation and change. This contradiction is made visible in the commercial architecture of London where pragmatism is the overarching attitude. If an institution or building fulfils its purpose, it remains; if it fails, it goes. This explains why there is so little of the eighteenth-century fabric left in the City, and why even examples from the nineteenth century account for a relatively small amount of City property. And yet given the short life-cycle of commercial buildings and high land values, it is surprising that there is as much Victorian office space as there is.

In London before the Great Fire of 1666, there was a physical connection between the port of London and the merchants who engaged in shipping goods in and out of the country. At that time London was the pre-eminent port in the country, with a vibrant import trade but with an equally buoyant trade in goods and supplies exported to the outposts of commerce throughout the world. Warehouses occupied the edge of the Thames and the streets running back from the river, but close to the wharves and the warehouses were also the counting houses where transactions were recorded and deals struck. During the seventeenth and eighteenth centuries, domestic space was often shared with productive work, especially in artisanal households. The mixing of domestic life and the world of business was evident in the counting houses of the same period, little evidence of which remains, although Wardrobe Place near St Paul's gives some idea of the intimacy of the many courts containing these houses (fig. 5.1).

The counting house combined office space at ground-floor and sometimes first-floor levels with domestic accommodation above. The principal in a business might live with his family in the house, but the young men engaged in the business would also eat and sleep on the premises. The young clerks would not necessarily be strangers to the family, but might be relatives or the sons of business associates. The

5.1 Wardrobe Place, *c.*1714.

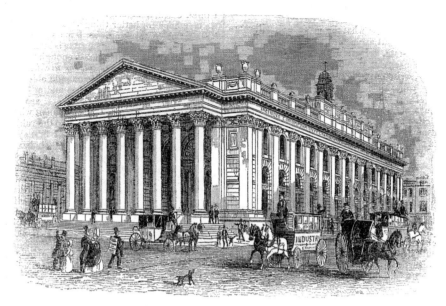

NEW ROYAL EXCHANGE.

counting house, therefore, assumed a special form of internal arrangement which allowed business and varying levels of intimacy to coexist together. From the few examples which are recorded, the ground floor usually consisted of a large counting office, where the clerks would work, and an inner parlour, where the principals would be able to converse confidentially with clients. On the first floor would be a dining room and kitchen and a drawing room for the use of the principal's family. How much the clerks participated in the family's life would depend on the individual household. If they were lodged in the attic, a secondary back stair could allow them to pass through the family's space without inconvenience.

Besides adapting the standard London house, some merchants built houses with the more specific purpose of using them for trade as well as household accommodation. One of these, which was well recorded early in the twentieth century but fell victim to bombing in the Second World War, was 34 Great Thames Street, the counting house of Capel Osgood and Hanbury, Virginia merchants. The house was built in a courtyard off the street, and was a generous five bays in width with three floors plus attic and cellar. On the first and second floors the windows were regular sash openings, but on the ground floor the windows of the room to the right of the entrance were double in width, giving a significant increase in light to the clerks' room. On each floor, four rooms were arranged around a corridor and staircase at right angles to the entrance front, providing either domestic or office accommodation depending on need.

Eighteenth-century inventories suggest similar furnishings in all counting houses, including counters, stools and clocks, but nothing else beyond what might be expected in any middle-class household of the time. The one piece of furniture of greatest importance, however, was the merchant's bureau, which formed the focus of the firm's filing system and guaranteed order in its dealings. Copies of correspondence and documents as well as account books were all kept within the bureau, which was the special preserve of the partners.

During the eighteenth century the location of the counting house close to the docks and the centres of financial news was important, so that the businessmen

5.2 Royal Exchange, Sir William Tite, 1841–4, *The Builder*, vol. 1, 21 October 1843, p. 447.

5.3 Bank of England, Tivoli Corner, Sir John Soane, 1804–7, and Sir Herbert Baker, 1936.

could keep up with not only their own interests but those of their competitors. The coffee houses and taverns of the City supplied one source of news, and it was the practice to visit those specialising in the relevant trade: for example, the Jamaica Coffee House in St Michael's Alley, off Cornhill, which carried news of the Caribbean trade. Besides information, the coffee houses also provided the location for lectures on topics such as Newtonian science, as well as the setting for socialising.

Although many banks and other institutions began in City houses, there emerged over time a public architecture to accommodate a range of financial activities. The Royal Exchange was one of the first, established in 1566 under the initiative of Sir Thomas Gresham, using the exchange in Antwerp as model. A version of the Continental bourse, it provided a public space where twice a day merchants gathered to transact business, an activity which had formerly taken place in Lombard Street. The new Royal Exchange, located nearby with its entrance on Cornhill, was distinguished by the regular Doric arcade within its walls, the rich marble of its columns and the classical entrance tower. After the Great Fire a new building was constructed to the designs of Edward Jerman in 1667–71 (see p. 27). This building followed the general arrangement of the first, with an internal courtyard and arcade at ground-floor level and rooms above. Classicising influences were even more evident, and a general air of substance prevailed. This building lasted more than 100 years, destroyed by fire in 1838 and rebuilt from 1841 by Sir William Tite. The scale was now Roman, perhaps with reference to the Roman Empire in relation to the quickly expanding British Empire, and the main entrance was reorientated towards the west with a giant Corinthian portico and pediment (fig. 5.2). Within, the arcade is retained, and in 1883 the court was roofed over. Not since 1939 has the Royal Exchange operated as a general trading venue, and today it is given over to retail (Walk 1).

Across Threadneedle Street is the Bank of England, which began in 1694 in the livery halls of the Mercers and then the Grocers. Thirty years later in 1734, it moved into its own premises designed by George Sampson near the Royal Exchange. Sampson employed a Palladian scheme in his seven-bay façade, with a rusticated basement, tall first-floor windows with pediments over, and giant Ionic attached columns on the projecting central bays. Extensions and changes were made in 1765–70 by Sir Robert Taylor, who added wings on either side of the original façade and provided spaces for specific functions such as the Transfer Office and Reduced Annuities Office. The latter was furnished with segmental arches and domes, lit from the side, inspiration for Sir John Soane's early work, which he undertook from 1788 when he was appointed architect. Over the next forty-six years, the bank's requirements and Soane's own creative vision transformed the Bank of England beyond recognition. He too designed rooms for specific functions such as the Consols Office (1797), the Accountants' Office (1805) and the Five Per Cent Office (1818), but he also designed the distinctive perimeter wall which 'spoke' of the desirable characteristics of security and solidity. The formidable wall was relieved by the Tivoli Corner at the junction of Lothbury and Princes Street, a feature retained by Sir Herbert Baker when from 1923 he recast Soane's building at a much grander scale (fig. 5.3) (Walk 1).

Nearby was the Mansion House, a commission acquired by George Dance Senior by virtue of his position as Clerk of the Works to the City of London (see p. 15) (Walk 1). This building is the residence of the Lord Mayor of London, elected annually from the aldermen of the City, and it functions as a site of ceremonial occasions as well as the Lord Mayor's home. Begun in 1739 and occupied in 1752, the

5.4 National Provincial Bank, Bishopsgate, John Gibson, 1864–5, *The Builder*, vol. 23, 23 December 1865, p. 909.

Mansion House, despite a very cramped site, manages to present a satisfactory Palladian façade to the prospect before it, opened up in the nineteenth century. In order to bring enough light into the building, Dance placed an open court centrally at first-floor level, although this was later covered over. The Mansion House, Royal Exchange and Bank of England ensured that this intersection eventually formed a financial and ceremonial hub of the City, which was later enhanced by the building of King William Street and the straightening of Princes Street in the 1830s, and the construction of Queen Victoria Street in 1867–71.

As time went on and London assumed the position of financial capital of the world, the more successful men in the City migrated to the West End and beyond, leaving their counting houses in the hands of managers. The Boyds are representative of such a commercial family, establishing themselves in the City after Augustus Boyd in 1738 returned from St Kitts, where he had spent nearly forty years trading and running plantations. From premises in Austin Friars he and his son John carried on colonial trade, providing goods and services to the colonies and finding markets for colonial products. Like many successful commercial men, John Boyd moved to a town house in the West End, 33 Upper Brook Street, designed by Sir Robert Taylor, the architect of the Bank of England and well known in City circles. About five years before, Taylor had designed Danson Hill House for Boyd, a country seat in Bexleyheath, Kent. By the end of the eighteenth century the exodus from the City had begun, leaving a greatly reduced population and also houses readily available for letting as office space.

House owners in the City of London found that the rooms in their houses became more valuable as office space than they were as space for retail or artisan activity, and as the housing boom began to take off in the inner suburbs such as Hackney and Islington, whole houses were let as offices. Advertisements began appearing in, for instance, the *Auction Register and Law Chronicle* of property which was on the cusp between residential and commercial, such as these two from 7 January 1813:

> *A very desirable Freehold Estate, consisting of a brick-built Dwelling House, No 26 Botolph-lane, with two rooms on each story, with a warehouse and counting house on the ground floor, now in the possession of Mrs. King, tenant at will, at the low net rent of £37 per annum.*

5.5 General Credit Company, Lothbury, G. Somers Clarke, 1866.

Porter-street Leicester sq. Consists of a spacious Leasehold brick-built Dwelling-House, in perfect repair, possessing every accommodation for a large family, or might be converted into capital Business Premises, being No 18, Porter's Street.

There was an interim period while house space was let out as offices, and some commercially minded owners used the rents as capital to set up their own businesses. Eventually, however, the speculative office building made its appearance in the City, and a new phase in commercial architecture began.

Banks and insurance companies had already started building their own premises, such as Hoare's Bank on the south side of Fleet Street, designed in 1829–30 by Charles Parker. The building still provided living accommodation for the Hoare family as well as banking facilities, but the scale has moved away from the domestic to a more monumental but restrained classicism. Hoare's was a private bank with its own wealthy clients, but in 1844 the Joint Stock Companies Act introduced a greater degree of competition into banking, which was made manifest in bank architecture. Though for the most part banks retained a classical face, they now acquired a monumentality that rivalled public buildings. The opulence of the façades and banking halls spoke not only of dependability, but also of the wealth sustaining the business.

A striking example of a confident bank building is the former National Provincial Bank in Bishopsgate of 1864–5 by John Gibson (fig. 5.4). Facing the street is a screen of fluted Composite columns topped by a heavy entablature, which in turn is surmounted by statues representing the towns served by the bank. The south end is rounded to Threadneedle Street in a curve reminiscent of Soane's Tivoli Corner, on the far side of the nearby Bank of England. Within, three large glass domes provided most of the lighting in the banking hall, where entablature and arches are supported on Corinthian columns of Devonshire marble. That the bank is in effect single storey, with just one row of very large, roundheaded windows, would have made it appear of a much greater scale to its five-storey neighbours, thus contributing to the appearance of monumentality.

After 1855 the success of the joint-stock bank led to a further development of the joint-stock discount companies with limited liability. Here, too, competition was important in the architectural sphere as well as the financial. One of these, the General Credit Company, Lothbury by G. Somers Clarke is worth considering (fig. 5.5). Although it was built in 1866 in a Venetian Gothic style, with the intimations of window tracery, stone balconies and decorative sculpture, the abstract treatment of the straightheaded, recessed windows, the areas of plain walling, and the three-dimensional geometry of the building all suggest a date forty years later.

Insurance companies competed with each other in the opulence of their premises as much as if not more than banks. As business practice became more complex and more abstract, especially in the fields of banking and insurance, there was an opportunity and a

5.6 Leeds and Yorkshire Insurance, demolished, W. B. Gingell, 1858, *The Builder*, vol. 16, 10 July 1858, p. 467.

5.7 Crown Life Office, New Bridge Street, demolished, Deane and Woodward, 1858, *The Building News*, vol. 4, 16 July 1858, p. 723.

challenge to create a new organisation within the office buildings. The sheer numbers of clerks required to deal with insurance and bank entries meant that premises needed to be much bigger than the old eighteenth-century houses allowed. On the other hand, size could not be allowed to compromise the amount of light entering the work space, and the architect had to reconcile extensive street façades with rows of large windows on every floor of the building (fig. 5.6). Most insurance offices included a public office on the ground floor together with the secretary's room. At first floor was the board room, decorated on an impressive scale, and there might be a floor for the numerous clerks that were necessary. In the basement would be the fireproof strong room, and also accommodation for a resident caretaker, if this were not in the attic. Quite often the arrangement left ample room for lettable office space, a practice that allowed insurance companies to build with more ambition than would ordinarily be the case.

Speculation in office building started in the 1830s, and that brought another element of competition into the production of this new type, since clients had to be persuaded to take office space in one building rather than another. This meant that architects had to be inventive in the design and construction of their buildings, and yet keep them flexible enough to suit the requirements of a varying clientele. One of the first speculative office blocks was Royal Exchange Buildings by Edward I'Anson (1842–4), immediately behind Tite's Royal Exchange. The Italian palazzo was

I'Anson's ordering model, one that was also the model for many of the new insurance blocks. On the ground floor behind a glazed arcade were purpose-built shops, an added bonus that came with the new building type. The first- and second-floor windows were of the same size, although the long row was given variety through alternating segmental and triangular pediments at first floor. At roof level was a prominent modillioned cornice over small third-floor windows. In 1906–10 I'Anson's building was replaced by a neo-baroque reworking by Sir Ernest George and Yeates.

The 1860s saw the introduction into the City of development companies, who built speculative office buildings purely for investment purposes. Nos 59–61 Mark Lane were put up in 1864 by the City of London Real Property Company (fig. 5.8). Their architect, George Aitchison Junior, provided an independent load-bearing screen wall, elegantly inscribed with Veneto-Byzantine decoration across its four storeys, while behind is an independent iron frame of cast-iron columns and wrought-iron beams. The frame construction gave the greater flexibility that speculative offices required. A sign of the times was another speculative building, this time at Nos 39–40 Lombard Street, in what had been traditionally the very heart of the private banking district of the City. This corner block of 1866–8 by F. and F. J. Francis takes the palazzo style to wild heights of exaggeration, and includes banded piers, columns, pedimented windows, entablatures at every floor and a modillioned cornice with balustrade above. The building indicates to what extent architectural style had come into the equation when plotting the success of a speculative venture.

The two requirements of an adequate natural source of light and a characterful façade pushed architects to look beyond the Italian palazzo which at mid-century dominated the street architecture of the City. In 1858, Deane and Woodward, the architects of the recently completed Oxford Museum, were responsible for the Crown Life Office, New Bridge Street, in which they were inspired by polychromatic Gothic (fig. 5.7). Portland stone, brick and red and grey granite were the materials which formed the colourful voussoirs over the large roundheaded windows at ground and first floors and over the double windows on the two floors above. Although this building was swept away with the coming of the railway in 1867, its influence continued, for example in I'Anson's No. 65 Cornhill of 1871, for Messrs King but

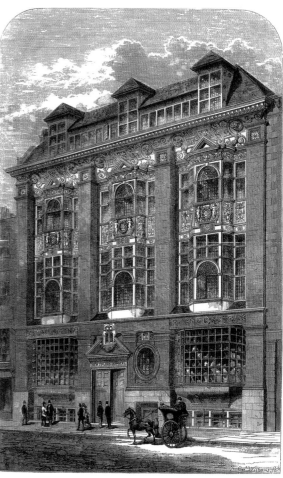

5.9 Hill and Evans, 33–5 Eastcheap, R.L.Roumieu, 1868.

5.10 New Zealand Chambers, Leadenhall Street, demolished, R. Norman Shaw, 1871–3, *The Builder*, vol. 31, 2 August 1873, p. 607.

with ample lettable space. Here decorative brick and terracotta signal a departure from I'Anson's usual Italianate to a textured but still disciplined Gothic. Three large windows with pointed voussoirs give light to each of three floors above the ground, and on the fourth floor six smaller windows are set in a diapered wall.

Street improvements provided a strong incentive to transform the old post-fire City into the new. We have noted that in the 1830s King William Street was laid out and continued along Princes Street to Moorgate. Here Sir Robert Smirke designed restrained blocks with some Italian details such as tall roundheaded windows at first floor, quoins and balustrade at roof level, all executed in stucco. Little remains of this planned set of façades except Nos 63–73 Moorgate.

A more ambitious scheme was the Holborn Viaduct, intended to facilitate traffic to and from the West End by bridging the Fleet valley. Work continued on this project from 1863 to 1869, and connected to it was the arrangement of Ludgate Circus (1868–72) after the arrival of the London, Chatham, and Dover Railway into the City. But the improvement which announced the full confidence of the City as the world financial centre was Queen Victoria Street (1867–71) (Walk 1), which linked the newly constructed Victoria Embankment and Blackfriars Bridge to the Mansion House. This was a broad avenue, which lent itself to a succession of fine façades, but given the period and its desire for show, there was more in the way of Gothic and Renaissance fantasies than distinguished architecture. Little remains, although one of the flat-iron blocks, Albert Buildings of 1873 by F. J. Ward, gives a flavour of the Gothic caprices that formerly lined the route. It could be said, however, that the strong horizontals of these buildings would have provided a fine visual sweep as the viewer proceeded along at speed in a carriage.

For centuries the City had been the repository of commodities coming into the port of London. Although we associate warehouses with the docks, such as those by Philip Hardwick of 1828 around St Katherine's Docks or along the Thames at Wapping, or even on the periphery of the City at Clerkenwell, warehouses continued to be built within the City well into the second half of the nineteenth century. Eastcheap has some particularly good examples, such as Nos 23–5 by John Young and Son. This block was built in 1861–2 for Messrs Hunt and Crombie, spice merchants, and while the ground and first floors were given over to offices, the ebullient upper floors of polychromatic brickwork housed the produce. A little further east are Nos 33–5 of 1868 by R. L. Roumieu for Hill and Evans, vinegar makers of Worcester (fig. 5.9) (Walk 1). The façade is truly startling, with a three-dimensional treatment of the Gothic detail consisting of decorated mullions and heavy transoms, together with richly articulated gables. Red and blue bricks, stone and marble ensure colour as well as texture. In 1987 the ground-floor arches were restored, returning the façade to its full effect. At Nos 2–16 Creechurch Buildings in Creechurch Lane is a former tea warehouse of 1886–7 which approximates more closely to our view of warehouse architecture. Here each bay of three lights is separated by narrow brick piers, and the general impression is of more window than wall, an indication that utilitarian concerns were overriding stylistic ones.

In the architectural culture at large, historical styles were giving way to a greater interest in the vernacular, especially in domestic buildings. How this movement could be incorporated into commercial building was more problematic, although evidence that it could be achieved appeared in Norman Shaw's 1871–3 New Zealand Chambers in Leadenhall Street (fig. 5.10). Red brick piers and great quantities of small-paned windows were surmounted by a cornice and plastered cove decorated in Renaissance motifs. Similar buildings were more likely to be found outside the City, for example Shaw's red brick and stone dressed block of 1882–3 for the Alliance Assurance at Nos 1–2 St James's Street (Walk 6). As time went on, further examples did penetrate the City, such as T. E. Collcutt's Nos 45–7 Ludgate Hill for the City Bank in 1890. Red brick, buff terracotta and a proliferation of gables, domes and turrets were the accepted accoutrements of commercial buildings in the West End. Still Gothic but taking advantage of the brick and terracotta fashion was Alfred Waterhouse's Prudential Assurance Building in Holborn of 1879 (fig. 5.11) (Walk 4). The building attests to the confidence and assertiveness of successful insurance companies at this time, since not only is it very large and very red, it occupies a very prominent site.

5.12 Institute of Chartered Accountants, Moorgate Place, John Belcher, 1888–93, and J.J.Joass, 1930.

5.13 Law Union and Rock Insurance, 5–7 Chancery Lane, A.C.Blomfield, 1911.

About the same time as Collcutt's building on Ludgate Hill, there appeared in Moorgate Place the Institute of Chartered Accountants by John Belcher, where the architect introduced with great confidence and skill the neo-baroque (fig. 5.12) (Walk 1). A symmetrical façade of regularly spaced windows provides the setting for many sculptural features such as heavy blocking at ground floor, a sculpted frieze under the second-floor windows, and a Doric order running from a band above the first-floor windows to a Corinthian entablature above. At the corner a domed and columned oriel is surmounted by a statue of Justice. As the City moved into the new century, it was the elaboration of this style, currently known as the Edwardian baroque, which came to dominate.

The intentions behind the nineteenth-century rebuilding of the City were to provide suitable office accommodation in buildings of striking appearance for the purposes of efficiency and prestige. But these premises also increased the land use of their sites, so that they produced greater profits for their owners than the post-fire houses. The advantage of a neo-baroque façade was that while keeping a generally classical schema thought appropriate for the City, a significant change in scale could be achieved. Visually within a rusticated basement, a full ground and first floor could be incorporated, as A. C. Blomfield did at Friars House of 1907–8 in New Broad Street. Above these were another two floors linked by double Ionic columns, and above that again was a floor of arched windows and one of dormers. An added frisson to Blomfield's façade was that it screened a concrete frame using the system of Julius Kahn.

There are many instances of this mode of rebuilding, for example Ernest George and Yeates's reworking of I'Anson's Royal Exchange Buildings, as mentioned above. Another example is Blomfield's Nos 5–7 Chancery Lane of 1911, where he took advantage of the corner site by incorporating fully articulated French baroque detail on the two exposed façades (fig. 5.13). The apogee of the neo-baroque style is perhaps the Port of London Authority building of 1912–22 by Sir Edwin Cooper, which speaks of London's confidence as the centre of world trade just at the moment when that predominance began to falter. The building replaced 60 houses, and dominates the west side of Trinity Square. Six giant Corinthian columns *in antis* in the central block support an entablature and an elaborate tower, consisting of decorated base, clusters of square columns and pilasters, and arched niche. To either side are subsidiary ranges dressed in a similar fashion. Although the neo-baroque did not entirely disappear with the First World War, the need for greater economy and recognition of a change in the financial climate led to the eventual emergence of a more modern agenda.

There were intimations of this more 'modern' approach to commercial architecture even before the First World War. H. P. Berlage, the Dutch architect, designed Holland House for the shipping firm W. H. Muller between 1914 and 1916. The building, in Bury Street just behind Norman Foster's Swiss Re block, is five storeys, but it looks taller because the floors are not differentiated and the bays are separated by narrow vertical piers, faced in grey-green faience and indicating the steel structure behind (fig. 5.14) (Walk 1). From some vantage points the building looks transparent, while from others it appears solid, and in scale it anticipates the larger buildings of the next decades.

Two buildings of the same date but of different ethos are Adelaide House, London Bridge, by Burnet and Tait and Lutyens's Britannic House in Finsbury Circus, both of 1921–5. Lutyens's building for the Anglo-Persian Oil Company presents a great curve on the north-west side of Finsbury Circus and could be two buildings,

with a three-storey heavy masonry base and, above, another three storeys slightly recessed with their own more decorative baroque scheme (Walk 7). Given Lutyens's commitment to the classical idiom, this is one solution to the conundrum of a classical treatment for a large-scaled building. Adelaide House, on the other hand, introduces an abstract solution more in keeping with the building's scale (fig. 5.15). This ten-storey block stands detached on its site overlooking London Bridge, and is divided as American architect Louis Sullivan divided his office blocks in the 1890s into entrance and ground floor, equally spaced office floors, and decorative cornice. Despite the heavy cornice, verticality is achieved by the thin mullions evenly spaced between the narrow windows. At the time, Adelaide House was considered 'modern' in its expression, but although it has escaped the neo-baroque still evident in Lutyens's building, classicism continues to hang about it.

Real intimations of modernism were to be found outside the immediate confines of the City in the areas of London where new types of businesses were developing. In the late nineteenth century newspapers began to cluster in Fleet Street between the City and the legal district. By the late 1920s the popular press had enough money and influence for some of the papers to wish to build forward-looking premises. The former Daily Telegraph building of 1928–31 was by Elcock and Sutcliffe with Thomas Tait, and is at once cheerful and monumental, with a screen of 'Egyptian' columns to the street (fig. 5.16). More striking is the former Daily Express building by Sir Owen Williams with Ellis and Clarke (Walk 4). Here in 1930–3 Williams produced the first true curtain-walled building in the country, using a concrete frame hung with black vitrolite set in chromium strips. The west corner was cantilevered to form a loading bay, and here the structure can be seen in the soffit.

At 33 High Holborn is a surprisingly modern block of 1930 by Frederick Etchells and Herbert A. Welch. This was for Crawford's Advertising Company, and besides the black marble ground floor contrasted with the cement render of the upper floors, modernity is intimated by the bands of strip windows. Back in the City, a much larger building of 1937 which still can shock by its long streamlined façades is Ibex House at Nos 41–7 Minories by Fuller, Hall and Foulsham. The cream and black faience of the facing and the continuous strip windows, together with the glazed stair towers, contribute to a feeling of bright modernism not reflected in its neighbours. Indeed, these examples stand out as exceptions to the general run of commercial buildings, of which there are many examples of merit, but nearly all with heavy masonry façades.

Sir John Summerson wrote in his essay on building in the City in *The Unromantic Castle* (1990): 'The eye of the 1930s saw the City as dead: a petrified theatre of bad architectural rhetoric.' The great catalyst for change was the bombing during the Blitz in the Second World War. By virtue of its proximity to the river and the docks, the City was particularly badly hit, and whole swathes of buildings around St Paul's and the Barbican were flattened. When construction was permitted once more, a programme of rebuilding was obviously necessary, but this was the high moment of town planning, and the destruction was seen as an opportunity to modernise the City and increase the density of land use at the same time.

Two projects stand out as significant post-war redevelopments, and both of them have recently been swept away by subsequent rebuilding. The first was the scheme for the area immediately to the north of St Paul's and designated Paternoster Square (Walk 1). For this sensitive area around the cathedral, Sir William Holford conceived a layout which would satisfy a number of planning concerns of the post-war period. First, the separation of pedestrians and cars was an important

5.15 Adelaide House, London Bridge Approach, Sir John Burnet and Tait, 1921–5.

5.16 Former Daily Telegraph Building, 135–41 Fleet Street, Elcock and Sutcliffe, with Thomas Tait, 1928–31, and Mersey House, 1904–6.

factor in designing the office blocks on a podium with parking beneath. Although it was never executed, there was a scheme to join up the podium to a series of aerial walkways planned around London Wall and the Barbican. Another accepted idea was that building a mixture of tall and medium-sized buildings freed up the space at the base of the blocks and ensured a pleasant environment within the offices. Given Summerson's horror of the rhetoric of the City's architecture, simplicity in the design of the blocks themselves was also desirable at the time. More controversially, Holford refused to open up the view to St Paul's from Ludgate, using Juxon House to screen the view of the complete façade until the last moment.

The scheme was executed by Trehearne and Norman, Preston and Partners, using a simple formula for their blocks which included Portland stone facing of the end walls and frames around the glazed bays. A curtain-walled tower of sixteen storeys stood at the north-west corner, but the other blocks were arranged asymmetrically to form open spaces at podium level. When in 1985 it was proposed to redevelop the area, neither the blocks nor the windswept spaces around them had acquired enough affection to prevent their ultimate destruction. However, lack of consensus about how an area so close to St Paul's ought to be treated led to the acceptance and discarding of a number of schemes by well-known architects. The initial competition was won by Arup Associates in 1987, but a rival scheme by John Simpson was subsequently adopted in 1989 on the strength of its reliance for effect on a pastiche of historical styles. Terry Farrell and Co. were the master planners, and they devised a scheme which reverted to the pre-war street pattern, rejecting completely the post-war planning consensus. In the event, a simplified scheme by Sir William Whitfield was adopted, and although the buildings are by

5.17 Paternoster Square, rebuilding, Sir William Whitfield, from 1996.

different architects around a large piazza, the higher density and the retained open space has provided a compromise solution (fig. 5.17).

The other post-war scheme was London Wall between Moorgate and Aldersgate Street (Walk 7). This was one of the most heavily bombed areas of the City, and in 1955 it was decided, according to a scheme of the LCC and City of London, to realign the street at this point with a dual carriageway. Along the route a series of towers and slab blocks were planned to stand at angles to the street, so that again there would be a sense of the buildings within their own space rather than in a continuous street façade. In order to separate the pedestrians from the traffic, aerial walkways were planned to run the length of the development and into the Barbican to the north. The six tower blocks were built, four on the north side and two on the south, together with the slab blocks, all of them by different architects but following the general guidelines of the master plan and all of them constructed with glass-curtain walls. The result was a quarter of a mile of modern life, used by Michelangelo Antonioni in his 1966 film *Blow-Up* to signify the modern face of London.

The rationality and coherence in the original London Wall scheme has now been lost through redevelopment which started in the 1990s. The first building to be replaced was one of the tower blocks, Lee House, by Bernard Gold and Partners of 1961–2, giving way to the greatly inflated Alban Gate by the Terry Farrell Partnership which spans the road at Wood Street. Thus the new building not only uses the cleared site, but also the air space over the road. Alban Gate reflects the so-called 'postmodern' style of the 1980s, but since then office design has fragmented and the design of subsequent rebuilt blocks along London Wall covers a spectrum of styles (see p.18).

Redevelopment, as we have seen, has been part of the long history of commercial building in the City of London, and its extent at any one time indicates the liveliness of the financial sector. One mark of the post-war years was the removal of commercial building out of the confines of the City to other parts of London, and

5.18 Economist Building, St James's Street, Alison and Peter Smithson, 1962–4.

5.19 45–6 Albemarle Street, Erno Goldfinger, 1955–7.

even into the suburbs. In the Marylebone Road in 1955–60 Gollins Melvin Ward and Partners produced in their Castrol House a very credible version of Gordon Bunshaft's Lever House in New York. A similar podium and tower provided an element of American glamour at the historically sensitive intersection of Haymarket and Pall Mall. New Zealand House (1957–63), by Robert Matthew, Johnson-Marshall and Partners, rises 255 feet (68.6 metres) above the pavement, a stone's throw from Trafalgar Square. Less admired is Centre Point (1959–66), an infamous speculation of the time, at the bottom of Tottenham Court Road. Designed by R. Seifert and Partners, its thirty-four-storey tower still looms over the east end of Oxford Street, but it was never really in the right place and did not prosper as an office block. More successful was Alison and Peter Smithson's Economist Building (1962–4) in St James's (fig. 5.18) (Walk 6). Three buildings of different heights are arranged around an open space raised above the street. The scale and proportions of the blocks ensure that the complex does not intrude on the surrounding buildings, and the Portland stone cladding is particularly sympathetic with this part of London. In the same district is Erno Goldfinger's Nos 45–6 Albemarle Street (1955–7) (Walk 6), an elegant reworking of the commercial and retail street façade (fig. 5.19).

Commercial buildings were also introduced during the 1960s as a means to generate economic activity in areas well beyond the City and the West End. As one

of these areas, the Elephant and Castle became the site of Erno Goldfinger's Alexander Fleming House, two seven-storey blocks and a thir-
teen-storey tower, much larger than his Albemarle Street offices. The
buildings have concrete frames, expressed by pilotis and in the grid of
the façade. But this complex of buildings has proved unsustainable as
an office development and has been converted to residential use. Even
further afield, extensive office development around East Croydon Station during the boom of the 1960s has managed to prosper, acquiring enough momentum to attract more recent development.

The event of the last twenty years which has made the most
impact on the City was the 'Big Bang', the deregulation of trading in
stocks and shares. London was well placed geographically to benefit
from deregulation, since with the innovations in electronic communications the markets were open in the morning at the same time as
those in the Far East, and then in the afternoon at the same time as
those in North America. The need now was for trading floors, large
undifferentiated spaces, and – while computers still required them –
deep floors to carry the necessary cables. Property developers were
very active in producing buildings which were much denser with
larger footprints than previously. This new boom also coincided with
a revulsion at the anonymous glass curtain-walled blocks of the
1960s, and many of these were either replaced or reclad. During the
'postmodern' 1980s, the cladding was more likely to be millimetres-
thin marble in imitation of masonry construction. An example of
this approach is Minster Court (1987–91) by Gollins Melvin Ward
and Partners.

Despite the speculative boom, there were still businesses that felt
the need of a building which expressed their own particular identity
and stood out from the rest. The National Westminster Bank started
off with the tallest tower in the City, which is still unrivalled (see
p.153). Then the insurers Lloyd's of London, after a competition,
commissioned Richard Rogers to design their new building (Walk 1).
They knew the Pompidou Centre in Paris that Rogers had designed
with Renzo Piano, but they had made the decision to court the future
and they were not disappointed. With the services on the outside and
its dramatic atrium inside, the Lloyds Building became instantly
recognisable (fig. 5.20).

Another development was the release of land which had had
other previous uses, with the result that the area within the City
dedicated to offices expanded. The Broadgate office development
colonised a large tranche of redundant railway property on the
northern periphery of the City. Here a number of architects, including the American firm of Skidmore Owings and Merrill, designed buildings of high density around Liverpool Street Station
(Walk 7). A mixture of styles was the result, with SOM adopting an
American retro façade to Bishopsgate reminiscent of 1930s
Chicago, with a much more muscular building, Exchange House,
behind (fig. 5.21). Although Broadgate seemed on the edge, this
was nothing to the next area of development, the redundant docks
on the Isle of Dogs.

5.20 Lloyds Building, Leadenhall and Lime Street, Richard Rogers Partnership, 1978–86.

5.21 Exchange House, Broadgate, Skidmore Owings and Merrill, 1990.

5.22 Canary Wharf, general view from Greenwich.

Since the closure of the large nineteenth-century docks (see p. 32) in the 1960s and the move down river to the container docks, the regeneration of 'Dockland' had been an issue. During the 1980s a new initiative was tried by the creation of the London Docklands Development Corporation. The purpose of this organisation was to facilitate new enterprise zones within these vast areas, where businesses were promised tax breaks and exemption from planning regulations. While many were still thinking of small-scale offices and workshops, in 1985 G. Ware Travelstead, an American developer, proposed a much more ambitious scheme. The chosen site was the docks at the top of the Isle of Dogs, known as Canary Wharf, and here they proceeded to prepare the site for a cluster of office towers. In 1987, before construction began, Travelstead bowed out, and the Canadian developer Olympia and York stepped in. At the time the scheme devised for them by SOM seemed megalomaniac, with a tall tower by Cesar Pelli and many large blocks in SOM's retro style, and this proved to be the case when the development opened in the 1990s. A downturn in the markets and lack of adequate transport to an area that had long been a backwater meant that Canary Wharf remained for a number of years a stage set with few players. However, with the upturn in the market and the completion of the Jubilee Line extension, the fortunes of the area revived dramatically, with the result that a whole new crop of buildings have gone up in a style more in line with current taste (fig. 5.22).

Canary Wharf has presented the first real challenge to the City of London for pre-eminence as London's financial centre, since its density is such that it can generate competing levels of business. Perhaps this has led to yet more redevelopment in the City itself with building going on in several areas, such as the gradual impinging on the edges of Spitalfields. Wherever there is a space, it is soon filled. For example, the Baltic Exchange, destroyed by an IRA bomb, was replaced by another

5.23 General City view from the Monument with Swiss Re Tower, St Mary Axe, Norman Foster and Partners, 2003.

Foster building, the Swiss Re (2003), fondly named the Gherkin (fig. 5.23)(Walk 1). This building is distinctive in shape, but also claims to have a sustainable internal climate, a concern that will surely be expressed in future buildings.

The current issue is one of height, with some factions envisioning the City as a mass of distinctive towers, of which the Swiss Re is but the beginning. Others are more convinced of the need to keep the skyline as it is, with enough open sight lines so that the dome of St Paul's remains visible from different directions. In the meantime, commercial London continues to refashion itself, and nowhere more so than in the City, where buildings continually have to assert their right to exist in what is a highly competitive space.

Chapter 6 CAPITAL LONDON
Building for government and display

King James I, Great Britain's Solomon who had united the crowns of Scotland and England, was apotheosised in the paintings by Rubens set into the ceiling of the Whitehall Banqueting House. Twenty years earlier, in 1615, James had drawn attention to his imperial ambitions in one of a series of proclamations by which he attempted to restrict new building and to specify form and quality:

> *As it was said of the first emperor of Rome, that he had found the city of Rome of brick and left it of marble, so Wee, whom God hath honoured to be the first of Britaine, might be able to say in same proportion, that we had found our Citie and suburbs of London of stickes, and left them of bricke, being a material farre more durable, safe from fire and beautiful and magnificent.*

Roman achievement has been a recurrent point of reference for the regulators and critics of London building. John Evelyn invoked Augustus in his address to Charles II in 1680, and James Elmes in 1827 was equally fulsome in his praise:

> *Augustus made it one of his proudest boasts, that he found Rome of brick and left it of marble. The reign and regency of George the Fourth have scarcely done less, for the vast and increasing metropolis of the British Empire: by increasing its magnificence and its comforts; by forming healthy streets and elegant buildings, instead of pestilential alleys and squalid hovels; by substituting rich and varied architecture and park-like scenery, for paltry cabins and monotonous cow-lairs; by making solid roads and public ways, scarcely inferior to those of ancient Rome, which have connected the extremest points of the empire, and have brought its provinces and seaports, many days journey nearer to the Metropolis, instead of the miry roads through which our respected ancestors ploughed their weary ways, from London to Bath, 'by the blessing of God, in four days'; and by beginning, and continuing with a truly national perseverance, a series of desirable improvements, that bid fair to render London, the Rome of modern history.*

6.1 Greenwich, from Island Gardens, showing the buildings of the former Royal Hospital for Seamen and the Queen's House.

6.2 King William Building of the Royal Hospital for Seamen, west front, 1701–8.

6.3 King William Building, doorway to the dining room beneath the Painted Hall, 1701–8.

The inexorable growth in state activity throughout the nineteenth century resulted in the demand for administrative space constantly outstripping supply. However, even when the need for improvements was acknowledged, there were tensions regarding implementation: style, degree of grandeur and cost were all contested subjects. The question of the appropriateness of grandeur is recurrent in the discussion of publicly funded architecture. Nicholas Hawksmoor in 1728 had reminded critics of Greenwich Hospital of Queen Mary's 'fix't intention for magnificence' in the foundation of a building which was designed not merely as an almshouse for aged and infirm naval pensioners, but also to send out a celebratory message concerning the power and benevolence of the state on one of the main public routes into London (fig. 6.1) (Walk 12). Here was a very visible manifestation of the reach and authority of the Royal Navy, protecting national interests and commerce around the world, and demonstrating the charitable impulse of a grateful nation which cared for those who had suffered in its service. All the architects who worked on the fulfilment of Christopher Wren's plan for Greenwich, from Hawksmoor at the beginning to Philip Hardwick in the mid-nineteenth century, had recourse to the argument for an appropriate magnificence whenever costs were questioned (figs 6.2 and 6.3). Even later, following the transfer of responsibility to the Royal Naval College in 1873, the new Pepys Building, which merely comprised courts for racquets and fives, was given an improbably rich screen front with a giant order of Doric pilasters, paired Ionic columns, and roundels containing the busts of national naval heroes. Its prominent location to the west of the hospital, facing the river, demanded this continuation of splendid display.

In the later eighteenth century, Sir William Chambers had essayed a comparable magnificence in the government service at Somerset House, erected principally for the Navy Office but also including revenue offices and, on the Strand front, housing learned societies: the Royal Society, the Society of Antiquaries and the Royal Academy (Walk 3). Palatially built on the site of a former royal palace between 1776 and 1801, Chambers married elements of the architecture of John Webb's Palladian riverside gallery of 1661–4 (fig. 6.4), which he reproduced at the entrance on the Strand (fig. 6.5), with the contemporary French classicism which informs the design of the long riverfront. The dome and portico which serve perfectly well on the shorter courtyard side (fig. 6.6) are too modest to provide an appropriate central accent towards the Thames, and this front was further compromised by the construction of the Victoria Embankment in 1864–70. The Embankment severed the direct connection with the river, obscuring and rendering redundant the great river

6.4 Somerset House, S. Wale's view (published 1761) of John Webb's riverfront building of 1661–4; the steeple of James Gibbs's St Mary le Strand (1714–17) is shown to the east, aligned with the water stairs.

6.5 Somerset House, William Chambers, 1776–1801, Strand front.

6.6 Somerset House, courtyard looking south.

6.7 (below) Somerset House, the Nelson (Navy) Stair at the west end of the south (river) range.

arch and water gates, but in an oblique view from the terrace, ever a popular viewpoint for scenographic artists, the proportions are magnificently harmonious. The financing of such splendour in the public service inevitably occasioned surveillance and criticism, but as John Harris (1970) describes, Chambers had Edmund Burke on his side in 1781: 'no man who looked at the ... works going on' could doubt 'the honesty and care of the application of sums that parliament had granted ... [Somerset House] did honour to the present age, and would render the Metropolis of Great Britain famous throughout Europe.'

Later, regarded as 'handsome but not over-elaborated' (fig. 6.7), Somerset House was recommended as an appropriate model for government buildings. An ornamental exterior in a large building added proportionally little to the cost, it was argued. As Sir Charles Edward Trevelyan, permanent secretary to the Treasury and advocate of purpose-built offices in Whitehall, observed in 1856 (quoted in M. H. Port's comprehensive study, *Imperial London*):

As it costs little more to build handsome public offices than unsightly public offices, [it is] very desirable on general national grounds to take this opportunity of embellishing the town ... we have a very important national duty to perform in this respect; this city is something more than the mother of arts and eloquence; she is a mother of nations; we are peopling two continents ... we are organising, christianising and civilising large portions of ... Africa and Asia; and it is not right that when the inhabitants of those countries come to the metropolis, they should see nothing worthy of its ancient renown.

Colonel Clarke, Director of Engineering Works at the Admiralty, submitted a plan for the complete demolition and rebuilding of the west side of Whitehall in 1865–6, producing a model in 1869, with the eastern (river) side of a widened Whitehall given over to first-class residences, leaving the Banqueting House in splendid, islanded isolation. The need to impress the visitor with the architectural ambition which denoted an appropriate seriousness of intent and due regard for the significance of governmental process was reiterated in 1900: 'Here the wishes of an imperial people are registered and enforced. From these buildings goes forth the motive force which moves armies and navies, and controls the destinies of millions in every part of the world. And it will be satisfactory to know that these high purposes are not wanting in grandeur and dignity.'

Trevelyan argued the case for a range of purpose-built offices concentrating the work of departments close to the Houses of Parliament, so that ministers and officials could remain in proximity and contact, and communication between departments could be facilitated. As they grew, these departments spread over several sites, often adapted from domestic use, with consequent problems of inadequate sanitation, light and ventilation. The Treasury – occupying William Kent's purpose-built building of 1733–7, together with many surrounding later buildings of the eighteenth and nineteenth centuries, all hidden behind the rich, symmetrical Whitehall front added by Charles Barry in 1844–7 – was likened in 1888 to a rabbit warren:

The ground floor contained a few really good rooms, including the famous Board Room ... reserved for the heaven-born, but most of the staff lived in dens and holes, some in the basement, some in remote attics, some at the end of long passages or dark staircases. If a senior officer wished to see one of his juniors ... the usual procedure was to put in a ferret in the shape of a messenger to find out if that particular rabbit was in his burrow and bolt him. If one young rabbit wished to commune with another young rabbit, he had to track him as best he could through the labyrinth.

Even new purpose-built offices could be criticised; indeed it is remarkable when they are not. G. G. Scott's Italianate Foreign and Commonwealth Office of 1862–75 (with the Home and Colonial Office on the Whitehall side and the India Office facing St James's Park, on which he collaborated with Matthew Digby Wyatt) had ranges of offices to either side of central corridors which in the days of gas lighting were either dark or badly ventilated (fig. 6.8) (Walk 2). There were also complaints about the height of rooms. How to accommodate low-ceilinged rooms with high rooms is a recurring architectural problem where grand rooms are required but ease and expense of construction favours continuous floor and ceiling levels. Scott believed that this difficulty would be better overcome in the Gothic style, in which exterior form followed interior function. The desirability of irregularity, enabling different parts to fulfil different purposes, had been promoted by Ruskin and lay behind the development of the English Free School in the mid-nineteenth cen-

6.8 The Foreign and Commonwealth Office, Whitehall, George Gilbert Scott, 1862–75.

6.9 Turret on the Parliament Square front of the New Government Offices, now the Treasury, J.M. Brydon, 1899–1915.

tury, a response to the need for public buildings of increasing complexity. But Scott had been encouraged to attempt to rival the Banqueting House with a number of grand first-floor spaces, with the consequence that a lot of cubic capacity was wasted in those rooms which were unnecessarily high. Stale air hung around above the windows, and according to one official, 'I not only cannot hear what others say to me, but very often I cannot hear what I am saying myself.' This was the price paid by officials for the inclusion in the design of conference rooms of considerable if oppressive grandeur.

Scott's Foreign and Commonwealth Office was a key building in the Battle of the Styles, the architect's initially successful Gothic design being overruled by Prime Minister Palmerston, who was opposed both to 'gloomy looking Buildings in the Gothic style' and to Scott's desperate 'mongrel' Italo-Byzantine alternative. A classical pattern had been set by the Banqueting House, and it had even been suggested in 1856 that the whole of Whitehall might be rebuilt using Inigo Jones's seventeenth-century Whitehall Palace proposals. Such extreme historicism mercifully was avoided, but the circular court from Jones's scheme appeared in the last great Whitehall building of the late Victorian period, John M. Brydon's New Government Offices on the corner of Whitehall and Parliament Square. Designed in 1898 and begun the following year, the building was not even above-ground when Brydon died in 1901, to be succeeded by the government architect Sir Henry Tanner. He broadly followed Brydon's plan, but a contemporary critic found the building 'shorn of some features which would have added greatly to its dignity'. This caveat notwithstanding, it is an imposing pile with corner towers and cupola-turrets in the centre of the long fronts (fig. 6.9). Completed in 1915, this was the last of the sequence of successively larger and grander classical buildings on the west side of Whitehall which began with Barry's Old Treasury building and continued with Scott's Foreign and Commonwealth Office.

The War Office on the east side of Whitehall, just north of the Banqueting House, was begun in the same year as Brydon's building but was completed in 1906. Hitherto, the War Office had been spread over eleven sites in Pall Mall and elsewhere.

6.10 The Old War Office, Whitehall, from the north, with the Banqueting House beyond, William and Clyde Young, 1899–1906.

6.11 Royal Hospital, Chelsea, 1682–91, designed by Wren for invalid and veteran soldiers, the front facing the river.

6.12 The Banqueting House, Whitehall, 1619–22, from the north, with the staircase compartment of 1808–9 by James Wyatt. The statue of Spencer Compton Cavendish, 8th Duke of Devonshire, statesman, by H. Hampton, was erected in 1910.

6.13 The Ministry of Defence, front to Horseguards Avenue (left), Vincent Harris, 1939–59.

With a staff of 498 in the mid-1870s, the distribution within the buildings ranged from 2 to 160. This was inefficient, expensive and led to inferior work. It was also unhealthy – as M. H. Port recounts, the secretary of state, under-secretary and assistant under-secretary had all died within a few months of each other in 1861–2, 'and there can be little doubt that a contributory cause, if not the chief cause, was the awful sanitary condition of the War Office'. By 1886–7, the department had grown to employ 958 staff, of whom 164 were messengers, the invisible cohort indispensable in a paper-driven service. But it was not until 1899 that a new building was begun, to the design of William Young. He died the following year, and his son Clyde took over with the Office of Works architect Sir John Taylor. Image came before function. Service (1977) quotes Clyde Young's recollections:

> My father's first thought on receiving the commission was, very naturally, of the style to be adopted for the new building; and the position of the site ... quickly decided him upon a Classic treatment. The question whether that treatment should be free or orthodox was a problem more difficult to solve. The influence of the Banqueting House, was, however, too great to be resisted and he decided on the more difficult and dangerous course ... of trying to produce a design which would harmonise with its beautiful neighbour ... The dimensions of the order, the level of the cornice, and the height of the building were accordingly made to line with the Banqueting House as nearly as the internal arrangements would permit.

This is a striking building, completed in 1906, perhaps not quite so harmonious as its architect hoped, being considerably more baroque than the Banqueting House, but fulfilling rather more complex requirements and answering the needs of a more difficult location (fig. 6.10). The corner turrets mask the fact that there are no right angles on the site, and they also act as focal points in views along the street since they are sited at the point where the alignment shifts, allowing Trafalgar Square to appear in views to the north.

Throughout this intense period of government building, the question of appropriate style was recurrent. As the capital of a great imperial nation, an appropriately impressive image for late nineteenth-century London was a paramount requirement, not least in order to emulate or exceed the ordered grandeur of Paris, just as two hundred years before, the Royal Hospital at Greenwich and Wren's

earlier Chelsea Hospital (fig. 6.11) (Walk 9) for army veterans had been built to rival the Hôtel des Invalides. At Greenwich, Wren's plan had to take cognizance of Inigo Jones's Queen's House (Walk 12). This small but perfectly formed building had been begun in 1617 for Queen Anne of Denmark and completed for Queen Henrietta Maria in 1638 (see p.228). It served as a royal retreat for occasional use on the edge of Greenwich Palace for only four years before the Civil War wrecked the precarious equilibrium of the state. But when Queen Mary granted the use of the former palace and its grounds for the establishment of the hospital in 1694, she specifically excluded the avenue which led from the Queen's House to the river. This strip of land remains the property of the Crown, and Wren's buildings perforce frame the view to an iconic building which is far too small to provide a strong central accent in a great baroque composition that represents a magnificent triumph over unavoidable difficulty.

Inigo Jones's Banqueting House in Whitehall, built for James I in 1619–22, has presented the same disabling challenge to subsequent architects who have had to work in a shadow which is literally small but metaphorically huge (fig. 6.12). Architects from William Kent and Thomas Ripley in the eighteenth century to Barry, Scott, Brydon and Young in the nineteenth have all worked in Italianate styles which follow the classical agenda set by Jones. Even Vincent Harris's enormous Ministry of Defence, built 1939–59, although appearing to make few concessions to the Banqueting House, raises pedimented corner blocks which recall the towers of John Webb's Jonesian Wilton House of the mid-seventeenth century (fig. 6.13). The problem of form and function was addressed by a Treasury study group, which, as Port recounts, concluded in 1944 that it is 'difficult not to fall amongst several stools in any attempt to create a building which shall be a modern office, a piece of monumental architecture designed to typify the solidity and permanence of the Nation and the authority of the Government, conform to an inconvenient site contour, and harmonise externally with Georgian and Victorian buildings of the same class – which is the problem in Whitehall'. Consideration was given shortly afterwards to replacing Scott's Foreign Office with something more modern and efficient, but the building survived. It was threatened again in the 1960s by the LCC's 'megalomaniacal scheme to rebuild the whole of Whitehall for the convenience of civil servants', the defeat of which in 1972, chronicled by Gavin Stamp, was a great spur to the conservation movement.

The Banqueting House is a building of great sophistication, but an inspiration rather than a model (Walk 2). In John Newman's sober judgement, this was 'a monumental and ordered architecture based on antiquity and the Italian Renaissance', harnessed by its architect 'to the expression of the grandeur of his monarch'. This was a building designed, like the Queen's House, as an adjunct to an existing and rather sprawling royal palace, paying no stylistic or structural heed to its surroundings. It was intended for occasional display and ceremony, thereby allowing its architect the licence for an architectural demonstration, in which respect it has more in common with such (reconstructed) festival buildings as Mies van der Rohe's Barcelona Pavilion and Le Corbusier's *Pavillon de l'Esprit Nouveau* than it does with buildings for permanent occupation and use. Built before Jones had produced his unexecuted designs for a complete rebuilding of Whitehall Palace, the Banqueting House was designed for the enactment of fantasy and ritual through the court masques. As characterised by Stephen Orgel, these celebrations represented a 'vision of nature controlled by the human intellect'. In the parallel reality which King Charles I occupied when ruling without Parliament, these were, in the view of Jane Roberts, both 'expressions of the royal will and mirrors of the royal mind'. Their performance here ceased with the installation in 1635 of Rubens's magnificent ceiling paintings glorifying King James I, after which events involving smoky torchlight took place elsewhere, with masques held in a timber masquing house built behind the Banqueting House in 1637.

The innovatively rational classicism of the Banqueting House was celebrated in the early eighteenth century by Colen Campbell in his three-volume compendium of British architectural achievement, *Vitruvius Britannicus*. Here Jones is extolled as having 'out-done all that went before', including the great Palladio who had arrived at 'a Ne plus ultra of his Art'. But Campbell's engraving of the Banqueting House gives little idea of the sculptural vigour of its exterior modelling and the exuberance of its detailing, far from the Palladian stylistic straitjacket in which its architect has been imprisoned by commentators since the eighteenth century (fig. 6.14). It also could give no idea of its original polychromy: the white Portland stone of the columns and entablature stood out against the buff Oxford and honey-coloured Northamptonshire stone of the walls. This facing was replaced by pure, unsullied Portland stone in works by Sir William Chambers (1774) and Sir John Soane (1829–33), who, along with all those who have worked on the very few surviving buildings by Jones, found themselves in pursuit of an idea as much as a real building. The remarkably untrammelled critical reception of the work of Inigo Jones is not just a function of its innovative quality, or even, in the case of the Banqueting House, of its beauty and harmony. It is a reflection of the view we hold of the doomed Stuart court which Jones served as architect, masque-maker and connoisseur. The premature death of Henry, Prince of Wales, Jones's first royal patron, and the removal of the head of his brother King Charles I, who stepped to the scaffold on 30 January 1649 from a window of the Banqueting House, have imbued this period with the aura of romance which pertains when men die young and brilliant promise remains unfulfilled. As Jane Roberts has noted: 'The death of Charles I on the scaffold ... has bestowed a particular pathos and fascination on both his life and his portraiture', to which might be added the architecture with which he was associated.

The English Civil War provided a rich source of inspiration for those nineteenth-century artists who specialised in historical genre painting, both sides in the conflict supplying matter fit for representation in the service of an emerging middle-class

6.14 The Banqueting House, Whitehall.

public which, for Roy Strong, had become 'saturated with history' through history writing by Henry Hallam, John Lingard and Thomas Macaulay, and through the historical fiction of Sir Walter Scott and others. Ernest Crofts was a particularly enthusiastic exponent of historically meticulous scenes from the period, rarely producing anything else; his work includes a representation of Charles I on the scaffold outside the Banqueting House – *Whitehall: January 30th 1649* – exhibited at the Royal Academy in 1890. Following Thomas Carlyle's publication of Oliver Cromwell's letters and speeches in 1845, his image was transformed as he came to be recognised as a man of integrity, sincerity and faith, the defender of English liberties, joining Charles I, the hero and martyr of chivalry, as a dominant figure in the public memory. Even before his death, the king had been depicted as the chivalrous knight in Rubens's *Landscape with St George and the Dragon* (1629–30). Charles was declared a martyr by Parliament in 1660 and added to the calendar of Anglican saints: prayers were said on the anniversary of his death until the practice was discontinued by the Church of England in 1894. Between 1820 and 1900, about 175 paintings connected with Charles I and his family, Cromwell and the Civil War were exhibited at the Royal Academy. Inside the new Houses of Parliament, the preoccupation with the subject was seen at its finest in Charles West Cope's monumental series of Civil War paintings of the 1850s and 1860s.

Cromwell's image was forever fixed in the great unfinished 'pimples warts & every thing as you see me' prototypical portrait miniature by Samuel Cooper, which was followed most notably by Peter Lely. Charles's self-fashioning, especially through the agency of Van Dyck, whose genius transformed the 5 foot 4 inch (1.63 metre) king into God's representative on earth in appearance as well as belief, had by contrast been designed to demonstrate his divinely inspired occupation of that high ground identified by Roland Barthes in his analysis of electoral photography in which the candidate reaches an 'Olympus of elevated feelings, where all political contradictions are solved'. These consummate portrayals have long outlived the purpose of their making. In Richard Ollard's neat encapsulation, 'the visual arts that Charles I sought to harness to his politics have in the end carried him out of them'. When we think now of Charles I, we follow Barthes's formulation and imagine the Van Dyck portraits with the soaring gaze of the king 'lost nobly in the future'. It is a gaze tinged with fashionable melancholia, which later was read as the tragic premonition of martyrdom. It is through his sophisticated patronage of painting and architecture that Charles has come to be celebrated, rather than through the catastrophic manoeuvring which precipitated the Civil War and undermined the trust of his people.

Inigo Jones's Banqueting House, with Rubens's apotheosis of James I within, is as potent a monument to the monarchy as the court paintings by Van Dyck, a man who 'gladly acceded to the mythology of an Arcadian realm ruled by an enlightened monarch'. Here in these paintings was the manifestation of the 'myth of stability' identified by Arthur Wheelock. Jonesian classicism similarly was deliberately used to express the magnificence, authority and stability that was a prerequisite for this new royal building on the road known at that time as King Street. Seen in this light, and notwithstanding the reality of the political ineptitude of the early Stuarts (well understood in the nineteenth century), to question the place of the Banqueting House and its architect in the national story would have been tantamount to contemplating an architectural regicide. Even Wren, provided with circumstances which elicited a response far more prolific and various than that of Jones, has never invited this reverence: he did not work for a king sanctified by

martyrdom. In initially offering Gothic at the Foreign and Commonwealth Office, Scott believed that he was offering a rational answer to a problem, but in the context of Whitehall the question was as incapable of rational response as an enquiry concerning religious faith.

In Parliament Square, in the context of Westminster Abbey, a different response was possible. The classicism which traditionally stood for the authority of secular government or, as at the British Museum (Walk 3) and National Gallery (Walk 2), for high culture was here deliberately eschewed. The old Palace of Westminster, an accretive group of buildings with alterations and additions by Wren and Soane, was largely destroyed by fire in October 1834, a scene recorded as an apocalyptic vision of the sublime in the painting by J. M. W. Turner (*The Burning of the Houses of Lords and Commons*, Philadelphia Museum of Art). This provided the occasion for a competition for a new Houses of Parliament which specified the Gothic or Elizabethan style. The commission was won by Charles Barry, who together with A. W. N. Pugin provided a building which married Tudor-Perpendicular Gothic detailing with classical symmetry in a supremely logical plan arranged along a north–south spine and bracketed by two towers: the Victoria Tower upstream to the south (fig. 6.15) and the Clock Tower downstream to the north, housing the great bell, Big Ben, with an octagonal spire over the Central Lobby. This great public building, erected 1839–60, manages to fulfil day-to-day functional requirements of considerable complexity within the armature of imposing grandeur necessary for such a political and national statement, without the customarily commensurate intimidatory quality of great government buildings (Walk 2). Here, however, as in Whitehall, there was no shortage of instant criticism at the time of building – all succeeding architects must envy Wren his foresight in shrouding the works at St Paul's in scaffolding and wattle screens to deter premature and ill-informed comment. Anthony Trollope, writing in 1855–6, offered a corrective to the criticism:

> Now that our Houses of Parliament are nearly completed it is of course the fashion to abuse them. They are too low, too much burdened with decoration. Perpendicular ornamentation is found to be unsuited for so long a frontage. The towers are, or will be, too heavy. There is no point from which to see it,

6.15 The Victoria Tower of the Palace of Westminster, from Victoria Tower Gardens, with the Gothic memorial fountain of 1865–6 designed by S. S. Teulon and Charles Buxton MP in commemoration of the latter's father, Sir Thomas Fowell Buxton, a slave-trade abolitionist who led the Anti-Slavery Party. It was resited here from Parliament Square in 1957.

6.16 Whitehall from Trafalgar Square.

and nothing worth looking at if such a point were found. Such are the judgements pronounced by architectural critics of the present age, and yet it may be doubted whether many nobler piles have ever yet been built by the hands of man, or blessed with a better site than this will be found to have when the bridge over the river shall have been finished ... But English critics of this age are indignant if ready made palaces do not fall from heaven into grounds prepared for them in a night by legions of angels. It is not some twenty years since the plans for the present Houses of Parliament were approved of, and men seem to think it wondrously shameful that everything belonging to the building is not completed. Do they ever reflect how long it took to build St Peter's? How long the Duomo of Florence?

It is notable that Barry's efforts elevated him into the select pantheon of architects celebrated in niches on Aston Webb's Cromwell Road façade (1899–1909) of the Victoria and Albert Museum, in company with William Wykeham, John Thorpe, Inigo Jones, Christopher Wren and William Chambers.

Parliament Square was not laid out until after the completion of the Houses of Parliament, although the ground which it occupies had been cleared in the early nineteenth century in order to make a setting for the monuments to church and state: Westminster Abbey and the Houses of Parliament. At the other end of Whitehall, Trafalgar Square had been formed in the 1820s at the angle between the route from governmental and monarchical Whitehall and Westminster to the south (fig. 6.16) and Fleet Street and the City, beyond the private palaces of the Strand, to the east. Notwithstanding this role as fulcrum, it is as much destination as route, an iconic site of immense significance. As well as being a gathering point for tourists, it has long been a site for celebration and popular political assembly and protest, which – flanked by Canada House to the west and South Africa House to the east, with Nelson surmounting the central column – is also paradoxically an imperial arena. This is a complex and contested space. Its architectural history presents a case study in the reluctance of the administrative and political classes to engage with the notion of magnificence in public architecture, however much critics might dream of Augustan Rome.

At the top of rising ground on the north side of this rather amorphous monument to empire (Walk 2), William Wilkins's neoclassical National Gallery, by common although unfair consent, fails to provide the anticipated climax: 'Let us grant that the National Gallery is a poor erection', said Trollope. Like Chambers's Somerset House, it appears to be too long, too small in scale for its extent, with a central emphasis too modest for declamatory gesture (fig. 6.17). Also like Somerset House, it is the oblique view – along the front past the fine portico and steps towards James Gibbs's church of St Martin-in-the-Fields – which most impresses. But such criticism begs the question of how Wilkins might have produced a more dramatic design in such a context, on top of a notional escarpment. He would have preferred to build fifty feet further south, but that would have blocked the view of St Martin's, so he was left with the task of providing a piece of harmonious, classically impeccable scenography which closes the view rather than dominating it. In fact, when built in 1833–8 on the former site of William Kent's proportionally comparable Royal Mews, this was little more than a screen. St George's Barracks and St Martin's Workhouse, respectively to the west and east behind, prevented the new gallery from being more than one room deep, with the recently acquired national collection occupying the top-lit upper-floor galleries in the west wing and the Royal Academy,

removed from Somerset House, in the east. Here the Royal Academy remained in rooms allegedly regarded by King William IV, according to Hutchison, as 'a nasty little pokey hole', beginning the great tradition of sensitive royal architectural criticism on this site, until it was removed to an enlarged Burlington House, Piccadilly, in 1869.

London was unusual in the early nineteenth century in being the only major European capital where the public had no right to see Old Master paintings: the royal collection was private and so remains. In establishing the National Gallery in 1824, voting £60,000 for the purchase of the thirty-eight paintings which had belonged to the banker John Julius Angerstein housed at 100 Pall Mall, Parliament was specifically providing a place where the public could see great paintings, a privilege whose defence, like freedom itself, requires eternal vigilance. The nucleus provided by the Angerstein collection was soon enhanced by further acquisitions, including the collection of Sir George Beaumont. Angerstein's old house was neither grand enough nor big enough to hold the collection, let alone to stand the inevitable comparison with the Louvre, but tenancy was brief. With the building works on Trafalgar Square barely begun, the collection had to move into an equally small house, 105 Pall Mall, as the construction of the Carlton Club put 100 Pall Mall and its contents at risk.

Further expansion on the Trafalgar Square site to house a rapidly growing collection did not take place until after the departure of the Royal Academy and the removal of first the workhouse and then eventually, in 1901, the barracks. Expansion to the east was carried out by E. M. Barry in 1872–6; in the centre first by James Pennethorne and then by Sir John Taylor in 1885–7; and to the west by H. N. Hawkes in 1907–11. Before this apparently logical, phased expansion had been agreed, consideration had been given in the course of two parliamentary commissions to the removal of the National Gallery to a more salubrious site, less subject to the central London smoke which was begriming the pictures. The discussions were protracted and repetitive, rendered the more complex through being entangled with the future of the Royal Academy, a long political, institutional and procedural story recounted with great precision by M. H. Port. A new gallery was proposed in distant, suburban Kensington associated with Prince Albert's desire to establish a cultural centre; this proposal was promoted by the 1851 Exhibition Commissioners, a body chaired by the prince. Here, in the later nineteenth and early twentieth centuries, the Natural History, Victoria and Albert, and Science Museums were erected.

A recurring theme in the National Gallery discussions was the balance between conservation and access. Smoke (with every room having a coal fire), ventilation (in the most polluted city in the world) and crowds (some as now just sheltering from the rain) provided reasons for moving west, but, as Port observes, 'the instruction and improvement of the intellect and the moral condition of the people' demanded a central location. It was regularly reported that 'the laborious and responsible classes' went to the National Gallery 'to forget their cares'. The serving of guardianship, access, scholarship and social purpose are perpetual issues in the housing and presentation of great public collections, and the satisfaction of potential conflicts is not lightly achieved. Treasury approval of the purchase of the Kensington site in 1856 merely presaged the establishment of a Royal Commission, which embarked on market research the following year: seventy-five major employers were invited to ask their employees about visits to public institutions and thirty-five replied. The result, according to Neil MacGregor, was 'a complete vindication of a free Gallery in Central London': the 338-strong workforce of Jackson the Builders had visited the National Gallery 583 times in 1856. Hooper the Coachmakers, whose forty-six employees had made sixty-six visits, quoted one of their workmen who hoped that the National Gallery would not move since 'working men could not afford to lose much time in going a long way to some suburb of London'. The education of the working man and his family won the day, for reasons encapsulated by Mr Justice Coleridge in 1857 (quoted by MacGregor, 2004):

> *if it were demonstrable that the pictures in their present position must absolutely perish sooner than at Kensington, I conceive that this would conclude nothing. The existence of the pictures is not the end of the collection but a means to give the people an ennobling enjoyment. If while so employed a great picture perished in the using, it could not be said that the picture had not fulfilled the best purpose of its purchase or that it had been lost in its results to the nation.*

It stayed in the centre of the city, accessible to all, although a condition for remaining in Trafalgar Square was that the pictures had to be glazed. They remained so for nearly a century until the installation of air conditioning.

Deliberations on the future of the National Gallery had been given greater urgency by the terms of the Turner bequest. One of the codicils of the artist's will allowed ten years from his death in December 1851 for building a gallery for his pictures. By a decree in the Court of Chancery in 1856, all the paintings, drawings and sketches from Turner's own hand that were in his possession when he died were given 'for the benefit of the Public', to be retained for the time being in the National Gallery. Housed temporarily in South Kensington, the paintings arrived in Trafalgar Square in 1876. Following the foundation of the Tate Gallery on Millbank (Walk 2) as an annexe to the National Gallery in 1897, a large number of British pictures were transferred. These were followed by the Turner bequest in 1910 after Sir Joseph Duveen had provided rooms for the reception of the paintings. Basement flooding at the Tate in 1928 prompted the transfer of the drawings and sketchbooks to the British Museum.

The expansion of the National Gallery to the north was mooted in 1962, began in 1970 and was completed in 1975 to the design of James Ellis of the Department of the Environment. The ground-level entrance without steps – an innovation considered worthy of remark in Michael Levey's 'Directors's Report' – provided access to exhibition rooms, facilities for relaxation (including a smoking room), seminar and lecture rooms, and space on the uppermost floor for the scientific and conservation departments. The new main road which was projected along Orange Street at this time encouraged an elegant stone-faced austerity, relieved by the glazed entrance and capped by the powerfully articulated overhanging offices and workshops. The siting of the northern extension at the rear, and the controversial later developments to the west, have conspired to inhibit appreciation of a building of restrained authority.

The Hampton furniture store site to the west of the National Gallery had been left vacant after bombing during the Second World War, and then was bought by the government in 1958. In 1981, in tune with the pusillanimous and niggardly spirit of the age, an architect/developer's competition was announced, inviting designs for top-lit galleries which were to be financed by high-quality private development on the lower floors. The developer would provide the galleries rent-free during the course of a 125-year lease (at a peppercorn rent), after which the building in the time-honoured London leasehold fashion would revert to the landlords, in this case the Crown. As Peter Buchanan observed at the time of the competition (1982), it was 'sad that public life should be reduced to a commercial spin-off'. It was more than sad, it was utterly outrageous that the building of an extension for one of the premier galleries of paintings in Europe, one of the most important cultural monuments in the western world, intended to house an incomparable Early Renaissance collection, should be piggybacked on top of an office block.

6.18 The National Gallery, south front, with the Sainsbury Wing, Venturi, Rauch and Scott Brown, 1987–91.

Seventy-nine designs were submitted, from which seven semi-finalists were chosen. Models and drawings by the seven practices were exhibited for two and a half weeks to 78,000 visitors, a further remarkable demonstration of the pre-eminent place of the Gallery in the national imagination. As Buchanan observed: 'The importance of the National Gallery competition cannot be overstated. Suddenly architecture in Britain is once again a subject of public interest and debate.' Ten thousand voted, although it was not necessarily clear what they were voting for since they did not have the benefit of the architectural brief – but the architects themselves had not been fully informed of the requirements either, since dialogue between architects and clients is not permitted under RIBA competition rules. In these foggy circumstances, the democratic process resulted in the design by the Richard Rogers Partnership being voted both most and least popular. Rogers's inspired urbanism created an explicit visual and physical connection between Trafalgar Square and Leicester Square, and by placing a tower between the extension and the Wilkins building reflected Gibbs's St Martin-in-the-Fields in contemporary terms. As Buchanan lamented, this might have become 'a fitting monument to an age of optimism, now fast fading, in which the imaginative use of technology was to have made available to all the benefits of modern life – including culture'. But the five advisers judging the competition for the Secretary of State for the Environment rejected it, and invited three practices to modify their designs before finally settling upon Ahrends Burton Koralek (ABK), ignoring the unanimous opposition of the director and the trustees, who thought that Skidmore Owings and Merrill (SOM) had provided the best setting for pictures. The winners of this scandalously bungled competition, in which it was the architectural team rather than the design which was victorious – a situation which invited claims of 'breach of competition' from the losers – were then able at last to enter a dialogue with the clients about the preferred hang for the paintings. More problematically, they were required to produce a distinguished building capable, in the words of the editor of *The Burlington Magazine*, of fitting in with 'the distressingly undistinguished architecture of the National Gallery and Canada House'. Although SOM allegedly had failed to demonstrate their

6.19 The National Gallery, Sainsbury Wing gallery with Cima's *The Incredulity of St Thomas* of *c*.1502–4.

ability to produce an architecturally distinguished exterior, 'it is hard to credit the charge that any elevation is too banal to stand in the company of Trafalgar Square'.

ABK's new design, which now included a glazed access tower, was presented in December 1983. The practice was on the point of winning approval from both the planners and the public when Prince Charles addressed the Royal Institute of British Architects at its 150th anniversary celebration at Hampton Court on 30 May 1984. In his self-appointed role as the guardian of traditional values, he likened the ABK design to 'a kind of vast municipal fire station' before sentimental anthropomorphism provided him with one of the sound bites of the era: this was 'a monstrous carbuncle on the face of a much-loved and elegant friend'. The ABK design could not survive this expression of royal disapprobation (recorded by Farrelly) in a thoroughly bleak period in politics and architecture: planning permission was refused after an enquiry.

In March 1988 the Prince and Princess of Wales attended the ceremony of laying the foundation stone for the National Gallery extension. The recently appointed director, Neil MacGregor, who had expressed such scathing views about the bungled competition as editor of *The Burlington Magazine*, was on hand to witness an event which represented a remarkable turnaround in the fortunes of the Gallery, as well as releasing the government from a hook of its own making. In 1985 the Sainsbury brothers, celebrated in *The Architectural Review* as a 'winged triumvirate of beneficence and patronage', in an act of 'unprecedented generosity' paid for a new building entirely for the Gallery's use without recourse to supporting commercial developments. The architectural practice of Venturi, Rauch and Scott Brown, chosen from a shortlist of six practices in 1986, unveiled a design the following year for the extension, which for Paul Goldberger, architectural critic of *The New York Times*, 'may be the most significant architectural commission in Europe ever awarded to an American architect' for 'one of England's greatest, but most difficult, urban spaces'.

The contextualism which Venturi had promoted in his theoretical writing is made manifest in the Sainsbury Wing (fig. 6.18). The firm had, according to the architect, 'decided to respect the much-loved friend' in attempting to fulfil the requirements of a brief which, for the writer in *The Architectural Review*, required the making of a statement while giving 'due deference to a host building whose self-importance, while largely undeserved, was inviolable'. The concluding sentence of Venturi's *Complexity and Contradiction in Architecture* (1966) informs the approach of his firm to Trafalgar Square: 'And it is perhaps from the everyday landscape, vulgar and disdained, that we can draw the complex and contradictory order that is valid and vital for our architecture as an urbanistic whole.' One man's complexity is another's desperate eclectic historicism, and Venturi's design has been properly criticised for a mannered approach in which elements of the Wilkins building are deployed as motifs, demonstrating the connection between old and new and best appreciated in an oblique view: clusters of pilasters fussily stutter across the angle of the façade like runners making a false start. The building, however, eschews grandeur in its homage to context, and much of it works. The ground-level entrance is clear and non-hierarchical, the spaces within are rationally disposed: we see where we are supposed to go without excessive signposting. The basement galleries for special exhibitions are distressingly dark and claustrophobic, but the upper galleries for the permanent collection, lit through clerestory windows, are dignified and humane (fig. 6.19). Completed on time in 1991, the Sainsbury Wing represents a significant conclusion to a salutary and often painful saga.

6.20 The British Museum, Great Court, Foster and Partners, 1997–2000.

The introduction of National Lottery funding in 1994 to the construction and reconstruction of cultural institutions throughout the country has prompted further consideration of purpose, and has brought an unexpected competitiveness into the provision of 'ennobling enjoyment' – which in the mantra of contemporary politics is less elegantly known as 'access'. Accompanying the pedestrianisation of the north side of Trafalgar Square in 2002–3, a notable contribution to public health and safety, the National Gallery presented a master-plan by Dixon Jones for a major refurbishment including a new entrance, a lower hall meeting place, an atrium and new ground-floor galleries at the rear. The implementation of this scheme, drawn up during the directorship of Neil MacGregor, was begun by his successor Charles Saumarez Smith. In Hugh Pearman's report, he emphasised the need for the National Gallery to be kept up to date rather than being perceived as 'frozen as a historical collection in a nineteenth-century building' – suffering perhaps from comparisons with the extraordinarily successful Tate Modern on the South Bank (Walk 5) or Norman Foster's Great Court at the British Museum (fig. 6.20) (Walk 3). Both of these have become meeting places as well as repositories for collections. As Paul Goldberger has noted, 'the museum can continue to be a treasure house and a place of scholarly research, but surely it is also more and more, the public square of our age, the place of our coming together'. In the evocative *London Perceived*, V. S. Pritchett in 1962 celebrated the absence of accidental social contact familiar to the habitués of the *grande place* or piazza: 'Londoners do not meet, do not gather, and reject the peculiar notion that people like "running across each other" in public places.' In a city where much has remained constant and current, this sounds now like a message from a barely discernible past.

The story of the development of the National Gallery is significant in illustrating the ambivalent attitude of successive British governments towards the architectural provision for major cultural monuments which are celebrated as soon as they no longer need to be funded. Here is a building and collection which is fundamental to our idea of capital and nation, and central to our idea of a shared public realm, yet even this building has been prey to the political and economic imperatives which bedevil public works and subject to the potentially destabilising interventions of the powerful. This case is emblematic of an approach to national life which in emphasising measurable process over elusive visions falls far short of fulfilling the expectations of those who would recall antique glories. But it is not unique. The saga of the British Library – of painful genesis and triumphant conclusion – is a yet more telling example in which changes of site, uncertainties of funding and unhelpful official intervention resulted in a design and building programme of over thirty years.

Since the library provision at the British Museum had been long outgrown, in 1964 Sir Leslie Martin and Colin St John Wilson presented a new design for a site in Bloomsbury south of the museum, in two parts to either side of Hawksmoor's St George's Church (Walk 3). This was abandoned in 1967 by a government sensitive to conservation pressure, and a second Bloomsbury scheme was produced by Wilson alone for the British Library, newly established by Act of Parliament in 1972 as an institution independent of the museum. This proposal also foundered on grounds of conservation of historic buildings and the lack of space for expansion. Wilson's subsequent design for a library to the north of the museum on the site of the former Somers Town railway goods-yard, next to St Pancras Station, was produced in 1975, with building commencing three years later. Completed in 1997, this major monument will now be one of the first sights of London for visitors arriving at the new international station next door, a fortuitous outcome and

a belated rebuke to those critics who considered this site too remote from established centres of culture (fig. 6.21).

Wilson brought from the Bloomsbury scheme the horizontal layering of floors on the east block of the new library, but this is a highly legible and precisely detailed site-specific building which is thoroughly in tune with location and function. It comprises two strongly differentiated ranges on its wedge-shaped site, with science reading rooms and offices to the east along Midland Road, humanities reading rooms in the range to the west, set back behind the forecourt required by the local authority as a public amenity. At the centre of the design, a six-storey tower of bronze and glass reflects the history of the library in displaying the leather and vellum bindings of the King's Library, the collection of George III. Beneath the main ranges, four storeys of basement book storage accommodate 340 kilometres of shelving.

The irregularity of the building as well as the use of brick (on a concrete frame) acknowledge Scott's adjacent Midland Grand Hotel and Wilson's belief in allowing the required function to determine the overall form, fulfilling the different requirements of readers in the humanities and science. The central foyer, a superb light-filled public space further enhanced by Ron Kitaj's great tapestry *If not, not*, serves both groups as well as providing access to exhibition galleries. The Gothic-inspired English Free School, denied to Scott in nineteenth-century Whitehall, is here superbly deployed by Wilson, who in his writing identified this as the

6.21 The British Library, courtyard with Eduardo Paolozzi's Newton monument, and Scott's Midland Grand Hotel to the east.

6.22 The British Library portico, Euston Road, Colin St John Wilson, 1978–97.

6.23 The National Theatre, South Bank, from Waterloo Bridge, Denys Lasdun, 1967–76.

source for an alternative modernism, asymmetrical and organic. The asymmetrical tone is set from the outset with public entrances through the great portico to the south-west (fig. 6.22) and by a lesser entrance to the south-east, the axes of movement intersecting at Eduardo Paolozzi's monumental bronze sculpture of Newton.

Wilson, fully aware of funding difficulties, anticipated building the new library in self-contained phases. In fact we now have half a building, with the remainder of the site to the north remaining empty. The architect likened the length of time spent on the project to that spent on St Paul's Cathedral, although he believed that Wren had not suffered the 'irresolution of authority that has dogged our project'. The inability to 'ring-fence' the finance for building, an obvious strategy which was achieved for the new Jubilee Line, the tendency of politicians to assume that election confers the right to engage in the architectural criticism of the unfinished, and the (at the time) inevitable unhelpful contribution of the Prince of Wales (likening the half-built library to an academy for secret police) exerted a pressure which might have scuppered a less resilient project. At the unveiling of Wilson's design, Sherban Cantacuzino anticipated the 'translation of man's complex needs into life-enhancing architectural form'. At its completion, Peter Blundell Jones welcomed a building of 'long-term and fundamental quality'. A decade on, the vicissitudes of its fraught history fading in the memory, the British Library is now recognised – along with Sir Denys Lasdun's National Theatre (fig. 6.23) (Walk 5), a building with a comparably lengthy gestation and triumphant conclusion – as one of the two finest public buildings of late twentieth-century London: persistence pays in the realisation of a public architecture commensurate with the expectations of the capital city.

Chapter 7 LONDON CHURCHES

The City churches and the 'Fifty New Churches'

Churches in London have tended to be built in groups in response to political and religious need and informed by contemporary theory. In 1631–5 before the Great Fire, Inigo Jones's St Paul's Covent Garden (fig. 7.1) (Walk 3) had been built as a one-off as part of the Earl of Bedford's suburban residential development outside the City, but the first great wave of post-medieval church building took place as a result of the fire. Wren and his office rebuilt fifty-one churches in the City from *c*.1670, with work on some of the towers continuing into the early eighteenth century (Walk 1). Wren had been unable to implement his new post-fire street plan, because of the City's need to get back to work as swiftly as possible on its existing medieval plots. So the churches, with the exception of St Mary-le-Bow (see p. 27) on Cheapside, the major shopping street, were rebuilt in confined spaces. In order to allow them to be seen from a distance, towers and spires were raised, giving London its distinctive skyline in which St Paul's Cathedral and the City churches appeared to soar above the workaday commercial and residential buildings which lined the rebuilt narrow streets and courts (see p. 27). The effect was a cumulative and sublime scenography now lost in London's exponential growth.

Wren's churches, on which his main collaborator was Robert Hooke, display great variety in their planning, with single cells, galleried basilicas, nave and aisles, and domed central plans often reusing existing foundations and exploiting irregular sites with considerable structural inventiveness. They were intended to be auditories and naturally lit through clear glass, with the congregation all able to see the preacher and hear the lesson – contrasting with Roman Catholic practice in which, in Wren's possibly exaggerated view, 'it is enough if they hear the murmur of the Mass, and see the Elevation of the Host'. Few of the churches survive in their entirety, following the losses and refittings of the nineteenth century (removal of box pews and the addition of stained glass) and the destruction of the Second World War, but enough remain to give an idea of the quality and extent of the achievement. The wood carving of pulpits and fonts is especially notable, and in St Stephen

7.1 St Paul's Covent Garden, Inigo Jones, 1631–5.

7.2 St Stephen Walbrook, Christopher Wren, 1672–80, interior with central altar by Henry Moore (1972).

Walbrook there is at least one translucent design of genius, fit to stand with the best of contemporary European architecture (fig. 7.2).

The role of Nicholas Hawksmoor, Wren's pupil, in the design of the churches remains elusive. He worked in the churches office from 1684 to 1701, but when he came to design churches in his own right under the Act of 1711, the monumental results were very different from those of his teacher. He did have the benefit, however, of Wren's advice, and he was able in most cases to build on new, open sites. Looking now at Hawksmoor's London churches, we see the interrelationship between ancient architecture, its modern interpretation, political imperatives, and the liturgical requirements of Anglicanism. These are rational buildings designed to a coherent programme in the service of church and state which, in demonstrating the relationship of theory and practice, might be taken as a historical model of how architecture at its best should work. According to the obituary written in 1736 by his son-in-law Nathaniel Blackerby, treasurer to the Commission for the Fifty New Churches (quoted in full by Downes, 1979), Hawksmoor was 'perfectly skill'd in the History of Architecture, and could give an exact Account of all the famous Buildings, both Antient and Modern, in every Part of the World ... He was bred a Scholar ...'. He was in fact fulfilling the polymathic Vitruvian requirement for the architect, paraphrased by Henry Wotton in *The Elements of Architecture* (1624). Vitruvius, Wotton wrote, 'commendeth in an Architect, a Philosophical Spirit; that is, he would have him ... to be no superficiall and floating Artificer; but a Diver into Causes, and into the Mysteries of Proportion'. John Webb, Christopher Wren and Nicholas Hawksmoor were all Divers into Causes, looking for the roots of architecture and practice, an early Enlightenment search which found expression in the 1721 publication by Hawksmoor's Austrian contemporary, Fischer von Erlach, of *Entwurf einer historischen Architectur*. Hawksmoor had a copy of this pluralist volume with its imaginative reconstructions of ancient Roman, Assyrian, Egyptian, Turkish and Chinese buildings. Wren's 'Discourse on Architecture', one of his five 'Tracts', begun in the 1670s but not published until 1750, covered similar ground: the Tower of Babel, the Temple of Solomon, the Pyramids, the Mausoleum at Halicarnassus – a considered enquiry into ancient and distant sources. Because of what we might readily perceive as the emotional power of Hawksmoor's buildings, there has been a temptation to look in his work for the triumph of dark, mystic forces over logical procedure, but it is this fusion of the worlds of sensory and rational experience which characterises great art.

The church of St Alfege in Greenwich, the second to be built on the site where Alfege, the Archbishop of Canterbury, was killed by Danes in 1012, was ruined during a severe storm in November 1710. The roof collapsed because one of the piers had been weakened by the numerous excavations undertaken for burials. The parishioners petitioned Parliament on the grounds that for forty years they had contributed to the building of St Paul's Cathedral and the City churches by a 'Duty of Coals', and they asked for £6,000 or 'such other sum as the House shall think fit' for rebuilding their church. The year 1710 also saw the fall of the Whigs from power, and in a High Church Tory House of Commons this occasioned a discussion on the whole question of church building in London. Wren's churches had catered for the needs of the City, but districts outside the area rebuilt after the Great Fire were ill-served for places of worship. In an age when the parish played a key role in the maintenance of law and order, the church had a social and political function, particularly in areas more Nonconformist than High Anglican. In those areas, according to the anonymous incumbent of one of the outer parishes in *c*.1714:

Many Score Thousands of People ... scarcely in their whole lives so much as Peep into a Church ... [and here] ... the Vilest People, Highwaymen, House-Breakers, Felons of all Degrees, Impudent Women, and Persons Disaffected to His Majesty's Government, take Harbour, and Fly to their Haunts therein, as Vermin to their Kennels, after they have taken their Prey.

The committee appointed to review the St Alfege petition was invited also to 'consider what churches are wanting within the Cities of London and Westminster, and Suburbs thereof'. The answer, with the assent of Queen Anne, was enshrined in the Act of 1711, which imposed a duty on coals for the purpose of 'Building ... Fifty New Churches of Stone and other proper Materials, with Towers or Steeples to each of them; and for purchasing of Sites of Churches and Church-Yards, and Burying-places, in or near the Cities of London and Westminster, or the Suburbs thereof'. One of these was to be at Greenwich, and following this success others also petitioned, among them the parishioners of St Mary Woolnoth in the City, patched up after the Great Fire and now on the point of collapse. Although fifty was a good round number and reminiscent of Wren's achievement, there was never enough money to build so many churches of the grandeur and ambition of those commemorating Queen Anne: twelve were achieved.

The commissioners in 1711 solicited views from vestries to enable them to decide which should benefit. Wren was one of the commissioners, and in his 'Letter to a Friend on the Commission for Building Fifty New Churches', he set out the results of forty years of experience: the churches should be of good brick or stone, in places of heaviest population on large and open streets; fronts should be adorned with porticoes, the other walls left plain, with handsome spires or lanterns rising above the neighbouring houses; they should be large and galleried, but everyone should be able to see and to hear; and, learning from St Alfege, burials should be in cemeteries on the outskirts of town rather than within the church. He cited his own St James's Piccadilly of 1676–84 as a model (fig. 7.3) (Walk 6). Sir John Vanbrugh's proposals differed from those of Wren in rhetoric and degree rather than substance: the new churches should be 'Monuments to Posterity' of the piety and grandeur of Queen Anne, 'Ornaments to the Towne, and a Credit to the Nation', 'High and Bold Structures' with 'the most Solemn and Awfull Appearance both without and within'.

The commissioners chosen in 1711 to implement the Act appointed Hawksmoor and William Dickinson, another colleague of Wren, as salaried surveyors. The following year, Hawksmoor, in tune with the archaeological bent of his High Church Anglican patrons, produced a plan for 'The Basilica after the Primitive Christians' for a site on the corner of Brick Lane and Hare Street (now Cheshire Street). In the event, the site was not acquired, but Hawksmoor showed himself to be fully in tune with early Christian practice in his recreation of the 'Manner of Building the Church as it was in ye fourth Century in the purest times of Christianity'. Set on an insular, prominent site, the church fulfilled requirements by being orientated east–west, with a font large enough to permit full immersion – a practice which some churchmen wished to revive – and an enclosure for a vestry building and houses for the minister, the clerk and sexton, and the reader, all set behind a wall designed to 'keep off filth Nastyness & Brutes'.

Hawksmoor remained in post until the 1730s, but Dickinson resigned after two years without building anything. He was succeeded by James Gibbs, a Tory nominee who designed St Mary le Strand in 1714, his first important commission after spending several years in Rome as the pupil of Carlo Fontana. This is a spatially simple church

7.3 St James's Piccadilly, Christopher Wren, 1676–84.

7.4 St Mary le Strand, James Gibbs, 1714–24.

7.5 St Martin-in-the-Fields, James Gibbs, 1721–6, from Trafalgar Square.

in which the architect very successfully brought Italian decorative elements to bear on a small scale (fig. 7.4) (Walk 3). With the Whigs once more in government, Gibbs lost his post in January 1716. His later church, the galleried St Martin-in-the-Fields (1721–6), was not one of the 'Fifty New Churches', but was more influential than any of them, being prominently sited and published by Gibbs in 1728 in *A Book of Architecture* (fig. 7.5) (Walk 2). He combined the portico, which was concurrently occurring elsewhere in designs by Hawksmoor and John James, with a steeple inspired by Wren's City churches.

By the time of the appointment of John James, Gibbs's replacement and a long-time collaborator with Hawksmoor, most of the designs had been prepared, but he did produce one notable building, St George Hanover Square (1721–5), with internal galleries and an imposing portico (fig. 7.6). He also collaborated with Hawksmoor on two rather plain, simple, barrel-vaulted nave and aisles churches with galleries, designed to cost nearer £10,000 than the £30,000–40,000 expended on some of the others. Both were characterised by highly idiosyncratic towers: St Luke Old Street and St John Horsleydown of 1727–33, with respectively an obelisk and a tapering Ionic column. After several years at risk, St Luke has been rescued (fig. 7.7). The original interior has gone apart from some vestigial pilasters, and a new interior was completed in 2003 by the architects Levitt Bernstein for the London Symphony Orchestra. St John, on a site near the south end of Tower Bridge, was gutted in 1940 and demolished in 1948. Its foundations have been reused in Nasmith House (London City Mission), built 1972–6 to the designs of John D. Ainsworth and Associates. The rectories survive at both churches.

Of the remaining eight churches, six were designed by Hawksmoor and two by Thomas Archer: St Paul Deptford (1712–30) (fig. 7.8) and St John Smith Square (1714–28) (fig. 7.9), the two most indebtedly Continental of the group. These might lack the tension of the centralised churches of the full Roman baroque, but St Paul, recently restored and richly decorated, presents an interesting solution to the problem of combining the central plan with galleries. Archer placed his galleries behind a giant order, and put boxes at the canted corners of the central square which align not with the opposite corners but with the centres of the opposite sides, setting up minor cross axes. Outside, very fine staircases lead to the side entrances, and at the west end a curved portico, inspired perhaps by Pietro da Cortona's Santa Maria della Pace in Rome, is combined with the steeple, an idea which was to recur at St Mary le Strand, although there the steeple was a difficult afterthought. St John's, indebtedly Italianate in its baroque detailing and superbly sited, closes the view at the end of Lord North Street (Walk 2). Archer's interior does not survive: it was twice altered before being gutted in 1941 and rebuilt as a concert hall in 1965–9 by Marshall Sisson.

Hawksmoor's six churches were less obviously centralising in tendency than those of Archer, but nevertheless combined a central focus with an east–west axis. This is clearly apparent at St Alfege, the church which began the whole process (Walk 12). Hawksmoor's design, approved in 1712, has transepts which emphasise the cross axis and the side entrances, with the main west entrance undramatically placed

7.6 St George Hanover Square, John James, 1721–5.

7.7 St Luke Old Street, Nicholas Hawksmoor and John James, 1727–33.

7.8 St Paul Deptford, Thomas Archer, 1712–30.

7.9 St John Smith Square, Thomas Archer, 1714–28, from Lord North Street.

at the base of the tower. The east end portico, borrowed possibly from Wren's giant order portico design for St Paul's, derives ultimately from the temple of Bacchus, Baalbek (Lebanon), which Hawksmoor drew on the basis of engravings and travel accounts (fig. 7.10). The deeply cut windows and the sharply defined labels and keystones point to the similarity between this church and Hawksmoor's Clarendon Press building in Oxford, also begun in 1712. There is the same effect of achieving a sense of volume and mass through cutting back the wall in parallel planes, giving the sculptural impression of immense thickness of masonry.

Within this hall with galleries, Hawksmoor's ceiling appears to float miraculously, not supported from the floor but suspended from tie beams. This was reconstructed by Sir Albert Richardson in 1953 following wartime gutting. James

7.10 St Alfege Greenwich, Nicholas Hawksmoor, 1712–30, east end.

7.11 St George in the East, Nicholas Hawksmoor, 1714–29.

7.12 St Anne Limehouse, Nicholas Hawksmoor, 1714–30.

Thornhill's illusionistic apse painting, making a shallow recess look much deeper, has been repainted by Glyn Jones. Instead of Hawksmoor's new tower, in keeping with the church, parishioners had to settle for a recasing by John James of the original medieval tower, completed in 1730.

By this time, Hawksmoor's tower had been built on the other side of the Thames, at St George in the East (fig. 7.11), one of the three great Stepney churches on new sites which were all begun in 1714 and completed in 1729–30. These are extraordinary, dramatic and intense buildings, with towers which once dwarfed their original surroundings. It would be difficult to conceive a clearer manifestation of the power and authority of church and state being brought to the overcrowded suburbs than these three buildings. The site of St George in the East originally was more constrained than now, with houses to the south which Hawksmoor tried unsccessfully to remove. The church was gutted in 1941, and a new smaller church was built within the walls by Ansell and Bailey in 1960–4. Both here and at St Anne Limehouse, restored in 1850 by Philip Hardwick after a fire, Hawksmoor defined the central space with columns, creating embryonic Greek crosses within rectangles, although neither church can be entered on the transverse axis. Both have side galleries and chancels reached through depressed arches, emphasising the east–west axis, in tune with the demands of the liturgy.

Externally, the design of St George in the East evolved slowly, Hawksmoor's drawings showing the tower beginning as a two-stage belfry with an octagonal pepper pot lantern. It later acquired a third belfry stage, and the lantern derived from Greenwich became an open octagon reminiscent of Perpendicular Gothic churches, but here with classical details. The pepper pot quadrupled and in an elongated form appears over each of the four staircase turrets. The west tower seems to break through the roofline. At St Anne, the tower does not burst through a broken pediment, but rises above a vigorously modelled circular portico (fig. 7.12).

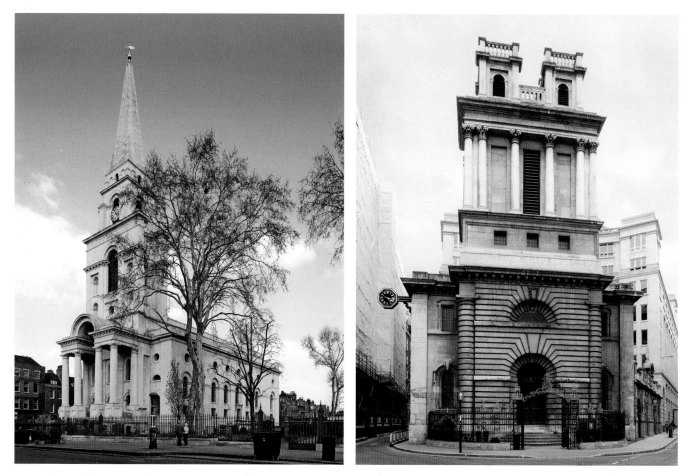

7.13 Christ Church Spitalfields, Nicholas Hawksmoor, 1714–29.

7.14 St Mary Woolnoth, Nicholas Hawksmoor, 1716–27.

Neither of these two churches is especially large, only 20 feet (6 metres) longer than St James's Piccadilly, but they are immense in scale. Christ Church Spitalfields (Walk 7) is wider and 20 feet (6 metres) longer. Here is the 'Solemn and Awfull Appearance' required by Vanbrugh. An excellent restoration, overseen by Red Mason and completed in 2004, has brought the church back as nearly as possible to its original form. The design was developed over a number of years, and it was not until 1723–4, when the body of the church was completed, that the original design of a flat front with box tower and lantern was abandoned in favour of the massive and unprecedented Venetian-window portico and spire (fig. 7.13). The window motif was repeated above as well as at the east end, where it is more to be expected. The tower is the same width as the portico, and deeply scooped out at the sides, revealing the volume. The spire was stripped of its ornament of crockets and dormers in 1822–3. The body of the church is unadorned, with windows with minimal mouldings which seem to have been punched out of the wall. When the galleries and box pews were removed by Ewan Christian in 1866, he unaccountably lowered the main windows and removed the lower ones, so the heavy keystones were anachronistically placed. The windows and the south doorway to the churchyard have been restored. This had been blocked by Christian following the removal of the central north door in 1743 when Fournier Street was extended west, upsetting Hawksmoor's cross-axial intentions. Christ Church is predominantly a longitudinal church, with a flat beamed ceiling and a five-bay Composite arcade rising from high bases the height of the original pews, leading to a straight architrave carrying the royal arms, which separates the body of the church from the chancel and

7.15 St George Bloomsbury, Nicholas Hawksmoor, 1716–31.

reconstructed reredos, a screened separation which follows early Christian practice. Hawksmoor did, however, emphasise the central area by delimiting it with clusters of columns and making the central bays of the arcade slightly wider. His fine rectory of 1726–9 survives next door on Fournier Street.

Away from the East End, Hawksmoor built two highly idiosyncratic churches on constrained sites, both beginning in 1716. The old church of St Mary Woolnoth was demolished in the same year, making way for Hawksmoor's smallest church (fig. 7.14) (Walk 1). Both its exterior context and its internal arrangement have been changed, but it is still a building of great impact. Until the cutting through of King William Street in the nineteenth century, the plain south wall with deeply recessed windows could be seen only in deep foreshortening, and later it was again obscured by the outworks of Bank Underground Station. The north wall with its remarkable concave aedicules is clearly different; as Wren stated and Hawksmoor agreed: 'In things to be seen at once much variety makes confusion ... In things that are not seen at once ... great variety is commendable.' At the west end, twin towers are fused into a single mass; the upper part is surprisingly shallow in relation to its width and the columns go all the way round.

Inside, St Mary is a square within a square defined by triplets of columns, although this appearance has been compromised by the removal of the galleries by William Butterfield in his reordering of 1875–6. The interior is monumental, large in scale and small in size, but the original sense of dark enclosure, lit by big semi-circular windows from above, has been lost with the removal of the galleries and pews. The Solomonic columns of Hawksmoor's *baldacchino* recall Bernini at St Peter's, but ultimately hark back to the archetypal Christian church, the Temple of Jerusalem.

Hawksmoor was working in a tradition, but he brought to it an extraordinarily powerful imagination, which caused his achievement to be derided during the great age of Taste. Looking at the tower of St George Bloomsbury in 1734, the Palladian critic James Ralph observed: 'the builder mistook whim for genius, and ornament for taste ... the execrable conceit of fitting up the king on top of it, excites nothing but laughter in the ignorant and contempt in the judge'. St George has suffered many trials but restoration, and the reinstatement of the original orientation, is now complete (fig. 7.15) (Walk 3). The area was new and fashionable, and a church was badly needed to serve a rapidly growing population. The site, however, was small and so hemmed in by other buildings that Vanbrugh considered it impossible to have an east–west orientation, but Hawksmoor nevertheless managed it, providing access up steps to each side of the tower. The central square, like St Mary Woolnoth, raised a clerestory in order to provide light on the restricted site. The orientation was always problematic, and for all the grandeur and expense the accommodation was tight. According to the vestry, as Meller relates, it seated 447, of whom only 313 could see and hear, so in 1731 they built a gallery on the west side and asked the commissioners to pay. They, in their turn, responded with different figures, and the affair degenerated into hair-splitting about the number of 'largest sized men', 'lesser men

7.16 Grosvenor Chapel, South Audley Street, Mayfair, Benjamin Timbrell, 1730–1.

7.17 St John Church Row, Hampstead, John Sanderson, 1745–7.

and women' or 'lesser and more bulky together' that could be accommodated, noting that the vestry had failed to mention the two galleries to north and south for which the commissioners had paid. The provision of more seats was considered again in 1762, 1776 and 1781, when Isaac Mansfield's richly ornamented eastern apse was screened off (to be rediscovered in 1838) and the altar moved to the north, where the gallery was removed. This change in orientation suppressed the axial conflict which lay at the heart of Hawksmoor's design.

Hawksmoor's portico for St George, whose design preceded those at St George Hanover Square and St Martin-in-the-Fields, possibly alludes to the Pantheon in view of the doubling of the pediments. The tower has an equally hallowed source, the fourth-century BC tomb of Mausolus at Halicarnassus, one of the seven wonders of the ancient world. This was mentioned by Vitruvius and drawn by Hawksmoor after Wren's reconstruction, following the account in the *Natural History* of Pliny the Elder in the first century AD: 'above the colonnade rises a pyramid as high again as its substructure, tapering in twenty-four stages to its apex. Here there stands a four-horse chariot in marble made by Pythius.' In the *Hypnerotomachia Poliphili* of 1499, the stupendously high, dreamed reconstruction was topped by an obelisk and the statue of a nymph with beautiful face, plump calves and two open wings who revolved at every breath of the wind. Hawksmoor, in contrast, rather soberly has the statue of George I on one of his recurring classical motifs, a Roman altar. The accompanying lion and unicorn adorning the north and south faces were removed in 1871 during the restoration by G. E. Street and put back in 2006. The statue of the king was paid for by parishioner William Hucks, the MP for Abingdon and brewer to the royal household, who recognised perhaps better than the Palladian critic James Ralph that it is not always easy to draw lines of separation between church, state and monarchy, still less between the 'strong reason and good fancy' which Hawksmoor considered, when joined with 'experience and tryalls', to be fundamental to the practice of architecture.

Late eighteenth- and nineteenth-century churches

English church architecture as developed by Wren and Hawksmoor tended to emphasise rationality and reliance on the word, whether written in the Bible or the Prayer Book or spoken from the pulpit. Given the recent history of the previous century, 'enthusiasm' was the last emotion they wanted to evoke in the congregations: the Grosvenor Chapel exemplifies this simplicity (fig. 7.16). Parish churches nonetheless held an important position in people's lives because of their administrative role: they continued until the 1830s to record births, deaths and marriages, and the vestrymen were responsible for public works such as roads through the rates and public order through poor relief. During the second half of the eighteenth century, as the former villages around the City were transforming into suburbs and their populations rapidly expanding, many of the old parish churches were replaced by larger churches more suited to the contemporary liturgy of the word. Most of these churches were built in brick, with classical details in stonework and often, if affordable, a tower and steeple. Within, there was little differentiation between the altar area and the rest of the church, and generally they were galleried. An example of this type of parish church can be found on the edge of the City in St Leonard's Shoreditch of 1736–40, designed by George Dance Senior. The brick church is faced by a stone façade with a Tuscan portico, and, above, a stone tower is surmounted by a cupola, an elongated version of that at St Mary-le-Bow (see p.27). Other examples include St John in Hampstead (1745–7) by John Sanderson (fig. 7.17) ((Walk 10), St Mary in Islington (1751–4) (Walk 8) by Launcelot Dowbiggin, and St John in Hackney (1791–4) by James Spiller. The distinctive tower of the latter was added in 1810–14.

The later years of the eighteenth century saw a renewal in the Anglican church through the initiative of the Evangelical movement. This movement was fostered by a group of commercial families living in Clapham, known as the Clapham Sect and including the Wilberforces and Macaulays, and inspired by the Evangelical clergyman, the Reverend John Venn. At this time it was necessary to obtain an Act of Parliament to build a new parish church, and the Clapham Sect managed to achieve this in 1774 for the building of Holy Trinity on the north side of Clapham Common. Their building was designed by Kenton Couse in the accepted plain brick, with stone quoining and turret, surmounted by a domed cupola. Originally the pulpit stood in the middle of the church, indicating the importance of the sermon for the Evangelicals.

The Evangelicals attracted the growing commercial and professional elites of society, and their strong belief in the benevolent influence of the church in social affairs led to the initiative of the 1818 Churches Act. Under this Act £1,000,000 was set aside to build churches in the newly populous parts of the country which were without church accommodation (fig. 7.18). By 1830, thirty-eight new churches had been built in London, mostly in the new suburban areas. Three of these were by Sir John Soane: St Peter's Southwark (1823–5), St John on Bethnal Green (1825–8), and Holy Trinity in Marylebone Road (1824–8). The latter was a short distance from Thomas Hardwick's recent St Marylebone parish church, but the pressure of the new residential districts of Marylebone and Regent's Park was such that another church was considered necessary. Holy Trinity was the most expensive of the commissioners' churches at £24,708, and is distinguished by a façade of Bath stone consisting of an Ionic portico with Greek key pattern over, and a tall tower and cupola above.

7.18 All Souls Langham Place, John Nash, 1822–4.

Not far down the road is St Pancras, which was not a commissioners' church but was built after obtaining an Act of Parliament in 1816 to replace the old parish church. It was designed by William Inwood and his son Henry, who had travelled to Greece in order to learn from the antique remains in Athens. As a result the portico, with its six fluted Ionic columns, was derived from the Erectheum on the Acropolis. In addition, two projecting wings were graced by four caryatids by J. F. C. Rossi, again inspired by the Erectheum, although one of the originals was available for study in London in the collection amassed by Lord Elgin which is now in the British Museum. Above the portico is a replica of the first century BC Athenian Tower of the Winds, placed like Gibbs's tower and spire at St Martin-in-the-Fields.

The Inwoods' St Pancras was a very expensive building at £90,000, but St Mary (1822–6), the church they designed for the Church Commissioners in nearby Eversholt Street, had the virtue of cheapness (fig. 7.19). It is a stock brick box with very elementary Gothic details in stone, and resembles a two-dimensional drawing. Similarly, the three commissioners' churches designed by Charles Barry in Islington are also stock brick Gothic, but their articulation and details demonstrate a greater sophistication. St John Holloway Road and St Paul Essex Road (both 1826–8) are similar, while Holy Trinity Cloudesley Square (1826–9) is more like the collegiate chapel of King's College in Cambridge (fig. 7.20).

It might seem strange that Gothic was chosen for the commissioners' churches, given its previous associations with irrationality and the old religion; however, new associations of national identity were beginning to accrue to an architecture which no longer seemed a threat. In Chelsea James Savage had used in his St Luke Sydney Street (1820–4) what was up to then the most elaborate version of the Gothic style. Although the church retained its galleries within, it has a stone vaulted roof, and on the exterior this is supported by flying buttresses. As St Luke is built in Bath stone, it looks more substantial than the stock brick churches of the Church Commissioners, but despite its striking west tower, there is something stiff and constrained about it.

The cause of Gothic architecture in church building was to gain impetus under the impact of A. W. N. Pugin's writings and works of the next couple of decades. In 1836, Pugin published *Contrasts: Or a Parallel between the Noble Edifices of the Fourteenth and Fifteenth Centuries and Similar Buildings of the Present Day ...*, in which he pointed out the differences between the picturesque architecture of the Middle Ages and the utilitarian buildings of his own day. Shortly after, in *The True Principles of Pointed or Christian Architecture* (1841), Pugin put forward the argument that Gothic was in fact more rational than classical architecture, because its flexibility ensured that it could embrace any functionality. By Gothic, however, he did not mean that of the commissioners' churches, and he used St Mary Eversholt Street as a bad example. Instead, he urged the study of the many medieval buildings which remained, often in obscurity and poor repair. This call appealed to the Cambridge Camden Society, a group set up in 1839 to study medieval antiquities, particularly the many buildings within easy reach of Cambridge University where the society was based. Later in 1845 the society changed its name to the Ecclesiological Society and developed two aims: to identify and study existing medieval buildings and to encourage the development of a contemporary Gothic style.

This interest in Gothic architecture coincided with the rise of the Oxford Movement, a group of clergy at Oxford University who wished to explore the Catholic tradition of Anglicanism, which they felt had been overtaken by the Protestant strand. The Tractarians, as they were called after the *Tracts for the Times* published from 1833, were considered to be on dangerous ground because their interest in

Catholic tradition could easily lead to conversion to Rome, as it did in the case of John Henry Newman. With time the external manifestation of the Tractarians' religious quest led to a greater interest in Catholic ritual, and this meshed very well with the Ecclesiologists' mission to reinstate ritual within a medieval church layout. They advocated the separation of clergy and congregation by raising the chancel above the nave and by installing a rood screen between the two. Instead of the light, clear preaching box advocated by Wren, the ritualists yearned for a church of contrasts of light and dark, colour and texture. The consequence of this desire was an architecture which incorporated a plethora of decorative arts including stained glass, metalwork, incised decoration, painted tiles and murals.

The Ecclesiologist was established in 1841 as the journal of the society, and this proved an influential means of disseminating the ritualist ideas which gradually began to appear in churches during the 1840s. One of the first in London was St Stephen Rochester Row (1847–50) by Benjamin Ferrey, a gift of Baroness Burdett-Coutts in memory of her father, and built in a poor district of London, as so many of the ritualist churches were. In contrast to the early sketchy versions of Gothic, this is a scholarly rendering of the Decorated style of the fourteenth century, and the building sits comfortably on its site. When economy was important, a neo-Romanesque style was adopted by architects such as Lewis Vulliamy in St Peter with St Thomas Bethnal Green (1840–1), although this was not strictly approved by the Ecclesiologists (fig. 7.21) (Walk 11).

The Ecclesiologists themselves sponsored All Saints Margaret Street (1849–59) (Walk 6), and the architect they chose for this, their model church, was William Butterfield, who worked in conjunction with one of their prominent members, Beresford Hope. The building is ingeniously designed on a very tight urban site, and positioned behind a tiny courtyard which separates it from the street (fig. 7.22). The main materials are red and black brick, with stone for details such as window tracery. On either side of the courtyard are a school on the left and a clergy house on the right, both of them extensively patterned in coloured brick. Looming over all is the tower and very tall, very thin spire clad in green slate. The entrance is tucked away in the north-west corner of the courtyard, and within is a riot of colour, pattern and texture (fig. 7.23). Because the building is hemmed in, there are windows at clerestory level at the west end and on the south aisle only; where they would appear in the north aisle, their place is taken by colourful murals. The aisles are separated from the nave by three wide arches, and the nave from the chancel by arch and decorated wall.

The inspiration for the intensely decorated interior of All Saints came from the highly coloured medieval churches of Italy, and it was John Ruskin who directed architects to look abroad beyond English Gothic for their inspiration. His *Seven Lamps of Architecture* was published in 1849, with *The Stones of Venice* appearing from 1851 to 1853; although it can be debated just how influential he was for architects, the aestheticisation of Gothic in his writings gave licence to break the bonds of national constraints. Certainly, G. E. Street did not confine himself to English Gothic, particularly in his London churches. St James the Less Vauxhall Bridge Road (1859–61), a complex funded by the daughters of Bishop Monk of Gloucester, is a big, generous building in red and black brick with a large campanile derived from Italian churches. The interior is wide with an apsidal chancel and a

7.22 All Saints Margaret Street, William Butterfield, 1849–59.

7.23 All Saints Margaret Street, interior.

7.24 St Mary Magdalene Paddington, G. E. Street, 1868–78.

7.25 St Saviour Aberdeen Park, Islington, William White, 1865–6.

7.26 St Saviour Aberdeen Park, interior, *The Builder*, vol. 25, 27 July 1867, p. 550.

three-bay nave divided by notched and moulded brick arches. This church was also intended to serve a poor part of the city, as was St Mary Magdalene Paddington (1868–78), another of Street's London churches (fig. 7.24). St Mary's was put up by the incumbent, Reverend Dr Richard Temple West, who had been a curate at All Saints Margaret Street and had ritualist sympathies. Street provided a distinctive, octagonal belfry in stripes of red brick and stone, capped by a stone spire, thus signalling the presence of the church over the neighbouring houses, now long gone. Here too the site was constrained and also on a slope, so Street inserted concrete vaults under the body of the church, where he was then able to locate the vestry.

Butterfield and Street both took the form of the ritualist church far beyond the confines of antiquarianism into the realms of Victorian eclecticism. Another architect whose churches explored form was J. L. Pearson, whose St Peter Vauxhall (1863–4) was also one of those built among the poor. The stock brick church is much plainer than planned, but the simple lines of both the exterior with its bold apse and the interior with its brick vaulted ceiling are impressive. Much more elaborate is Pearson's St Augustine Kilburn of 1870–7, though the very tall stone spire was completed only in 1898. The church is constructed of red brick and stone, and the interior is beautifully articulated, with a tall brick vaulted nave supported by internal buttresses. A passage gallery is carried over the arches of the inner aisles, and this emphasises the sense of three-dimensional space within.

Although we find much to interest us in the inventiveness of the best of the ritualist churches, their appearance was not without controversy. When residents of Islington tried to initiate the building of a ritualist church in 1856, they stirred up a controversy which led to acrimony on both sides. The Reverend Daniel Wilson owed his incumbency as vicar of Islington to his Evangelical family, and he had been instrumental in establishing the Islington Protestant Institute in 1846 to counteract what they saw as the growing influence of the Roman Catholics. In Wilson's eyes, the Tractarians and ritualists were even worse than the Catholics, because they were betraying the reformed church and they were doing it through 'music, painting, poetry, architecture, eloquent appeals to the feelings', as he points out in *Our Protestant Faith in Danger*. It was no wonder then that he should refuse permission for a ritualist church, and Islington was without this form of worship until 1865, when William White built a very inventive church in Aberdeen Park for the Reverend W. D. Morrice, the owner of the estate.

White's church is worthy of note because, although ritualist, it was built within a comfortable middle-class suburb as the estate church (fig. 7.25). The owner of the development was a rural clergyman living at this time in Wiltshire. However, the Reverend Morrice had had a long association with White and the Ecclesiologists, and was indeed connected to White by marriage. Although the church is relatively small, its height and inner articulation give the impression of a much larger space. Breaking up into the nave is a high lantern just before the chancel, which is separated from the nave by a low arch (fig. 7.26). Aisles crowd on either side, and the main source of light is from the west window and the clerestory, emphasising the height of the interior space. The predominating material is Aylesbury red and buff brick with stone for the tracery, but even now when the church has been transformed into artists' studios, there are around the chancel fine floral motifs delicately painted across the brickwork.

The great number of London's nineteenth-century suburban churches attests to the importance of the church to the social as much as the spiritual life of Victorian London. Many of these churches are competent but undistinguished, for example George Godwin's St Mary The Boltons (1849–50), which he designed as architect for the Gunter estate in Kensington. Nonetheless, these churches and their ancillary buildings have become integral to their neighbourhood, and provide the site for local amenities such as nursery schools. As with White's St Saviour, some of these churches are noteworthy, such as the remarkable St Martin in Vicars Road, Gospel Oak (1864–5) by E. B. Lamb. Unlike most of the churches looked at so far, this is inspired by broad church principles where great store was set by internal visibility, so that the plan is broad and unobstructed. Above, however, is an oversailing wooden roof with hammerbeams dominating the inner space. Not far away in Shirlock Road is All Hallows (1889–1901) by James Brooks, whose design fosters the sublime over the picturesque, with great buttresses in Ancaster stone expressed on the exterior. Within, the form adopted is the hall church – that is, the aisles and the nave are the same height – and the columns supporting the ribs of the vaulting are without capitals.

7.27 Immaculate Conception Farm Street, Mayfair, J. J. Scoles, 1844–9, *The Builder*, vol. 7, 2 June 1849, p. 258.

The religious controversies of earlier in the century and the architectural responses to them became less strident with time, and the result was that churches became the repositories of some very fine Arts and Crafts design as aesthetics were given precedent over dogma. One of the founding members of the Art Workers' Guild, J. D. Sedding, was responsible for Holy Redeemer Exmouth Market (1887–8), unusually based on an Italian Renaissance design (Walk 8), and Holy Trinity Sloane Street (1888–90), with the west front reminiscent of King's College Chapel in Cambridge. The latter church, though simple in plan, is the repository of carving, metalwork and stained glass executed by decorative craftsmen of the time. Similarly, St Cyprian in Clarence Gate (1902–3) by Bucknall and Comper has a very simple nave free of pews, but a richly elaborated altar area with gilded and painted furnishings designed by Comper.

A background to the religious controversies within the Anglican Church was the increasing freedoms being given to Roman Catholics and dissenting churches during the nineteenth century. The 1829 Act of Emancipation gave Catholics freedom to worship, and in 1850 they were allowed to re-establish their hierarchy. Although Catholic chapels had existed throughout the seventeenth and eighteenth centuries, Catholic churches could now be built openly. Since the Catholics did not have to make the point about ritual, they tended to be more eclectic in the styles they chose for their churches. J. J. Scoles's St John the Evangelist in Duncan Terrace, Islington (1841–3) presents a large red brick neo-Romanesque façade to the street with two square towers, one higher than the other (Walk 8). The interior of the church is large but barn-like, and was greatly disliked by Pugin, who would have preferred something more like a medieval English parish church. A few years later in 1844, Scoles designed Immaculate Conception in Farm Street for the Jesuits in a Decorated style reminiscent of Beauvais in France (fig. 7.27). This has since been added to, and is now much more elaborate with, for example, Flamboyant arcading of 1898–1903 by W. H. Romaine-Walker around the left-hand chapels.

Cardinal Newman himself preferred Italian baroque to English Gothic, and
this was the style adopted for the Oratory of St Philip Neri in Brompton Road for
the Oratorians, the order to which Newman belonged. Herbert Gribble's design won
the 1878 competition with a scheme based on the Gesù in Rome, employing a large
dome over the crossing and side chapels in place of aisles. Despite its Roman baroque
antecedents, new building methods were introduced in the form of concrete vaults
in the nave, inset with three glazed domes, and a steel frame in the main dome.

In 1885 there was another competition, this time to replace the Spanish embassy chapel of 1793 on a site just to the north of Manchester Square. Edward
Goldie won the competition for St James Spanish Place, this time with a design
incorporating French and English Gothic. The church is tall and striking in white
ashlar, vaulted throughout, and with interior decoration begun by J. F. Bentley in a
rich and convincing style. It was Bentley who became the architect of the foremost
Catholic church in London, Westminster Cathedral in Victoria (Walk 2). In 1894
Cardinal Vaughan asked Bentley for designs, specifying an early Christian basilica.
Bentley preferred Gothic, but managed to persuade the cardinal that Byzantine
would be more appropriate. The cathedral is striped in vibrant red brick and Portland stone, with a very tall campanile to the side (fig. 7.28). In contrast, the body

of the building sits broadly on the site with many repetitions of rounded arches of various types. The interior is truly impressive, more so because it remains unfinished, since through lack of funds the mosaics intended for the upper walls and the internal domes were never executed. The result is that the upper reaches are dark, bare brick and give intimations of infinity.

During the second half of the nineteenth century, Nonconformist congregations were increasingly able to build substantial churches of their own. Especially noteworthy are the Congregationalist churches, which returned once more to the principles of freedom for all the congregation to see and hear. In Islington, the Union Chapel of 1876 is an impressive example by James Cubitt. The clock tower dominates that part of Upper Street, and the large roof over the octagonal central space looms over the rest of Compton Terrace. The main hall within is a very expansive space, top-lit and with seating for 1,650. Two other Congregational churches of note are by Alfred Waterhouse. In 1883–4 he built the large church at the corner of Lyndhurst Road and Haverstock Hill, using purple brick and terracotta (Walk 10). The generous interior spaces have lent themselves to reuse as concert hall and recording studios. Waterhouse's other Congregational church, King's Weigh House Chapel just off Oxford Street, has also found a new use as the Ukrainian Catholic Cathedral (Walk 6). This church dates from 1889–91, and its red brick and terracotta complement the Grosvenor estate preference for these materials. Romanesque in inspiration rather than Gothic, its oval auditorium is expressed externally to the east, behind the two irregular towers of the west end facing Duke Street (fig. 7.29). Nonconformist churches in central London often make surprising appearances, for example the Welsh Baptist Chapel (1889) by Owen Lewis in Eastcastle Street to the

7.29 Former Congregational church (now Ukrainian Catholic Cathedral), King's Weigh Street, Mayfair, Alfred Waterhouse, 1889–91.

7.30 Welsh Baptist Chapel, Eastcastle Street, Marylebone, Owen Lewis, 1889.

north of Oxford Street (fig. 7.30). This domestic-scale building in a humdrum commercial area has a portico and monumental stairs up to the first-floor entrances.

The suburbs, however, are particularly the location for Nonconformist churches, and during the twentieth century until the Second World War, new churches were more likely to be Nonconformist than Anglican. No one style prevailed, and the results could be inventive, such as the former Presbyterian church at Muswell Hill by G. and R. P. Baines of 1903. It is difficult to ignore the contrasting grey flint and bright red Ruabon brick of this art nouveau façade. The one architect of Anglican churches of the inter-war period that stands out is N. F. Cachemaille-Day. His strategy was to abstract the elements of the traditional church and to put them together in an original way, with emphasis on bringing light into the sanctuary area. The result is at once archaic, reminiscent of fortified churches of southern France, and modernist. Notable examples are his St Saviour's Eltham (1932–3), credited with being one of the first London churches to be built in a modern style, and St Mary Becontree (1934–5), with other examples in the northwest suburbs.

In his churches, Cachmaille-Day was interested in bringing the congregation closer to the altar, a theme developed by the new Liturgical Movement which started in Germany before the Second World War. After the war, there was much activity in rebuilding or replacing churches that had been damaged in the bombing, especially in the East End. St Paul in St Paul's Way, Bow Common (1956–60) by Robert Maguire and Keith Murray was one of these, and in their new church the architects introduced an open, geometrical plan, top-lit over the central sanctuary area, which is otherwise distinguished from the seating only by a slight change in floor level. Not only was the plan shocking at the time, but the materials were unadorned and semi-industrial. Few new churches have been built recently, although a notable exception is St Paul in Wightman Road by Inskip and Jenkins (1988–93). This church replaces one of 1890 destroyed by fire. Here Peter Jenkins has dramatically abstracted the elements of the traditional Gothic church – the steeply pitched roof, the sharp gable end, the monumental west front – and assembled them in a composition which commands the road at the top of a rise.

The great Anglican church building in London of the nineteenth century has produced innumerable buildings which are no longer required for worship, or which are free to be taken over by other Christian sects and religions. There is a long history of churches passing through numerous hands, such as the former Huguenot church in Fournier Street off Brick Lane, which has been subsequently a Methodist chapel, a synagogue, and now the Great Mosque (see p. 207). Churches have held an important place in the cultural life of London, but they have also been the occasion for theorising and speculation by architects about the nature of their art. They have given expression to important moments in architecture, whether the churches of Hawksmoor in the eighteenth century or the neo-Gothic and Arts and Crafts churches of the nineteenth.

Chapter 8 OPEN SPACES
Parks, the Metropolitan Board of Works, and sports

Parks and pursuits

In its report on the opening of Finsbury Park in August 1869, *The Times* noted the inaugurating remarks of Sir John Thwaites of the Metropolitan Board of Works, in which he yoked together health and economic benefits:

> *There could be no doubt that these open parks were not only conducive to health but to the moral improvement of society. They were calculated to invigorate the frame and enable the workman to sustain that labour which was one of the greatest sources of our national wealth, and in these days of furious competition nothing ought to be overlooked which tended to invigorate and strengthen the mass of the London population.*

London's parks and other open spaces – notwithstanding vicissitudes in fortune, management and funding – continue, in the words of Ken Worpole, to be fundamental parts of 'the vital public connective tissue of the twentieth-century city'.

The creation of municipal parks was a nineteenth-century initiative designed to provide open space and recreational facilities for an enormously expanding population in urban centres throughout the country where there was, following enclosure, no longer access to common land. The increasing enclosure of fields and common land throughout the eighteenth century, a process fundamental to agricultural improvements, removed the commons from the public domain, pauperising the newly disinherited in a process excoriated by William Cobbett in his *Rural Rides* (1830). In the words of the anonymous verse: 'The law locks up the man or woman / Who steals the goose from off the common / But lets the greater felon loose / Who steals the common from the goose.'

The Enclosure Acts of 1836 and 1845 set limits on enclosure according to the distance of the land from urban centres and stipulated the amount of land to be set aside for recreation according to the size of the population. The process of official recognition of the need to preserve open space for recreation had begun in 1833 with the report to Parliament of the Select Committee on Public Walks which, Hazel Conway (1991) relates, 'provided the first survey of accessible open space in the major towns and cities of England and recommended action for the future'. A succession of major Acts of Parliament followed, promoting the development of urban parks, beginning with the 1847 Towns Improvement Act which enabled urban authorities to obtain land for recreation. In the following year, the Public Health Act empowered local boards of health to provide, maintain and improve land for municipal parks. Further legislation in the 1850s and 1860s included provision for recreation grounds and playgrounds; the levying of rates for maintaining public walks, parks and playgrounds; the protection of neglected town gardens; and in 1866, by the Metropolitan Commons Act, all commons within fifteen miles of the centre of London were protected and regulated. Kennington Common, a popular site for preachers and political meetings as well as a pasture for horses and cattle, had become a public park in 1852.

Before the creation in the nineteenth century of municipal parks throughout London, the royal parks were the best-known open spaces, although their location

8.1 Finsbury Circus, the only significant public open space in the City, laid out by William Mountague, 1815, with bowling green added in 1909; the NatWest tower is beyond.

8.2 Hyde Park, public since *c*.1630; Rotten Row, a place for fashionable parade, was laid out in 1690 as a 'route du roi' from Kensington Palace to St James's; photograph *c*.1905.

Rotton Row, Hyde Park.

in a West End which already had a number of squares and other gardens was not much use to East Enders or those from the City (fig. 8.1) or from south of the river. For Jerrold, 'the picturesqueness of the St James's and Regent's Parks, and of Kensington Gardens, is not to be matched by any capital with which I am familiar, or of which I have heard. In these open places there are sylvan recesses and sylvan views, that carry the mind and heart hundreds of miles from the noise and dirt of Cheapside.' Hyde Park, the largest, has been open to the public since the 1630s (fig. 8.2). St James's Park and Green Park followed, with layouts formalised by Charles II. St James's was particularly popular, centrally placed for the London stroller, especially during the eighteenth century when Boswell was a regular visitor, contributing to its reputation as a disreputable venue for Londoners of all classes. John Nash was involved in redesigning St James's in the 1820s; he came to the task from Regent's Park, on which he worked from 1811 until 1826 on land that had just reverted to the Crown. Laid out as a landscaped open space with private villas, Regent's Park is bounded by unified palace fronts which conceal regular terraced houses, best appreciated as scenography, in the verbally expressed view of Reyner Banham, at 20 miles per hour. The picturesque asymmetry of the park recalls the contrivedly natural landscaped grounds of contemporary country houses in which it was easy to get lost, the first time at least, a conceit lampooned by Thomas Love Peacock in *Headlong Hall* in 1816:

> 'Allow me', said Mr Gall. 'I distinguish the picturesque and the beautiful, and I add to them, in the laying out of grounds, a third and distinct character, which I call *unexpectedness*.'
>
> 'Pray sir', said Mr Milestone, 'by what name do you distinguish this character, when a person walks round the grounds for the second time?'

Regent's Park was intended to satisfy the profit motive as well as the aims of beauty, health and convenience, but the building of the villas was curtailed and profits were far below Nash's estimates. Designed as a public park and influential in later municipal park development, Regent's Park was opened progressively to the public from 1835 until the 1860s, by which time a new gymnasium at the northern corner, contemporary with Edward Gruning's remarkable surviving German Gymnasium of 1864–5 at King's Cross, was attracting crowds of youths and boys. In recent years the building of a series of predominantly classical, gated villas by Quinlan Terry, complementing Nash's original group of five, has revived the original public/private idea, emphasising the latter with the full panoply of modern surveillance and intrusive security.

The Zoological Gardens in the north-west corner of Regent's Park were laid out from 1827 to the designs of Decimus Burton, who had worked with Nash on the Regent's Park terraces; the first animals arrived in 1828. Admission was restricted to members of the Zoological Society of London and their guests until 1846 when the general public was admitted. Burton continued as architect until 1841, designing buildings which have been described as 'follies set in an elegant garden for entertainment and curiosity', in keeping with Nash's picturesque park. His Giraffe House of 1836–7, a handsome Tuscan barn fit to rival St Paul's Covent Garden, was largely rebuilt in 1960–3 (fig. 8.3). None of the other early animal houses survives, but much of the later work has the innovative quality of the best festival architecture, most notably Lubetkin's Gorilla House (1932–3) and the currently disused Penguin Pool (1934), Hugh Casson's Elephant and Rhino Pavilion (1962–5) (fig. 8.4), and the spectacular Northern (Snowdon) Aviary (1962–4) designed by Tony Armstrong-Jones with the architect Cedric Price and the engineer Frank Newby (fig. 8.5).

Greenwich Hospital pensioners and local residents were granted access to the royal Greenwich Park in 1705, when the first group of aged and infirm seamen arrived at Wren's new hospital. The park was also opened to the general population on public holidays, becoming a popular venue at Easter and Whitsuntide during the eighteenth century when the Greenwich Fair attracted large crowds of south Londoners (fig. 8.6). However, numbers were so increased – to c.250,000 after the introduction of river steamers and trains from London Bridge in 1836 – that local pressure was increased to close a 'three days' fever', recorded by Dickens, 'which cools the blood for six months afterwards'. The protesters achieved their aim in 1857 when this 'old market of vice and debauchery' was abolished.

Greenwich Park, hugely popular in the nineteenth century, was, as stated in an anonymous press report of 1846, used by all classes 'from the unwashed sweep to the clean confectioner; the mealy baker to the fan-tailed coalheaver'. It became a fully public amenity during the 1830s at about the same time as the Select Committee on Public Walks recommended an increase in the number of open spaces for

8.3 Giraffe House, London Zoo, Regent's Park, Decimus Burton, 1836–7.

8.4 Elephant and Rhino Pavilion, London Zoo, Regent's Park, Hugh Casson, 1962–5.

8.5 Northern Aviary, London Zoo, Regent's Park, on the north side of the Regent's Canal, Tony Armstrong-Jones, Cedric Price and Frank Newby, 1962–4.

poorer Londoners in order 'to wean them from low and debasing pleasures'. It was argued that workmen were driven to drinking houses, dog fights and boxing matches for want of 'rational recreation' which served to refresh the mind and spirit in manners other than alcoholic. Ideas of rational recreation may be interpreted as evidence of a middle-class desire to control activities of which they disapproved under the guise of knowing what was best for others. It was the rowdiness and horseplay of the crowds, discomforting the neighbours, which later led to the refusal of a licence and consequent closure of Highbury Barn in north London in 1871, as the middle-class suburb developed alongside. Entertainments here had included Blondin on the high wire, the gymnast Leotard, music hall, a large supper room, pyrotechnic displays and splendid illuminations. The Highbury entertainments had appealed in the early nineteenth century to the middle and tradesman classes, but the introduction in the 1850s of dancing every evening brought a rather more ebullient clientele and discouraged local support. The scandalous exhibition in June 1870 of 'French dancing', the high-kicking Can Can by the Colonna troupe, proved to be the last straw for the local authorities.

The rational municipal parks were the successors of commercial pleasure gardens, recreational venues of which Highbury Barn was a late survivor. The most famous London pleasure gardens had been established as the Old and New Spring Gardens at Vauxhall at the Restoration, taking their name from earlier pleasure grounds near Charing Cross. They were situated just to the east of modern Vauxhall Bridge, on the opposite side of the river from the present Tate Britain Gallery. Pepys was a frequent visitor to this initially free attraction, travelling by water, taking pleasure in walking in the gardens, 'observing the several humours of the citizens', and on one occasion 'pretty merry' in company, seeing 'a fellow that imitated all manner of birds and dogs and hogs with his voice, which was mighty pleasant'. Here also he ate a lobster, and later in the same month of July 1668 he ate, walked and deplored the rude and pushy behaviour of some young gallants. The gardens really took off as a public attraction between 1728 and 1767 under the management and later the ownership of Jonathan Tyers, who transformed them from a 'rural Brothel' into one of London's most fashionable nightspots, although complete decorum remained elusive. He introduced artifice and more commercial possibilities, with supper boxes around a quadrangular grove, ruins, a cascade, a music room, an orchestra and Chinese pavilions. One shilling was charged for admission, raised to two shillings in 1792. The pavilions and fifty supper boxes – following the promptings of William Hogarth, who was keen to bring English art to a wider public – were decorated with paintings after designs by Francis Hayman and Hogarth himself, who allowed his popular set of four paintings, *The Times of the Day*, engraved in 1738, to be reproduced. Other members of his circle produced designs for tickets and vignettes for song sheets. Hayman's rococo decorations of 1741–2 drew for their subject matter on children's games, popular pastimes, rural traditions and scenes from plays and novels, offering commentary, according to John Brewer, on 'the transitory character of human life and admonitions to incautious youth'. Hayman later provided four Shakespearean pictures for the Prince of Wales Pavilion at Vauxhall in *c.*1745 (named in acknowledgement of the site's landlord) and four large contemporary history paintings in 1761–4, celebrating victory at the extremes of the British Empire in Canada and India. These were displayed in the saloon, the annexe to the rotunda, the music room which Tyers had built in the late 1740s in order to counter the attractions of Ranelagh Gardens, which had opened in 1742 on the north bank of the river, east of Chelsea Hospital (Walk 9).

8.6 *Greenwich Park with the Royal Observatory on Easter Monday*, published 1804 after a drawing by Pugh.

8.7 *An Inside View of the Rotunda in Ranelagh Gardens*, engraved by Nathaniel Parr, 1751, after Canaletto (Guildhall Library, City of London).

Since music was one of the main attractions of pleasure gardens, Tyers did much to turn Vauxhall into a significant venue with a varied repertoire. He commissioned the most notable work of art in the gardens, Louis-François Roubiliac's informally posed life-size statue of Handel (Victoria and Albert Museum). The first public statue of a British artist, it was unveiled in 1738, presiding 'where his Harmony has so often charm'd even the greated Crouds into the profoundest Calm and most decent Behaviour'. In 1749, in a stroke of entrepreneurial brilliance, Tyers pre-empted the inaugural performance of Handel's Music for the Royal Fireworks in Green Park, in commemoration of the Peace of Aix-la-Chapelle, by staging a highly successful public rehearsal at Vauxhall before a jostling crowd of 12,000 people.

Both Vauxhall and Ranelagh were depicted in 1751–4 by Canaletto in search of modern buildings and pursuits, including two precisely delineated views of the interior of the Ranelagh rotunda (fig. 8.7), a rococo colosseum of frivolity, with the fashionably dressed patrons on parade. Ranelagh claimed to be more exclusive than Vauxhall and certainly was more expensive: 2/6d. (12½ pence) for admission. Boswell in 1763 felt 'a glow of delight at entering again that elegant place. This is an entertainment quite peculiar to London. The noble Rotunda all surrounded with boxes to sit in and such a profusion of well-dressed people walking round is very fine.' Casanova, visiting during the same summer season, also admired William Jones's spectacular galleried rotunda in which he ate bread and butter, drank tea and danced a minuet or two. He found Vauxhall more to his taste, however, not only because it was less than half the price for admission: 'the pleasures to be had there were great. Good food, music, strolls in dark walks where the bacchantes were to be found, and strolls in lantern-hung walks where one saw the most famous beauties in London, from the highest rank to the lowest, side by side.'

The Ranelagh rotunda was demolished in 1805 and the grounds incorporated in those of the Royal Hospital. Vauxhall continued in business rather fitfully until 1859; the grounds were then built on. These were the most famous of the many pleasure gardens in the suburbs of London providing entertainment and spectacle throughout their most flourishing period in the eighteenth century. Those which continued into the nineteenth century, before being swept away by changes in taste, increases in the value of land and the disapprobation of the neighbours, had increasingly to rely (as Highbury Barn did) on such spectacular and staged amusements as tightrope walkers, performing dogs, fire-eaters, balloon ascents and, in the case of Vauxhall, Greek chariot races and a re-enactment of the Battle of Waterloo. Cremorne Gardens in Fulham opened as a stadium in 1832 with an alternative approach, offering tuition in such 'skilful and manly exercises' as swimming, rowing, shooting, fencing and boxing. This pedagogical strategy was unsuccessful, and Cremorne reopened as pleasure gardens in 1843 with a banqueting hall, a theatre, an American bowling saloon, an orchestra, grottoes and bowers. Further entertainments included fireworks, balloon ascents and various sideshows, but the age of the pleasure garden had passed. Cremorne, condemned as the 'nursery of every kind of vice', was closed in 1877. Lots Road Power Station was built on the site in 1902–4 to provide electricity for the Underground.

Although with the demise of pleasure gardens the time was ripe for rational recreation, by the time of the Festival of Britain in 1951, another turn of the wheel found the frivolity of Vauxhall at its best inspiring the Festival Gardens in Battersea Park. Laid out in 1854–6 to the design of James Pennethorne, the park had been turned over to wartime allotments and a cricket pitch. Funded substantially by the sponsorship which was not allowed on the South Bank site of the festival, the Battersea Festival Gardens offered hedonistic pleasures, fireworks and illuminations, a shopping parade with luxury goods which acted as an antidote to pervading postwar austerity, restaurants, bars and three pubs: all tastes, all ages and all pockets were accommodated. The gardens included an amusement park with American fun fair and paddle boat, two theatres, a dance pavilion and a children's zoo. Chandeliers in the Chinese taste and 'Chinese Gothic' arcades provided the inevitable nod towards the exotic in this pursuit of what the organisers intended to be a classless world of 'elegant fun' in a setting historically associated with carnivalesque pleasure. Like Vauxhall, Battersea Fields (before the creation of the park) had been a popular place of resort with a wide range of diversions, exhibitions and drinking opportunities, easily accessible by river steamer. The weight of historical precedent was too great to resist for long, and the inescapable and inevitable raffishness of the Festival Gardens, where 'sleaze ... was rampant', was recognised and gleefully exploited by John Harris (later the esteemed curator of the RIBA Drawings Collection) when he was employed in 1953 in manning the entrance to Schweppes's Grotto of the Four Elements, creaming off the takings to this 'enchanted underworld of technicolour caverns and fragrant scents'.

The need for parks in east and south London had been acknowledged by the Select Committee on Public Walks. Kennington and Battersea Parks were both created in the 1850s as part of a national initiative to bring green oases to serve the expanding population, countering the negative effects of excessive development and providing improving, healthy recreational facilities for working families. Momentum had been slow to build after the Select Committee's report in 1833, as Conway notes, with reliance initially on 'the liberality of individuals'. It was a royal grant which provided funds for the purchase of land for a park in the East End, following a petition to the queen in which the living conditions and high mortality rates of the 400,000 people in the area were unfavourably contrasted with those in the West End who had the benefit (among other things) of the royal parks. Victoria Park, on the fringes of Hackney and Bethnal Green, opened as a royal park in 1845; it was designed by Pennethorne, who had worked with Nash on Regent's Park. The combination of healthy open space with speculative housing development, which had been attempted at Regent's Park, was the model for Victoria Park, but the failure to secure funding for the intended roads west to the City and south to the river at Limehouse inhibited investment. Development of the park was slow but by the early

8.8 Finsbury Park boating lake, c.1910.

8.9 Finsbury Park, the gardens, c.1910.

1860s, thanks to the efforts of John Gibson, a skilled gardener appointed park super-intendent in 1849, the planting had been increased, with more trees as well as floral displays in ribbon borders and geometric beds, and the landscape diversified: there were two lakes for bathing and two gymnasia. Gibson was responsible also for the improvements to the landscaping and planting at Pennethorne's Battersea.

Pennethorne's greatest public park remained on paper. This was the 500-acre Albert Park proposed in 1851 for a site extending north from Highbury, with an esplanade on the banks of the New River. Albert Park was a development of a pro-posal in the previous year for a 300-acre 'Islington Park' to serve an area which was notoriously short of open space. This deficiency was noted by an anonymous writer in 1850: 'if the parks be the lungs of London then has the northern district of the metropolis no respiratory organs'. In the eighteenth century there had been dozens of pleasure gardens in Clerkenwell and immediately north at the southern end of Islington, including Sadler's Wells (Walk 8), a spring promoted as 'full of strength and virtue and able to cure consumption and melancholy'. Development following the construction of new roads to the north swallowed up these open spaces.

Albert Park would have been larger than Regent's Park and similarly would have provided land for building on the perimeter. It would have occupied an impor-tant strategic position in the ring of parks around the central built-up area, but a change of government scuppered the proposal and speculative building, rolling like a carpet across north London, filled the void. Highbury Fields, acquired as public space in 1885, is the remnant of these grandiose plans for Highbury, which although relatively modest remains the largest public open space in the borough of Islington.

Finsbury Park, to the north of Highbury, was a small consolation for the loss of Pennethorne's grand design. The enabling act for the park was secured in 1857 by the recently established Metropolitan Board of Works. The original scheme included part of the site of the proposed Albert Park, south of the Seven Sisters Road. How-ever, this was reduced to the 115 acres north of the road in the modern borough of Haringey, occupying the site of part of Hornsey Wood, a well-known duelling ground – some way from the borough of Finsbury whose constituency it purported to serve. Financial difficulties delayed the construction of Finsbury Park – the prom-ised government grant was not forthcoming – and it eventually opened in 1869 at the same time as Southwark Park, both designed by Alexander McKenzie, the land-scape gardener attached to the Board of Works. Planting in parks takes many years to develop and Finsbury Park was rather prematurely criticised (figs 8.8 and 8.9). As early as 1876, its landscape-garden style, affording pretty views, was acknowl-edged by James Thorne, but it 'would be pleasant if there were a little shade, and

walking were not confined to the gravel paths'. Later well known for its annual chrysanthemum shows in a purpose-built glasshouse, this was a park intended for activities, constructed following the agenda of improvement. The London County Council in 1906 recorded the recently erected buildings and developing facilities: 'every possible provision in the way of games and recreation is made for the rapidly increasing population'. As well as the flower beds, rockeries and glasshouse, there was a boating lake, refreshment house, bandstand, an aviary, gymnasia, a bowling green, tennis courts, and provision for cricket, football, croquet, hockey and lacrosse: the full range of typical park buildings and pursuits. As the number of permitted activities in parks increased through the nineteenth century (in Victoria Park cricket grounds dated from 1849, but football was not allowed until 1888), so did the emphasis of the authorities shift from suppression to control, with the introduction of standardised rules which for Conway 'reinforced class identity and gender distinctions'. Some parks developed specialisms: cycling at Battersea was a fashionable pursuit and open-air bathing, for men only, was popular in the lakes at Victoria Park from the late 1840s, although it was not until 1898 that the eastern lake had all the necessary accessories.

Outdoor bathing had been possible in London at the Serpentine in Hyde Park and from 1743 at the Peerless Pool, Finsbury, developed by the jeweller William Kemp. Situated just north of St Luke's Old Street, this was on the site mentioned by John Stow in 1603 as 'Perillous pond, because divers youths, by swimming therein, have been drowned'. It was advertised in the early nineteenth century as a 'Grand Pleasure Bath, where Gentlemen may without Danger learn to swim'. This they did until the pool closed in 1850. There were also two fishponds, a library and a bowling green. In 1833 an outdoor swimming bath, with mass concrete sides and bottom, designed by Joseph Kay, was opened at Greenwich Hospital Schools for the instruction of trainee seamen, in order to counter the traditional inability of sailors to swim. This was covered in 1874–5 by a sky-lit timber and wrought-iron construction.

By the later nineteenth century there were swimming lakes not only at Victoria Park but also at Brockwell Park, Plumstead Common, Clapham Common and Hampstead Heath. Of these, only the Hampstead Heath men's, ladies' and mixed ponds remain, in vigorously defended continuing use (fig. 8.10). They form part of a chain of twenty-three ponds originally dug as reservoirs in the seventeenth and eighteenth centuries and cleaned up by the LCC in 1893 and 1906. The swimming opportunities were put onto a more formal basis at Victoria and Brockwell Parks with the creation of lidos in 1936 and 1937 respectively during a halcyon period when Herbert Morrison, chairman of the LCC, determined to make London 'a city of lidos'. By 1951 there were over sixty open-air pools in Greater London. The areas around them often provided space for sunbathing and spectating – creating, as Worpole notes, 'new spaces of public informality in the city' and helping to 'break down the barriers between men and women in public, especially in minimal attire and part-nudity'. The belief in the benefits of fresh air and sunlight was an abiding theme of early twentieth-century modernism, and the provision of lidos in the 1920s and 1930s owed much to the consequent liberation of the body, inspired in part by the international success of Hans Suren's *Man and Sunlight*, published in Germany in 1924 and in English in 1927. Billy Butlin's holiday camps with their organised games, mass fitness exercises and ubiquitous swimming pools, developed first at bracing Skegness in 1936, were part of the same health-seeking movement described by Worpole: 'the holiday camps democratized the body in an institutional setting, as the beach had democratized it decades earlier in a state of nature'.

A change of fashion followed the Wolfenden Report on Sport in the Community in 1960, which recommended indoor swimming baths and proposed the construction of indoor leisure centres catering for a variety of activities. This new impetus, coupled with the increasing availability of package holidays to warmer water, began the decline in outdoor provision. The fate of many lidos was sealed when responsibility for their maintenance was passed to local authorities, for whom they were an expensive luxury, upon the replacement of the LCC by the GLC in 1965. The open-air pool at Highbury Fields, built in 1923, was closed in the 1980s and is now an indoor pool. The Victoria Park lido closed in 1989 and is now a carpark. Brockwell Park lido – 'Brixton Beach' – continues with a loyal and socially mixed clientele, supported financially through the use of additional buildings which provide for community activities in the close season. According to Janet Smith's comprehensive national listing, Brockwell is one of only eight open-air pools surviving in London, in addition to the long-established Serpentine and Hampstead Heath ponds.

Even though lidos have dramatically declined in number and the provision of facilities in local authority parks has been subject to erosion through municipal cost cutting, healthy open spaces are still at a premium in the city and we might hope for a revival in fortune. Just as the use of lidos declined with the onset of package tourism, so they might be revived as politics and economics render air travel less attractive and encourage staying at home.

The Metropolitan Board of Works

Victoria, Kennington and Battersea Parks were all managed on behalf of the Crown until 1887, when their status changed as control was passed to the Metropolitan Board of Works (MBW), established in 1855, with funding provided through the rates (fig. 8.11). The management of these newly municipal, formerly royal parks, as well as those which had been established under the auspices of the Board of Works, then passed to the London County Council (LCC), established in 1889. The LCC Parks Department, created in 1892, managed them until the LCC was replaced by the Greater London Council (GLC) in 1965. With the demise of the GLC at the hands of a vindictive national government in 1986, the management of London's municipal parks was fragmented as responsibility was passed to the relevant local authorities, subject to the vagaries of funding and shifting priorities.

The prime purpose behind the establishment of the MBW was the provision of a unified body charged with countering threats to public health. Asiatic cholera had reached England in 1831. Five thousand died but nothing was done apart from holding a day of prayer and fasting. The Thames was polluted. Salmon could be caught until 1800, but by the 1830s the wider provision of piped water by private water companies led to the growing use of toilets which flushed water into the sewers rather than into cesspits, and so into the Thames. But the water companies also piped their water from the Thames between Chelsea and London Bridge. The bacteriological explanation for disease was unknown at this time.

Edwin Chadwick, who in 1834 secured the Poor Law Amendment Act establishing the workhouse system, next considered disease and appointed physicians to investigate. Thomas Southwood Smith found that urban improvements had hitherto been confined to the rich, with nothing done to improve the conditions of the poor. This now obvious perception informed Chadwick's *Sanitary Condition of the Labouring Population of Great Britain*, published in 1842, in which he proposed the creation of a national public health authority to direct local boards of health; the latter would be responsible for providing clean water, drainage, cleansing and paving on the rates, with comprehensive new sewage and drainage systems, the collection of liquid sewage for recycling on sewage farms as fertiliser, and the abolition of cesspits. He proposed a single Crown-appointed Commission for London, a suggestion which was denounced as tyrannically centralising. In 1847 a Royal Commission was set up to look into the problem – a delaying tactic – but the threat of further cholera prompted the recommendation that there should be a single Metropolitan Commission of Sewers (established 1848) for the whole of London, except the City, which had its own commission.

8.12 Crossness Pumping Station, beam engines by James Watt, 1865 (© The Crossness Engines Trust 2007).

The British Public Health Act of 1848 created the General Board of Health to oversee town councils across the country, which were permitted to raise revenue through the rates, becoming responsible for drainage and water supplies and for appointing medical officers of health. This did not apply immediately to London, where medical officers of health did not become compulsory until 1855. The City had gone its own way and appointed John Simon as medical officer in 1848, and he did much to improve the situation in his area of authority by improving water supplies, introducing better street cleaning and suppressing cesspools. In the cholera outbreaks of 1849 and 1854, the City was largely unscathed. In the light of this example, the need for change, despite the opposition of the anti-centralisers, became unarguable.

The Metropolitan Board of Works was founded for the 'better management of the metropolis in respect of the sewerage and drainage, and the paving, cleansing, lighting and improvements thereof'. A new metropolitan administration was set up, but many of the ancient vestries, the long-established bodies of local government, were retained, with the power to elect the members of the new Metropolitan Board. Although this was a cumbersome and undemocratic system, it continued for thirty years and brought some much needed co-ordination to municipal administration.

The urgent task in the prevention of disease was to stop sewage going into the Thames, but it was not until the 'Great Stink' of 1858, which forced the panicking

8.13 Crossness Pumping Station, upper level of engine house (© The Crossness Engines Trust 2007).

8.14 Crossness Pumping Station (© The Crossness Engines Trust 2007).

House of Commons to adjourn, that a spur was given to the endeavour. Ten thousand cholera cases in Whitechapel was one thing, but a potential disaster so close to the parliamentary home was quite another. Further powers were rapidly granted to the MBW. The chief engineer Sir Joseph Bazalgette set about creating the system which, completed in 1875, is still in use. By this time consensus had emerged that cholera was carried in water: Dr John Snow showed that all the cholera victims in Broadwick Street, Soho, had drawn water from the same pump – hence the pub named in his honour, one of the greatest accolades available to the popular hero.

Thomas Cubitt had already suggested ways to direct the sewage in his *Suggestions for Improving the State of the River Thames and the Drainage of London*, published in 1843. He recommended conducting it to reservoirs in the east, with gates and sluices allowing it out into the river on the ebb tide, thus preventing it coming back into London. This is what Bazalgette did: eighty-three miles of main sewers were built, intercepting the old sewers at right angles. Rainwater and sewage were taken in underground pipes to the river's edge, then into large sewers running west to east under a newly built Thames Embankment. North of the Thames the sewage was discharged via Abbey Mills, Stratford, to the Northern Outfall Works at Barking Creek. The polychromatic Italian Gothic-cum-Byzantine Abbey Mills, which opened in 1868, designed by Charles Driver, has been dubbed 'the cathedral of sewage'. South of the river, intercepting sewers led to the Southern Outfall Works at Crossness on the Erith marshes, opened in 1865. There is now a modern sewage treatment plant, which came into service in 1963, at Crossness, but the magnificent beam engines by James Watt and Son survive, one of them now lovingly and beautifully restored by expert volunteer enthusiasts (figs 8.12 and 8.13). There are no better examples than these monumental pumping stations and engines of the pride, celebration and functionality which Bazalgette and his associates brought to the public service in this concerted metropolitan endeavour (fig. 8.14). An overall total of 1,300 miles of new sewers was eventually built, together with the Victoria and Chelsea Embankments. Much of this was possible because there was no infringement of property rights. As the system spread into the suburbs in the late nineteenth and early twentieth centuries, the new sewers not only serviced existing settlements but frequently determined the layout of new streets. There was less success in dealing with the private water companies, who were forced to introduce filtration systems but were not municipalised until 1902.

The MBW was responsible also for road improvements, laying out Southwark Street (the first, in the 1860s, to have all its services constructed below the surface at the same time), Commercial Road, Clerkenwell Road, Shaftesbury Avenue, Charing Cross Road and Piccadilly Circus.

With housing, the MBW was less successful because it had the power to demolish but not to build. It was required to dispose of compulsorily purchased land to those who were prepared to build for the poor, and there was rather generous compensation provided for slum landlords. It was not until the establishment of the London County Council in 1889 and the Housing of the Working Classes Act of 1890 that much was achieved: by 1914 the LCC had housed 25,000 people.

Sport

The decline in participation in sporting activities in the later nineteenth century was bemoaned by Jerrold. The archery grounds had fallen to speculative builders; 'quarter-staff and single-stick, foot-ball and bowling-alleys are lost English games, which have gone the way of bull and bear baiting, prize and cock fighting'. But the Boat Race and Derby Day provided opportunity for the spirited enjoyment of non-participatory spectator sports, and in the twentieth century it was the development of sport as mass entertainment – stationary and often sedentary rational recreation – rather than as an activity requiring individual participation that had the greatest impact on the environment and upon the economics of leisure.

Sport as a spectacle, involving large crowds legitimately gathered together, rather than as a participatory pursuit was given a great boost in the early decades of the twentieth century through the development of the cantilever roof. This encouraged the building of large stadiums with uninterrupted views of the entertainments provided for a mass audience, which could travel considerable distances to see them on the developing public transport system. There was a downside: Dorothy Nicholson in 1944 noted the deplorable propensity for betting on dog racing and on football (through the football pools companies established in the 1920s and 1930s), but was consoled by the thought that this was 'steadily superseding the Londoner's old propensity for drink'.

GREYHOUND RACING   H. S. Williamson's evocative poster invited punters to the newly opened Harringay Park greyhound racing track in 1927: 'Book to Finsbury Park – thence by tram or bus' (fig. 8.15). 'Thence', commonly used in London's transport advertisements at that time, underpinned the air of anticipation and sophistication which the floodlit image embodied, the stands in shadow and the dogs strung out along the brilliant yellow track. Dog racing, a spectacle imported in the 1920s from the United States, where the first track had been laid out in Emeryville, California in 1919, once had over twenty tracks in the London area, of which Harringay was the second after White City. Greyhound racing, in which the dogs chase an electrically propelled mechanical hare, was an outgrowth from the traditional sport of coursing, in which dogs

8.15 Harringay Park, by Harold Sandys Williamson, 1927 (London Transport Museum © Transport for London).

8.16 Walthamstow Stadium, entrance range to Chingford Road, 1932, with neon lights installed to illuminate the lettering and greyhound, 1951.

had hunted by sight rather than by scent. Class-conscious promoters, fighting its working-class image, sought to promote its social cachet, desperately noting the support of many titled people, including ex-Queen Sophie of Greece, the widow of King Constantine. By 1932 there were 220 dog tracks in Britain with an attendance of 50 million per year by the late 1940s. This is a pursuit which has scarcely survived the century. By the late 1990s, national attendances had fallen to four million. Among the best-known tracks, White City Stadium was replaced by the BBC Headquarters in 1989–90, Wembley closed in 1998 and Catford in 2003. Walthamstow, notwithstanding its status as the British Greyhound Racing Board 'Racecourse of the Millennium', has been at risk of sale and redevelopment since housing is potentially more remunerative than dog racing, but listing in 2007 has preserved a building of considerable panache (fig. 8.16). Built in 1932 and dramatically lit at night, the stadium has a long concrete frontage and stepped central parapet, below which a black greyhound in relief advertises the delights within. Stands with cantilevered roofs and original tote boards with art deco profiles contribute to a rare survival.

Harringay was built on spoil left from the excavations for the Piccadilly Line, completed as far as Finsbury Park in 1906. In 1930 the track had the distinction of housing the first automatic-odds equipment to be installed in England. Magnificent to behold, this complex, labour-intensive, electro-mechanical marvel of levers, pulleys, belts, ticket-issuing machines and display boards was a development by George Julius of his original 'automatic totalisator', invented in 1913 and first put into service in New Zealand. Betting on the 'tote', the pari-mutuel, in which the odds are calculated in strict relation to all the bets made by others and so are not finalised until just before the race begins, was generally offered on the enclosed 'up-market' side of the track, where scampi and chips were also available. More serious gambling, with winnings paid out at the odds laid at the time of betting, required consultation with the open-air tick-tack men. All this, including the still functioning totalisator, was swept away after closure in 1987 to make way for Sainsbury's and its carpark.

FOOTBALL The 'New Home of Woolwich Arsenal Football Club', advertised as 'London's most accessible ground' and located immediately opposite Gillespie Road Underground Station (see p.77), was said to be reachable from any part of London in a few minutes. The station opened in 1906, and the original name is still prominently picked out in the recently restored tiling along the walls of the platforms. The fine arcaded front was replaced when the station was renamed after the club in 1932, providing it with free advertising throughout London.

Just as at Harringay, the new terraces at Arsenal's Highbury Stadium were constructed from the earth excavated for the Piccadilly Line. The club, named after the Royal Arsenal workshops at Woolwich, had been founded in 1886, turning professional in 1891 and joining the Football League two years later. Based in Plumstead in south-east London, it failed to establish itself as a leading force before the First World War and went into voluntary liquidation in 1910. Chelsea, Tottenham Hotspur and Fulham all had better grounds, bigger crowds and access to better transport.

A good deal of sentimental nonsense concerning 'the beautiful game' bemoans the loss of football's working-class roots. But to progress from park to stadium has always required considerable financial clout and political skill as well as vociferous and dedicated supporters. Arsenal was bought by the property developer Henry Norris, chairman of Fulham, who moved the club to Highbury in 1913 where he had secured a lease from the Church of England to take over the playing field of St

John's College of Divinity. Resisting the objections of both Tottenham and Clapton (now Leyton) Orient to unsporting competition in north London, a new ground was built to the designs of A. G. Kearney, working for Archibald Leitch, a specialist who had already designed grounds at Stamford Bridge (Chelsea), White Hart Lane (Tottenham) and Craven Cottage (Fulham). The first match was played on the unfinished ground in 1913, but following the outbreak of war, competitive football stopped two years later with Arsenal lying fifth in the Second Division. After the war, the Football League expanded the First Division by two clubs. Logic suggested that Chelsea and Tottenham, who had finished bottom in 1915, should stay up with extra places going to the top two in Division Two, but Norris, now Sir Henry and an MP, a ruthless man of enormous influence, exercised his negotiating skills and secured Arsenal's promotion at the expense of Tottenham. The club has been in the top division ever since. Norris cemented his success by buying the entire Highbury site and bringing the most successful manager of the era, Herbert Chapman, from Huddersfield in 1925, laying the foundation for a string of honours – five League Championships and two FA Cups during the 1930s – and an epoch-making ground.

Highbury Stadium, designed by Claude Waterlow Ferrier in partnership with William Binnie, was a corporate headquarters as much as a football ground, symbolising metropolitan affluence and capable of being built lavishly precisely because of the availability of cheap labour and materials during a period of high national unemployment. Building the stadium provided stable employment for labourers who were accustomed to short-term engagements. The West Stand, by Ferrier, opened in 1932, and Binnie's imposing art deco East Stand, five storeys high and looming over the late Victorian terraces of Avenell Road, followed in 1936 at a cost of £130,000 (fig. 8.17). These were then the most lavish pieces of football architecture ever built, and in their proximity to housing were typical of football grounds throughout the country, which drew their support and some of their players from the close surrounding community. Here were the famous marble halls, the panelled boardroom and Epstein's bust of Chapman, completed in 1936, two years after the manager's unexpected death. Only the rebuilding of the North Bank in 1992–3 by the Lobb Partnership, with a cantilevered upper tier and art deco styling,

8.17 Highbury Stadium, the East Stand, Avenell Road, William Binnie, 1936.

8.18 Emirates Stadium from Hornsey Road, HOK Sport, 2006.

approached the quality of the innovative work of the 1930s, as well as rivalling Darbourne and Darke's dramatic steel-framed, cantilevered East Stand at Chelsea's Stamford Bridge of 1972–4. The latter was once perceived, according to the pre-eminent commentator on football grounds, Simon Inglis, after coming in late and over-budget, as a 'ruinous icon'; now in the era of Roman Abramovich it is approaching the status of historic monument.

The economics of modern football has prompted Arsenal's move to a new stadium nearby in order to accommodate crowds of up to 60,000, no longer possible at Highbury since the introduction of all-seater stadiums after the Taylor Report into the Hillsborough disaster of 1989. The site chosen, at Ashburton Grove, formerly occupied by industrial units and the municipal rubbish dump, now houses the new Emirates Stadium, named for the eponymous airline which sponsors the club. This enormous structure, with two emblematic cannon at the entrance, opened at the beginning of the 2006–7 season (fig. 8.18). It was designed by HOK Sport, who skilfully shoehorned the building onto a tight plot between railway lines, and constructed by Sir Robert McAlpine at a cost of £390 million. Within, the undulating roofline – created to direct airflow onto the pitch – and the raking seating providing spectacular uninterrupted views restore the dramatic expectations which have been lowered upon arrival by the banality of the circulation spaces and claustrophobic staircases, whose architectural lineage might be more readily found in the multi-storey carpark than in any theatre of dreams. In *Sightlines*, his tour of stadiums around the world, Inglis posed the question: 'what better way … to raise the general public's awareness and appreciation of quality design than to offer them the very best buildings in the one area of life that seems to touch them the most?' But the football supporter, like the architectural critic, is doomed to eventual disappointment, with dreams always partially unfulfilled. It is perhaps at the most ambitious and successful clubs where expectations are highest that disappointments are felt most keenly. Watching top-flight football in the hysterical, over-analysed and overhyped age of the Premiership is too tense to provide relaxed rational recreation for season-ticket holders risking impoverishment through their commitment. Arsenal's supporters have brought to the Emirates Stadium the notorious solemnity which gave their previous ground the sobriquet 'Highbury – The Library'.

The Emirates development received the enthusiastic endorsement of the local authority, anxious to retain the club within the borough. When Arsenal first came to Highbury, both Islington Council and local residents objected because of the undesirable elements of professional football and fears for property prices. Football now enjoys unprecedented cultural status, although some of the local residents remain to be convinced of its community benefits. Highbury Stadium is under redevelopment for flats and houses with token retention of the façades of the East and West Stands.

HOK Sport are specialist stadium architects who have been responsible also, together with Foster and Partners and engineers Mott MacDonald, for the new Wembley Stadium which opened in 2007. Built to accommodate crowds of 90,000 at a cost of over £750 million, this new national centre replaces the reinforced concrete oval stadium built for the British Empire Exhibition of 1924. The old stadium was demolished in 2002 after some sentimental thought had been given to retaining the emblematic but undistinguished twin towers, now replaced as focal point by the great arch which has the functional purpose of supporting the roof. A far better building than the old stadium, the adjacent British Empire Pool (Wembley Arena), with reinforced concrete arches innovatively spanning seventy metres, was designed by Sir Owen Williams as an addition to the exhibition site in 1934. Recently renovated and embellished by the addition of interactive coloured fountains in front, this is now a concert venue.

CRICKET The financial power and ambition, verging on hubris, of contemporary football has no direct equivalent in the allegedly staid and gentlemanly world of cricket, which, as Mark Girouard (1981) has shown, in the past provided one of the necessary keys to Society and to the select preserves of male-dominated fellowship. In recent years, this most traditional of pursuits remarkably has sponsored some of the most prominent modern architecture in London in refashioning the so-called 'home of cricket', Lord's. The initial impulse inevitably was driven by the changing economics of the game. The need for corporate sponsorship and hospitality boxes resulted in the design by Michael Hopkins and Partners, completed in 1987, of the new Mound Stand. This tented structure with a polyester roof, reworking the idea of the village green marquee, is anchored to the ground by six steel masts. They allow it to hover above the massive brick arcading of the original stand of 1899 by Frank Verity which Hopkins extended along the St John's Wood Road, so providing a contextually sensitive solution to the demands of tradition and the site: this is hallowed ground.

Thomas Lord leased the land for his first cricket ground in St Marylebone, forming the Marylebone Cricket Club (MCC) in 1787, but was forced to move in 1811 for the development of Dorset Square. Taking his turf with him, he established the club on the north side of Regent's Park but had to move again in 1814, with his turf, to the present site with the coming of the Regent's Canal (Walk 8). The canal was cut in 1812–20 to link the Grand Junction Canal at Paddington with the Thames at Limehouse (fig. 8.19). The oldest surviving building, Thomas Verity's sober brick and terracotta Pavilion of 1889–90, the third on the site (refurbished in 2004), was followed first by the old Mound Stand, then in 1925–6 by Sir Herbert Baker's Grandstand. Kenneth Peacock added the cantilevered Warner Stand in 1958 and the Tavern Stand ten years later. After his new Mound Stand, Hopkins returned with the raked, concrete Compton and Edrich Stands, completed in 1991, named in commemoration of the two great Middlesex post-war batsmen for whom this was the

8.19 The Regent's Canal.

8.20 Grandstand, Lord's Cricket Ground, Nicholas Grimshaw and Partners, 1998.

8.21 The Media Centre, Lord's Cricket Ground, Future Systems, 1999.

home ground. Nicholas Grimshaw and Partners then supplied the riposte to Hopkins's Mound Stand in a new Grandstand (fig. 8.20), replacing Baker's and structurally comparable with Hopkins's, in which two 50-metre-span roof trusses are supported by three columns in a design both elegant and timely in its moment: it was opened in 1998, the year in which the gentlemen of the quasi-feudal MCC, embracing modernity, fully accepted the arrival of the twentieth century and voted to admit women members.

The latest addition to Lord's, the Media Centre for commentators and journalists (completed in 1999), is a semi-monocoque aluminium structure, supported high above the ground on two concrete access towers (fig. 8.21). The vast glazed wall overlooking the field, appearing to frame the scene like a camera viewfinder, is set at an angle to prevent reflections dazzling the players. This adds a vertiginous quality to the view from within the pod to add to the difficulties reported by commentators of seeing the TV monitors as they look straight into the late afternoon sun. Such problems notwithstanding, this is a stunning design by Future Systems, with a nod towards Dan Dare, engineered by Ove Arup, although possibly, as Samantha Hardingham notes, 'in the realm of the futuristic rather than in the future'.

At the Kennington Oval, where cricket has been played since 1846 on land leased from the Prince of Wales, Surrey County Cricket Club has greatly improved the provision for spectators in its reconstruction of the Vauxhall Stand at the opposite end of the ground from T. Muirhead's Pavilion of 1895–7. Completed in 2005, this steel-framed stand with a curved steel roof in the form of a crescent rises from a concrete substructure; it adds a note of architectural drama to a ground where hitherto it has been signally lacking. Designed by HOK Architects and the Miller Partnership, with engineering by SKM Anthony Hunts, the stand incorporates a media centre and the now inevitable hospitality boxes with their banal advertising signage. It has long been an understandable complaint of architects that they lose control of the appearance of their creation after the handover of the building: the demands of commerce and security are currently the worst offenders in the erosion of the impact of good design.

CONCLUSION

In his concluding remarks to his magisterial account of the small house in eighteenth-century London, Peter Guillery refers to the perpetual coexistence of the vernacular and polite in a London 'where improvers have rarely been all that rigorous or systematic'. Herein lies London's strength and its enduring appeal. It has incorporated the best efforts of great architects, and assimilated the often far-reaching attempts of planners, politicians and engineers to impose a necessary, often desirable order. But it has remained haphazard, far from the dream of the Augustan city. There can be no resounding conclusion to a continuing narrative of this coexistence of the formal and the informal, the planned and the accidental, and the accommodations, compromises and manoeuvring required to create and maintain a liveable city. Historical approaches to the subject, as here, may be analytical or synoptic, focusing on significant details which might fleetingly illuminate a bigger picture, like coin-operated lights in a baroque chapel, or essaying a broad sweep of circumstances, intentions and results. In a city as rich, vast and various as London, with an accompanying commentary too large to compass in one lifetime (22 million hits on Google for 'London books'), all approaches will be selective. In making their selections, as Guillery has noted, historians risk investigating only that which is known and taking cognizance only of that which they have sought. Since this book is intended as an introduction to London buildings and to ways of looking at them for the benefit of students and visitors, we have courted this risk and followed established themes. But in broadening the scope of available examples from the grand to the everyday, we hope that we will have prompted the reader to look further into the impulses and forms which have shaped our shared environment. As Wren noted, 'the Project of Building is as natural to mankind as to Birds, and was practis'd before the Floud'. This quotidian ubiquity demands our engagement and our continuing investigation, in the archive and library, on foot or, following Hollar, from some convenient bird's-eye vantage point.

WALK 1 THE CITY

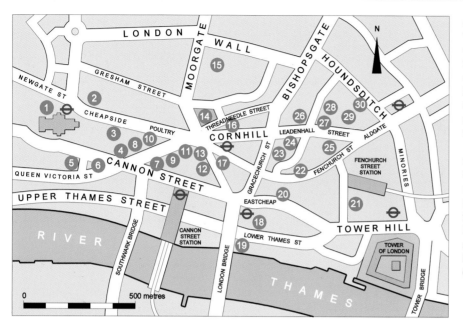

An area of extraordinary richness and density, the 'one square mile' is the oldest part of the capital, with continuous development since the founding of the Roman town in the first century AD. The architectural heritage reflects the vibrancy of a mercantile centre whose public, commercial and religious buildings have been subject to processes of considerable change while retaining examples of remarkable survival.

The medieval St Paul's Cathedral and 87 of the 107 City churches were destroyed in the Great Fire of London in 1666; 51 were rebuilt under the direction of Sir Christopher Wren, paid for out of the Coal Tax (c.1670–90). One-third of the tax was allocated to each of the following: churches, St Paul's Cathedral and City streets. Seventeen of these churches had gone by the Second World War; there are 24 left plus 6 solitary towers.

1 St Paul's Cathedral and environs

Sir Christopher Wren's masterpiece (1675–1711), with his accompanying three-storey Chapter House of 1712–14 to the north. The imposing grandeur and iconic status of the building – and the problem-solving genius of its architect, who lived long enough to conceive and execute a building which has become an enduring national symbol – have daunted all who have tried to build in its shadow. The injunction on the memorial tablet over Wren's grave in the crypt – 'Si monumentum requiris, circumspice' (if you are expecting his monument, look around you) – has inhibited more than it has encouraged. Originally St Paul's was pressed around by housing and the shops of the book and print trade, above which rose much of the upper screen walls, cornice line, towers, drum and dome. This was a building whose rich detailing could be appreciated close-to, but the whole could be seen only from a distance.

The surrounding buildings, devastated during the Blitz of the Second World War, were replaced by the more open, traffic-free Paternoster precinct of 1962–7, following the masterplan by Lord Holford. This was largely demolished (one small block survives above St Paul's Underground Station) and replaced after protracted discussion, the inhibiting intervention of Prince Charles, and the forging of an unholy alliance between market forces, architectural political correctness and sentiment: this is a no-win site. The new Paternoster development

(see p.110) master-planned by Sir William Whitfield, who also designed the deferentially stone-clad Juxon House at the south-west corner, was completed in 2004 by the arrival of the resurrected Temple Bar (fig. W1.1). This was brought back from exile at the edge of Theobalds Park in Hertfordshire, where it had been rebuilt following its removal in 1878 from its original site at the west end of Fleet Street where it marked the boundary between the City and Westminster. Built in 1670–2, possibly to Wren's design, this once vigorously modelled gateway had been designed with a political purpose for a potentially contested site; in its new and anachronistic location it looks like stage scenery: emasculated and far too bright. From within the square, artful contrivance permits fragmentary views of St Paul's (see p.28). The uncharacteristically bland sculpture by Elizabeth Frink, *Paternoster – Shepherd and Sheep* (1975), serves to confirm the difficulty of measuring up to Wren's great building.

Inside the cathedral, once past the ticket barrier and the queues, and notwithstanding the later mosaics and stained glass, it is still possible to appreciate the exhilarating drama of light and space framed by cut stone that was contrived by Wren and his craftsmen. There is nowhere better than the crossing of St Paul's to appreciate the power of great architecture to move and exalt, beneath the dome which manifests the supreme fusion of aesthetic intention and technical realisation

W1.1 Temple Bar, resited at the corner of Paternoster Square. The original west side, shown here, has John Bushnell's statues of Charles I and Charles II; the former east side has his statues of Elizabeth I and James I.

W1.2 St Mary Aldermary, from Queen Victoria Street, and York House of c.1873.

W1.3 St Mary Aldermary.

that was Wren's great contribution to English architecture. There are, in fact, two domes, acknowledging that the height required for the view from distance would have been much too high for the view from within. The inner dome of brick, supported by the stone drum, and the outer dome of lead-covered timber are separated by a brick cone which carries the weight of the stone lantern. Glimpses of this virtuoso performance provide the first reward for those who climb to the lantern; the views from the top of the dome provide the second.

2 St Vedast Foster Lane

The medieval church, restored in 1669–72, was rebuilt to the design of Wren in 1695–1701, incorporating medieval walls within an irregular plan shape. The tower was rebuilt by Wren on new foundations to the south-west, with a baroque spire of 1709–12 (see p.12). Burnt out 1940; restored by Dykes Bower 1953–63. Dramatically undercut carving in the reredos from St Christopher le Stocks (demolished 1782) and the pulpit from All Hallows Bread Street (demolished 1878). East window glass by Brian Thomas (1961) depicts scenes from the life of St Vedast, a sixth-century Bishop of Arras in Flanders.

3 St Mary-le-Bow

On Cheapside, the main City shopping street, with the tower and steeple standing apart from the body of the church on a Roman roadway which provided appropriate foundations and also allowed for distant views (see p.27). The doors, framed by Tuscan columns, are set in rusticated niches. The church was built to the design of Wren (1670–80) over an eleventh-century crypt, an important survival which now accommodates a small café. The church was burned out in 1941, but the crypt, tower and steeple survived; it was rebuilt by Lawrence King (1954–64), reproducing Wren's design.

4 St Mary Aldermary

Built in 1679–82, this church is reached by crossing medieval Watling Street, which offers an excellent view of St Paul's Cathedral. St Mary was Wren's only Gothic rebuilding, incorporating earlier masonry. Much of the cost came from a benefactor, thus allowing the parishioners more say than usual in the style of the rebuilding. The tower was rebuilt by William Dickinson in 1701–4 in a classicist's interpretation of the Gothic (fig. W1.2). Stone refacing in 1876–7 followed the laying out of Queen Victoria Street. Inside, the spectacular plaster fan vaulting, classical font and sword-rest (1682), and west door-case imported from St Antholin (demolished 1876) are notable (fig. W1.3). The bench pews and floor tiles are of c.1876, the reredos 1914 and the stained glass 1950s. The late seventeenth-century pulpit is set on a base of 1876.

5 Bracken House

Sir Albert Richardson's steel-framed, sandstone and brick *Financial Times* headquarters of 1955–9, for which the architect claimed Guarini's late seventeenth-century Palazzo Carignano, Turin, as a source. When the printing press moved to Docklands in the 1980s, this became the first post-war building to be listed (1987) in order to save it from demolition; this was partially successful. Hopkins and Partners (for the Obayashi Corporation) retained Richardson's flanking office wings, but replaced his central printing hall in 1988–91 with new offices radiating from a central atrium. The result is an object lesson in the reconciliation of old and new.

6 Credit Lyonnais
7 Albert Buildings
8 No 60 Queen Victoria Street

Here for **Credit Lyonnais** the rounded corner on the wedge-shaped site was reinterpreted in 1973–7 by Whinney, Son and Austen Hall, with engineering by Ove Arup and Partners (fig. W1.4). No longer occupied by the original clients, this five-storey building with an innovative, prefabricated, glass-fibre reinforced cement façade remains startlingly and spikily elegant – of its date but not dated.

Queen Victoria Street was cut through in 1867–71 at a cost of £1,076,000 as a continuation of the Metropolitan Board of Works' Victoria Embankment of 1864–70; Blackfriars Bridge was rebuilt at the same time to the design of Joseph Cubitt. At the lower, south-west end, the new street incorporated an earlier uncompleted route of the 1850s. The oblique alignment of the street resulted in elongated triangular sites; some of the 1870s buildings

W1.4 Credit Lyonnais.

survive (see p.15), but the majority were replaced after the Second World War. F. J. Ward's **Albert Buildings** at Nos 39–53 is a grandly arcaded Gothic survivor (with some original shopfronts), criticised at the time for its pretentious medievalism; Nos 68–72 and 74–82 (York House) (fig. W1.2) are good triangular blocks of *c.*1873 in the established classical commercial style. **No 60 Queen Victoria Street** is a striking bronze-clad office block designed by Peter Foggo Associates (1995).

9 Bucklersbury House

Designed by O.Campbell Jones and Sons (1953–8) and one of the bulkiest office buildings of the 1950s, this was the first City design to abandon the street line in favour of a new planning formula which envisaged an architecture of slabs and towers arranged with picturesque asymmetry around gardens and courts. The result here is a building of fourteen storeys with three six-storey wings incorporating naturally lit offices to each side of central corridors. Set at right angles to Bucklersbury, Temple Court, completed in 1962 to the design of O. Campbell Jones and Ronald Fielding, is a tall slab for Legal and General Assurance (now occupied by the SMBC Bank).

Excavations for Bucklersbury revealed the second-century AD Roman Temple of Mithras, now resited to the west with a different orientation and set on a terrace at an anachronistically high level above-ground. The central Mithraic belief concerns the god's slaying of a bull in a cave – the triumph of light and life over darkness, which is experienced by going down into a subterranean cavern. Classical sculpture from the site is displayed in the Museum of London.

10 No.1 Poultry

This wedge-shaped plot with fronts onto Poultry and Queen Victoria Street was the site of a major planning battle – the highpoint of opposition to wholesale redevelopment. A group of High Victorian buildings, including the turreted Mappin and Webb, were demolished to make way for a development instigated by Lord Palumbo, who wished to create a new square – Mansion House Square – with an eighteen-storey tower by Mies van der Rohe (designed 1962–8 but delayed by lease acquisitions). This scheme was rejected in 1985, and the strongly articulated, stridently postmodern, colourful, wedge-shaped building, with playfully arch detailing, by James Stirling, Michael Wilford and Associates, was erected 1986–98 (see p.15). There are good views of the City from the rooftop garden.

11 City Magistrate's Court, No 1 Queen Victoria Street

A good palazzo-style building by John Whichcord, built 1873–5 as the National Safe Deposit and including four storeys of armoured safe deposit vaults underneath, partly converted to cells for the new courtrooms (1988–91) (see p.15).

12 St Stephen Walbrook

A superb building, designed by Wren (1672–80), the first domed church in Britain (see p.135). The plan effects a balance between the liturgical longitudinal axis and classical centralisation: read from the west the side colonnades appear to be regular, but beneath the dome the bays are wider. The centrality is now overemphasised by the Henry Moore altar (1972, with kneelers by Patrick Heron and beechwood seating by Andrew Varah). The marble of the altarpiece is indented as if moulded by hand, in response to the play of light from above which Moore observed during lengthy preparatory sittings. The steeple was added to the tower in 1713–15. War damage was made good in 1948–52, including the repair of the coffering of the dome (plaster on wood, clad in copper). The church was further restored in 1978–87 by Brandt Potter and Partners. The pulpit and tester, reredos and font are all of the 1670s and the organ case of 1765; the pews were removed 1886–7.

13 Mansion House

Designed by George Dance Senior (1739) as a residence for the Lord Mayor, with accommodation for the mayor and his household, civic entertainments and a Justice Room where the mayor presided as Chief Magistrate of the City (see p.15). Later additions include an extra attic storey, while alterations to the front have reduced the grandeur of the entrance – twin double flights of steps flanking a small forecourt were removed in 1867 with the building of Queen Victoria Street. Robert Taylor's celebratory pediment carving shows the personified City of London wearing a crown and supporting the City's coat of arms, trampling on Envy and receiving the benefits of Plenty brought to London on the River Thames.

Opposite the Mansion House, forming one side of the vista from the Royal Exchange towards Queen Victoria Street, are two confidently classical banks: the Midland Bank headquarters, now HSBC, by Sir Edwin Lutyens (1924–39), steel framed with Italianate detail; and at the corner Sir Edwin Cooper's colonnaded National Provincial of 1929–32, now the National Westminster. Implicit in both is the idea that your investment is safe, a seductive note to strike during a decade of financial uncertainty.

14 Bank of England

Founded in 1694, the first purpose-built building on Threadneedle Street, completed in 1734 to the design of George Sampson, was first extended by Sir Robert Taylor and then rebuilt by Sir John Soane behind massive screen walls in his masterpiece of 1788–1827. Soane's work was swept away in Sir Herbert Baker's bombastic rebuilding of 1921–39, in which he raised seven storeys of offices behind Soane's perimeter walls, fronting them with a vast hexa-style portico with coupled columns, raised like the upper tier of a wedding cake (fig. W1.5). At the north-west corner of this large site, Soane's elegantly arranged Tivoli Corner columns survived Baker's onslaught (see p. 98). There is public access on the east side from Bartholomew Lane to the Bank of England Museum (free admission), where Higgins Gardner in 1986–8 reconstructed Soane's top-lit Bank Stock Office of 1792–3.

15 Institute of Chartered Accountants, Moorgate Place and Great Swan Alley
John Belcher and Beresford Pite's building of 1890–3 announces the arrival of the free neo-baroque in the City (see p. 106). Within a classi-cally ordered façade there is every sort of licence: blocked Doric columns at ground floor are echoed by smooth Doric at second-floor level, while the cornice is Corinthian without the frieze. There is a richly sculpted band between the upper columns under the second-floor windows, while at the corner of the building, above an elaborate domed oriel, is a niche containing the figure of Justice by Sir Hamo Thornycroft. J. J. Joass extended the building six more bays along Swan Alley in 1930, and further exten-sions were made by William Whitfield (1964–70).

16 Royal Exchange
Sited at the physical and functional heart of the City with the Bank of England across the street and the Mansion House opposite (figs W1.5 and p. 98). This is the greatest of the City's nine-teenth-century exchanges, built to the designs

W1.5 The Bank of England and the Royal Exchange.

of Sir William Tite (1841–4). This is the third ex-change on the site, following previous merchant-trading halls of 1566–70 and 1667–71 (see p. 27). Originally open, the arcaded central courtyard was roofed in 1883. General trading stopped in 1939, replaced by specialist exchanges else-where. It was converted by Fitzroy Robinson in the 1990s into an upmarket shopping centre with some interiors preserved together with an important group of paintings of 1895–1922 around the walls of the ground-floor courtyard. These are largely obscured by the shops. The intrusive security tends to inhibit investigation. The sculpture (1842–4) in the pediment on the west front is by Richard Westmacott Junior: Commerce holding the Exchange Charter is flanked by discrete groups of figures glorifying Trade. In front, Aston Webb's Great War me-morial was unveiled in 1920, and Sir Francis Chantrey's equestrian statue of the Duke of Wellington was erected in 1844.

17 St Mary Woolnoth
One of the 1711 'Fifty New Churches' for Queen Anne. Unlike the Wren churches, many of these were on new sites, so a grandeur of size and scale was possible. St Mary Woolnoth differs in being an outstandingly inventive rebuilding of an originally medieval church, partly rebuilt 1670–5, with a remarkably powerfully modelled exte-rior which brings a largeness of scale to the constrained site (see p. 140). Designed by Hawksmoor and built 1716–27, the plan is a square within a square, defined by columns which raise a clerestory with lunettes. The origi-nal galleries were removed by William Butterfield in 1875–6; the gallery fronts have been applied

to the walls. Butterfield also raised the chancel – thereby raising the original *baldacchino*, whose cornice line is consequently higher than the cor-nice of the building – removed the high pews and lowered the pulpit.

18 Monument
Erected 1671–6 to the design of Wren and Robert Hooke 'as a perpetual memorial to pos-terity', commemorating the Great Fire of 1666 and celebrating the largesse of King Charles II in remitting taxes in order to allow the City to be restored to a greater beauty. The fluted stone Doric column, with drum and flaming urn on top, is 202 feet (61.5 metres) high, with 311 spi-ral steps to an observation platform which ini-tially was railed but was caged in 1842 following a number of suicides (see p. 26). This is a stiff climb, rewarded on return by the presentation of a certificate. Samuel Beckett was here in 1932 in unhappy, temporary exile from Paris: 'and curse the day caged panting on the platform / under the flaring urn' (*Serena I*, published in *Echo's Bones*, 1935). The allegorical sculpture on the pedestal is by C. G. Cibber (1674).

19 Adelaide House
A handsome office and warehouse block of 1921–5 by Sir John Burnet and Tait, prominently sited at the southern edge of the City on the approach to London Bridge (see p. 109).

20 Nos 33–5 Eastcheap
The showiest in a pretty showy line of com-mercial façades (see p. 104). Built by R. L. Roumieu (1868) as a vinegar warehouse for Hill and Evans of Worcester, the main material is red brick with blue stripes and diapering, but the overall impression is derived from the white stone detailing. At ground floor are five bays of pointed arches, while the next two storeys, both sides of the central bay, are encased in an arrangement of transoms, trefoil arches and spindly attached columns. At roof level are two gables with finials, filled with decorative brick-work, while filigree ironwork and coloured tiles make their contribution. When it was built this neo-Gothic exuberance was already ten years out of date.

21 Nos 59–61 Mark Lane
An early block of speculative offices built in 1864 to the design of George Aitchison for the Innes Brothers, who had just set up the City of London Real Property Company (see p. 103). To ensure maximum flexibility the structure com-prises wrought-iron beams on cast-iron columns with fireproof brick-arched floors, as in contemporary warehouse construction. The façade is a load-bearing screen wall of refined design thought to be inspired by Ruskin's *Stones of Venice*. Over the segmental headed

W1.6 Bolton House, Cullum Street.

W1.7 19–21 Billiter Street, detail of the façade.

openings at ground floor is a band of sgraffito, while above, the round-headed windows in the upper floors are enclosed with abstract plant motifs. The general effect is of a reticent Venetian Gothic.

22 Bolton House, Nos 14–16 Cullum Street
A modest but refreshing example of Edwardian free style by A. I. Selby (1907), according to Murphy. The materials are blood-red glazed brick and blue and white faience, notably the foliage frieze (fig. W1.6). An insouciant eclecticism allows trefoil arches over the first-floor windows and straightheaded sash windows at second-floor level, decorated by blue faience surrounds. The two symmetrical entrances are likewise distinguished by blue and white faience tile decoration. This façade was incorporated by Gollins, Melvin, Ward in the erection of the adjacent building in Fenchurch Street, when the steep roof was added above the cornice.

23 Leadenhall Market
Designed by the market specialist Sir Horace Jones (1880–1). Open-ended, timber-trussed, glass-roofed alleys on a cross plan; two storeys with offices above shops reached by spiral staircases; octagonal domed crossing (see p.92). Originally a wholesale food market (Nos 1–5 have nineteenth-century shutters and racks for hanging game). Restored 1990–1, the cast-iron details are now emphasised in rich colours. There has been a market here since the fourteenth century, when this was the place where non-Londoners could sell poultry. The market stands partly over the site of the east end of the great second-century AD Roman assembly hall.

24 Lloyd's of London
In the late seventeenth century shipowners and merchants transacted business at Edward Lloyd's Coffee House, out of which grew the insurance organisation. The present consistently innovative and extremely striking building by Richard Rogers Partnership (architects) and Ove Arup and Partners (engineers) (1978–86) was surprisingly groundbreaking for a long-established City institution (figs W1.9 and p.112). The concrete frame structure with precise and smooth stainless steel cladding houses a central, glazed atrium trading floor with offices around. Services and lifts are on the outside to free the internal space, which thanks to security concerns is no longer easily accessible to the general public. There is a nod to tradition in the otherwise daring design by the retention as a screen of Sir Edwin Cooper's Leadenhall Street frontispiece to the premises built here in 1925–8.

Lloyd's Register of Shipping, which shares common roots with the insurers, was completed by the Richard Rogers Partnership in 2000. This is an accomplished dense development soaring above a small entrance forecourt on a cramped site off nearby Fenchurch Street, with the same trademark external glazed lifts as its predecessor.

25 Nos 19–21 Billiter Street
Inspired by the Renaissance palaces of Italy, this slightly concave façade by Edward Ellis (1865) is anchored at both ends by bays of alternate courses of white and red stone rustication. Over the arches in these bays are segmental pediments carved with ships, cornucopia and busy putti, indicative of marine commerce (fig. W1.7).

The windows at ground floor have segmental heads; then each succeeding floor alternates between round and segmental arches over double windows in each bay. The central entrance dates from the 1930s.

26 Commercial Union Building
Across the street from Lloyd's, completed to the designs of Gollins, Melvin, Ward and Partners (1963–9), is an elegant Miesian tower twenty-eight storeys high, with a forecourt and recessed ground floor (fig. W1.10). This gives us some idea of what was missed in the defeat of the contemporary Mies van der Rohe proposal for Mansion House Square. The building was reclad by RHWL following bomb damage in 1992.

27 St Andrew Undershaft
In the contemporary context of Lloyd's and Swiss Re, this medieval nave and aisles church illustrates the extraordinary juxtapositions of age and type which still characterise the City (fig. W1.10). The prominent tower is from the fifteenth century, with the pinnacles and turret added in 1883. The interior, which dates from 1520–32, includes notable decorative features: grisaille paintings of the life of Christ by Robert Brown (1724–6) in the spandrels of the arcade, and an east window of 1875–6 by Heaton, Butler and Bayne depicting the Crucifixion and the Ascension.

28 Swiss Re Tower, 30 St Mary Axe
Replaced the Baltic Exchange, demolished after the severe IRA bomb damage suffered in 1992. Designed by Foster and Partners for Swiss Reinsurance and completed in 2003, this is a paradoxical building: from a distance, its forty storeys and curving ('gherkin') shape have imposed the building on the London skyline, rivalling in visual impact Richard Seifert's nearby Tower 42 (the former NatWest Tower, completed in 1981), but closer to the building, the apparently bellying curve first confounds the viewer's sense of scale and then, closer still, obscures the upper storeys – we lose all sense of the tower's great height and the drama of its spiralling form, both of which are better appreciated from afar (fig. W1.10 and pp.18, 114). As a pure form the building should ideally flow into the ground without interruption, but this is not Los Angeles where a basement carpark would be the main entrance: pedestrian London requires a relationship with the street, and this is provided here by triangular cut-outs in the outer skin which act as a caesura in the otherwise smooth lines, providing a walkway and access to the recessed entrance on the inner face.

Across Leadenhall, on the east side of Lime Street, facing Lloyd's, is yet another Foster and Partners contribution to the skyline: the twenty-nine-storey concave tower of the Willis Building

(2006–7), with steps and roof terraces at the six-teenth and twenty-third floors. This complex, which includes a ten-storey block behind, facing Billiter Street, provides a good illustration of how speculative development works: British Land, the owners of the site, in collaboration with Stanhope, the developer, were granted planning permission for an office development before identifying the occupier – the Willis Insurance Group.

29 Holland House, Bury Street

Now National Employer's House, behind Swiss Re, an outstanding steel-framed building, clad in grey-green faience, designed by Hendrik Berlage, was completed in 1916 for the Kroller-Muller shipping firm (see p.107). In an oblique view the projecting mullions allow the building to be read as a solid, windowless wall of tiling. Round the corner, the prominent ship's prow was carved by J. Mendes da Costa.

30 Spanish and Portuguese Synagogue, Bevis Marks

This is the oldest surviving English synagogue, built for Sephardic worship in 1699–1701. The design, which may be by carpenter Joseph Avis, is a simple brick box with internal galleries, so it has much in common with the churches and chapels of the day, with especially fine wood-work and superb brass chandeliers. It is set back behind a small courtyard since Jews were for-bidden from building on a high street.

On the continuation to the south of Bevis Marks, on Duke's Place, is the neo-baroque façade of the Sir John Cass School of 1908, designed by A. W. Cooksey (fig. W1.8). It incorporates the figures of charity children in niches, perhaps taken from the original school founded by the eponymous benefactor in the early eighteenth century.

W1.8 Sir John Cass School, Duke's Place.

W1.9 Lloyd's of London, the corner of Leadenhall Street and Lime Street.

W1.10 The Commercial Union Building, Leadenhall Street, with the Swiss Re Tower and St Andrew Undershaft.

WALK 2 WESTMINSTER AND WHITEHALL

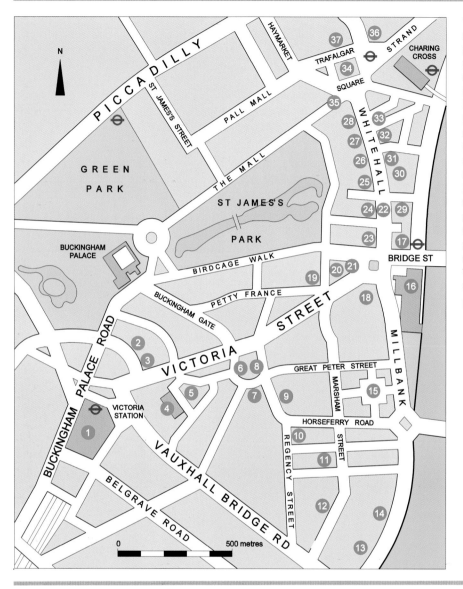

Westminster is the historic centre of church and state, and Whitehall, site of a former royal palace, has been the administrative centre of government since the eighteenth century. Here are buildings designed to impress and central to the promotion of an image of empire, albeit stylistically contested. Elsewhere in London, it was the architecture of Wren that was represented during the Edwardian period as the style of authority, notably at E. W. Mountford's Central Criminal Court – the Old Bailey of 1900–7 in the City – but here in Whitehall the presence of the Banqueting House encouraged a classicism which looked further back to Inigo Jones. South and west of the historic heart of Westminster towards Victoria, there are a wide range of domestic and commercial buildings as well as the great Roman Catholic cathedral. North of Whitehall, Trafalgar Square, with the National Gallery on the north side, is London's traditional place of public assembly.

1 Victoria Station

A monument to commercial rivalry: the London, Brighton and South Coast Railway and the London, Chatham and Dover Railway arrived side by side in 1860. Both were given grand showfronts fifty years later: the red brick Italianate Brighton side of 1906–8, designed by C. D. Collins, was upstaged in 1909–10 by the stone-faced Edwardian baroque of the Dover line by Alfred Blomfield and W. J. Ancell. Around the corner on Buckingham Palace Road, the Grosvenor Hotel of 1860–2, by J. T. Knowles, Senior and Junior, was not the first railway hotel (preceded at King's Cross and Paddington) but one of the earliest and the grandest of its date,

although privately built and not acquired by the railway until 1900.

2 Stag Place

The site of Watney's Brewery, replanned 1959–64 by Howard, Fairbairn and Partners, now occupied by Portland House (1960–2), a thirty-storey tower with tapered ends, and Eland House (1994–5) by EPR Architects. Between the two, to increase public amenity and break up the wind tunnel effect of the surrounding buildings, *Big Painting Sculpture* by painter Patrick Heron, architect Julian Feary and structural engineers Ove Arup and Partners was installed in 1998: aluminium yacht masts with

stainless steel rigging support coloured plastic, glass-reinforced flat disks, illuminated at night by neon tubes (fig. W2.3). The intended walk-through has been compromised by the addition of unsympathetic paving.

3 Victoria Street

Cut through slum housing in 1847–51 and redeveloped from the 1950s and 1960s onwards in uniform blocks to a uniform height. On the corner of Stag Place, Cardinal Place (EPR Architects, 2005), a mixed office and retail development with a prominent anteater snout, snuffling towards Victoria Station, replaces Esso House (1962, demolished 2003) (fig. W2.2).

W2.1 Westminster Roman Catholic Cathedral.

W2.2 Cardinal Place, Victoria Street.

4 Westminster (Roman Catholic) Cathedral

A neo-Byzantine longitudinal, domed basilica by John Francis Bentley (1895–1903), with a tower 284 feet (86 metres) high; Bentley had wanted two (fig. W2.1). The style chosen deliberately differed from the medieval Westminster Abbey, the baroque St Paul's Cathedral and the Italianate Brompton Oratory, although the plan, with central nave – here exceptionally wide – and side chapels, draws like the last on the same Roman precedent, the Gesù, the sixteenth-century mother church of the Jesuits, with the addition of further side aisles. Bentley's masterpiece was not entirely finished according to his proposals. He wanted all the internal walls to be covered with marble and mosaic, but much fortunately remains undecorated, although many of the fittings, including the remarkable *baldacchino*, were completed to his designs after his death in 1902. Collection boxes encourage donations to complete the building along the lines indicated in the illustration on the wall at the west end, but it is the impressively bare brick and the awe-inspiring scale of the building which contribute powerfully towards its profound spirituality. Happily, this austerity remains uncompromised by the demands of tourism which overwhelm the Abbey and St Paul's. The fourteen reliefs, the *Stations of the Cross* by Eric Gill, were carved and installed in 1913–18. The piazza in front of the cathedral was created in 1975.

5 Ashley Gardens

Mansion flats (1890–3) in a powerful, repetitive design in red brick with stone stripes which precedes but complements the cathedral.

W2.3 *Big Painting Sculpture*, Stag Place.

W2.4 Fire Station, Greycoat Place.

6 Artillery Row

Westminster Palace Gardens, red brick mansion block of 1897–9 by C. J. Chirney Pawley; and Artillery House, modernistic, scenographic stone-faced offices with buttresses (1928–30) by Maurice Webb and H. A. Dawson.

7 Grey Coat Hospital

Founded as a boarding school in 1698; moved here in 1701 into a workhouse of c.1664. Rebuilt in 1955 by Laurence King following Second World War bomb damage. It is an object lesson in the difficulties of designing buildings in a historicist style outside their own time, a problem acknowledged by the architect himself, who referred to this as a contemporary version of the Queen Anne style, although it might more properly be regarded as a contemporary pastiche.

8 Fire Station, Greycoat Place

Opposite the hospital, this attractive and wholly convincing granite and red brick building of 1905–6 by the London County Council is built in a newly invented recreation of the style of c.1700 and so succeeds where pastiche fails (fig. W2.4). The free interpretation available in the Queen Anne style was particularly well suited to the humane architecture deployed by the LCC for housing and public utilities in the period up to the First World War.

9 Channel 4, Horseferry Road

By the Richard Rogers Partnership (1991–4), with Ove Arup and Partners and YRM Engineers. A glazed, concave centrepiece is flanked by two five-storey office wings, with basement studios and projecting stair and lift towers.

10 Regency Café, Regency Street

A good example of a vitrolite façade on a post-war building type threatened by the relentless colonisation of the landscape by Starbucks and its fellow travellers.

11 Grosvenor Estate, Page Street

Nothing prepares the visitor for this extraordinary council estate by Sir Edwin Lutyens of 1929–35, replacing dilapidated courts on land provided by the Duke of Westminster. Built of brick with white rendering to create a chequerboard pattern to break up the monotonous regularity of the seven five- and six-storey blocks, with concrete balconies in the internal courtyards (figs W2.5 and p.69). The effect may be variously interpreted as playful, hallucinogenic (how do you find your way around?) or simply patronising. The classicising detailing of the door-cases with dates in Roman numerals, the classical gatepiers and the pyramid-roofed lodges, masquerading as shops and barbers, are refugees from a country estate, with the implied *de haut en bas* relationship of squire to tenant.

12 Millbank Estate

London County Council (1897–1902): red-brick working-class flats on a large scale for 4,430 people, aligned symmetrically on the axis of the Tate Gallery, on the site of the former Millbank Penitentiary. Along with the LCC's contemporary Boundary Street Estate in Shoreditch (Walk 7), Millbank represents one of the highpoints in social housing provision in London. Unlike Boundary Street, Millbank is well preserved and maintained, a reflection of subsequent public and private funding rather than a function of the architecture itself. Lacking Boundary Street's wilful stylistic inventiveness, the designs are logical and homogeneous without being repetitive, with excellent detailing: the courtyard porch at Lawrence House, for example, in its inventive Mackintosh-like approach to three-dimensional form is one of the lesser-known highlights of London architecture, which a century later retains its power to thrill (see p.62). As Susan Beattie, the historian of LCC housing, observed, such details expressed 'a joyous determination to apply to council housing the same standard of architectural grace, the same depth of design, that at present benefited only the rich and fashionable'.

13 Tate Britain

Founded by Sir Henry Tate, who had made a fortune from his patented invention of sugar cubes, the Tate Gallery was designed as an annexe to the National Gallery for the display of British art, of which Tate himself had a significant collection that he donated. Designed by

W2.5 Grosvenor Estate, Page Street.

W2.6 Millbank Tower, from Lambeth Bridge.

W2.7 The Houses of Parliament and Portcullis House, from Parliament Square.

Sydney R. J. Smith, the gallery opened in 1897 on the site of the former Millbank Penitentiary (demolished in 1892–3) after earlier proposals to house the collection in South Kensington had been rejected. In 1917, the Tate (which did not become fully independent until 1954) was constituted as the National Gallery of Modern Foreign Art as well as British Art, a responsibility which continued to be discharged in this building until the establishment of Tate Modern (Walk 5) and the rebranding of the institution. Numerous successive extensions to Smith's original building, beginning in 1909–10, have been made possible through the generosity of Sir Joseph Duveen, his son Lord Duveen (twice), and the Calouste Gulbenkian Foundation. A new entrance designed by Allies and Morrison was completed in 2001 on the Atterbury Street side. The most architecturally significant addition, the Clore Gallery, funded by the eponymous foundation to house the Turner Collection, was completed in 1986 to the seriously playful design of James Stirling, Michael Wilford and Associates. Behind the Tate, the former Queen Alexandra Military Hospital of 1903–6 houses the gallery's administrative offices.

14 Millbank Tower

By Ronald Ward and Partners for Vickers (1960–3); thirty-two storeys, reinforced concrete with grey-green curtain walling with projecting stainless steel mullions, this was briefly London's tallest building (387 feet or 118 metres) (fig. W2.6). The concave sides to east and west and convex to north and south catch and reflect the changing riverside light. Since this is such a prominent landmark, later builders might have been expected to have learned more from its scenographic success. It was listed in 1995 and remodelled in 2000–1.

15 St John Smith Square and Lord North Street

Developed in the early eighteenth century, the square originally was entered only from the east and north. Lord North Street is one of the finest Georgian streets in London, all genuine except Oliver Hill's neo-Georgian College House of 1930–3 on the north-west corner. Wartime signs point to air-raid shelters under the pavements.

St John was the most expensive of the Queen Anne churches, costing over £40,000, by Thomas Archer (1714–28). A wonderful piece of Italianate urbanism, this is one of the greatest English baroque buildings, with broken pediment, decorative triglyphs, curved surfaces and circular corner turrets closing the view at the end of Lord North Street (see p.138). The plan originally was a variation on the Greek cross, but internal columns were lost after a fire in 1742; further alterations were made in 1824–5. The interior, burnt out in 1941 was rebuilt by Marshall Sisson in 1965–9 as a very good concert hall.

16 The Palace of Westminster (Houses of Parliament)
17 Portcullis House

The Palace of Westminster was gutted by fire in October 1834; Westminster Hall (Norman with a hammerbeam roof of *c*.1400) survived the conflagration. The new Parliament building by Barry and Pugin (1839–60), required to fulfil both national and international requirements in the capital of the empire, triumphantly married grandeur with accessibility, establishing Gothic not only as a national style but also as a parliamentary style, later employed in both Ottawa and Budapest (see pp. 30, 124).

On the other side of Bridge Street, linked by subway to Parliament, **Portcullis House**, by Michael Hopkins and Partners, architects, and Ove Arup and Partners, engineers, was completed as parliamentary offices in 2001 (fig. W2.7). Designed to fit into the context provided by Barry and Pugin to the south and Norman Shaw's late nineteenth-century New Scotland Yard to the north, this initially shocking building looks ever more contextually appropriate as familiarity increases. Shaw's Metropolitan Police headquarters was remodelled as parliamentary offices in 1973–9 after being vacated by the police, and now has a pedestrian link with Portcullis House. At the heart of Hopkins's building, an arching roof of laminated oak and glass covers an internal courtyard landscaped with pools and trees; a first-floor gallery gives access to workaday committee and seminar rooms, above which rise the offices for Members of Parliament. The stubby 'chimneys' on the roof act as flues for the ventilation system. Below, the wonderfully Piranesian Westminster Underground Station was completed by the same architects in 1999 as part of the Jubilee Line extension.

W2.8 Westminster Abbey, the west front.

W2.9 Methodist Central Hall, from Broad Sanctuary.

W2.10 Middlesex Guildhall, east front.

18 Westminster Abbey
19 The Methodist Central Hall
20 The Queen Elizabeth Conference Centre
21 Middlesex Guildhall

Westminster Abbey, a new church on an earlier foundation, begun 1245 with building continuing into the sixteenth century. This is a building unique among abbeys for its connection with monarchy and state – the coronation and burial place for kings and queens. The west towers were not completed until the early eighteenth century – begun 1735 to the design of Nicholas Hawksmoor, completed by John James in 1745; a proposed crossing tower was never built (fig. W2.8). In a building rich in architecture and sculpture, it is the breathtaking Henry VII Chapel of 1503–10, at the east end beyond the Sanctuary, which alone justifies braving the crowds of tourists and the red-coated attendants. The pendant fan vault of the chapel is the most perfect existing example of its type. It is the only large-scale fan vault (spanning 35 feet or 10.6 metres) comprised wholly of jointed masonry, each stone shell pared down to a depth of only 3 to 4 inches (8 to 10 centimetres), with the filigree decoration possibly all carved in advance before installation. This is scarcely believable, virtuoso stone-cutting (see R. Evans, 1995).

The Methodist Central Hall by Lanchester and Rickards (1905–11) (fig. W2.9) and **The Queen Elizabeth Conference Centre** by Powell, Moya and Partners (1981–6) are on potentially sensitive sites, but they do not defer to Westminster Abbey by attempting stylistic compromises: they are characterised by an assertive nonconformity.

In all the excitement of Westminster Abbey and the Houses of Parliament, and the perilous business of crossing the road, the unusual art nouveau **Middlesex Guildhall** is easy to overlook (fig. W2.10). Built in 1912–13 by J. G. S. Gibson and Partners, this high-quality building, with striking frontispiece and muscular tower, has been most recently in use as a Crown Court and is now being converted to house the new Supreme Court.

WHITEHALL

W2.11 Cenotaph, with the Foreign and Commonwealth Office, Whitehall.

Whitehall refers to the street of government offices between Parliament and Trafalgar Squares and occupies the site of lands owned by Westminster Abbey which subsequently came into the possession of Henry VIII. The palace buildings were a rambling assemblage rather than especially grand. Optimistic seventeenth-century proposals by Inigo Jones and John Webb for a classical palace of absolutist extent stretching from Charing Cross to Westminster and from the river to St James's Park were not carried out. Wren made additions and alterations in the later seventeenth century, but there was no attempt to rebuild after a major fire in 1698 destroyed most of the buildings. Only the **Banqueting House** by Inigo Jones (1619–22), built for the masques and formal spectacles of the royal court before he produced designs for a complete palace, survives (see pp.121–2). This is a highly wrought casket whose sophisticated deployment of the classical orders suggests a two-storey building, but within, above a fine vaulted undercroft, there is one single 'double-cube' room, 55 x 55 x 110 feet. Until the present staircase was added in 1808–9, access to this was by a temporary timber stair, which has been taken to imply that Jones was intending to carry the building further. The compartmented Venetian ceiling, an innovation in England, was decorated by Rubens with paintings installed in 1635 which celebrate the reign of King James I. Commissioned by his son Charles I, this is the largest Rubens decorative ensemble to remain *in situ*. The paintings are aligned in order to be seen from specific points: from the doorway, the centrepiece *Apotheosis of James I* flanked by processions of cherubs; from within the room, the *Peaceful Reign of James I* above the throne flanked by *Reason subduing Intemperance* and *Bounty triumphing over Avarice*; from the throne, the *Union of England and Scotland* above the door flanked by Minerva as *Wisdom conquering Ignorance* and Hercules as *Heroic Virtue triumphing over Discord*. The whole spectacle became a fully baroque *tableau vivant* only when Charles I was seated on the throne, a short-lived possibility since it was from a window of the Banqueting House that he stepped onto the scaffold for his execution in 1649. The Banqueting House became a Chapel Royal in 1698 and a museum in 1890. It is used now for presidential visits, fashion shoots and other such occasions of pomp and circumstance.

22 Cenotaph
By Sir Edwin Lutyens (1919–20), the chief national war memorial, originally created in timber and then in permanent Portland stone form, succeeds through its merciful reticence and explicit absence of symbolism (fig. W2.11). There are no monuments or religious references and no vertical or horizontal lines – all are curved.

GOVERNMENT BUILDINGS ON WHITEHALL, WEST SIDE FROM THE SOUTHERN END

A monumental group of three buildings erected between 1844 and 1915 reflects the need to accommodate the increasing amount of government business during the nineteenth century and to house those activities in a grand manner, imparting confidence in the efficiency and probity of the decision makers.

23 New Government Offices
Home, Health, Education and Local Government, now the Treasury, by J. M. Brydon (1899–1915), the last and largest of the group, commanding the corner of Parliament Square (see p.119).

24 Foreign and Commonwealth Office
By George Gilbert Scott (1862–75), originally with the Home and Colonial Office on the Whitehall front and the India Office, with picturesque tower, on the St James's Park side. A key building in the Battle of the Styles with Scott, originally proposing Gothic, being pressed to follow the well-established classical mode of Whitehall government buildings (see p.119). Decorative allegorical sculpture on the Whitehall front illustrates Home and Colonial concerns: Literature, Commerce, Manufacture, Science, Art, Agriculture and Law are followed by Government, Europe, Asia, Africa, America, Australasia and Education.

25 Old Treasury
Now the Cabinet Office, completed by Charles Barry (1844–7), whose rich, symmetrical front to Whitehall (originally housing the Board of Trade, the Home Office and the Privy Council) conceals a complex group of eighteenth- and early nineteenth-century structures, including William Kent's Treasury of 1733–7.

26 Dover House
Scotland Office, by James Paine (1754–8), remodelled in the later eighteenth century by Henry Holland.

27 Horse Guards
By William Kent and John Vardy (1750–9), combining barracks and offices, and presenting a 'neo-Palladian' counterpoint to Jones's 'Palladianism' opposite, a cautionary lesson in the slippery notions of stylistic analysis (fig. W2.12).

28 Old Admiralty
By Thomas Ripley (1723–6), the oldest government office on Whitehall for the once largest department, with screen by Robert Adam (1759–61).

GOVERNMENT BUILDINGS ON WHITEHALL, EAST SIDE FROM THE SOUTHERN END

29 Richmond House
Housing the Department of Health, completed in 1987 to the design of Whitfield Partners, presents an asymmetrical front to the early nineteenth-century range behind.

30 Ministry of Defence

Designed by Vincent Harris in 1915, but not built until 1939–59, an enormous wedge-shaped building, largely unrelieved save for the top-floor colonnades and the pedimented corner blocks which are peculiarly reminiscent of Wilton House, designed in the mid-seventeenth century by Inigo Jones's pupil John Webb and thus in thrall to the idea of Jonesian classicism (see p.121). In front, Field Marshals Montgomery, Alanbrooke and Slim give notice of intent.

31 Banqueting House and Gwydyr House

For the Banqueting House, see above. Gwydyr House next door is now the Welsh Office, built c.1772 with a recessed link to the Banqueting House. Government offices since 1842, attic storey added 1884–5.

32 Old War Office

By William and Clyde Young (1899–1906), designed to harmonise with the Banqueting House but using the same classical language, this is a far busier design, with corner turrets (see p.120).

33 Office of Woods and Forests

Now the Department for Environment, Food and Rural Affairs at 55 Whitehall, Edwardian classical by J. W. Murray (1906–9), with cornice height aligned with that of the War Office.

34 Trafalgar Square

Formed in the 1820s following the idea of John Nash, who proposed a straight road from here to the British Museum (Charing Cross Road was eventually formed in the 1880s). Situated at the angle on the route from governmental and monarchical Whitehall and Westminster to the south and the City and Fleet Street, beyond the private palaces of the Strand, to the east. This has become the main gathering point in London for demonstrations, celebration and performance, but in recent years 'security' has overwhelmed spontaneity. The removal of traffic from the north side, and the construction of grand stairs into the square in front of the National Gallery, have greatly improved the space as a public amenity, but it remains a collection of features rather than a wholly coherent urban experience – and crossing the road on the south side remains a hazardous procedure.

Canada House (west side of the square) was built 1824–7 as Union Club and Royal College of Physicians by Sir Robert Smirke, becoming Canada House in 1924; South Africa House (east side) by Sir Herbert Baker (1930–3).

The monuments in Trafalgar Square include the equestrian bronze of Charles I by Hubert Le Sueur (1629–33) on the south side, and a Roman James II of 1686 by Grinling Gibbons in front of the National Gallery. The centrepiece, Nelson's column (1839–43) by William Railton (170 feet or 52 metres high), is surmounted by the statue of the national hero by Edward Hodges Baily; the lions are from designs by Sir Edwin Landseer (1858–67).

35 Admiralty Arch

By Sir Aston Webb (1908–11), conceals the change of axis between Trafalgar Square and The Mall, and heralds the beginning of the ceremonial route to Buckingham Palace which Webb refaced during the same period, along with the building of the Victoria Memorial.

36 St Martin-in-the-Fields

Built by James Gibbs (1721–6) (see p.137). An imposing, galleried church, not one of the Queen Anne churches although built at about the same time, but every bit as grand and considerably more influential, being published by Gibbs in his *Book of Architecture* (1728). The temple front portico was present in contemporary designs by Nicholas Hawksmoor (St George Bloomsbury) and John James (St George Hanover Square), but in combining it with a steeple inspired by Wren's City churches, Gibbs was devising a new and for some an anachronistic formulation. The combination of portico and tower was enormously influential both in Britain and the United States.

37 National Gallery

By William Wilkins (1833–8), built to house the Angerstein collection of paintings (and other publicly owned pictures) purchased by the government; mid-nineteenth-century interiors survive (see pp.126–9). The north wing, to the rear, was completed in 1975 to the design of James Ellis. The extension to the west (the Sainsbury Wing), completed after a protracted and painful process of competition and deliberation, was built 1987–91 to the design of Venturi, Rauch and Scott Brown, developing a theme based on Wilkins's classicism. The National Portrait Gallery is to the east by Ewan Christian and J. K. Colling (1890–5), with a rear wing of 1998–2000 by Dixon/Jones which considerably improves the circulation.

W2.12 Horse Guards, Whitehall.

WALK 3 BEDFORD SQUARE TO SOMERSET HOUSE

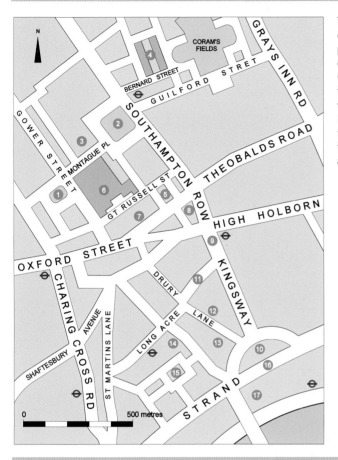

The London square – with regular terraces around a central, originally gravelled but later planted space – is often regarded as an eighteenth-century phenomenon, but it began earlier and finished later. The first, which was not entirely according to the later four terraces model, was Inigo Jones's Covent Garden of 1629–37; Bedford and Russell Squares were among those which followed. These developments were built according to the leasehold system, which from the sixteenth to the twentieth centuries has been the basis of London house building. The system is one of deferred gratification in which the ground landlord lets plots for building, at a low ground rent, the houses then being sold or rented for a set leasehold period (up to ninety-nine years), after which they revert to the estate of the original ground landlord.

1 Bedford Square

This square of 1775–86 has come to symbolise Georgian London at its most regular and composed, partly because of the completeness of its survival – other early squares have all been wholly or partly rebuilt. Here, only one corner house, No. 39, has been reconstructed. Initially lived and worked in by lawyers, described by Byrne as 'the aristocracy of the City and the Inns of Court'. These were followed in the nineteenth century by doctors and architects, but today the square is mainly offices. The first impression is of a complete entity: brick houses with a stucco facing for the ones in the centres of the sides, with Coade stone decoration around the doors. This gives the impression, on the east side especially, of a palace front with prominent centrepiece (see p.13). There are numerous variations, however, within this apparent uniformity – differing fanlights and ironwork balconies, differing first-floor window heights, irregular plot sizes. Such variations in detail are typical of London terrace house development, in which it was unusual either for one architect

to lay out the whole or for one builder to build it.

The main plan type on Bedford Square and the adjacent streets is the one which was in common use until the late nineteenth century: front door, on the left- or right-hand side of the façade, giving onto the passage to the staircase; two main rooms to each floor, one front and one rear, the grandest being the first (upper) floor (which often retains its original decorative plasterwork ceiling, best seen in Bedford Square from the pavement in early evenings in winter when the lights are on). The longevity of this plan type throughout London derived from its flexibility: the house could be occupied by one family or several, one to each floor; the ground floor could be used for business with living accommodation above. Here, No. 1 is the exception to this type, having a central projecting entrance, flanked by niches, which gives onto a large hall.

2 Russell Square

Begun in 1800, the largest square of its day, laid out by Humphry Repton. Its central gardens were restored in 2002. Only a short stretch of

houses survive in their original state, at the north end of the west side. The houses on the south and north were decorated with terracotta in the 1890s. On the east the houses were replaced by two enormous late nineteenth-century hotels, one of which survives: the Hotel Russell of 1898, C. Fitzroy Doll's giant version of a French château. The undistinguished hotels to the south date from the 1960s. On the north side, the Institute of Education, clad in anodized aluminium panels, is part of a handsome composition by Denys Lasdun for the University of London (1965–76) (fig. W3.1). On the west side, terracing steps down to a landscaped area in front of his library for the School of Oriental and African Studies.

3 Senate House

Built 1932–7 to the design of Charles Holden for the University of London's library, council rooms and halls for academic gathering and ceremony. The set-back upper storeys go some way towards mitigating the potentially overbearing Portland stone massiveness of the building, in a

W3.1 Institute of Education, from Russell Square.

W3.2 Sicilian Avenue, from Bloomsbury Square.

W3.3 The British Museum, south front.

manner comparable with the architect's earlier London Transport offices at 55 Broadway, Westminster (see p.80).

4 Brunswick Centre

To the east of Russell Square, Patrick Hodgkinson's megastructure of housing, shops and cinema was built 1968–72 as an alternative to the high-rise during a brief period of optimism about new approaches to urban living (see p.75). It was originally intended to be twice the length which eventually was achieved, with the terraces of flats offering two contrasting views from the balconies: the sky above and the linear concourse below. In recent years the latter has appeared very bleak indeed and confirmed Richard Sennett's view (*The Fall of Public Man*, 1974) that this was an area to pass through rather than to use, but the successful recent restoration and letting of the shops have contributed to a revival of public life. The flats now are partly private and partly local authority housing.

5 Bloomsbury Square

The site occupied by this square was first laid out by the Earl of Southampton in 1661, in front of his own house on the north side. Some eighteenth-century houses survive on the west side. The terraces on the north side of the square, replacing Southampton House, and on Bedford Place, which runs north to Russell Square, are of c.1800. On the east side is the grand rear of Victoria House (1921–34) by Charles W. Long for the Liverpool Victoria Friendly Society.

To the west of the Southampton development, Montagu House was built by the Duke of Montagu (1675–9), and rebuilt (1686) after a fire, on the site now occupied by the British Museum.

6 The British Museum

Established by Act of Parliament after the death of the collector Sir Hans Sloane in 1753. The collections were opened to the public in Montagu House in 1759 as the first public museum in Europe with a collection accepted as a national responsibility. As the collections grew, so did the need for a new building. Sir Robert Smirke's monumental neo-classical design was built around a central courtyard (1823–52) (fig. W3.3), to which the innovative round reading room was added to the design of Sydney Smirke, Robert's brother, and the principal librarian Anthony Panizzi (1852–7). Additional wings followed – the notably handsome block to the north (1907–14) by Sir John Burnet, and the Duveen gallery, for the Parthenon marbles, to the west in 1938 by John Russell Pope, although not opened until 1962. The pediment sculpture, by Sir Richard Westmacott, illustrates the progress of civilisation from primitive life on the left, through paganism to astronomy in the centre; arts and sciences are on the right, terminating in natural history. It illustrates the original scope of the museum before the building of Waterhouse's Natural History Museum in South Kensington in the 1870s, to which the relevant collections were transferred. A blue background and gilding were part of the original scheme.

With the departure from the museum of the British Library in 1997 to the fine new building at St Pancras by Colin St John Wilson (see p.132), the opportunity was taken to restore the round reading room and to open up the central courtyard, which had been filled with temporary structures and not open to the public, the reading room being accessible (only to accredited readers) through a utilitarian passage. Foster and Partners' design (1997–2000), now known as the Great Court, has roofed over and paved the courtyard, added exhibition space, shops and restaurant, and enabled far easier access to all parts (see p.131). It has occasioned controversy for using the wrong sort of stone (French limestone rather than English Portland stone) on the reconstructed south portico, but this is far less significant than the overall achievement of a popular and efficient new public space. The curving profile of the roof is best appreciated from the first-floor window of the new south portico. The removal of the British Library collections has enabled the fine King's Library in the east wing to be restored as the new Enlightenment gallery, with appropriate displays which underline the rational, humane and questioning traditions that underpin this great and freely accessible institution.

7 St George Bloomsbury

Built 1716–31, this superb church by Nicholas Hawksmoor, one of the 'Fifty New Churches', has undergone many trials, but following a restoration completed in 2006 it is so far as possible back to its original appearance and internal orientation (see p.141). Deeper on the north–south axis than on the east–west, the original positioning of the altar was changed from east to north in 1781 in order to accommodate a larger congregation. The excellent portico presents a grand show-front to the street, but it was never the main entrance: these are on the north and south sides of the tower. The stepped pyramid of the tower was based on the tomb of Mausolus at Halicarnassus, one of the wonders of the ancient world, to which Hawksmoor added a statue of George I, with lion and unicorn supporters, remade as part of the recent restoration.

8 Sicilian Avenue

An elegant and self-contained pedestrian shopping street with offices above, built to the design of Robert J. Worley for the Bedford estate

W3.4 Bush House, Aldwych, from Kingsway.

(1905–10), capitalising on the commercial opportunities attendant upon the creation of Kingsway (below) and the regeneration of Holborn which followed (fig. W3.2). The Ionic screens at each end reinforce the feeling of privileged private enclosure.

9 Kingsway
10 Bush House

Cut through a slum area in 1900–5, **Kingsway** was the grandest of the London County Council's street improvements of the late nineteenth and early twentieth centuries. It is a great canyon lined by tall, stone-faced buildings (erected over a period of twenty years), running south from Holborn and culminating at the grand Aldwych crescent. This connected the new street with the Strand, the main route between Westminster and the City, which was narrow and congested at this point. The new development not only improved traffic circulation but also performed a political and moral function in sweeping away the notorious Holywell Street, a historic pre-fire street of picturesque timber-framed, lath and plaster houses, described in detail by Nead. This inappropriate survival in the modern imperial capital was the site of the radical book trade, which by the mid-nineteenth century had become associated with obscene publications. Building on the large new site at the southern end of the new thoroughfare, in a variety of classical styles, continued until 1935. The best building here, facing Kingsway with a theatrically climactic entrance exedra, is **Bush House** of 1920–3 (fig. W3.4), by the New York architect Harvey W. Corbett of Helmle and Corbett, which was praised at the time by

W3.5 Freemasons Hall, Great Queen Street.

Professor C. H. Reilly: 'Here is honesty, simplicity, faith in, and hope for the future.' Built for exhibitions of commercial products, with flexible office space, for the international shipper Irving T. Bush, the building is now occupied by the BBC. Corbett also designed the Bush Terminal Building (now Bush Towers) in 1916–18 at 130 West 42nd Street, New York City, a thirty-storey Gothic tower, for the same purpose of encouraging manufacture and trade.

11 Great Queen Street

William Newton's innovative terrace of fourteen large houses (1637) on the south side of this important route between Covent Garden and Lincoln's Inn Fields does not survive, but there are six good houses of the eighteenth century on the north side, with ground-floor shops, at Nos 27–9 and 33–5. Opposite, the great stone bulk of the Freemasons Hall, by Ashley and Newman, was erected 1927–33 in a classical revival style (fig. W3.5).

12 Wild Street Peabody Estate

Built in 1880–1, following H. A. Darbishire's generic design, in an area which had declined into a slum and was scheduled for rebuilding in 1877 by the Metropolitan Board of Works.

13 Theatre Royal, Drury Lane

This is the fourth theatre on this historic site since 1663 and the longest lived. Built in 1810–12 to the design of Benjamin Dean Wyatt, it has a fine series of front-of-house spaces, although the auditorium itself was rebuilt in 1921–2 in an Edwardian classical style. The Catherine Street entrance porch, with uncompromising coupled piers, was added in 1821, and the cast-iron colonnade on Russell Street in 1831.

14 Royal Opera House

Also the fourth on its site, this vast ensemble was begun by E. M. Barry, who built the classical, porticoed theatre on Bow Street (1857–8), and followed it with the glass and iron Floral Hall next door (1858–60), an adjunct to Covent Garden Market. Extended to the west by GMW Partnership (1980–2), restoration and further extensions to the south by Dixon/Jones and BDP were completed in 2000. The east end of the Floral Hall, now housing the public foyer, has been incorporated within the Opera House, raised on a basement (fig. W3.6) (the façade of the west end has been re-erected at Borough Market – Walk 5). A new studio theatre, ballet studios and backstage facilities fill the remainder of the block towards Russell Street.

15 Covent Garden

Built to the design of Inigo Jones for the Earl of Bedford (1629–37), Covent Garden was a notable attempt at regular town planning, with terraces to north and east, the church of St Paul to

W3.6 The Floral Hall, incorporated within the Royal Opera House.

the west, flanked by houses, and the garden behind the landowner's own house to the south. Jones's piazza design was indebted to recent Continental precedents in Livorno, Paris and Madrid, with the arcaded façades of the houses perhaps also inspired by Sansovino's superb mid-sixteenth-century, non-residential Fabbriche Nuove di Rialto in Venice. The church, restored in 1795 after a fire, was designed as a simple box with a Tuscan portico: 'the handsomest barn in England' (see p.134). The door in the portico is blind since this is the altar end, and east–west orientation required the entrance to be at the west where there was less need for architectural display. None of Jones's houses survives: the arcaded block on the north side by Henry Clutton (1877–9) gives a good idea of the appearance of the original, to a larger scale. The colonnades and shops at the north-east were built as part of the recent restoration and extension of the Royal Opera House. To the northwest at the end of a street with good Georgian houses, the restored 43 King Street of 1716–17 by Thomas Archer is outstanding.

The original Covent Garden development was not fashionable for very long, acquiring a justified reputation for raffish and exuberant behaviour, prompting the better-off to move west: 'Here oft' my Course I bend, when lo! from far, /

I spy the Furies of the Foot-ball War' (John Gay, *Trivia*, 1716). A market was established in the central area in 1671. The surviving market buildings, the best preserved of their period in England, were built to the design of Charles Fowler in 1828–30. They were restored and converted to shop and restaurant use in 1977–80 after the successful conclusion of a long conservation battle that had followed the removal of the fruit and vegetable market to Nine Elms, Vauxhall, in 1974 (see pp.14, 89).

16 St Mary le Strand

Designed in 1714 by James Gibbs as one of the 'Fifty New Churches' and consecrated in 1724, this is a spatially simple building with richly detailed exterior and elaborate decoration within, giving it the character of a jewel box (fig. W3.7). The semi-circular porch and the classical tower make the most of the scenographic possibilities afforded by the view down the Strand towards the island site (see p.137).

17 Somerset House

Somerset House is a superb building of 1776–1801 framing the finest Georgian square in London (see p.117). It is customary to refer to the building's having been rescued from use as government offices, but that was its original

W3.7 St Mary le Strand.

function and in fact the Inland Revenue is still in substantial occupation. Designed by Sir William Chambers, principally for the Navy Office, with learned societies and the Royal Academy in the range facing the Strand, it now houses the Courtauld Institute of Art and

W3.8 Somerset House, rear of the Strand front, north side of the courtyard.

Gallery on the Strand front, with further galleries on the river front. The building occupies the site of the grand sixteenth-century house begun by 'Protector' Somerset, regent for the young King Edward VI, which was taken over by the Crown on his death in 1552. John Webb added an arcaded riverside gallery to this palace in 1661–4, and this provided Chambers with his inspiration for the design of the Strand front of the new government offices (fig. W3.8 and p.117). Here he recreated the serene façade that he believed to be by Inigo Jones, placing at the centre a superb Doric vestibule which recalls the entrance to Palazzo Farnese in Rome (fig. W3.9). Trained in Paris and Rome, Chambers – in addition to his Palladian homage

to Jones – produced a design that was learned, rational, modern and wonderfully well detailed, in the spirit of the best contemporary French classicism with which he was closely familiar. With the construction of the Victoria Embankment in 1864–70, the direct relationship between the building and the river was severed, to the detriment of the overall massing. Within the courtyard there is no such problem, and even the dome, which looks far too small on top of the long riverfront, seems to be in harmony with the whole. The riverfront was made even longer than Chambers intended with the building of an additional wing on Lancaster Place for the Inland Revenue by Sir James Pennethorne (1851–6).

Following the arrival of public collections from the late 1980s onwards, the interiors of the Strand and river ranges may be visited, as well as the terrace with views of the river and St Paul's. Chambers had a genius for staircases: the former Royal Academy staircase, now leading to the Courtauld Gallery, rises vertiginously in a semi-circular top-lit well, but it is the former Navy Stair (now renamed after Nelson) at the west end of the south range which is incomparably spectacular, with two curved flights followed by a straight flight which launches itself across the space, concluding with one long flight which hugs the curving wall of the well beneath the oval skylight (fig. W3.10 and p.117).

W3.9 Somerset House, Strand front vestibule.

W3.10 Somerset House, the Nelson (Navy) Stair, ground floor.

WALK 4 LEGAL LONDON

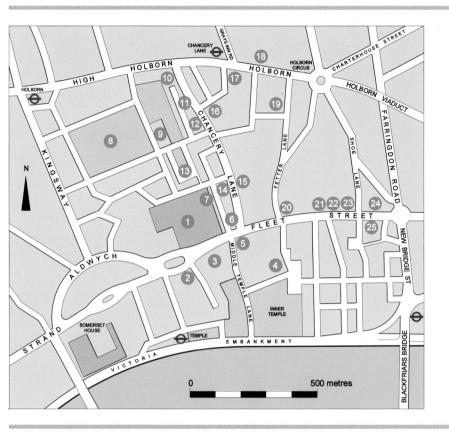

The east end of the Strand and the west end of Fleet Street have been dedicated to the law since the late Middle Ages. The Inns of Court, Lincoln's Inn, Gray's Inn and the Temple occupy much of the area, as do lesser inns such as Staple Inn just off Holborn. The completion of the Royal Courts of Justice in the Strand in 1882 continued the concentration of the law in the area; it also acted as an attraction for the nation's press, which became established in the last decades of the nineteenth century further east in Fleet Street, a long-established centre for the printing trade. Perhaps the conservatism of the law has meant that there are many relics of the past among the buildings in the area, and the wealth of the law has enabled a high level of preservation. The press in Fleet Street has proved more ephemeral, with its exodus during the later 1980s led by the removal of *The Times*, *Sunday Times*, *Sun* and *News of the World* to Wapping in 1986. Nonetheless, there is a rich mix here of old and new, well worth investigating.

1 The Royal Courts of Justice

By G. E. Street (1871–82), dominates the north side of the east end of the Strand and is the last large public building designed in strict Gothic style (fig. W4.1). The entrance façade, leading to the great hall, is surprisingly symmetrical with a composition of elements inspired by both French and English thirteenth-century styles. The material is white Portland stone, given texture through decorative carving, while spires, pinnacles and chimneys lend a spiky appearance to such a substantial building. At its eastern end is the distinctive clock tower with hipped roof, completing the long street façade.

Across the Strand on the south side was the site of large houses and gardens prior to the Restoration and the general move west.

2 Essex Street

Built 1675–82, carved from an estate by Nicholas Barbon, the seventeenth-century developer. No. 19 on the west side remains as do Nos 32 and 34 on the east side, but more redolent of the early development is the arched gate at the end of the street, which was meant to separate the houses from the commercial wharves on the river side.

3 Middle Temple

Barbon sweetened the lawyers of Middle Temple by building New Court (1667) and the passage leading to it from Essex Street, Devereux Court. The lawyers' chambers are of domestic scale in red brick with regular symmetrical sash windows, a model followed throughout the Inns of Court. From New Court, steps lead into Fountain Court, from which the backs of Barbon's houses in Essex Street may be seen (see p.39). To the left is Middle Temple Hall, the best-preserved Tudor hall in London. The material is dark red brick, but there are six large four-light windows with mullions and transoms, separated by brick and stone buttresses. The arch on the north side of the Fountain Court just opposite the hall leads to Brick and Essex Courts. The date over the arch on the west side is 1677, and the brick-built chambers with pedimented door-cases demonstrate the entrenchment of the seventeenth-century model.

4 Inner Temple
5 Middle Temple Lane
6 Former branch of the Bank of England
7 Bell Yard

On the east side, across Middle Temple Lane, an arch leads into Pump Court, **Inner Temple** (fig. W4.2), with a pleasant group of late seventeenth-century chambers at the west end, while at the east end is Sir Edward Maufe's Cloisters (1949–52). These open on to Church Court and the Temple Church, much restored in the nineteenth century and also after bomb damage in the Second World War. The oldest part of the church is the twelfth-century circular nave in the Templar tradition to memorialise the Church of the Holy Sepulchre in Jerusalem, while the rest of the church is of the thirteenth century. The passage at the east end of Church Court emerges into King's Bench Walk (see p.42), and on the east side is a range of chambers from 1670. No. 2 is particularly worth noticing for its five-bay, red brick façade and door-case, hipped roof, and wooden cornice, the architecture of London's main streets at the end of the seventeenth century. Further down on the left are Nos 9–11 (1814) by Sir Robert Smirke, in severe grey stock brick with little decorative detail. Across to the west is Paper Buildings (1838), also by Smirke in buff brick with stone dressings and a fully stone-faced façade to the north. The red brick range opposite is all post-war replacement by Worthington and Sutcliffe after bomb dam-

W4.1 The Royal Courts of Justice, The Strand, G. E. Street, 1871–82.

W4.2 Pump Court, Temple, c.1680.

W4.3 Hare Court, Temple, T. G. Jackson, 1893–4.

W4.4 19 Lincoln's Inn Fields, Philip Webb, 1868–9.

age. Back into Church Court and up to the right at the west end leads into Hare Court (fig. W4.3). Nos 2 and 3 are by T. G. Jackson of 1893–4, where flaming red facing and rubbed bricks contrast with the more sober No.1 of about 1680.

Passing through No. 3 Hare Court leads into **Middle Temple Lane** (see p.38), and up to the right a rare example of timber-fronted buildings with a jettied first floor, recalling the London street architecture of the period before the Great Fire. Then through the gate into Fleet Street, where the site of Temple Bar, removed in 1878 (now installed in Paternoster Square), is marked by Horace Jones's Memorial, erected in

the middle of the road in 1880. Immediately across Fleet Street is a former branch of the **Bank of England** by Sir Arthur Blomfield (1886–8) in a full-blown Italian Renaissance style, which contrasts with the neighbouring Law Courts, only just finished when this building was going up.

Between the Bank of England building and the Law Courts is **Bell Yard**, and on the left is the red brick and white stone of the rear elevations of the Law Courts. On the right is the 1874–6 rear extension of Thomas Bellamy's former Law Fire Office with firemen's helmets in the spandrels of the arches.

8 Lincoln's Inn Fields

Reached via Carey Street and Serle Street is this generous open space in a very dense urban area, first developed from 1640 by William Newton. On the south side all the early houses have gone, to be replaced by institutions, notably the Royal College of Surgeons by Sir Charles Barry (1835–6), which reused the six Ionic columns from the previous building on the site by George Dance the Younger. On the west side at Nos 59–60 is Lindsey House of 1639–41, employing the Palladian motifs of a rusticated ground floor and giant Ionic order above. On its left is the later Nos 57 and 58 (1730), whose façade is similar but in stone. Both houses were divided into two sometime after building. Newcastle House at No. 66 is a seven-bay aristocratic house dating from 1685–9, and completed by Wren in 1694. On the north side are Nos 12, 13 and 14, acquired by Sir John Soane, who transformed these into his own house and museum from 1792 to 1824. Further along are Nos 17 and 18 for the Equity and Law Assurance (1871–2) by Alfred Waterhouse in stone-faced Gothic with a light touch. A little earlier is No. 19 by Philip Webb (1868–9), a relaxed combination of Gothic and Queen Anne in red brick and stone (fig. W4.4).

W4.5 New Hall and Library, Lincoln's Inn, Philip Hardwick, 1842.

W4.6 Stone Buildings, Lincoln's Inn, Sir Robert Taylor, 1774–80.

9   Lincoln's Inn
10 Stone Buildings
11 Old Square

Lincoln's Inn is entered on the east side of Lincoln's Inn Fields. Immediately on the left is the New Hall and Library by Philip Hardwick of 1842 (fig. W4.5). Red diapered brick, crenellation, and mullioned windows announce a Tudor model, and the façade to the garden on the east presents a very picturesque front. In contrast is the adjacent **Stone Buildings** by Sir Robert Taylor of 1774–80 (fig. W4.6). The stone-faced west façade has a 21-bay central section with two 5-bay end pavilions adorned by a giant Composite order of attached columns. The court side behind is similar, but with large entrances to the chambers reached across bridges over the very wide area. Immediately to the south is **Old Square**: on the west by Sir George Gilbert Scott (1874) and on the east by J. Oldrid Scott (1886). There is an echo here of Hardwick's Tudor New Hall, but also the actual Tudor Old Hall on the other side of the chapel.

12 Lincoln's Inn Chapel
13 New Square

The chapel has a very distinctive undercroft, and is reached up a stair at the west end of the building. Behind the chapel is Old Buildings, where Nos 21–4 on the south side are Tudor. **New Square**, which opens up to the south, was begun in 1680 as a private development. When the lawyers objected, it was agreed to build chambers for their use, and these form a very coherent red brick group, with broken segmental pediments over the door-cases. In the south-east corner is a gateway into Carey Street.

14 The Law Society
15 The former Public Record Office
16 Southampton Buildings

17 Staple Inn
18 The Prudential Assurance Building
19 No 80 Fetter Lane
20 Crane Court
21 Cheshire Cheese
22 Nos 135–41 Fleet Street
23 Mersey House
24 Nos 120–9 Fleet Street
25 Reuters and Press Association

The Law Society is sited on the corner of Carey Street and Chancery Lane (fig. W4.7). The older section (1829–32 and later) is by Lewis Vulliamy, whose Ionic portico *in antis* lends gravitas to the building. The extension at the corner (1902–4) is by Charles Holden, who elaborated the classical theme with the dramatic use of Palladian windows, which take up most of the first-floor elevations. The blockiness of the building is emphasised by the cutting back of the corners above.

Across Chancery Lane is **the former Public Record Office** by James Pennethorne of 1851–96. The building was intended to hold government records, and the size of the bays is determined by this requirement. The style is Gothic of sorts, with Tudor ogee domes at the top of the Chancery Lane façade, but the scale is massive, with a further long wing within the gateway at right angles to the west range. The building now houses the library of King's College.

Chancery Lane provides examples of the eclectic façades of nineteenth-century commercial buildings, and the visual impact that many City streets would have had before redevelopment. Near the top on the east side is **Southampton Buildings**, where No. 25 is the old Patent Office, with a complex building history but mostly nineteenth-century Tudor. From there, steps lead down into the garden of Staple Inn.

From the garden of **Staple Inn** a passage leads into a small, treed court, where there is the hall in the south-west corner and brick chambers on the other sides (fig. W4.8). Nos 7–9 are the only original eighteenth-century chambers,

W4.7 The Law Society, Chancery Lane, Lewis Vulliamy, 1829–32 and later, and Charles Holden, 1902–4.

W4.8 Staple Inn, Holborn, c.1750, rebuilding after war damage, Sir Edward Maufe, 1954–5.

while the others were rebuilt by Sir Edward Maufe in 1954–5 after bomb damage. Holborn is reached through a passage on the north side of the court, and the façade facing the main street is an impressive surviving example of half-timbered Elizabethan houses.

Across Holborn on the north side is the **Prudential Assurance Building** (see p.105) by Alfred Waterhouse (1876–9, 1885–8 and 1899–1906); the earliest part was rebuilt in 1932 by Messrs Joseph. The materials are vibrant red brick and terracotta, which give such a large building a hallucinatory quality. The style is unapologetically Victorian Gothic. The central court,

W4.9 'Alere flammam', Red Lion Court, Fleet Street, 1820s.

now called Waterhouse Square, is accessible from Holborn and is entered from a smaller court under a wide, dramatic arch. Its effect is almost overwhelming.

Back across Holborn, **80 Fetter Lane** is by Treadwell and Martin (1902) for Buchanan's Distillery, with a great deal of decorative carving and the odd scale characteristic of art nouveau.

South on Fetter Lane, great cliffs of glass are rising, but at the south end and around the corner off Fleet Street in **Crane Court** are Nos 5 and 6, the earliest known houses by Nicholas Barbon (1670), although substantially restored. In the adjacent Red Lion Court, at No. 18, occupied by printers since the 1760s, is the sign of Abraham Valpy, who printed books here in the 1820s: a hand pouring oil into a Greek lamp with the motto 'alere flammam' – to feed the flame (fig. W4.9).

Back in Fleet Street, a relic of earlier times is part of the **Cheshire Cheese**, formed from two small seventeenth-century houses each comprising one room per floor and a staircase compartment. It is worth investigating this internal arrangement.

Further east on the same side is **135–41 Fleet Street**, the former Daily Telegraph Building by Elcock and Sutcliffe with Thomas Tait, and Owen Williams as consulting engineer (1928–31) (see p.109). The street façade has something of Selfridge's about it, with a screen of giant columns in a Graeco-Egyptian fashion, but 'moderne' is the word that comes to mind here.

There are many examples along Fleet Street of the sort of narrow fronted office speculations

which gradually replaced the wooden framed and brick houses during the nineteenth century. An interesting example at 133 Fleet Street, next door to the Daily Telegraph, is **Mersey House** (1904–6), built to the design of an unknown architect to house the London offices of the *Liverpool Daily Post*. The whole composition, with a large arch at ground floor and a curved façade above flanked by buttresses, is reminiscent of C. Harrison Townsend.

On the other side of Shoe Lane, at **120–9 Fleet Street**, is the former Daily Express Building of 1930–3, largely by Sir Owen Williams, who employed a concrete frame providing unobstructed width in the basement printing hall. The west corner is cantilevered to form a loading bay, and here it is possible to see the elements of construction under the overhang. Provocatively clad in black vitrolite set in chromium strips, with a fine art deco entrance hall by Robert Atkinson, the building conveyed a striking image of stylish modernity.

Almost opposite across Fleet Street is Lutyens's **Reuters and Press Association** of 1934–8, bringing together the international and provincial news agencies. Here is Lutyens at the 'high game', with the top and bottom of Doric pilasters peeping out of rustication on the ground and mezzanine floors, where there is a wide entrance niche with the figure of Fame. Then an entablature with cornice, triglyphs and guttae, broken at the corners, while above this are four floors of simple casements. At the top is a balustrade, but beyond is a two-storey concave block topped by a rotunda.

WALK 5 THE SOUTH BANK

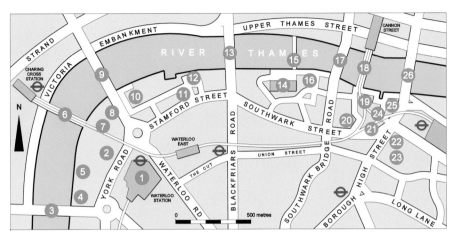

London is divided by the River Thames, with 'south of the river', notwithstanding its complex history and large population, regarded by visitors and north Londoners alike as liminal – a way into the capital rather than a destination in its own right. Southwark was noted from the medieval period for inns to accommodate travellers and for the town houses of church dignitaries, and from the sixteenth century for bear-baiting, theatres and prisons. Industrial enterprises and philanthropic institutions followed in the eighteenth century as the borough became heavily built-up. Despite this rich history, the South Bank, from Westminster Bridge (Lambeth) to London Bridge (Southwark), has for a century been regarded as a patient in need of attention, the focus for periodic bouts of regeneration. County Hall, the Festival of Britain, the Hayward Gallery, the National Theatre, Tate Modern and the London Eye have all contributed to the cultural renaissance of a once active and industrial riverfront which fell into decline during the twentieth century. As a result, it is at last a tourist destination with a traffic-free walk along the river, although few attempt to penetrate the hinterland.

W5.1 County Hall (on the right), the London Eye and the Shell Centre, from the Victoria Embankment.

1 Waterloo Station

Dating from 1901–22 (incorporating earlier station buildings of the mid- and later nineteenth century), by engineers J. W. Jacomb Hood and A. W. Szlumper, with a fine baroque façade by J. R. Scott. Built on a difficult site at a time when the large shed allowing dispersal of smoke and steam was no longer required with the introduction of electric trains, the emphasis here shifted to the spacious, well-serviced concourse, the beginning in England of the station as a meeting place and a setting for commerce.

The contrasting international terminal by Nicholas Grimshaw and Partners and YRM Anthony Hunt Associates, completed in 1993, recalls nineteenth-century glories (see p. 82). This steel and glass shed on a concrete base is constructed as a series of intersecting arches, longer on one side than the other, enabling the shed to curve along the very long platform required for Eurostar trains. After a long period of decline in public transport provision, this station, along with the Jubilee Line, restored faith in the redemptive possibilities of public service architecture. It is regrettable that the future of the terminal is now in doubt following the opening in November 2007 of the new high-speed line to St Pancras.

2 Shell Centre

Built 1953–63, by Howard Robertson and R. Maynard Smith, partly ten and partly twenty-six storeys high, of reinforced concrete with a steel-framed tower, all stone faced (fig. W5.1). The small windows, designed to light small offices, are not large enough in scale on the outside

W5.2 The Royal Festival Hall, from Hungerford Bridge.

view to deliver on the promise of such a big building on such a notable site.

3 Westminster Bridge
The original stone bridge by Charles Labelye (1738–50), a much-illustrated wonder of its age, was replaced by the present bridge of 1854–62, designed by Thomas Page.

4 County Hall
The building of a new headquarters on a new site for the London County Council, to reflect its status and to accommodate its expanding responsibilities, was a lengthy procedure which involved the acquisition of several tenanted older properties (fig. W5.1). The competition for the design was won by Ralph Knott in 1908, and building began four years later but was then interrupted by the First World War. Opened in 1922 but not completed until 1933, the building's prominent position on the south side of Westminster Bridge within sight of the Houses of Parliament kept it in the mind of a government determined to abolish the LCC's successor body, the Greater London Council. The GLC went in 1986, and the Inner London Education Authority followed four years later. So this fine building, with its grandly sweeping concave colonnade to the riverfront, topped by a peculiarly inconsequential cupola, passed out of public ownership and now accommodates a variety of private commercial enterprises in inappropriately august grandeur.

5 London Eye
This is the largest observation wheel ever built at 135 metres (443 feet) in diameter, with thirty-two glass-panelled capsules (fig. W5.1). It differs from the Ferris wheel in being supported by steel legs on one side only, allowing it to overhang the river and provide, on clear days, spectacular views. Designed by David Marks and Julia Barfield and opened in 2000, the Eye has been a great popular success which has contributed significantly to the revitalisation of the South Bank.

6 Hungerford Bridge
Brunel's suspension bridge of 1841–5 provided a pedestrian way from the South Bank to Hungerford Market. When the market site was taken over by Charing Cross Station, the bridge was replaced by John Hawkshaw's iron-girder railway bridge of 1860–4, which rises from Brunel's brick piers; it was widened in 1882–8. New pedestrian suspension bridges to each side by Lifschutz Davidson and WSP Group Engineers are strapped to the original stanchions. Completed in 2002, these are a major improvement on the previous highly uncomfortable and often intimidating narrow footbridge which was attached to the north side only.

7 Royal Festival Hall
Designed by Robert Matthew, Leslie Martin, Peter Moro and Edwin Williams for the 1951 Festival of Britain, this is the only building on the main festival site to survive (although Lansbury, the 'Live Architecture' component of the festival, is still there in Poplar, east London). It is perhaps difficult now to appreciate the thrillingly innovative qualities of a building erected during the drab post-war period of austerity and shortages. Here is the first major British public building in a modernist idiom, designed and detailed with considerable panache and great technical skill (fig. W5.2). The 3,000 seat auditorium is placed above-ground, floating above the multi-level foyers, insulated from the sound and vibration of the nearby railway line into Charing Cross. Alterations by Hubert Bennett in 1962–5 added new service buildings to the rear and pushed the riverfront forward, enlarging the foyer and restaurant. Refurbishment, including the addition of shops at the lower level, was carried out by Allies and Morrison in 2006–7.

8 Hayward Gallery, Queen Elizabeth Hall and Purcell Room
Built 1965–8 to the design of the GLC Architect's Department, this is exciting architectural sculpture, although the elevated walkways and reinforced concrete can appear forbidding on grey, rainy days, making this group of gallery and concert halls an acquired taste. But they work well, the Hayward being particularly successful for big art with the power to hold its own in challenging surroundings. The Richard Rogers Partnership's proposal to put a roof over the whole lot, giving it 'a climate like Bordeaux', has been abandoned, but the apparently endless discussions on upgrading the area continue. The National Film Theatre nearby, also by Leslie Martin, was constructed in 1956–8 under the south arch of Waterloo Bridge.

9 Waterloo Bridge
John Rennie's great granite bridge of 1811–17, its strength symbolised by the coupled Doric columns attached to the piers, was replaced in 1937–42 by this elegant essay in reinforced concrete by Sir Giles Gilbert Scott and Rendel, Palmer and Tritton, engineers.

10 National Theatre
Sir Denys Lasdun's masterpiece (1967–76), this superb building was the result of a long saga which had involved consideration of sites in Bloomsbury, South Kensington and Jubilee Gardens (in front of the Shell Centre). There are three theatres: the amphitheatrical Olivier (1,160 seats), the proscenium-arched Lyttleton (890), and the experimental Cottesloe (200–400, depending on layout), which has a separate entrance towards the rear of the building. Internally, the foyers of the two main spaces do not interconnect, the compensation for which lies in the pleasure of unexpected views and the drama of sudden changes in height. (The lobby areas were revised by Stanton Williams in the late 1990s to improve the circulation.) The building is roughly square with diagonal routes and alignment of supporting members. There is a deliberate evasion of symmetry – an aesthetic of broken forms: broad fly towers, terraces to the river, entrance turrets housing lifts and services, raking struts – all in grey concrete with the sensual imprint of exposed shuttering (fig. W5.3 and p.133). Lasdun admired the architecture of Nicholas Hawksmoor – there is more than a hint here, in a lateral view, of the tower of St Anne Limehouse. Remarkably, Lasdun had the opportunity to extend the terraced theme of the National Theatre next door in the IBM London Marketing Centre (1978), although there the supporting struts are vertical rather than raked.

W5.3 The National Theatre, from Waterloo Bridge.

W5.4 Broadwall (Coin Street development) and the Oxo Tower.

11 Coin Street development

Initially warehousing, cleared after the Second World War, was to be succeeded by a comprehensive office development planned in the 1970s, but successful opposition from local residents culminated in the purchase of the site by Coin Street Community Builders. Broadwall by Lifschutz Davidson (1995) is one of the scheme's three distinct housing developments (fig. W5.4). It comprises flats in a block of nine storeys to the north and in two four-storey blocks which bracket a row of eleven three-storey houses, a highly effective reinterpretation of the London terrace.

12 Oxo Warehouse

Now one of the Coin Street development properties, the building accommodates a restaurant and shops whose rent contributes to the cost of the houses, workshops and flats. Beef extract production here has ceased, but the tower of 1928 by A. W. Moore continues to advertise the food flavouring cube which, the manufacturers claimed, 'gives a meal man appeal' (fig. W5.4).

13 Blackfriars Bridges

Robert Mylne's stone bridge of 1760–9 was replaced in 1860–9 by Joseph Cubitt and H. Carr's

iron bridge on granite piers, with squat red granite columns. Of the two adjacent railway bridges, the east (1884–6) remains in use; the striking piers of the west bridge (1862–4), with powerful Romanesque columns, survive as midriver sculpture (fig. W5.5). The cast-iron insignia of the London, Chatham and Dover Railway, dated 1864, remains at the abutment.

14 Tate Modern

Although this huge steel-framed building with a central tower/chimney 325 feet (99 metres) high, directly opposite St Paul's Cathedral, is now a fundamental part of the central London

W5.5 Blackfriars Bridges and St Paul's Cathedral.

W5.6 Millennium Bridge and St Paul's Cathedral.

W5.7 Winchester House, Clink Street.

tourist itinerary, it was not until its conversion from its original function as an oil-burning power station that most people knew it was there. The successful reinvention of Sir Giles Gilbert Scott's monolithic masterwork of 1947–63 (with the engineers Mott, Hay and Anderson) as the premier national gallery of modern art, completed in 2000, has ensured its celebrity and that of its architects, Herzog and de Meuron. Greatly improved walkways along the South Bank and across the river on the Millennium Bridge have added accessibility to visibility.

15 Millennium Bridge

The first completely new pedestrian bridge for a century, this is a wonderful addition to London's amenities (fig. W5.6). Designed by Foster and Partners, with Ove Arup, engineers, and Anthony Caro, this 'Blade of Light' is a shallow suspension bridge which opened in 2000 but famously wobbled in heavy use. Dampers were applied and the bridge was successfully brought back into popular service in 2002. The smooth passage from street to bridge on the north side is not replicated to the south, where there is apparently insufficient space to allow a flowing termination, and height problems cause the bridge to turn uncomfortably back on itself, depositing the pedestrian next to the river rather than next to the Tate.

16 Globe Theatre

A reconstruction of the thatched-roof, wooden Tudor theatre of 1598–9, built close to the original site in as authentic a manner as possible by the architects Pentagram Design. Completed in 1995, this is the place to experience both the atmosphere and the rudimentary comfort afforded by the Shakespearian playhouse, but it does raise the question of the nature of theatrical authenticity and the manner in which the requirement might be satisfied.

17 Southwark Bridge

Rennie's cast-iron bridge on granite piers (1815–19) had only three spans, the central one, of 240 feet (73 metres), being the largest ever achieved in cast iron. It was replaced by the present steel-arched bridge by Mott and Hay, engineers, and Sir Ernest George in 1912–21.

18 Alexandra Bridge (Cannon Street Railway Bridge)

Constructed in 1863–6 to the design of John Hawkshaw to serve Cannon Street Station on the north bank; it was widened in 1886–93. The bridge has suffered aesthetically through the loss of ornamental elements, just as the station itself has suffered through the loss of its arched shed between the two monumental towers, which now frame an anachronistic and over-scaled block of 1987–91 supported by piles driven through the platforms.

19 Winchester House

The early fourteenth-century window of the great hall of the Bishop of Winchester's town house is a remarkable survival: a hexagon with eighteen cusped triangles around a smaller hexagon, with radiating daggers (fig. W5.7).

20 Cromwell Buildings, Redcross Way
21 Central Buildings
22 W. H. and H. LeMay Hop Factors

On a constrained site in a landscape fractured by railways and roads, **Cromwell Buildings** is a sturdy block of flats with elegant cast-iron galleries by Sydney Waterlow's Improved Industrial Dwellings Company (1864), possibly to the design of Matthew Allen, with floor plans based on the pairs of model cottages designed by Henry Roberts for the Great Exhibition of 1851 (see p.59).

Southwark Street was laid out in 1862 by Sir Joseph Bazalgette. This was the first street in London with a duct for water, gas and telegraph services in the middle of the road. Some of the original High Victorian commercial buildings lining the street survive, including a good five-storey block at Nos 51–2, with hoists and loading bays at each end. The superb **Central Buildings** was erected as the Hop Exchange in 1866 to the design of R. H. Moore, with a handsome exchange hall with offices opening off the galleries (fig. W5.8). The top two floors were removed after a fire in 1920. This area was a centre for the hop trade – the decorative façade of **W. H. and H. LeMay Hop Factors** survives nearby at 67 Borough High Street.

23 George Inn, Borough High Street

Southwark historically was noted for its inns, and this is the fragmentary sole survivor of the original galleried courtyard type, built after the Southwark fire of 1676 (fig. W5.9).

W5.8 Central Buildings (Hop Exchange), Southwark Street.

W5.9 The George Inn, Borough High Street.

W5.10 Southwark Cathedral, with ancillary buildings to the north.

24 Borough Market

This substantially mid-nineteenth-century group of buildings, with additions from 1932, had its origins as a fruit and vegetable market in the thirteenth century. It has been on this site since 1756, and has recently been revamped as a retail market with the addition on the Stoney Street front of the restored iron and glass façade from E. M. Barry's Covent Garden Floral Hall of 1859 (Walk 3).

25 Southwark Cathedral

An Anglican cathedral since 1905, this was the church of St Mary Overie whose tower provided the viewing point for seventeenth-century panoramas. The original twelfth-century church was damaged by fire *c*.1212. There have been many later rebuildings and major nineteenth-century restorations: choir and retrochoir 1215–60; north transept thirteenth century; south transept fourteenth century; nave 1895. The east wall of the choir has a striking progressively restored early sixteenth-century stone reredos with tiers of canopied niches with figures. Notable monuments include the Austin monument by Nicholas Stone (1633) and the languid Lionel Lockyer (1672), a quack doctor: 'His virtues and his PILLS are soe well known / That envy can't confine them under stone.' Ancillary buildings to the north of the cathedral were completed in 2001 to the design of Richard Griffiths Associates (fig. W5.10).

26 London Bridge

The Roman timber bridge – the first permanent crossing of the river, connecting Roman Londinium with the suburb of Southwark – was the first of a series of timber bridges which were succeeded *c*.1200 by the famous stone bridge with houses. This, the only bridge across the Thames until the building of Westminster Bridge (1738–50), was rebuilt in 1823–31 to the design of John Rennie and replaced in 1967–72 by the present concrete cantilever bridge by Mott, Hay and Anderson. Rennie's bridge was re-erected in Arizona.

WALK 6 MAYFAIR AND MARYLEBONE

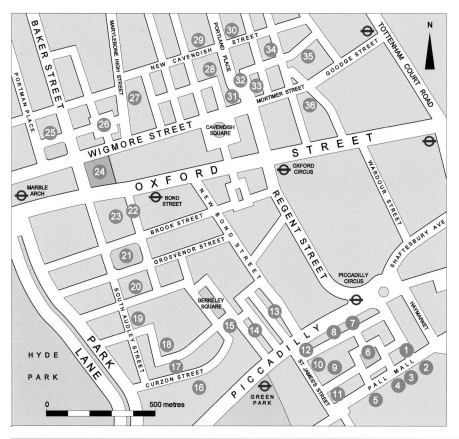

Mayfair and Marylebone were built up over the eighteenth century, and became the fashionable 'West End' residential district in relation to the City. They are both close to Westminster as well, and once Parliament secured its predominance in government, the West End was where the powerful wanted to live. Nobility clustered around Piccadilly and Mayfair, and the wealthy middle class inhabited the substantial streets of Marylebone. There is still a surprising amount of residential property in both areas, although professional and commercial activities have moved in, along with leisure pursuits of every sort. This was also the area of many of the estates of landed families, and the names of the streets and squares such as Grosvenor and Cavendish Squares attest to this.

W6.1 Shepherd's Market, Mayfair, Edward Shepherd, 1735–46, rebuilt 1860s.

1 Waterloo Place and Pall Mall
2 United Service Club
3 Travellers' Club
4 Reform Club
5 Royal Automobile Club
6 St James's Square
7 St James's Piccadilly

Waterloo Place and **Pall Mall** are at the lower end of John Nash's great urban intervention from 1813, which included the residence of the Prince Regent, Carlton House, and the sweep north of Regent Street, culminating in Regent's Park and its terraces. Carlton House was demolished and replaced in 1827–33 by Carlton House Terrace, facing St James's Park. Waterloo Place is monumental in scale, with the Duke of York's column and steps at the south end and Piccadilly Circus framed by Lower Regent Street at the north end.

Pall Mall is the site of 'Clubland'. No. 2 on the south-east corner of the intersection is the former **United Service Club** by John Nash (1826–8), with Victorian additions by Decimus Burton (1858–9). The double-height portico of Doric columns below and Composite above announce

a Roman model, while opposite on the west side of Waterloo Place is the Athenaeum (1827–30) by Decimus Burton (see p.62). Here, as the name suggests, is a more Greek design with a portico *in antis* of coupled and fluted Doric columns.

Next door to the Athenaeum, to the west, is the **Travellers' Club** (1829–32), Charles Barry's first club, where he introduced the Italianate palazzo style (fig. W6.2).To the rear the mood shifts with a lighter Venetian façade of vermiculated rustication around the ground-floor windows, shells within the arches of the first-floor windows, and balconies projecting on brackets.

Next to the Travellers' is the slightly later **Reform Club** (1838–41), also by Barry and now demonstrating a fully assured Italianate style. The nine-bay façade is symmetrical around the central entrance and is arranged hierarchically from rusticated basement to small upper windows under wide eaves.

On the same side of Pall Mall is the fifteen-bay **Royal Automobile Club** (1908–11) by Mewès and Davis, which is on the scale of a palace but is devoted to the automobile and its

enthusiasts. As so often with these architects, the inspiration is the French classical tradition.

Across Pall Mall is the south-western entrance into **St James's Square**. This was the first West End square to be developed after 1660, and was laid out by Lord St Albans with the intention of building superior town houses for those wishing to be close to the restored court and Parliament. Nothing is left of the original houses, but there still remain examples of eighteenth-century replacements. No. 20 is by Robert Adam (1771–4), and on a scale of his Edinburgh houses in the New Town. No. 15 is Lichfield House (1764–6) designed by James 'Athenian' Stuart, where he incorporated into the town house giant Ionic half columns and pediment (see p.41). Nos 9–11 on the north side are by Benjamin Timbrell (1735–6). The square retained its status with the result that these houses were later altered by architects Henry Flitcroft and Robert Adam. Across Duke of York Street, No. 7 is an insert by Lutyens of 1911–12 in Georgian mood. No. 5, Wentworth House, is by Matthew Brettingham Senior (1748–9), while No. 4 of 1726–8 is by Edward

W6.2 Travellers' Club, Pall Mall, Charles Barry, 1829–32.

W6.3 Nos 31–5 Bury Street, R. J. Worley, 1901–2.

W6.4 Ely House, 37 Dover Street,
Sir Robert Taylor, 1772–6.

Shepherd, a local builder and developer. Norfolk House at No. 31 by Brettingham is no longer standing, but its very fine rococo music room is re-erected in the British Galleries of the Victoria and Albert Museum, and gives some idea of the magnificence of the eighteenth-century interiors.

The north end of the square exits into Duke of York Street, at the top of which on the north side of Jermyn Street is St James's Piccadilly by Wren (1676–84) (see p.136). Despite changes made over the years and Sir Albert Richardson's restoration after bomb damage in 1940–1, it retains the general arrangement of the 'auditory' church favoured by Wren. Five galleried bays are divided by square piers, on which are placed Corinthian columns supporting the barrel vault. Externally the church is red brick with stone dressings, and sits well in the domestic surroundings of the houses it was intended to serve.

8   Jermyn Street
9   Bury Street
10   Economist
11   Alliance Assurance
12   St James's Street
13   Albemarle Street

Jermyn Street formed part of Lord St Albans's estate, and was begun from 1661. A few older houses remain together with shop fronts, but they are relics amid a continual rebuilding. However, the eighteenth-century roof line has been retained in many cases with judicious additional building behind parapets. To the east of St James's Church is the rear of Nos 203–6 Piccadilly, the former Simpson's (now Waterstone's bookshop) (1935–6) by Joseph Emberton, demonstrating a convincing and elegant modernism with a fine open-well staircase. Further to the west, on the north side of Jermyn Street, is the opening to Princes Arcade by H. Kempton

Dyson of 1930–3. This was the last of the West End shopping arcades, which started with the Royal Opera Arcade (1816–18) behind Her Majesty's Theatre, Haymarket, followed shortly after by the Burlington Arcade (1818–19) on the opposite side of Piccadilly, next to Burlington House (see p.83).

A left turn into Bury Street, where there is a row of former West End hotels and chambers. No. 15 was the Hotel Meurice by Paul Hoffmann (1911) in a restrained baroque, and Nos 12–14 was the Marlborough Hotel by G. D. Martin (1897–8). Further down on the right, Nos 37–8 are chambers by William Butterfield (1870), the neo-Gothic architect. Here he has produced complementing façades of stock brick with red stripes decorated with blue bricks. More light-hearted are Nos 31–5 by R. J. Worley (1901–2) in red brick and pink terracotta, sporting segmental oriels (fig. W6.3).

At the corner of Ryder Street with St James's Street is the Economist group of buildings by Alison and Peter Smithson (1962–4) (see p.111). Three blocks of different heights stand around an open podium raised off street level, and offer a reinterpretation of Mies van der Rohe's central core recessed at ground level behind the supporting piers. The blocks are of expressed concrete frame construction with Portland stone facing, and the arrangement of the three solids in space makes a distinguished modernist intervention.

At the bottom of St James's opposite St James's Palace is the former Alliance Assurance of 1882–3 for fans of Norman Shaw. Domestic red brick striped with stone, but there are many overscaled details such as the tall mullioned first-floor windows, corner canted turret, and two large stepped Dutch gables with volutes in the angles.

North of the Economist Building St James's Street proceeds past Boodle's Club next door

and White's Club further up. Then Piccadilly and to the left W. Curtis Green's former Wolseley Motors of 1920–1, and beyond that Mewès and Davis's Ritz Hotel of 1903–6. Both these and the buildings opposite gave Piccadilly its character of moneyed luxury in the early years of the twentieth century.

Across Piccadilly is Albemarle Street, carved out in 1683 from part of the site of Clarendon House, Roger Pratt's ill-fated house of 1664–7 for the Lord Chancellor. On both sides of the street there are examples of eighteenth-century houses, such as No. 50 (c.1717–19), the home of the publisher John Murray from 1812. Other interventions include No. 3 by C. H. Townsend and C. H. B. Quennell (1914), and across the street Nos 45–6 by Erno Goldfinger (1955–7) (see p.111). At Nos 20–1 is the Royal Institution, founded in 1799 for the advancement of scientific knowledge. In 1837–8 No. 21 was given its screen of giant Corinthian half-columns by Lewis Vulliamy. At No. 22 is a house by Sir Robert Taylor, and there is more of his work of the 1770s around the corner at Nos 4–6 Grafton Street.

14 Dover Street

This is the continuation of Grafton Street; at No. 37 is the very fine Palladian Ely House of 1772–6, also by Taylor, for Bishop Keene of Ely (fig. W6.4). Then down Hay Hill where on the south side are red brick mansion flats by Macvicar Anderson (1898–9).

15 Berkeley Street
16 Shepherd's Market

Berkeley Street is at the bottom of Berkeley Square, where some substantial eighteenth-century houses are still extant on the west side. But the pedestrian precinct Lansdowne Row leads to the very eclectic Curzon Street, which in its turn leads to Shepherd's Market (fig. W6.1).

W6.5 Electricity substation, Duke Street, Mayfair, Stanley Peach with C.H. Reilly, 1903–5.

W6.6 Welbeck Street, Marylebone, eighteenth and nineteenth centuries.

W6.7 Langham Court Hotel, Langham Street, Marylebone, Arthur E. Thompson,

This is an enclave of miniature streets of shops and houses, built 1735–46 by Edward Shepherd. Many of the original buildings have been replaced, but the atmosphere of intimacy remains.

17 Chesterfield Street
18 Charles Street
19 Grosvenor Chapel
20 Mount Street
21 Grosvenor Square
22 Duke Street
23 Brown Hart Gardens
24 Selfridge's
25 Portman Square
26 Manchester Square
27 Hinde Street Methodist Church
28 Queen Anne Street

Chesterfield Street proceeds north from Curzon Street, and was laid out by John Phillips in 1755 on land belonging to the Curzon estate. Phillips was also responsible for much of Charles Street, although there is here, as in other parts of Mayfair, much infill.

The west end of **Charles Street** narrows and at the end is the Red Lion pub (see p.46). A short way up Waverton Street is Hill Street, built between 1745 and 1750 by many of the builders already encountered such as John Phillips and Benjamin Timbrell. At the west end of Hill Street is South Audley Street, at this point part of the Grosvenor estate, still eighteenth century, but further north appears the red brick and terracotta favoured by the estate. On the east side of the street going north is **Grosvenor Chapel** (see p.142), built in 1730–1 as a proprietary chapel and part of the Grosvenor estate. The chapel is practically free-standing and has a broad five-bay, yellow brick west end with Doric

porch. The stucco details around the windows are later, as are the quoins on the projecting tower, both of which add to the chapel's diminutive, almost toy-like character.

Beyond the chapel is **Mount Street** and a complete change of pace (see p.63). It was rebuilt in 1880–97 in pink terracotta and in the manner of the Flemish Renaissance. The predominant type is flats with shops on the ground floor. Nos 104–13 are by George and Peto, the builders of the florid Harrington Gardens in Kensington, while the pink terracotta of Nos 87–102 by A.J. Bolton (1889–91) is especially characteristic. At the corner with Carlos Place is the Connaught Hotel of 1894–6 by Isaacs and Florence.

Carlos Place leads north to **Grosvenor Square** (1725–31), the first square in London to employ uniform façades, as had been done previously in Queen Square, Bath. Only three houses, Nos 4, 9 and 38, remain from before the twentieth century, and the square is dominated on the west side by Eero Saarinen's United States Embassy of 1957–60.

Out of the north-east corner of Grosvenor Square is **Duke Street**, where on the left is found a curious electricity substation by Stanley Peach with C.H. Reilly of 1903–5, designed as a neo-baroque folly with two domes resting on a large podium (fig. W6.5). On the right side of the street is the former King's Weigh House Congregational Church (1889–91), since 1965 the Ukrainian Catholic Cathedral (see p.150). The architect was Alfred Waterhouse, and the materials are rich red brick and terracotta. Although the front façade is asymmetrical at the upper level where the two towers are differentiated, below – despite first impressions – all is regular. Duke Street heralds the commercialism of Ox-

ford Street with a plethora of shops and flats, some of them by the Improved Industrial Dwellings Company (now Peabody Trust).

In **Brown Hart Gardens** to the west, the Grosvenor estate insisted on red brick façades and scalloped tiles on the roof of the improved dwellings, while in Balderton Street is an earlier block, Clarendon Flats (1871–2), which are of the same model as Leopold Buildings in Bethnal Green.

At the top of Balderton Street is Oxford Street, and on the north side is **Selfridge's**. This largest of West End department stores was conceived by Chicago entrepreneur Gordon Selfridge in 1906. The store was begun in 1908 and continued to expand until 1928 (see p.84). The design is credited to a number of different architects, but the motif that dominates Oxford Street is the screen of giant Ionic columns that rests on the large ground-floor display windows. The monumental sculpted figure over the central entrance is the Queen of Time.

On the west side of Selfridge's is Orchard Street, which leads into **Portman Square**, laid out around 1765 by Henry William Portman (see p.40). No. 20 in the north-west corner is by Robert Adam, a fine example of his town house architecture. The house is restrained on the exterior, but within is a sequence of grand rooms and well-placed service spaces. The branching staircase is especially fine within its circular, top-lit well. No. 21 is by James Adam (c.1772), and although it has been altered, it forms a pleasing unit with its neighbour. Otherwise the tone of the square is set by Portman and Orchard Courts, neo-Georgian eight-storey blocks by Messrs Joseph (1929).

From the north-east corner of Portman

Square and across Baker Street is Fitzhardinge Street, which leads into **Manchester Square** (see p.40). This square was laid out in 1776, and there are still some terraces intact from 1776–88. On the north side is Hertford House, to which Sir Richard Wallace added a gallery wing at the rear in 1872 for his art collection. Now open to the public, the Wallace Collection houses an outstanding range of European paintings and furniture of the eighteenth and nineteenth centuries.

Hinde Street leads out of the east side of Manchester Square and across Thayer Street, which is the south end of Marylebone High Street, transformed into a substantial shopping street after Lord Howard de Walden took control of the Portland estate in 1879. On the northeast corner of the crossing is **Hinde Street Methodist Church** by James Weir (1881–7), carefully detailed with a smaller version of the double portico of St Paul's Cathedral.

The Portland estate developed Marylebone during the eighteenth century with streets of substantial houses. Under de Walden, many domestic scale flats in red brick and terracotta were interspersed between the older houses, so that the streets to the east of Marylebone High Street offer a fine display of urban domestic architecture of the late nineteenth century. **Queen Anne Street** is reached across Marylebone Lane by way of Bentinck and Welbeck Streets (fig. W6.6). No. 2 Queen Anne Street, at its far end, is Chandos House (see p.41) built in 1769–71 by Robert Adam for the Duke of Chandos. The house is distinguished by its cool, grey stone façade and square-cut window openings. Back a few steps in Mansfield Street is more Adam, with speculative houses of 1770–5. No. 13 was the home of Edwin Lutyens with a very nice fanlight over the entrance.

29 New Cavendish Street

The usual mixture of eighteenth-century houses of the Portland estate, with the later additions and interventions encouraged by the de Walden estate. Nos 61–3 were built by John Johnson in 1776–7 and treated as if they formed one façade.

30 Portland Place
31 The Langham Hotel
32 Broadcasting House
33 All Souls Langham Place
34 Langham Street

Laid out as a speculation by the Adam brothers in 1773, **Portland Place** was eventually incorporated into John Nash's grand scheme from Regent's Park to Carlton House Terrace. The width of the street was determined by Foley House, on the site of the present **Langham Hotel**. At the top of the street is Nash's Park Crescent, and a few Adam houses remain, particularly between New Cavendish Street and Weymouth Street, although their size has meant they have become offices or schools; others on the west side of the street have been mutilated. At No. 66 is the headquarters of the Royal Institute of British Architects by Grey Wornum of 1932–4. The Langham Hotel (1863) at the bottom of Portland Place was designed by Giles and Murray in vaguely Second Empire style, using buff brick and stone dressings. Opposite the Langham Hotel is **Broadcasting House** by G. Val Myers (1931), while on its eastern and northern flanks is the new extension by MacCormac Jamieson Pritchard and Sheppard Robson.

The curve of Broadcasting House echoes the circular porch of **All Souls Langham Place** (1822–4), by which Nash cleverly masked the change in alignment between upper Regent Street and Portland Place (see p.143).

Between Broadcasting House and All Souls is **Langham Street**, leading across Great Portland Street and Great Titchfield Street, near the corner of which is No. 35, built as a nurses' home and now the Langham Court Hotel, by Arthur E. Thompson (1901) (fig. W6.7). Surprising for the date, the style is Gothic, but in glazed white bricks picked out in black.

35 Foley Street

The continuation of Langham Street; here are some eighteenth-century houses, but No. 40 demonstrates an Arts and Crafts/art nouveau treatment, continued to the south in Candover Street (fig. W6.8) where are to be found Belmont House, Tower House, York House (1903) and Oakley House, all in the same style.

36 Margaret Street

Reached via Nassau and Wells Streets, here is the extraordinary All Saints, William Butterfield's Gothic Revival church of 1849–59, which marked the coming of age of the style (fig. W6.9 and p.146). Designed as a model for ritualist churches, it was sponsored by the Cambridge Camden Society and supervised by Beresford Hope. The site is very constricted, but Butterfield managed to provide a forecourt to his church, as well as clergy house on the right and choir school on the left. The material is red brick, but striped with black and relieved with stone tracery around the windows. A tall tower and narrow broached spire complete the impressive exterior. Within all is colour and, because of the restricted number of windows, a dim glow. The tall nave is divided into three bays, with two additional bays in the chancel. Coloured tiles, painted stone and polished Aberdeen granite cover every surface, so that the effect on first encounter is overwhelming. The figures on the tiles of the north wall were designed by Butterfield himself, although executed by others. Here in this model urban church, Ian Nairn found 'the

W6.8 Boulting and Sons, Riding House and Candover Streets, Marylebone, H. Fuller Clark, 1903.

force of *Wuthering Heights* translated into dusky red and black bricks … the proportions and transfigured gilded violence … burn through any artificiality'. Butterfield also later designed the red brick Gothic All Saints Church House and School (1870) at No. 84 Margaret Street to the east.

W6.9 All Saints Margaret Street, William Butterfield, 1849–59.

WALK 7 THE BARBICAN TO BOUNDARY STREET

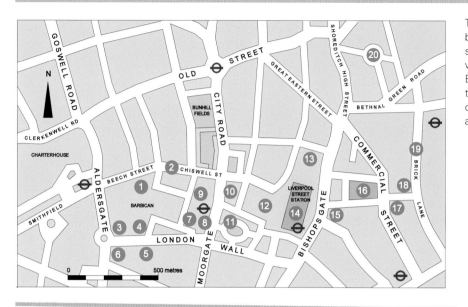

This slice through London north of the City is bracketed by two great housing developments, separated by less than a century in date but worlds apart in contemporary prosperity. Between the two there is a rich mix of nineteenth-century and modern commercial developments and in Spitalfields some of the best architecture of early eighteenth-century London.

1 The Barbican
2 Whitbread Brewery

A colossal project of enormous power, **The Barbican** is a masterpiece of asymmetrical, formal planning and architectural grandeur built in reinforced concrete and faced in hammered granite (see pp.18, 37, 74 and figs W7.1–3). Built on a post-Second World War blitzed wasteland by the architects Chamberlin, Powell and Bon, who were responsible also for the adjacent Golden Lane Estate to the north (1952–7), distinguished by the colourful sixteen-storey Great Arthur House, with water tanks on top shielded by a sculptural concrete wave. Both estates were carried out for the City Corporation. Planning the Barbican began in 1956, but work did not start until 1963; it was completed in 1981. This was a bold attempt by the City to finance new housing, schools and buildings for the arts. It was never going to be cheap – this is not workers' housing but rather intended for middle-class rental; most flats now are privately owned. There are 2,113 flats housing 6,500 people on a 35-acre estate: three towers 43 and 44 storeys high (Lauderdale, Shakespeare and Cromwell, the highest residential blocks in Europe at the time), powerfully articulated (partly, in their jutting balconies, in order to deflect the wind), and 11-storey horizontal slabs. This is a traffic-free 'megastructure', with elevated walkways offering thrilling views across the lake. Within the complex is the City of London School for Girls, the Guildhall School of Music and the restored church of St Giles

Cripplegate (1545–50, with nineteenth-century and modern restorations). The complex is picturesque in the sense that it has no single, commanding viewpoint but a multiplicity of views. The main public building is the Barbican Centre (1968–82). This has good internal spaces but is notoriously difficult of access, partly because functional requirements grew during the planning process and consequently had to be pressed into a smaller space than would have been ideal, but this does result in an interesting play with interior levels. The quality of the components in both the Barbican Centre and the flats is especially notable: the door furniture alone is an object lesson in architectural detailing (fig. W7.2).

To the north, the core of the site of the former **Whitbread Brewery** (famous for its horse-drawn drays) occupies both sides of Chiswell Street. The Partners' House (c.1700), originally of five bays, is on the south side next to the King's Head pub (see p.93); the yard behind, with the late-eighteenth century Sugar Room, is reached through archways on both Chiswell Street and (via a ramp) Milton Street. On the north side, buildings of 1867, which replaced those of 1771, frame a deep, narrow courtyard. The brewery closed in 1976.

3 The Museum of London
4 Alban Gate
5 No 88 Wood Street
6 No 1 London Wall
7 Moor House
8 Fox umbrella shop
9 City Point
10 Helicon block
11 Britannic House

By Powell and Moya (1968–76), the **Museum of London** was crammed into a corner of the Barbican site as part of the initial completion of London Wall. This is an invaluable collection for all concerned with London's history. A reordering of the entrance by Wilkinson Eyre was completed in 2004. Fragments of the original Roman/medieval City wall remain, most notably a corner bastion visible from both within and without the museum.

London Wall was redeveloped in the 1950s and 1960s as a broad route flanked by office towers, pictured in Antonioni's *Blow-Up* (1966) as a symbol of modernity, London's response to Godard's totalitarian vision of Paris in *Alphaville* (1965) (see p.18). We are now experiencing the second generation of towers, where buildings at the western end of the street offer a short essay in the office architecture of the last years of the twentieth century: Terry Farrell's postmodern **Alban Gate** (1991), with a rather compromised arrangement of ground- and first-floor levels; Richard Rogers's **88 Wood Street** (2000), with characteristic external lifts and colourful ventilation shafts; and Foster and Partners' curvaceous glazed **No 1 London Wall** (2003). The practice has also completed the rebuilding of the 1960 **Moor House** at the Moorgate end of the street, with a distinctive curved wall to the east. Next door at 118 London Wall, E. Pollard's

W7.1 The Barbican, view east across the lake to Gilbert House, with the Barbican Centre to the north.

W7.2 Barbican Centre, door handles.

W7.3 The Barbican, Shakespeare Tower, fire escape from the thirty-sixth floor.

black vitrolite and chrome façade of 1937 for the **Fox umbrella shop** is a remarkable survival (see p. 83). **City Point**, a reclad tower (previously the British Telecom HQ) visible from the Barbican immediately west of Moorgate, was refurbished and extended by Sheppard Robson International (1997–2000), a practice which was responsible also for the speculative **Helicon block**, completed in 1996 on the east side of Moorgate.

Moorgate was cut through in the 1830s in connection with the rebuilding of London Bridge. It runs north to the boundary of the City. At the north end, Moorfields was a place of resort in the seventeenth century. Bethlem Hospital, for the mad and melancholy, was built on its south side in 1675–6: this was a visitor attraction until the late eighteenth century. Finsbury Circus, laid out in 1815 on an oval plan, is the City's only significant public green space, with a bowling green added in 1909 (see p. 153). All of the early nineteenth-century houses have gone, to be replaced by offices, of which the most notable is Sir Edwin Lutyens's

Britannic House (1921–5) at the north-west corner next to Moorgate.

12 Broadgate
13 Exchange House
A substantial development, **Broadgate** was constructed to a master-plan begun by Arup Associates after the demolition of Broad Street Station in 1985. This is a case study in finance (electronic trading following financial deregulation), urbanism and issues of public/private space. Large blocks are placed around three pedestrian squares. Arups were responsible for the south and west, Skidmore Owings and Merrill for the north and east – particularly notable is their steel-framed **Exchange House** on the north side with parabolic arches, composed of straight members, carrying the weight over the tracks from Liverpool Street Station (see p. 112). Deep, flexible floor plans fulfil the needs of contemporary financial trading; prefabricated construction ensured rapid building and quicker returns on investment. This is a generally airy and originally humane environment (although becoming much less so as the ubiquitous security increases), animated by sculpture of varying quality including Richard Serra's well-sited *Fulcrum*, strangely delicately balanced in view of the massiveness of its steel slabs (fig. W7.4); Fernando Botero's opulently built, reclining *Broadgate Venus*; and Barry Flanagan's improbable *Leaping Hare*. The view from outside the complex, however, particularly from Bishopsgate, is less sympathetic: oversized and overscaled, clad in bronzed panels and granite, this is the embodiment of the crushing insensitivity of capital.

14 Liverpool Street Station
Built in 1875 and extended in 1890–4, with the Great Eastern Hotel to the south (1880–4, extended 1899–1901). Threatened with demolition in the 1970s, the station was refurbished by

W7.4 Richard Serra, *Fulcrum*, with Broadgate Square beyond.

W7.5 Liverpool Street Station.

Nick Darbishire (1985–91), alongside the Broadgate development. This is an excellent naves and aisles train-shed (fig. W7.5) with fine ironwork detailing, rather overpowered by the clamouring commercial concourse to the south with galleries and shops – more mall than station.

W7.6 Bishopsgate Institute.

15 The Bishopsgate Institute

Built 1892–4, this is a charitable educational foundation including open-access libraries and a lecture hall, housed on a deep and irregular plot behind this narrow façade (fig. W7.6). This is one of three remarkable and idiosyncratic buildings by Charles Harrison Townsend, who also demonstrated his eclectic style (drawing on Arts and Crafts, art nouveau and the North American work of H. H. Richardson) at the Whitechapel Art Gallery, Whitechapel High Street (1898–1901), and the Horniman Museum, Forest Hill (1897–1901). At Bishopsgate the buff terracotta lent itself to extensive moulded decoration above the entrance arch. The twin turrets, also decorated, suggest a fortified gate, an impression reinforced by the large arched entrance. Above the large, central four-light window, the name of the building appears in raised lettering. There are further fronts north and east to Brushfield and Fort Streets.

16 Spitalfields Market

Founded for fruit and vegetables in 1682, rebuilt 1883–93 and expanded in 1926–9, the market closed in 1986. In reduced form, it now houses independent retailers, cafés and bars, with the area to the west colonised and redeveloped as offices and shops to the design of Foster and Partners (with an earlier block of 1999 by EPR opposite Broadgate), as the insatiable City has leaped across Bishopsgate. To the north of the market, the handsome early eighteenth-century houses of Elder Street, many of which are only one room deep, were saved from demolition and commercial redevelopment after a vigorous campaign of preservation in 1977.

17 Christ Church Spitalfields
18 London Jamme Masjid

A sublime masterpiece by Nicholas Hawksmoor (1714–29), **Christ Church** is one of twelve churches built following the passing of the 1711 Act for Building Fifty New Churches (fig. W7.7 and p.140). The original intention here was a simple box tower and lantern, but late in the design process, after the completion of the body of the church, the monumental 'Venetian window' portico, tower (with sculpturally scooped-out sides) and tapering spire were built in fulfilment of the New Church Commissioners' requirement of 'plainest manner and least expense'. The church was reopened in 2005 after a major restoration programme, begun in 1976, under the architectural direction of Red Mason.

Next to Christ Church, Hawksmoor's fine Rectory was begun in 1726 as part of the development of Church Street, now Fournier Street, which forms part of one of the best surviving groups of early Georgian housing in London. The condition of the houses in Fournier Street and the adjacent Wilkes Street and Princelet Street declined during the impoverishment of the area in the nineteenth century and put them at serious risk of demolition and redevelopment in the twentieth. However, from the later 1970s, the Spitalfields Historic Buildings Trust, together with committed owners and imaginative financing and refurbishment schemes, have secured the fabric of this extraordinary architecturally and socially rich area (see p.42). Once populated by Huguenot weavers from France, then by Jewish and now by Bangladeshi immigrants, the successive waves of immigration into the area are epitomised by the **London Jamme Masjid** (Great Mosque) at the corner of Fournier Street and Brick Lane, which is a symbol of both multicultural London and architectural adaptability (fig. W7.8). Originally a Huguenot chapel of 1743–4, it became a Methodist chapel in 1819, a synagogue in 1897 and a mosque in 1975. Brick Lane, named in acknowledgement of the nearby claypits which were used for brick and tile making, was built up from the seventeenth century, but the buildings now date predominantly from *c.*1900.

19 Truman's Brewery

Once one of the largest in London, famous for its porter (black stout), the brewery occupied a large site on both sides of Brick Lane. The first brewhouse here (*c.*1666) for the Black Eagle Brewery was followed by significant expansion for Truman's in the eighteenth and nineteenth centuries, and modernisation in the twentieth. Much of the original fabric survives, including the eighteenth-century Director's House and the nineteenth-century Head Brewer's House to the west, and nineteenth-century Vat House, Engineer's House and stables to the east. The red brick boiler-house chimney, with the company name inset, dates from 1929 (fig. W7.9). Following closure in 1988, the brewery buildings have been redeveloped for arts, media and commercial functions.

20 Boundary Street Estate

North of Bethnal Green Road, this was the largest and most important of the early London County Council housing estates, completed in 1900, with 23 five-storey walk-up blocks housing 5,000 people (fig. W7.10 and p.61). The development included a laundry, two schools, shops, workshops and, on the central mound made of rubble from the demolished Old Nichol slum, a garden and bandstand. The flats were well built with the striking Arts and Crafts styling which was more usually to be expected in middle-class developments to the west. The rents were too high to accommodate the poorest from the demolished slums, the flats being occupied by the better class workmen and artisans, but this nevertheless proved to be an influential model development. It could be again if the borough of Tower Hamlets, one of the poorest in the country, could afford to make it so. Some of the buildings have been regenerated, but others are in poor condition, occupied by those with limited choices, just a short distance from the boundary of the City of London, one of the richest boroughs in the world. The contrast is profound – a comparable contrast shocked Jack London on his investigative visit to the East End in 1902, which he published the following year as *The People of the Abyss*, documenting poverty and desperation 'in the heart of the greatest, wealthiest, and most powerful empire the world has ever seen'.

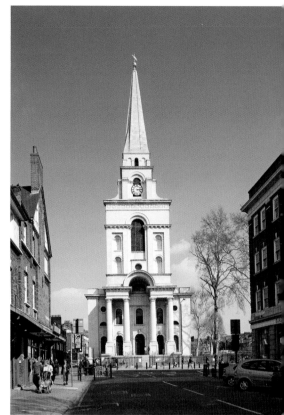

W7.7 Christ Church Spitalfields, from Brushfield Street, with Spitalfields Market to the left.

W7.8 London Jamme Masjid (Great Mosque), from Brick Lane.

W7.9 Truman's Brewery, Brick Lane, detail showing boiler-house chimney.

W7.10 Chertsey House, Boundary Street Estate.

WALK 8 ISLINGTON

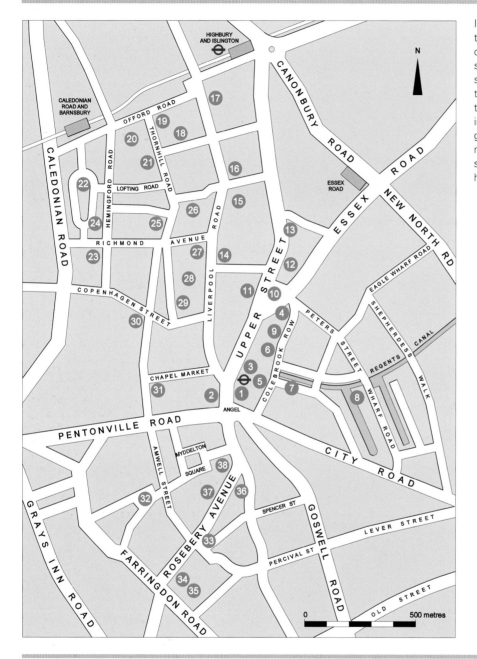

Islington developed alongside a medieval route to the north of England. This was not only a thoroughfare but also a centre for dairy farming and spas with natural spring waters. It was described in the mid-eighteenth century as an 'extensive and opulent village, and remarkable for the sweetness of the air'. Speculative building in the later eighteenth and nineteenth centuries greatly increased both population and commerce, and makes this a very good area to study the development of suburban terraced houses and squares.

1 Angel Underground Station
2 Angel Hotel
3 The Mall
4 Camden Head
5 The New River
6 The Roman Catholic Church of St John the Evangelist

Angel Underground Station was opened in 1901, reached now via an overscale block of 1987–91 designed by Rock Townsend. On the opposite (west) side of Islington High Street, on the site of an earlier galleried inn, the former **Angel Hotel**, which gives this small area its name, was built c.1880 and completed in 1899 by Eedle and Myers, who provided the distinctive, doughy dome (fig. W8.1). The adjacent stuccoed tower and cupola is all that remains of the Angel Picture Theatre, completed in 1913 by H. Courtney Constantine when Islington was a centre for entertainment. The cinema became an Odeon in 1963 and closed in 1972.

To the north of the Angel, the York public house of 1851 was rebuilt in Italianate style in 1872. Next to it, on an island site at the beginning of Upper Street, **The Mall** is a former Electric Tramway Transformer Station, designed by Vincent Harris for the LCC (1905–6), its powerful rustication inspired by George Dance's (the Younger) eighteenth-century Newgate Gaol in

W8.1 Angel Hotel, from St John Street.

W8.2 City Road Basin, Regent's Canal (the approach from the west).

the City, which was demolished in 1902. This was converted into a shopping arcade in 1979, predominantly for the antiques trade which also fills the shops (with eighteenth-century houses above) of nearby Camden Passage, the continuation of the High Street, running parallel with Upper Street. **The Camden Head** pub of 1899, with engraved interior glass, replaces an earlier one on this site. It was named after the first Earl Camden, Sir Charles Pratt (Lord Chancellor 1766–70), who was a landowner here as well as in Camden Town. Roderick Gradidge refurbished the pub in 1969.

Upper Street has a great variety of mainly nineteenth-century buildings above modern shops, with some earlier survivals of c.1700 at Nos 37–8 and 60–1. The partisan *Islington Gazette* in 1865 likened this fashionable shopping street to a Paris boulevard: 'no other street is so crowded nightly with innocent pleasure seekers, while the picturesqueness of the place is an exception to the dreariness of London'. There was, however, a low, disorderly rabble in the habit of offending the respectable before residents and shopkeepers, despairing of the feebleness of the authorities, armed themselves with sticks and gave the 'cads' a thrashing in 1870.

Duncan Terrace, east of the High Street, was developed piecemeal from the late eighteenth century. The houses originally overlooked **the New River**, whose site is now landscaped. The river was an aqueduct constructed 1609–13 to bring fresh water from Hertfordshire to the City. At the end of the terrace, **the Roman Catholic Church of St John the Evangelist**, with Romanesque façade, was built to the design of J. J. Scoles (1842–3) following the passing of the Catholic Emancipation Act in 1829. The nave and side chapels plan broadly follows the model of the Gesù in Rome; the asymmetrical twin towers were completed in 1877 by F. W. Tasker.

7 Regent's Canal

Cut by the engineer James Morgan (1812–20) to connect the Grand Junction Canal at Paddington Basin with the River Thames at Limehouse (see p.169). Almost all of the towpath can be walked apart from the Maida Hill Tunnel (near Little Venice) and the much longer 900 metres of the Islington Tunnel, which conducts the canal from King's Cross to Colebrooke Row (passing under the New River) where it can be reached via a steep path. The narrow-boats along the stretch of the canal between the tunnel and City Road Basin are officially allowed to moor for only fourteen days since, as the notice board advises, 'there are no facilities at Islington'.

8 City Road Basin
9 Charlton Place

City Road Basin is an important traffic centre for the transfer of goods from barge to road, it superseded Paddington as the main distribution point for London. Survivals here include the early nineteenth-century wharf cottage and the former Diespeker and Co. terrazzo factory of c.1908, with a tall chimney (fig. W8.2). Industrial use ceased in the 1980s: new housing and offices have followed. Originally there was a dual lock here, and the removal of one of them to accommodate a new apartment building for Grove Manor Homes has excited the wrath of canal heritage enthusiasts, who must now go to Hampstead Road (Camden) Lock for the only surviving example on the canal of working dual locks. A master-plan for the whole basin by Bennetts Associates Architects was agreed in 2004. This proposes a mixed development of new homes, leisure, business and green spaces, with public access all round and two new buildings at the southern (City) end of 'a vibrant and active waterspace'.

To return to Upper Street, leave the towpath

at Danbury Street. Noel Road, lined with three-storey terraces of c.1840–50, leads to Colebrooke Row, built on the east side of the New River. **Charlton Place**, with a crescent on the south side, named on the central plaque 'Charlton Crescent 1795', was laid out by the architect James Taylor.

10 Islington Green
11 Electric Cinema
12 Islington Chapel

A surviving patch of common land, **Islington Green** was railed in 1781. At the southern end, the statue by John Thomas of Sir Hugh Myddelton, creator of the New River, was inaugurated in 1862. To the north, the war memorial of 2006 by John Maine, a leaning ring of stone, is minimalist and rather provisional in appearance.

W8.3 Upper Street, the former Electric Cinema.

W8.4 Islington Chapel and St Mary's Church.

To the west, on Upper Street, the former **Electric Cinema**, now a shop, with small entrance dome and originally torch-bearing allegorical figure on top, was opened in 1909 by Electric Theatres Ltd, the first company to establish a chain of cinemas in London (fig. W8.3). It continued only until 1916, when competition from the much larger Angel Picture Theatre and the nearby Empress Picture Theatre (1910, then reopened in 1913) forced closure. The Empress became the Rex in 1951 and Screen on the Green in 1970. It was refurbished by Fletcher Priest in 1981.

North of Islington Green, the former **Islington Chapel** (dated 1888) is a handsome red brick corner block in Queen Anne style by H. J. Paull of Bonella and Paull, with a striking oriel window towards Upper Street (widened at this point during the same period by the Metropolitan Board of Works) (fig. W8.4). The chapel closed in 1979 and is now a recording studio.

13 St Mary's Church
14 Gibson Square
15 Milner Square
16 College Cross
17 Samuel Lewis Buildings
18 Barnsbury Park

St Mary's Church designed by Launcelot Dowbiggin (1751–4), replaced the medieval parish church. The tower and steeple survived the bombing in 1940 of the body of the originally galleried building, which was then rebuilt by Seely and Paget in 1954–6 as a plain, well-lit brick box. The original semi-circular porch was replaced in 1903 by the colonnaded porch by A. W. Blomfield that carries a relief of the Nativity.

On the opposite side of Upper Street, reached on Theberton Street, is the Milner Gibson estate, laid out by Francis Edwards from 1823, a very good example of nineteenth-century development behind the village roads made more accessible once the omnibus started running from 1828. The land was owned by the Milner Gibson family of Suffolk. The elements of design are established on the south side of **Gibson Square** in Theberton Street (1829–36), where Doric pilasters through the first and second floors mark the corners (see p. 44). Otherwise the terrace is stock brick, and each house is of two bays with rounded openings at ground floor and straightheaded windows above, although to mark the three central houses they are roundheaded at first floor. Cement render with channelling at basement and ground-floor level imitate stone facing. Gibson Square (1836–9), which extends to the north, is similar, and as a complete square was favoured by middle-class gentrifiers in the 1960s and 1970s. Within the central garden is a ventilation shaft for the Victoria Line by Raymond Erith (1968–9) in the shape of a classical pavilion.

W8.5 Milner Square, Roumieu and Gough, 1839–44.

W8.6 Thornhill House, Thornhill Road, East End Dwellings Company, 1902.

W8.7 Mountfort Crescent, 1837–47.

W8.8 Islington West Library, Thornhill Square, Beresford Pite, 1905–7.

W8.9 Stonefield Street, 1818–26.

At the top end of the square, the pattern changes in Milner Place in preparation for **Milner Square** by Roumieu and Gough (1839–44), which is unique in London house design (fig. W8.5). Here there is a very strong tripartite arrangement with rendered basement and ground floor, the first- and second-floor windows squeezed within what are in effect brick pilasters, and the attic storey of roundheaded windows and blind arches above a very heavy cornice. The height of the terraces, emphasised by the rhythm of brick pilasters to narrow windows, seems too great for the width of the square. It is surprising to find such effort in devising an original façade, despite such a peculiar effect.

Across Barnsbury Street to **College Cross**, where to the right is a Sutton Trust estate of 1926 by Henry Tanner on the site of the former Church Missionary College. Around 1827, Thomas Cubitt took five acres behind the college and built two still extant houses at right angles to the present line of the street, and also Manchester Terrace around the corner at Nos 202–66 Liverpool Road.

Further north across Islington Park Street on Liverpool Road are the **Samuel Lewis Buildings** (1909–10) (see p.62) by C. S. Joseph and Smithem. Six blocks separated by tree-lined yards are at right angle to the street. The large-scale blocks are of red brick with stone quoins and mouldings. Far from the bleak barracks of previous philanthropic housing, there is here a plethora of detail, such as canted bays (some of them topped by ogee domes) and roundheaded and pointed gables. The *Islington Gazette* in 1910 commented that the accommodation was 'very much more in character with West End structures of the sort than model buildings for the poor'.

On the west side of Liverpool Road, **Barnsbury Park** has a terrace on its south side where some effort has been made to vary the London terrace. A rhythm of two projecting and two receding houses gives some interest to these rendered façades. On the north side, No. 8 with five bays was the home of the vicar of Islington in the nineteenth century.

19 Thornhill House
20 Belitha Villas
21 Barnsbury Square
22 Thornhill Square
23 Richmond Avenue
24 Hemingford Road
25 Ripplevale Grove
26 Lonsdale Square
27 Stonefield Street
28 Holy Trinity Church
29 Cloudesley Road
30 The Barnsbury Estate
31 Chapel Market
32 Lloyd Square

Thornhill House was built by Samuel Barnett's East End Dwellings Company (1902) at the corner with Thornhill Road. The five-storey block is of red and yellow brick as are those in the East End, but most remarkable are the entrances, which have red glazed bricks at ground-floor level with a large bull's-eye over the door (fig. W8.6). The entrance bays also have a stepped gable at roof level.

Across Thornhill Road, the semi-detached houses of **Belitha Villas** of about 1845, possibly by James Wagstaffe, are unusual for Islington in having the sort of Italianate porches with Ionic columns that are found in Kensington.

Back down Thornhill Road, Nos 47–9 are worth noting as attractive, substantial houses. At the first right, **Barnsbury Square** (*c*.1834) is the centrepiece of the Bishop estate. At the west end is Mountfort House, a rendered five-bay façade, with shells over the arches at first floor and large brackets under the eaves. At the north-west corner of the square is Mountfort Crescent (1837–47), an attractive group of rendered semi-detached houses with two-storey rounded bays (fig. W8.7). On the other side of the square in the south-west corner is the short, Italianate Mountfort Terrace, faced by the double-

storey bay of the opposite villa.

From Barnsbury Square, Barnsbury Terrace leads into Lofting Road. To the right and across Hemingford Road is **Thornhill Square**, laid out by the estate surveyor, Joseph Kay, for the Thornhill family and built during the 1840s and 1850s. Thornhill Crescent at the top of the square is of 1846–52, with the rest of the square begun a year later in 1847. It has its own church, St Andrew (1852–4) by Francis B. Newman and John Johnson, with a sturdy tower and broach spire. Across from the church in Bridgeman Road is West Library (1905–7), a surprising Byzantine striped pink and yellow brick building by Beresford Pite (fig. W8.8).

At the bottom of Thornhill Square in **Richmond Avenue** are the earlier houses of the Thornhill estate, for example Nos 76–86 of 1829, and houses further east around Hemingford Road of the 1840s. Across Hemingford Road there are Egyptian sphinxes and mini-obelisks at the front of the houses.

North on **Hemingford Road**, on the west side, are stock brick linked villas of the 1840s with pediments over the shared gables. On the east side are similar houses which are rendered and whose entrances are not recessed. The first right is **Ripplevale Grove**, with ranges of cottages of 1839–41 running up the hill. At the top are some detached, double-fronted cottages which are particularly attractive.

At the top of Ripplevale Grove a left turn and a sharp right leads into Barnsbury Street. Bracketed between the houses in the north side terrace is the Drapers' Arms, part of the Drapers' Company estate of 1838–45, laid out by the estate's surveyor, Richard Carpenter. His son, the neo-Gothic architect R. C. Carpenter, was responsible for **Lonsdale Square** and its unusual Tudor façades (see p.57). Although of light stock bricks, the details such as pointed gables, hoods over the windows, and Tudor arched entrances all refer to English precedents.

At the bottom of Lonsdale Square and across Richmond Avenue is the Stonefield or

W8.10 Lloyd Square, W. J. Booth, 1833.

Cloudesley estate from 1812. On the west side of **Stonefield Street**, a street of generous width, double houses are linked to their neighbours with recessed entrances (fig. W8.9). **Holy Trinity Church** of 1826–9 in the middle of Cloudesley Square is by Charles Barry, and is one of three churches that he designed for Islington (see p.144). In the west exit from the square is Stonefield Mansions of 1903–4, designed for the local builders, Dove Brothers, by Horace Porter. **Cloudesley Road** is another wide street with former shops at the north end and early terraces in the rest of the street. On the east side are front gardens, and on the west a smaller concave terrace follows the street line. At the bottom of Cloudesley Road a sharp right into Copenhagen Street leads to Barnsbury Road. On the south-west corner is the **Barnsbury estate**, an LCC slum clearance estate of the 1930s (see p.68).

To the east of Penton Street, the southern continuation of Barnsbury Road, **Chapel Market** is a traditional London street market still in operation. Across Pentonville Road, a short detour to the west of Amwell Street leads to **Lloyd Square** (1833), part of the Lloyd Baker estate, planned from 1818 and built from 1825. The wide-fronted double houses are surmounted by a broad, low pediment, and the cumulative effect is an elegant urbanity (fig. W8.10). The large 'Queen Anne' building at the east side of the square is the former convent for the Society of the Sisters of Bethany (1882–4) by Ernest Newton.

33 Finsbury Town Hall
34 The Holy Redeemer
35 The Finsbury Health Centre
36 The Spa Green Estate
37 Laboratory Building

Finsbury Town Hall is on Rosebery Avenue, opposite Amwell Street, built as Clerkenwell Vestry Hall (1894–5 and 1899–1900) by Charles Evans Vaughan in a Flemish Renaissance style (fig. W8.11). Of red brick with elaborate stone dressings, the front is enlivened by a glass and iron street canopy, the rear by a fine curved corner with female figures and a carved frieze. There is a richly decorated public hall on the first floor. Local government use has been followed by conversion to dance studios.

Behind the former town hall, Baynes Row was renamed Exmouth Market in 1939 when a market was established there. Only a few stalls remain and the street, once full of second-hand bookshops, now has a number of fashionable restaurants and shops. Towards the south-west end, **The Holy Redeemer**, built in brick on a steel frame to the design of J. D. Sedding (1887–8), was completed in 1892–5 by H. Wilson, who later added the campanile, clergy house and church hall. This is a most unusual Victorian Anglican church in being an Italian Renaissance design rather than fashionably Gothic. The particularly striking high altar, under a domed *baldacchino*, is inspired by Santo Spirito, Florence.

Round the corner on Pine Street, **The Finsbury Health Centre** of 1935–8 by Lubetkin and Tecton was the first achievement of the 'Finsbury Plan', which was devoted to the betterment of living conditions in the overcrowded borough. A reception and waiting area with a curved glass-block wall has a lecture theatre behind, with consulting and treatment rooms in flanking, splayed wings. This is one of the key Modern Movement buildings in England: visionary architecture bringing light, air and optimism within a rational design in fulfilment of a social agenda. Repaired by Avanti Architects in 1994–5, it is now in need of another facelift.

Rosebery Avenue was built up in the 1890s. To the north **The Spa Green Estate** was designed before the Second World War by Lubetkin and Tecton for Finsbury Borough Council but was not built until 1946–50, on a slum clearance site near former eighteenth-century pleasure gardens. This was the most innovative public housing of the time: concrete

W8.11 Finsbury Town Hall, Rosebery Avenue.

W8.12 Spa Green, centre of façade of block facing Rosebery Avenue.

W8.13 Laboratory Building, Metropolitan Water Board, Rosebery Avenue.

W8.14 Sadlers Wells Theatre, Rosebery Avenue.

construction, aerofoil roof canopies to channel the wind to clothes-drying areas, bedrooms facing inwards, balcony overlooked by the kitchen and accessible from the living room, stainless steel sinks, ventilated larders, heated linen cupboards, and the first Garchey refuse disposal system in London, taking rubbish directly from the flat to the incinerator. The accommodation is arranged in three blocks, two of eight storeys and one of four, with flats ranging from one to four bedrooms (fig. W8.12 and p.70). The development has proved to be durable as well as attractive, nicely variegated in rhythm, texture and colour. It was refurbished by Peter Bell and Partners in 1978–80. In the adjacent public garden, the war memorial of 1921 carries the powerful bronze winged Victory by Thomas Rudge on a granite base. A bronze plaque shows the Finsbury Rifles attacking Gaza in 1917. Two other plaques have been lost and replaced by inscription panels.

Some early buildings, and ponds which survive as open spaces, remain from the termination of the New River. The modern buildings of the Metropolitan Water Board which are visible from Rosebery Avenue, most notably the fine **Laboratory Building** of 1938 by Easton and Robertson, with a semi-circular straircase projection (fig. W8.13), were converted into flats in 1997–8.

38 Sadlers Wells Theatre

The theatre traces its history back to Thomas Sadler's 'musick house' of 1683, next to the medicinal well. It was rebuilt on its wedge-shaped site by RHWL and Nicholas Hare Associates (1997–8) with National Lottery funding (fig. W8.14). Used principally for dance, this is a spatially uncompromising building of admirable simplicity and clarity. A large auditorium with adequate legroom, seating 1,500, is framed by plain brick walls; orientation is easy – the bar and staircase flank the large entrance hall; there are sufficient women's lavatories. It all seems so obvious.

At the north end of Rosebery Avenue and round the corner on St John Street leading back to the Angel are good rows of nineteenth-century brick and stucco terraced houses, with some rebuilding, and a good, tiled butcher's at the end of a row of small shops.

WALK 9 KENSINGTON AND CHELSEA

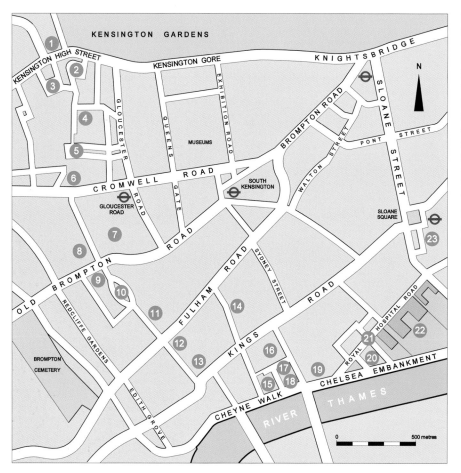

Kensington and Chelsea remained working suburbs of London until far into the nineteenth century. Once the Metropolitan and District Railway (1864–9) penetrated into the area, however, more and more landowners sought to increase their profits by granting building leases in what became one of the most desirable residential areas of London. By traversing the Royal Borough, a good overview can be gained of how nineteenth-century residential London came about, but in addition there are here many important examples of the London house from the late seventeenth to the nineteenth centuries. This is a long walk, although it is possible to interrupt it at any of the main roads crossed, such as Cromwell and Fulham Roads, and to resume the walk at a later date.

1 Palace Green

Forms the south end of Kensington Palace Gardens, and was laid out in 1843 by the Crown Commissioners on the site of the former kitchen gardens of Kensington Palace. No. 2 Palace Green (1860–1) was built by the novelist W. M. Thackeray in a style reminiscent of his preferred historical period somewhere around 1700. In contrast to the Italianate aspect of many of the neighbouring mansions, Thackeray's house is red brick, and brick forms the decorative detail such as keystones over and aprons under the windows. The Crown Commissioners accepted this distinctive treatment because it chimed with the architecture of Christopher Wren's Kensington Palace nearby. They were not so happy with Philip Webb's No. 1 next door, which he designed for George Howard in 1868. Again red brick predominates with fine brick mouldings, but they insisted that Webb include more stone details, which he did under protest. The tall narrow sash windows look forward to the emerging 'Queen Anne' style, and the size and location of the house ensured its subsequent influence.

W9.1 No 2 Kensington Court, T. G. Jackson, 1883–4.

W9.2 No 17 Kensington Square, Thomas Young, 1685–90.

2 Kensington Court

Albert Grant bought old properties facing Kensington Road, and built from 1873 to 1875 a very grand house designed by James Knowles Junior. Financial difficulties prevented Grant from ever living there, and his creditors, the Land Securities Company, took possession. In 1882 they made an agreement with Jonathan T. Carr, the developer of Bedford Park (1874–81), and after demolition of the big house, work began on Kensington Court, a residential enclave of middle-class houses and flats. Carr engaged J. J. Stevenson, who had designed the Red House in Bayswater in the increasingly popular 'Queen Anne' style. The site is triangular, built around the periphery, with two central island sites. Stevenson began his houses – Nos 3–25 on the east side – in 1883 and chose red brick and buff terracotta for his materials. The street façades give the impression of a relaxed informality; however, on closer inspection a repetitive pattern emerges of projecting bays with stepped gables, and various window treatments. Decorative details are in a playful Renaissance style. No. 2, at the top end, more elaborate but still in keeping, is by T. G. Jackson for Athelstan Riley (fig. W9.1). On the west side of the estate are a number of blocks of red brick flats, such as No. 34, Kent House by R. J. Worley (1896–7), and Roxburghe Mansions at No. 32 by Paul Hoffmann of the same date (see p. 64). A novel amenity in the houses were hydraulic lifts supplied with their power from a station in the south-east corner next to the stables, and in addition from January 1887 electricity was generated from a station in the north-west corner.

3 Kensington Square

At the bottom of Kensington Court a right turn leads into Thackeray Street and thus to Kensington Square, a seventeenth-century development built in what at the time would have been an unlikely location for such an urbane type of housing if Kensington Palace had not appeared nearby in the 1690s. Thomas Young, a joiner and wood-carver, acquired the fourteen-acre site in 1682 and began building houses in 1685. By 1736–7 the square was complete, and while some houses have been replaced and others have been refaced, the effect is still harmonious. Nos 44 and 45 date from 1685, and No. 17 was built by Thomas Young for himself in 1685–90 (fig. W9.2). Nos 11 and 12 are from a little later around 1700, and although not strictly part of Young's square, they are typical of contemporary house design: for example, the hipped roof with dormers, modillioned eaves cornice and shell-shaped hoods over the front doors. The building now occupying Nos 20–4 is the former Convent of the Assumption, designed from 1868 by George Goldie, the architect of numerous Roman Catholic buildings.

4 The Vallotton estate

Back into Thackeray Road and then south down Kensington Court Place to Stanford Road and the beginning of the Vallotton estate. Gradually over time from 1794 the family acquired land in the immediate vicinity, but full-scale development waited until the 1840s. Sewerage plans were submitted in 1842 and 1852 with the help of George Godwin, but design of the houses was in the hands of a variety of small builders.

Eldon Road provides a good example with a homogeneous group of 1851 by Henry Holland on the south side, where cement render allows play with quoining and a balustraded balcony over the canted bay (fig. W9.3). On the north side of the street, of 1852 by David Howell, the houses are less uniform.

5 Cornwall Gardens

Stanford Road was intended to continue south, but the Metropolitan and District Railway disrupted plans, so that the south end of the road is linked to Cornwall Gardens by a footpath. Cornwall Gardens was developed from 1862 to 1879, and is a good example of an estate colonised by the influential rich, many with imperial connections (see p. 44). The Broadwood family engaged Thomas Cundy III as their agent to lay out the estate in 1862–79. The north side of Cornwall Gardens was started in the same year by builders Welchman and Gale, with houses in a five-storey terrace plus basement and attic. The front porches are marked by three Ionic columns, while the rendered façades are given character with much detailing such as window pediments and quoining. On entering Cornwall Gardens from the footpath, the first houses across the road are of a later date, 1877–9, on land made available after the completion of the railway. Cornwall Mansions (fig. W9.4), No. 1 Garden House and No. 2 Cornwall House were designed by James Trant Smith and built by William Willett; with their steep mansard roofs and dramatic rounded bays to the communal gardens, they give a Second Empire character to their end of the estate. They are finished in fine white bricks, and the elaborate details are Portland stone.

6   Lexham Gardens
7   Harrington Gardens
8   Collingham Gardens
9   Bousfield Primary School
10 The Boltons
11 Harley Gardens
12 Park Walk
13 Chelsea Park Gardens
14 Nos 64 and 66 Old Church Street
15 Peabody Estate
16 Glebe Place
17 Cheyne Row
18 Nos 38–9 Cheyne Walk
19 Cheyne Walk

Exit from Cornwall Gardens is made from the south-west corner via Cornwall Gardens Walk and Lexham Walk. By carrying south along **Lexham Gardens** (fig. W9.5), some impression is gained of the Edwardes estate. At the beginning of the nineteenth century William Edwardes, first Baron Kensington, owned 250 acres, the largest parcel of land in the area. Development was begun in the west of the estate in Edwardes

W9.3 Eldon Road, Vallotton estate, Henry Holland, 1851.

W9.4 Cornwall Mansions, James Trant Smith, 1877–9.

W9.5 Lexham Gardens, from the 1870s.

W9.6 The Boltons, George Godwin the Younger, 1849–60.

W9.7 Harrington Gardens, detail, Ernest George and Peto, 1880–4.

Square in 1811, and continued in phases until the end of the century. The area around Lexham Gardens remained in agricultural use until the 1860s and the arrival of the railway. The houses along the eastern arm of Lexham Gardens date from the mid-1870s, and are typically large Kensington houses, in buff brick with generous cement detailing, such as the Doric columns supporting the porches and the balustraded balcony.

Across Cromwell Road and into Collingham Road, after St Jude's Church on the left, it is worth taking a detour east into **Harrington Gardens** to inspect Nos 20–6 on the north side, and Nos 35–45 on the south side (fig. W9.7).

These are very distinctive in the history of the London town house in introducing a Germanic element into the tall, rich brick manner of the 1870s. Ernest George and Peto designed these houses from 1880 to 1884, partly as speculation on the Alexander estate and partly as individual houses for named clients, such as W. S. Gilbert of Gilbert and Sullivan at No. 39. The exuberance of materials, the width of the broad fronts and the strangeness of the dominating gables all make for a novel experience.

Back west, **Collingham Gardens** was an attempt to repeat the success with two rows of smaller but similar houses of 1883–8, backing onto a communal garden (see p.47). These houses were built on the adjacent Gunter estate, but took a long time to fill.

Continuing south on Bolton Gardens towards Old Brompton Road is more of the Gunter estate, acquired together with land further south over an extended period from around 1800 until the 1860s. Bolton Gardens dates from 1865, and was built by John Spicer, a builder already engaged on the estate further south.

Across Old Brompton Road is The Boltons, but before carrying on, note should be made of **Bousfield Primary School** (1954–6) by Chamberlin Powell and Bon for the LCC. This is one of a new breed of post-war school for which the siting and landscaping of the building was part of an enlightened educational agenda. Colourful curtain walling is reminiscent of the same architects' Golden Lane Estate north of the Barbican on the edge of the City. The Boltons were laid out in 1849–50 by George Godwin the Younger, and building continued from 1851 to 1860 (fig. W9.6). The centrepiece is the two elongated crescents, the east built by Atkinson and Tidey (1851–2) and the west by Spicer (1857–60). The houses are large semi-detached

villas with very generous gardens, and they are distinguished by the elaborate rendered façades which contrast sharply with the stock brick flanks of the houses. A large balustraded wall between the front gardens and the street contributes to the homogeneity of the area. In Gilston Road houses on the east side are bracketed by two picturesque Italianate villas with belvedere towers (fig. W9.8). Behind in **Harley Gardens** are an attractive group of smaller semi-detached and terraced houses.

Across Fulham Road is Chelsea, less wealthy than Kensington in the nineteenth century and more heterogeneous. At the top of **Park Walk** on the Sloane-Stanley estate, there are plain stock brick cottages on the east side and later red brick flats on the west side. Further down is St Andrew's by Blomfield and then **Chelsea Park Gardens**, a domestic enclave laid out in 1913, but built 1923–8 by E. F. M. Elms and Sydney Jupp. Back to Elm Park Road on the way to Old Church Street, and a bewildering array of different house styles of differing dates bears witness to a hesitant building history. In Old Church Street, again a heterogeneous group, made even more so by **Nos 64 and 66 Old Church Street** (fig. W9.9). These are two modernist houses: No. 64 of 1935–6 is by Erich Mendelsohn and Serge Chermayeff, the architects of the De La Warr Pavilion at Bexhill, for their client Denis Cohen. A long, low elevation to the street screens the main living rooms on the garden side. This has survived better than No. 66 next door, where Walter Gropius and Maxwell Fry designed another modernist house for Benn Levy of the same date. This house is at right angles to the street, and much of the exterior wall has been faced with slate. Still, the composition of the two houses makes an urbane contrast with the surrounding domestic eclecticism.

W9.8 Gilston Road, George Godwin the Younger, 1850–2.   W9.9 No 64 Old Church Street, Erich Mendelsohn and Serge Chermayeff, 1935–6.

Across Kings Road, Old Church Street continues and further down on the left is Justice Walk, which leads into Lawrence Street. To the right is the familiar form of a **Peabody Estate** (see p.60), witness to the social mix of Chelsea in the nineteenth century, and to the left modest but attractive cottages. From there into **Glebe Place** (see p.47), where No. 35 was designed as a studio house for George Boyce by Philip Webb in 1868. The projecting entrance to the street dominates the façade, but behind can be seen Webb playing with differing width of windows in the red brick wall. An addition on the garden side dates from 1876.

Back down **Cheyne Row** (see p.39), where the Most Holy Redeemer Catholic Church by G. Goldie, of 1895 in an Italian Renaissance style, is followed by a row of houses dating from 1708, some with original details, including at No. 32 a door hood on carved brackets. No. 24 was the house of Thomas Carlyle and can be visited.

Around the corner, **Nos 38–9 Cheyne Walk** are the remnants of three houses by the Arts and Crafts architect C. R. Ashbee. The façades are handled individually using red brick and roughcast, and display a clever abstraction of window arrangement.

Across Oakley Street, **Cheyne Walk** continues with terraces of 1717–20 behind front gardens displaying some very pleasing details such as handsome iron gates and canopied balconies, along with some good door-cases (No. 4). The most celebrated house is No. 16 where Rossetti lived from 1862. Nos 7–11 are 'Queen Anne' interlopers of the 1880s.

20 Chelsea Embankment
The embankment of the Thames at Chelsea Reach was completed in 1874, when the Metropolitan Board of Works released eighteen building plots, which were taken for the most

part by individual clients who turned to fashionable architects such as Norman Shaw. These are handsome houses in red and sometimes yellow brick with red brick details. Two important Shaw houses are, first, No. 17, Swan House (1875–7) (see p.47), with a reticent ground floor and entrance, and then an exuberant jettied first floor with three big Ipswich windows and oriels at second-floor level. No. 8 further along Chelsea Embankment is Shaw's Clock House of 1878–80 with a complicated and rich façade. Again there is a reticent ground floor, but on the first floor a large central arch is flanked by two large windows opening onto a railed balcony, and at second floor there are three projecting Ipswich windows.

21 Tite Street
22 Royal (Chelsea) Hospital
23 Sloane Gardens
Laid out in 1877 as access to Chelsea Embankment, **Tite Street** attracted artists. Nos 28–42 on the west side formed a terrace of speculative houses (1878–80). No. 34 was Oscar Wilde's house. Further south Nos 44 and 46 were by E. W. Godwin, and both betray his originality. No. 46, the Tower House (1884), is especially striking, with the large studio windows in contrast to the adjacent small windows on the immensely tall façade. Across the street, Nos 31 and 33 are by R. W. Edis, No. 31 for the American artist John Singer Sargent (1878–9) (see p.48). These houses are distinguished by the use of contrasting red and yellow brick, and their relaxed 'aesthetic' composition. Further down the street, No. 35 is on the site of Godwin's 1877 house for Whistler, demolished in the 1960s. This was replaced by a simple white boxy house, which in its turn was demolished and replaced in the early 1990s with an eighteenth-century pastiche. Next door is an inter-

esting comment on Chelsea red brick houses by Tony Fretton in red sandstone (fig. W9.10).

The route to Sloane Square passes Wren's **Royal (Chelsea) Hospital**, built 1682–91 for the accommodation of veterans of the army, a function which the building continues to fulfil (see p.121). In the hospital chapel, to the east of the central vestibule is a fine *Resurrection* of c.1710–15, by Sebastiano Ricci. Beyond the Royal Hospital, from Lower Sloane Street, a slight detour into **Sloane Gardens** (1887) returns to the large red brick houses of Kensington Court, but now with very coarse details. These were part of the Cadogan estate, better represented by the Dutch gables of Cadogan Square and Pont Street to the north-west of Sloane Square. In the square itself the department store Peter Jones (1932–9) is one of the first and most elegant curtain wall buildings in the country (see p.86). It was designed by J. A. Slater, A. H. Moberly and William Crabtree, with C. H. Reilly.

W9.10 Red House, 37 Tite Street, Tony Fretton, 2001.

WALK 10 HAMPSTEAD

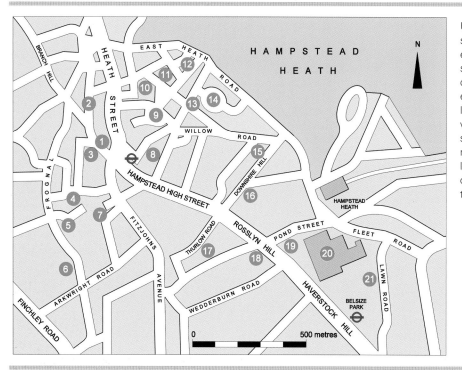

Until the end of the nineteenth century Hampstead retained its autonomy as a village on the edge of London. The atmosphere of the village still clings to the older streets, while in widening concentric circles around the core are important examples of middle-class houses of the mid- to late nineteenth century. For convenience the walk is divided into two – the west and east sides of the High Street – but this division also reflects a difference in character between the larger houses of the west side and the numerous cottages for a poorer population in nineteenth-century Hampstead on the east side.

WEST SIDE OF THE HIGH STREET

1 Holly Hill

The central intersection formed by Heath Street, High Street and Holly Hill was created in 1886–8. **Holly Hill** leads up to an area of large seventeenth- and eighteenth-century houses along with smaller houses in the twisting streets above Heath Street. At the top of the hill on the right is Romney's House (1797–8), built for the painter George Romney as a picture gallery. The weatherboard house was enlarged in 1807 to serve as Hampstead Assembly Rooms, and it was altered in 1929–30 by the architect Clough Williams Ellis as his own London house.

2 Fenton House

Across the little green at Hollybush Hill is **Fenton House** of 1693 (fig. W10.1). This is a double pile of brown brick with fine red bricks around the openings and at the corners as quoining. There is a pedimented Doric door-case to the south elevation, but the entrance is around the corner

W10.1 Fenton House, 1693.

W10.2 No 12 Church Row, early eighteenth century.

W10.3 St Mary's Roman Catholic Church, Holly Place, 1816.

in Hampstead Grove. The house contains a collection of musical instruments and as a National Trust property can be visited. Next to Fenton House on the green are three eighteenth- century houses – Windmill House, Bolton House and Volta House – all set back behind long front gardens and making an attractive composition. Overpowering the green on the west side is Mount Vernon, a former consumption hospital in French château style of 1880 by T. Roger Smith, converted to flats in 1997 by IKA Architects.

3 Mount Vernon to Holly Walk

On the right is eighteenth-century Mount Vernon House and on the left a nineteenth-century terrace, where Robert Louis Stevenson lived in No 7. Down Holly Walk and first on the left at No. 9 is the Watch House, built for the Hampstead Police around 1830. Then the pretty St Mary's Roman Catholic Church (1816) (fig. W10.3), built by the French émigré Abbé J. J. Morel and set within a terrace of around the same date. Further down, Benham and Prospect Place (1813) are at right angles to the walk, two terraces of small houses only one room deep. These houses look out over the green expanse of St John's churchyard extension of 1812 with its profusion of old headstones.

4 Church Row
5 Frognal Way
6 No. 39 Frognal
7 No. 6 Ellerdale Road

Church Row (see p. 42) was developed by Richard Hughes from 1713 to 1730 as accommodation for the fashionable, who were attracted to Hampstead during the summer months when the City became hot and unpleasant. The wide street led from the High Street via Perrins Court to St John's Church (1745–7) by John Sanderson (see p. 142). The two terraces provide fine examples of early eighteenth-century town houses of three storeys plus basement. Brown brick with red dressings around the openings is usual, although No. 5 has a weatherboard upper storey of a later date. Many doors have door hoods with carved brackets, and No. 12 has red brick Doric pilasters from the first floor on either side of the three-bay façade (fig. W10.2).

The church has been altered significantly from its original form, but now its modest brick exterior belies a very attractive interior arrangement and decoration. In 1843 R. Hesketh provided a western extension, while in 1877–8 F. P. Cockerell made improvements, including the re-orientation of the altar from the east end to the west, where it remains. The decoration of the chancel was designed by T. G. Jackson in 1883, and the choir vestry by Temple Moore dates from 1911–12. The setting within the old churchyard provides a suitable culmination to Church Row.

At the south-west corner of Church Row is **Frognal Way**, from which can be seen the rear of the houses in the Row and the various extensions which have been added to take advantage of the view, as the land falls away quite sharply here. No. 20 was built by Gracie Fields for herself in a vaguely Mediterranean style, but more importantly towards the bottom on the right is Sun House by Maxwell Fry of 1934–5 (see p. 55). The house has a nicely balanced façade of voids and white solids, with a flat roof and nautical railings around the balconies. Further down on the right and facing the main road is No. 66 Frognal (1937) by Connell, Ward and Lucas (fig. W10.4). The young architects took great pleasure in disturbing the neighbours with their modernist design, which included pilotis at ground level, nautical railings to the balconies at the rear, an abstract arrangement of windows and wall to the street, and of course a flat roof. The planter on the side of the house was a concession to local sentiment.

Many of the houses in the neighbourhood are substantial red brick suburban houses of the 1880s. **No. 39 Frognal** is Norman Shaw's house for the children's book illustrator Kate Greenaway

W10.4 No 66 Frognal, Connell, Ward and Lucas, 1937.

W10.5 No 6 Ellerdale Road, R. Norman Shaw, 1874–6.

W10.6 New End Hospital, H. E. Kendall, 1849, converted by Berkeley Homes, 1996–7.

W10.7 House in Well Walk, c.1880.

W10.8 Gainsborough Gardens, from 1884.

(1884–5). It is perhaps more conventional than expected, but does combine the red brick, tile hanging and white woodwork associated with Shaw's suburban work.

The Greenhill estate, Arkwright Road, was developed by George Henry Errington from 1871. T. K. Green was responsible for many of the houses, for example No. 13 Arkwright Road (1878) in a hybrid Gothic-Queen Anne style, and Gothic fantasies in Ellerdale Road. **No. 6 Ellerdale Road** is Norman Shaw's own house of 1874–6, which stands out among the other suburban villas (fig. W10.5). The tall façade reflects Shaw's free-style planning with the different levels expressed in the arrangement of the windows. On the left side a three-storey canted bay includes the double-height window to the dining room. A long staircase window divides the left side from the right, which is enlivened by an oriel of Ipswich windows with pargetting. Despite the details and variety of materials, the façade avoids fussiness.

EAST SIDE OF THE HIGH STREET
8 Flask Walk

This is flanked by early nineteenth-century cottages, and then at the bottom of the street is the detached Gardnor House of 1736. Further on facing Well Walk is Burgh House (1703), which is set back but presents a fine front to the garden, laid out by Gertrude Jekyll, innovative garden designer and collaborator of Lutyens.

9 New End Square
10 Christ Church

New End Square runs up beside Burgh House; a turn to the left on Streatley Place gives a glimpse of the very large baroque-style New End Primary School (1905–6) by T. J. Bailey for 612 children (see p.95). Back into New End Square and up to the left is the façade of the former workhouse and later New End Hospital (fig. W10.6) by H. E. Kendall (1849), now incorporated into new houses by Berkeley Homes (1996–7). This has a very grand broken pediment over the front entrance with two symmetrical wings to either side.

Christchurch Passage across the street leads past Christ Church School (1854–5) by W. and E. Habershon in grey brick Gothic. On the other side of the passage is **Christ Church** (1851–2) by S. W. Daukes, whose slim spire adds to the picturesque character of the neighbourhood. In front of the church is Hampstead Square, an informal group of eighteenth-century houses around a widening in the road rather than a square.

11 Cannon Place
12 The Logs (Lion House)
13 Well Walk

Cannon Place runs from Hampstead Square east in front of Christ Church. On the north side are some 'Queen Anne' houses of 1879, and then big blond brick semi-detached houses with red bricks over the openings. On the south side is No. 10, an Arts and Crafts vicarage of around 1900, and then Cannon Hall, a substantial eighteenth-century house with a stable block at right angles to the road, the childhood home of the novelist Daphne du Maurier. Even larger is Squire's Mount of 1714 (with later additions) at the end and across the road.

Cannon Lane runs downhill to Well Road, where a left turn leads to the corner with East Heath and **The Logs (Lion House)** (1867–8) (see p.48) by J. S. Nightingale for Edward Gotto, an engineer and developer. This is a phantasmagoria of turrets and bays enclosed within a wonderfully overgrown garden. Next door in complete contrast is a new house of cantilevered concrete and glass.

Back to Christ Church Hill and then left into **Well Walk**. The Wells Tavern is a pleasant four-square early nineteenth-century building, and on the same side are some Georgian houses, including No. 40, which was Constable's main residence, and No. 46, originally adjoining the Pump and Long Rooms associated with the spa. It is distinguished by a very nice gothick oriel. Across the road are some houses of c.1880 (fig. W10.7), in one of which, No. 13, lived Henry Hyndman, the socialist leader who died here in 1921.

14 Gainsborough Gardens
15 Nos 1 to 3 Willow Road

A private enclave begun in 1884, **Gainsborough Gardens** opens to the south of Well Walk (fig. W10.8). The houses are arranged around a central garden, the best examples along the west side. The houses are in the aesthetic fashion of the time and are by architects such as E. J. May, H. S. Legg and Horace Field, all experienced practitioners in the red brick style of house design.

At the bottom of Gainsborough Gardens a gate gives access to Heath Side and thus to East Heath Road. A right turn into East Heath Road leads to Downshire Hill and a sharp right here into Willow Road. **Nos 1 to 3 Willow Road**

W10.9 Nos 1–3 Willow Road, Erno Goldfinger, 1937–9.

(1937–9) are Erno Goldfinger's contribution to the form of the London terraced house (fig. W10.9). Unlike Fry's Sun House, Goldfinger used brick facing on his reinforced concrete structure, although he allowed the concrete as a frame around the windows at first-floor level. The structure allowed a flexible plan within, and since the National Trust has now acquired No. 2, it is possible to inspect the interior arrangement of this, Goldfinger's own house.

16 Downshire Hill
17 Rosslyn Park estate
18 Congregational Church
19 St Stephen's
20 Royal Free Hospital
21 Isokon Flats

Downshire Hill is a long straight street of early nineteenth-century semi-detached villas and cottages with lush front gardens. Along with Keats Grove it was developed from 1812 by William Coleman, with the attractive St John's Church added between 1818 and 1823. On the south side of Downshire Hill and hardly noticeable in its subtlety is No. 49a by Michael and Patty Hopkins for themselves: a steel and glass box of some size, but sunk below the road to which it is connected by a bridge at first-floor level.

At the top of Downshire Hill and across Rosslyn Hill is the **Rosslyn Park estate**, developed on land owned by the Dean and Chapter of Westminster from 1853 by Henry Davidson. Progress was slow, as can be seen by the variety of house styles, representing nearly fifty years of house design. In Thurlow Road on the north side are houses of grey brick with sub-stantial cement classical details such as the Doric porches. On the south side the houses are larger and more Gothic in inspiration. In Lyndhurst Terrace this inspiration spirals out of control with Gothic houses of the 1860s, for example Nos 1 and 3 by Alfred Bell of 1864–5. Lyndhurst Road is more mixed in its house styles, revealing an extended building period. At the corner with Rosslyn Hill and Lyndhurst Road is the former **Congregational Church** and Hall (1883–4) by Alfred Waterhouse. This is a large composition, made more striking by the prolific use of pale purple brick and red terracotta. Waterhouse's church has found a new use as concert hall and recording studio, but back across Rosslyn Hill **St Stephen's** (1869–73) by S. S. Teulon has not been so lucky. This is a large assured church by one of the nineteenth-century's more eccentric but able architects, and with its prominent tower, turrets and high west gable is an important landmark on this busy road. It was made redundant in 1977 and is still waiting for a new use.

An additional detour may be made to see the Lawn Road flats by Wells Coates (1934). By going down Pond Street to South End, the **Royal Free Hospital** (1968–75) by Warkins Gray Woodgate International is on the right. This hospital has a venerable history, having started in Hatton Gardens in 1828 and then in Gray's Inn Road from 1840. Now it takes up a significant site in this part of South Hampstead. From South End, Fleet Road leads off to the right and then it is right again into Lawn Road. Halfway up on the right are the **Isokon Flats** (fig. W10.10 and p. 66), commissioned by Jack Pritchard and his wife to provide minimal accommodation for

W10.10 Isokon Flats, Lawn Road, Wells Coates, 1934.

young professionals in London. The four floors of small flats with balcony access are sculpturally spare but impressive. Wells Coates believed in living with few possessions, and the fitted furniture he included in the flats was meant to keep possessions to the minimum. The flats have recently been restored by Avanti for Camden Council for key workers.

WALK 11 EAST END

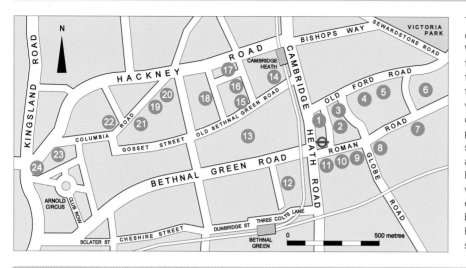

The East End of London was the location of industry and immigration up to the Second World War. From the end of the nineteenth century, efforts were undertaken to improve the lives of the workers, whether through philanthropy or through the efforts of local government, and it is very often the housing erected by these agencies that remains from that period. Similarly, public buildings of an improving nature such as schools, public libraries and churches remain as a testimony to the urge for civic improvement. Not much survives of the industrial East End, which was heavily bombed during the war, but efforts continued to improve lives through rebuilding the physical fabric of the area, which has become a repository of every description of style in the public provision of housing.

1 Museum of Childhood
On Cambridge Heath Road, by James Wild (1868–72) (fig. W11.1). This was a re-erection of the iron structure of the first, temporary museum building at South Kensington of 1855–6, the 'Brompton Boilers'. The idea was to improve the people of the East End by introducing them to art, and when it first opened the museum contained what is now the Wallace Collection in Manchester Square. Then, from 1885 to 1894, it housed the National Portrait Gallery while new premises were being built behind Trafalgar Square. Since 1974 it has been the Museum of Childhood. The iron structure was incorporated into a substantial red brick building of three large bays to the street and thirteen along its flank to the Green. This elevation is enlivened by sgraffito panels above the first-floor windows depicting occupations such as agricultural activities. Within, the iron frame is evident and divides the space into three: a central nave and two galleried spaces to the sides. The new entrance was designed by Caruso St John.

2 Victoria Park Square
3 Victoria Park Estate
4 Cyprus Street Estate
5 Cyprus Street

6 Cranbrook Estate
7 Globe Town Market
8 Butler and Digby Estates
9 Sutton Dwellings
10 Bethnal Green Estate
11 Public Library
12 Corfield Street
13 Canrobert Street
14 Minerva Estate
15 Old Bethnal Green Road
16 Keeling House
17 Claredale House
18 St Peter's Square
19 Jesus Hospital Estate
20 Guinness Trust
21 Columbia Road
22 Dorset Estate

In **Victoria Park Square**, facing the end of Museum Passage, is Montfort House for Samuel Barnett's East End Dwellings Company (1901) by Davis and Emmanuel (fig. W11.2). Barnett is best known for his involvement with the Toynbee Hall Settlement in Spitalfields. In this block of self-contained flats, the architects made an effort to avoid the barrack-like appearance of many previous philanthropic blocks, and chose red and yellow brick, fashionable at the time. The façade is given interest by two canted bays on either side of the entrance, which is marked by a rounded pediment and a stepped central gable at roof level.

To the left is Mulberry House, of a similar form for the same charity but a generation later by Arthur Kenyon (1934–6). This is a bright neo-Georgian block with red tile roof and large sash windows.

Nos 17 and 18 (c.1683–90) retain many original details (fig. W11.3). They have fine red bricks

W11.1 Museum of Childhood, Cambridge Heath Road, James Wild, 1868–72, new entrance by Caruso St John.

W11.2 Montfort House, East End Dwellings Company, Victoria Park Square.

W11.3 No 17 Victoria Park Square, c.1683–90.

W11.4 Victoria Park Estate, East End Dwellings Company, cottages in Globe Road, 1906.

W11.5 Sutton Dwellings, Cornwall Gardens, Joseph and Smithem, 1909.

around the openings, modillion eaves cornice and hoods on brackets over the doors. The houses are of five bays, but No. 18 is not symmetrical. No. 16 next door was built in 1888 by the University House Settlement, associated with High Anglican Keble College, Oxford, hence the small chapel which projects toward the street.

Up the side of No. 18 Victoria Park Square is Sugar Loaf Walk leading to Globe Road. In Globe Road is the **Victoria Park Estate** by the East End Dwellings Company (1901–6). Merceron House and Gretton House are similar to Montfort House described above. On the east side of the road the red brick cottages of 1906 (fig.

W11.4) are part of the estate, and although these are plain two-storey houses, they do have brick and render arches and hoods over the doors, which open directly onto the street.

Near the top of Globe Road a right turn leads into the **Cyprus Street Estate**, an attractive mixed development with a central garden by Shepherd Epstein. On the other side of the estate is **Cyprus Street**, formerly Wellington Street, of 1850–1 (see p.45). This is a beautifully proportioned street of two-storey cottages. There are rounded arches over the ground-floor windows and over the doors, which have Doric pilasters and heavy arches with keystones. The

cement string course and cornice give good definition, and all the houses have external shutters to the ground-floor windows.

A left turn at the bottom of Cyprus Street into Bonner Street leads to the corner with Old Ford Road. Across the street is St James the Less by Lewis Vulliamy (1842), Norman in grey brick. On the south-east corner is the entrance to the **Cranbrook Estate** by Skinner Bailey and Lubetkin (1961–8) (see p.73). This is a mixed development estate, with houses at the periphery, maisonettes further in, and six towers. The landscaping is generous, and a good sense of the estate can be gained by walking down the central walkway to Roman Road bordering on the south side.

Across Roman Road on the south side is what is now called **Globe Town Market**. This was laid out by Yorke Rosenberg and Mardall (1956–9), who designed the surrounding five-storey blocks. At the back of the market in Usk Street is the first of Denys Lasdun's cluster blocks (1955–8). This is formed by two angled blocks of eight storeys with a central access tower connected by bridges to the individual maisonettes.

At the west side of the market, Morpeth Street leads to Digby Street where there are two inter-war estates by E. C. P. Monson, a firm very active in local authority flat building in Bethnal Green, Finsbury and Islington. The **Butler and Digby Estates** are of 1934 and 1935 respectively, and both are five storeys, hipped roofed, and red brick with stripy channelling.

At the end of Digby Street is the southern section of Globe Road, and visible from here up to the right in Roman Road is a good example of a fire station of 1888–9 by Robert Pearsall for the Metropolitan Board of Works – now a Buddhist centre. Left on Globe Road and then first right across Sceptre Road leads to Braintree Street and Cornwall Avenue, where on the right is **Sutton Dwellings** (1909) by Joseph and Smithem (fig. W11.5). The William Sutton Trust was established on the death of Sutton in 1900 with a very generous endowment to build

W11.6 Bethnal Green Estate, Cornwall Gardens, Office of Works, Frank Baines, 1922–4.

W11.7 Temple Street, Winckley Estate, Charles Winckley, 1899–1904, detail of stairs.

W11.8 Minerva Estate, London County Council, 1946–8, refurbished 2003.

healthy homes for the poor. This example comprises three substantial blocks of red brick and roughcast with mansard roofs, roundheaded pediments and quoining. Next door is the **Bethnal Green Estate** (fig. W11.6), built under the first post-First World War housing Act in 1922–4 by the Office of Works under its chief architect, Frank Baines. These are plain neo-Georgian blocks of four storeys with hipped roofs. The stock brick walls are given some style with purple brick quoins, string course and arches over the large first-floor segmental opening.

Within Bethnal Green Gardens is the **Public Library** (1896), a remnant of the Bethnal House Lunatic Asylum. This is a nicely proportioned fifteen-bay red brick building, with brick Ionic pilasters at first floor, and straightheaded sash windows with aprons. It was adapted as a li-

brary in 1922, at which time the entrance was given terracotta Ionic squared columns.

Cambridge Heath Road is on the far side of Bethnal Green Gardens, and by proceeding south on the west side of this main road, Three Colts Lane is reached. Up this road between the railway lines are the remains of old East End industrial premises. A sharp right leads to **Corfield Street** (see p. 60) and a long stretch of the Improved Industrial Dwellings Company (1868–80) for Sydney Waterlow's philanthropic trust. These are five storeys of yellow stock brick with Italianate classical detail. The entrances open directly onto the street, and the stairs are semi-enclosed rather than open, as is usually the case with the IIDC's blocks. At the top, a left turn into Wilmot Street reveals even more elaborate façades with flights of front steps and half basements.

Across Bethnal Green Road and up **Canrobert Street** leads to Old Bethnal Green Road. Along here are many examples of post-war housing. At the top a right turn into Old Bethnal Green Road and on the other side of Temple Street is the **Minerva Estate** (1946–8) (fig. W11.8), one of the first estates built by the LCC after the war. The design was by the Valuer's Department, and construction consisted of concrete slabs over load-bearing concrete walls for economy and speed. The estate was refurbished in 2003, and demonstrates just how well housing of this date can look with some care.

Back west along **Old Bethnal Green Road** on the north side are four-storey dwellings with open staircases (fig. W11.7). These speculatively built flats were put up by Charles Winckley (1899–1904). Further along in Canrobert and Winckley Streets are three-storey houses with workshops behind, also part of Winckley's enterprise. These houses are plain red brick and open directly onto the street, but are neat and orderly; they would have provided an alternative to the philanthropic blocks at the time.

A complete contrast is **Keeling House** (1955–9) (see p. 72), up to the left along Temple Street and then into Claredale Street. This is Lasdun's mature version of his cluster block. Four arms of sixteen storeys each contain maisonettes and one floor of single-storey flats. They are connected to the access tower via bridges as in the Usk Street block, and on their south-facing sides there are balconies to the living rooms. Lasdun hoped that the configuration of the flats would lead to social interaction along the access balconies and in the drying areas in the central stair and lift tower. The building is now in private ownership after refurbishment by

W11.9 Durant Street, Jesus Hospital Estate, Henry Robert Abraham, 1862–8.

W11.10 Guinness Trust, Columbia Road, F. L. Pilkington, 1892.

Munkenbeck and Marshall (1999–2001) in consultation with Lasdun.

Across Claredale Street for Bethnal Green Local Authority is **Claredale House** (see p.70), a red brick block by E. C. P. Monson (1931–2) with large rendered panels and arched entrance, similar to a slum clearance estate in Islington the firm built a few years later.

At the end of Claredale Street, a left into Mansford Street and a right into St Peter's Close leads to **St Peter's Square**. Here amongst a well-detailed council estate is St Peter with St Thomas (1840–1) (see p.145) by Lewis Vulliamy in a Norman style reminiscent of that of St James the Less. Grey brick and knapped flint give the church a very sober air, but this is just part of the total ensemble of vicarage, former school and schoolmaster's house grouped around a small leafy yard.

Across Ion Square Gardens into Durant Street (fig. W11.9) and the network of streets of two-storey cottages that forms the **Jesus Hospital Estate**. The estate was laid out by Henry Robert Abraham around 1862–8, and forms a homogeneous neighbourhood of neat streets including Wimbolt, Baxendale and Elwin Streets. Proceeding down Wimbolt Street and back up Barnet Grove to Columbia Road gives a good idea of the area. Grey stock bricks, segmental headed openings, white string course and cornice provide strong but simple lines in what is a modest, but elegant urbanism.

At the top of Barnet Grove in Columbia Road, to the right is the one remaining block of the **Guinness Trust** housing of 1892 by F. L. Pilkington (fig. W11.10). To the left down **Columbia Road** on the south side are small houses and shops of the 1860s, now largely refurbished. On the north side is the Royal Oak public house (1923) (see p.93) by A. E. Sewell, then Columbia Primary School. Further down on the right is the **Dorset Estate** (1955–7) by Skinner Bailey and Lubetkin. The most distinctive feature of this estate is the two large eleven-storey Y-shaped blocks, in amongst smaller four-storey ones. Facing Columbia Road, of a later date (1964–6) and by Skinner and Bailey, is Sivill House, a tower which dominates its surroundings (fig. W11.11). Further down the road is Columbia Market Nursery School in a little weatherboard pavilion whose railings and gatepiers are all that is left of the Columbia Market, demolished in 1958.

23 Leopold Buildings
24 St Leonard's

Leopold Buildings is an impressive range of five and six storeys (1872) (see p.61), with the usual florid Italianate decoration for Sydney Waterlow's Improved Industrial Dwellings Company. The open staircases and balcony access of earlier blocks by the company are repeated here. Refurbishment in 1996 by Floyd Slaski Partnership has introduced colour to enliven the grey brick façade, and their new stair towers at the rear have freed the front balconies for a great show of potted plants.

Columbia Road ends at Hackney Road and the intersection with Old Street, Kingsland Road and Shoreditch High Street. Facing this busy intersection is **St Leonard's** (1736–40), Shoreditch parish church, by George Dance Senior. The church has an impressive stone fronted façade with a four-column, Tuscan portico, while the sturdy tower rises above with a tall, thin spire.

If the desire for public housing is not yet sated and it is more convenient to visit the Boundary Street Estate now, the walk through this estate, to the east along Calvert Avenue, is described in Walk 7.

W11.11 Sivill House, Columbia Road, Skinner and Bailey, 1964–6.

WALK 12 GREENWICH

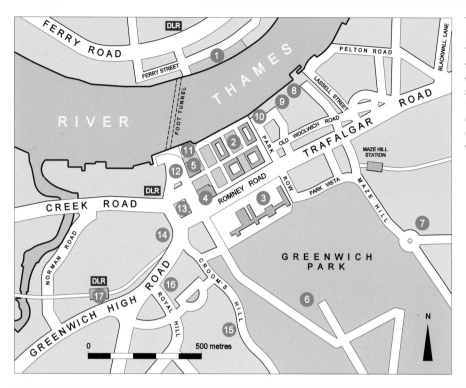

There is evidence of settlement here from the Roman and Anglo-Saxon periods, but it was following the building of the Tudor royal palace of Placentia that Greenwich grew as a significant town on the River Thames between the ship-building yards at Woolwich to the east and Deptford to the west. In the seventeenth century, Greenwich and Deptford formed the largest urban centre in England after London itself, Norwich and Bristol.

1 The view from Island Gardens

This view from the north bank of the river is one of the finest prospects in English architecture and landscape (see pp.21,115). From the gardens (reached by the Docklands Light Railway), which became a public amenity in 1895, we see the superb complex of buildings that originally formed the Royal Hospital for Seamen, with the Queen's House in the centre, Greenwich Park beyond and the Royal Observatory on top of the hill. To the east the view is terminated by the London Transport generating station, and to the west the town centre of Greenwich and the *Cutty Sark* tea-clipper in dry dock. Access to Greenwich from Island Gardens is through the foot tunnel, designed by Sir Alexander Binnie for the LCC and constructed in the river-bed in 1897–1902 to provide a route to the docks for workers from south of the river.

2 The former Royal Hospital for Seamen
3 The Queen's House
4 Infirmary
5 Pepys Building

The former Royal Hospital for Seamen (figs W12.1–W12.5 and p.116) and the **Queen's House** (fig. W12.6) is one of the greatest architectural ensembles in Europe, with work by many of the most celebrated English architects.

W12.2 Royal Hospital for Seamen (former), east (courtyard) front of the King William Building, 1701–8.

W12.3 Royal Hospital for Seamen (former), colonnade of the King William Building with the Nelson pediment, installed 1812.

W12.4 Royal Hospital for Seamen (former), the chapel, Queen Mary Building, refitted 1779–89 after fire.
LEFT W12.1 Royal Hospital for Seamen (former), the Queen Mary Building, 1735–42.

W12.5 Royal Hospital for Seamen (former), the Painted Hall, King William Building, built 1698–1707, painted 1708–12 (Painted Hall) and 1718–26 (Upper Hall).

Its history is as follows.

A house known as Bellacourt was built next to the Thames in the early fifteenth century by Humphrey, Duke of Gloucester, regent to his nephew, the young King Henry VI. He also built a small castle on top of the hill known as Duke Humphrey's Tower. After Humphrey's death in 1447, the house became the residence of Margaret, wife of Henry VI. It was rebuilt as a palace by Henry VII and renamed Placentia. Henry VIII made further substantial alterations during his reign (1509–47). During this period the palace became an important site for ambassadorial arrivals and departures, with associated ceremony.

The Queen's House was built as a private retreat in the grounds of the palace and the adjoining royal park. It is essentially a building of two halves, with a central bridge room spanning the originally public road which divided the palace from the park. It was begun in 1616 for Queen Anne of Denmark, wife of King James I, to the designs of Inigo Jones, and left only one-storey high at her death in 1619, then started again by Jones in 1629 for Henrietta Maria, wife of King Charles I; it was substantially completed by 1638, but interior decoration was still going on in 1642 when the Civil War broke out, sending the queen into exile and the king to his execution in 1649.

At the Restoration in 1660, King Charles II contemplated rebuilding the palace. He added two extra bridge rooms to the Queen's House, landscaped the park, then commissioned the architect John Webb, the pupil of Inigo Jones, to design a new palace. Demolition of the old palace started, and Webb built one wing of a new palace – the King Charles Building. Left incomplete internally and boarded up in 1672, this survives at the north-west of the complex.

In 1694 the King Charles Building and the adjoining grounds intended for a new palace were granted by Queen Mary for the building of a Royal Hospital for Seamen, more of an almshouse than a hospital in our contemporary sense of the word – that is, for the infirm and elderly rather than the sick. She kept the Queen's House for royal use and also retained the strip of land running from it to the river, so that she could have access by both land and water. This avenue, which remains in royal ownership, effectively divided the design into two halves, with two domes framing an open centre. Although Mary died at the end of 1694, her husband King William III kept the project alive.

Christopher Wren made the overall plan, although much of the design work, including the detail of the wonderful domes, was the responsibility of Nicholas Hawksmoor. Work went on in a piecemeal manner for well over fifty years, and some parts did not achieve their current form until the early nineteenth century. Other notable contributors to the buildings were Thomas Ripley, who designed the Queen Mary Building and the chapel; James Stuart, who designed the rebuilt chapel after a fire in 1779 had destroyed the earlier one, and the nearby **Infirmary** (later the Dreadnought Seamen's Hospital); James Thornhill, who painted the Painted Hall; and Benjamin West, who painted the chapel altarpiece (*The Preservation of St Paul after Shipwreck in the Island of Malta*) and designed the Nelson pediment, a celebratory commemoration in Coade (artificial) stone of the national naval hero, here delivered at the command of Neptune into the arms of Britannia.

The buildings of the hospital are very deliberately 'magnificent'. They are sending out celebratory messages on what was once one of the major public routes into London. These concern the power of the state, the authority of the Royal Navy in developing worldwide trading interests and protecting commerce, and the benevolence of a grateful nation which looks after those who have suffered in its service. The painted decoration is similarly celebratory, designed to deliver messages both to the resident audience of naval pensioners and to the visitors for whom this complex was a tourist destination even before it had been completed. Thornhill's Painted Hall, the finest decorative ensemble by a native painter, produced at the height of the fashion for baroque decorative painting in England, places the hospital's founders, Queen Mary and King William, at the centre of the ceiling, enthroned among the Virtues with Concord and Peace in attendance. King William, with his foot on Arbitrary Power (Louis XIV of France), hands the red cap of Liberty to Europe, and elsewhere Time exposes Truth while Wisdom and Strength destroy the Vices. Naval power, ensured by accurate navigation and guaranteeing trade, is celebrated at each end of the ceiling. In the Upper Hall, the Protestant succession is commemorated in the landing of William III, Prince of Orange, in 1688, and in the arrival of George I in 1714. On the ceiling, Juno, with her peacock, and Aeolus, god of the winds, command a calm, enabling Neptune to deliver his trident (and dominion of the seas) to the Lord High Admiral, Prince George of Denmark, consort of Queen Anne, depicted together in the central roundel. On the end wall, painted with the assistance of Dietrich Ernst Andreae, George I presides over Naval Victory, Peace and Plenty.

The hospital closed in 1869, and the buildings became the Royal Naval College in 1873. They served this function until the 1990s. The only significant addition to the complex during the tenure of the college was the **Pepys Building** of 1874–83, whose grand riverfront continues the theme of magnificence and greatly belies the humble function of the building, which originally housed fives and racquets courts, then a mechanical laboratory, and is now the Maritime Greenwich Visitor Centre. The occupants of the hospital buildings now are the University of Greenwich (in the Queen Anne, Queen Mary and King William Buildings, and in the former Infirmary, all converted by Dannatt Johnson Architects) and Trinity College of Music (in King Charles, converted by John McAslan). The site is administered by a charitable trust, the Greenwich Foundation.

The Queen's House became part of a residential school, the Royal Naval Asylum, and wings and Jonesian colonnades along the former road (which was moved north to its present site in the 1690s) were added in 1807–11 by Daniel Alexander. There were further extensions in the 1860s and 1870s. All the buildings on this south (park) side of the Romney Road were converted into the National Maritime Museum in 1933–7. The most notable recent addition was the creation of the Neptune Court (1998–9), designed by the Building Design Partnership and Rick Mather Architects.

W12.6 The Queen's House, south front from Greenwich Park, with colonnades along the former road added 1807–11.

W12.7 Vanbrugh Castle, Maze Hill.

6 Royal Observatory

On top of the hill, Flamsteed House, the Royal Observatory, was built to the designs of Christopher Wren and Robert Hooke in 1675–6 on the foundations of the demolished Duke Humphrey's Tower. From this prominent viewpoint, and from One Tree Hill to the east, generations of landscape painters have exploited the prospects to the Isle of Dogs and west to central London. The Royal Observatory – built, in Wren's words, 'for the observator's habitation and a little for pompe' – is now part of the larger complex of observatory buildings, no longer used for their original purpose of astronomical observation, but employed by the National Maritime Museum to tell the story of the search for longitude (through the mapping of the stars and the perfecting of sea-going timekeepers); the establishment here of the Prime Meridian (0 degrees longitude) and Greenwich Mean Time (GMT); and the techniques of modern astronomy. The time-ball on the east turret of Flamsteed House has indicated GMT since 1833 by dropping every day at 1 pm for the guidance of seamen on the river.

The most recent addition to the complex, the Peter Harrison Planetarium, designed by Allies and Morrsion, opened in 2007.

7 Vanbrugh Castle
8 London Transport generating station
9 Trinity Hospital Almshouses
10 Trafalgar Tavern
11 Greenwich Pier
12 *Cutty Sark*
13 Greenwich Market

To the east of the Royal Observatory, close to Greenwich Park on Maze Hill, Sir John Vanbrugh (surveyor to Greenwich Hospital 1716–26) built this picturesque and consciously medievalising house, **Vanbrugh Castle**, with battlements and corner turrets, for his own use in 1718–20 (fig. W12.7). Originally symmetrical, by 1724 the house had been extended by the architect into the asymmetry which made it the prototype for mock castles of the later eighteenth century. Further extensions followed and the house was converted into apartments by Gordon Bowyer and Partners *c*.1979. It is the sole survivor of a group of five houses which Vanbrugh built here for members of his family. It provides a notable illustration of a harmonious marriage between monumental grandeur and small size, and in its employment of the architect's favoured 'castle air' nicely counterpoints Wren's picturesque neo-Jacobean Royal Observatory.

On the riverside, to the east of the palatial hospital complex, the steel-framed **London Transport generating station** and accompanying coal jetty, constructed by the LCC in 1902–10, was a powerful demonstration of civic pride. It continues to provide a back-up source of electricity for London Underground.

Dwarfed by its neighbour, the quadrangular **Trinity Hospital Almshouses** of 1613 have an early nineteenth-century battlemented, gothick façade. At the west end of Crane Street, fronting the river, the **Trafalgar Tavern**, built to the design of Joseph Kay in 1837 on the site of the old George Tavern and famous in the nineteenth century for whitebait dinners, has survived numerous changes of fashion and fortune, including the possibility in 1931 of demolition to provide the site for a new town hall.

To the west of the hospital, **Greenwich Pier**

W12.8 Nelson Road (formerly Street), with the church of St Alfege.

was constructed for steamer traffic in 1836, the same year as the construction of the railway line from London Bridge, when Greenwich Fair, celebrated by Dickens, was a place of popular resort for south Londoners (see p.157).

Beyond the pier, the iron-framed *Cutty Sark*, under restoration in 2007–8, one of the last surviving tea-clippers and the fastest ship of her time, launched in 1869 for the China tea trade and subsequently employed in the Australian wool trade, was installed in the dry dock built by Sir Robert McAlpine in 1954.

Greenwich town centre, distinguished by stucco-fronted Regency terraces of shops and houses, was laid out to the design of Joseph Kay from 1827, and completed eventually by Philip Hardwick, his successor as surveyor to Greenwich Hospital, in 1849 (fig. W12.8). This regularisation and rebuilding of the older town centre effected the separation of the town from the adjacent hospital, and provided in College Approach (originally Clarence Street) a ceremonial route to the hospital's mid-eighteenth-century entrance lodges and gatepiers (topped by remarkable monumental globes), which were resited here in 1850. At the centre of the island site, **Greenwich Market**, begun by the hospital following the granting of a charter in 1700, was established in this new position in 1827–33. Designed by Kay, this retail market for the sale of meat, fish and vegetables was rebuilt in steel and glass in 1902–8, by which time the trade was primarily wholesale (see p.91). Now, in buildings dating predominantly from 1958–60, the trade is once more retail with a regular antiques market. The original entrance from College Approach carries a cautionary inscription from Proverbs: 'A False Balance is Abomination to the Lord but a Just Weight is his Delight.'

14 St Alfege
15 Our Lady Star of the Sea
16 The former Town Hall
17 Railway Station

The church of **St Alfege**, designed by Nicholas Hawksmoor in 1712, was the first of the proposed 'Fifty New Churches' to be begun following the Act of 1711. It replaced a church which was ruined beyond repair during a storm in 1710. The east end portico facing the High Road is an especially dramatic piece of late Roman scenography with an arch rising up into the pediment (see p.139). At the west end, above the entrance, the recasing by John James of the surviving medieval tower, completed in 1730, lacks the drama and vigorous modelling of the body of the church. Inside, Thornhill's illusionistic apse was repainted following the wartime gutting of the interior in 1941.

The rebuilding of St Alfege took place in the middle of a period of considerable prosperity in the town. This is made most obviously manifest in the surviving houses of Croom's Hill, a steeply climbing street which runs alongside Greenwich Park up to Blackheath. Here is an outstanding sequence of private houses, among the best in the whole of London, dating from the seventeenth, eighteenth and early nineteenth centuries, together with the Gothic Catholic church of 1851, **Our Lady Star of the Sea**, designed by William Wardell, with a handsome tower and spire, and decoration within by A. W. N. Pugin.

Towards the railway station on Greenwich High Road, **the former Town Hall**, now Meridian House, with a clock tower 165 feet (50 metres) high, is an imposing building of 1938–9, designed in the Dutch Modernist mode of the day by Clifford Culpin (fig. W12.9). The building was converted to private sector use in 1972–4, but the public halls survive to the rear.

George Smith's handsome classical **Railway Station**, built in 1840 as the terminus to the world's first suburban railway line (1836–8, from London Bridge), was rebuilt in 1878 when the platform layout was changed to accommodate the extension of the line to run east beyond Greenwich. Along with the new Cutty Sark Station, this is one of two stations in Greenwich served by the Docklands Light Railway.

W12.9 Meridian House, former town hall, Greenwich High Road.

BIBLIOGRAPHY

The bibliography for London is of necessity extremely long and varied. We have divided the entries into series of multiple volumes and single works, but in order to provide a guide to those sources we have found most useful, we have included a short bibliographical discussion for each of the chapters of the book, starting with an initial section on general sources.

GENERAL SOURCES
Multiple volumes
London is too large and it changes too rapidly for definitive publication. The topographical volumes of the *Survey of London* supply the most detailed and authoritative discussions of buildings and historical development, but the level of detail is such that completion of the whole of London will occur only in dreams. The *Buildings of England* London volumes are invaluable, readily available and comprehensive, although users need time to familiarise themselves with the format. They have been the single main source for factual information, but the pace of change is such that even they cannot be expected to supply all the answers. *The History of the King's Works* is the definitive account of public building from the Middle Ages to the mid-nineteenth century. *The Oxford Dictionary of National Biography*, now easily accessible online, has been the major source for modern accounts of historically significant figures: J. Morrill's Cromwell, M. Kishlansky and J. Morrill's Charles I, J. Newman's Inigo Jones and Kerry Downes's biographies of Wren (also available in book form in the VIP series, Oxford 2007), Hawksmoor and Vanbrugh have been especially useful.

Single works
The best single book on London's architecture, a well-written and witty thematic account, regrettably out of print, is by Harwood & Saint. Hebbert provides an excellent portrait of London from the perspective of a planner, exploring some of the 'picturing' themes of this book. For well-informed opinion, passionately expressed, Nairn's guide remains unsurpassed. Woodley's reliable contemporary guide has practical information for visitors as well as detailed descriptions. For modern and contemporary architecture, Allinson, Hardingham and Harwood all provide succinct analyses of individual buildings. In a brilliant, historically grounded polemic, Glancey celebrates the purposeful and targets the meretricious with argumentative verve. For discursive and beguiling accounts of London as a whole, see Pritchett (whose elegant prose is complemented by the atmospheric photography of Evelyn Hofer) and Rasmussen, the Danish architect who brought to the subject the objectivity and broader perspective of the outsider. On building types, Pevsner's groundbreaking survey (1976) of Western Europe and North America remains invaluable; C. Stevenson (2000) has considered one type, the hospital, in absorbing detail, paying attention as closely to the philosophical as to the architectural. The standard architectural history of British architecture remains Summerson (1983) and his often reprinted *Georgian London* the standard account of the eighteenth century: the 1988 edition was the last which he revised himself. McKellar and Guillery have enlarged the terms of reference for this period, the latter in an outstanding and innovative account (2004) of the hitherto less celebrated. For architects, Colvin (1995) provides definitive short biographical studies with lists of authenticated works. For the rich literature of architecture in English from the sixteenth to eighteenth centuries, E. Harris is indispensable. Dixon & Muthesius and Service (1977) provide good discussions of later developments, with lists of architects and works. For sculpture, both free-standing and architectural, see Read. For brief histories of streets, major buildings, institutions and much besides, see Weinreb & Hibbert. For simple but very effective maps of growth, great estates, transport, etc., see Clout. For general histories, Inwood and White (2001) are exhaustive and authoritative; Sheppard brings to the subject the knowledge and procedural skills of a former editor of the *Survey of London*; R. Porter's social history is indispensable, with a compelling narrative drive. Covering a narrower period with interdisciplinary panache and excellent illustrations, Nead sets a standard for all writers on perceptions of urban modernity.

THE BUILT HERITAGE
The Amsterdam Declaration (1975) is published in the Council of Europe collected texts (2002). Lord Duncan-Sandys's remarks were made in the last of the series of journals which commemorated European Architectural Heritage Year: these discussed *inter alia* the invading motor car, the problems of historic towns and the impact of tourism. Cormack's book, from the same period, presents a comparable threat-based analysis with a county by county 'Gazetteer of the Heritage'. Samuel (1994) offers the best and most eclectic description of

the British pluralist past and perceptions of heritage. Hewison lands several blows in his entertaining polemic in which he identifies the undefinable heritage as a manufactured commodity that everybody is eager to sell. Fowler provides illuminating juxtapositions of past, present and prescription. For underpinning sentiments and values, see the excellent Wiener. For a philosophical, historically grounded approach to the idea of the monument and the construction of identity, see Choay. Wright presents considerations of the national past and the elusive notion of the undefined heritage (1985), and provides in a further excellent collection of essays the apocalyptic view of London from Dalston, including life in the tower block (1991). The essays in Hunter, written with authority by those who have been engaged professionally in the subject (including Andreae, Saint and Stamp), provide the best succinct basis for a well-informed understanding of conservation. Delafons, a former civil servant in the Department of the Environment, offers an insider's views of the history and politics of preservation; this may be augmented by reference to Ross, a former Head of Listing in DoE; Hobhouse (1971a) provides a poignant record of what happened before all mechanisms were fully operational. As General Editor of the *Survey of London*, she also wrote the centenary history of the *Survey* which accompanied an exhibition at the Museum of London. Redundant historic buildings at risk and the strategy for bringing them back into use are discussed by P. Davies & D. Keate; English Heritage subsequently has published regular national 'Buildings at Risk' registers. The practical value of 'inherited' buildings was cogently expressed by Walter Godfrey, Director of the National Buildings Record 1941–60, who was a pioneer in the celebration of the familiar local scene. Rebecca West's monumental account of her prewar journey through Yugoslavia has much to say on English attitudes, offering comment and opinion on far more than her ostensible subject in one of the great books of the century.

PICTURING LONDON

Shakespeare Tower is the central tower in the group of three in the Barbican, between Lauderdale and Cromwell. On the Barbican see Cantacuzino's (1973) contemporary well-illustrated account with many plans, and the monograph by Heathcote. Michel de Certeau, on the 110th floor of the World Trade Center, considered himself a voyeur, out of the city's grasp – on the 36th floor of the Barbican it is possible to feel still in touch. Whitfield's well-illustrated survey was published to accompany a comprehensive exhibition at the British Library, which was enhanced by an excellent film of the taxi-driver's view, *Street Knowledge* (Noor Productions 2006), available on the BL website. For panoramic and topographical views, see Attoe, Harris (1979), Scouloudi's comprehensive

listing, and the exhibition catalogues by Blau & Kaufman, Bryant, Preston and Warner. For comment on panoramas in a wider context, see Nuti and the brilliant analysis of descriptive depiction by Alpers. On painters and paintings, see also the chronological, superbly illustrated coverage of London in Galinou & Hayes; on painters discussed, see Beddington, Cork, Croft-Murray, House, Links, A. MacGregor and Millar (1972). For Hollar, see Hind and Griffiths & Kesnerova. Eye-witness accounts are supplied by Evelyn and Pepys in the seventeenth century, Defoe and Boswell in the eighteenth and Jerrold (illustrated by Doré) in the nineteenth. Baedeker's 1900 guide is available in a modern reprint. The Blitz and its aftermath are considered in Holden & Holford, Lingard, Richards and Sebald. For St Paul's Cathedral see Downes (1998), Stancliffe, Stater and the compendious anniversary volume edited by Keene, Burns & Saint. For Wren's remarks on public buildings, see Soo as well as other Wren sources discussed below for Churches. On the seventeenth-century growth of London to the west, see the comprehensive Brett-James. On the Monument, see C. Stevenson (2005). Modernism was the subject of a comprehensive exhibition at the Victoria & Albert Museum (2006): Wilk edited the accompanying catalogue. The exhibition included the view from the air, for which see also Le Corbusier and Gropius for the architect's view; for the pilot's view, see A. de Saint-Exupéry for the poetry and J. Evans, inspired to write by the questions of passengers, for practical detail. For thoughts on perspective and the satisfaction of the needs of our eyes, see the outstanding dissertation by J. Rapp.

THE LONDON HOUSE AND FLAT

For houses and flats in London, it is important to refer to the architectural journals, especially in the case of inter-war flats. The most useful of these are: *The Builder, Building News, The Architect, Architectural Review, Architects' Journal* and *Architect and Building News*. Also indispensable are the London volumes of the *Buildings of England*, which identify across the capital the location of the many different types of dwelling.

The standard work on the social history of the English house is still Burnett. The pioneer work on the early years of our period is to be found in Summerson's *Georgian London* (first published 1945), and this has now been ably supplemented by McKellar and Guillery (2004). Also essential for these early years is Olsen's (1982) description of the development of the aristocratic estates. For the contemporary literature on the house in the eighteenth and nineteenth centuries, Archer is a valuable source. There is still little written on the High Victorian London house although information can be gleaned from more general studies, for example Muthesius (1982). The groundbreaking building history of Camberwell by Dyos is still worth studying. The best source for the Victorian villa remains Summerson's article republished in his 1990 publication, while the work of Norman Shaw and other 'Queen Anne' architects is dealt with in Saint (1976) and Girouard (1984a). The nuts and bolts of the Victorian house and its relation to health are discussed in Adams and Flanders.

Description of working-class housing in London is found in Tarn (1971 and 1973), and the early years of the LCC are well described by Beattie and later by Yelling. For the political dimension of working-class housing and how government became involved in its production, Englander and Swenarton are still useful.

For the twentieth-century London suburbs, see Jackson and Oliver et al., while in the volume edited by Silverstone, there are a number of stimulating essays on suburban life.

Indispensable for a study of the London flat in the nineteenth century is Perks. For the period between the wars, Darling provides an interesting discussion of modernity, and a contemporary argument for the flat can be found in Yorke & Gibberd. Hamnett & Randolph give a good introduction to the economics of the inter-war blocks of flats. The story of the post-war high rise, of which there are many examples in London, is told in Glendinning & Muthesius's monumental work, which is also a mine of information on sources. More recent developments such as the emergence of the owner-occupied flat are discussed in Hamnett.

SERVICING LONDON

For population see Clout and for the anthropomorphic image see McKellar.

Getting there: the Underground

Barker & Robbins deal with passenger travel as a whole and its role in London's development. On the Underground, Lawrence provides the best guide to the architecture, Halliday and Wolmar the most up-to-date histories, and Riddell an attractively illustrated collection of posters. Forty discusses London Transport design and corporate identity, particularly during the Frank Pick years. Rose's version of Harry Beck's map with the dates of opening of stations is invaluable as a guide to the relationship between the Underground and suburban growth. Collins, MacCarthy, Farr and Friedman, Silber et al. discuss the sculpture by Epstein and Gill on the London Transport headquarters. Hunter & Thorne, inspired by imminent redevelopment, provided a detailed analysis of the history and buildings at King's Cross and St Pancras. Simon Bradley's excellent monograph on St Pancras appeared shortly before the restored station reopened as St Pancras International in November 2007. All London's mainline stations were atmospherically illustrated in Betjeman & Gay.

Shopping

K. Morrison provides the best historical survey, well illustrated, of English shopping, from markets to malls, with a substantial account of department stores (including a useful development plan of the Harrods site); Draper-Stumm & Kendall present an attractive compilation of London shops. Grunenberg & Hollein include numerous essays and excellent illustrations on consumption and modernity to accompany an exhibition held in Frankfurt and Tate Liverpool. Rappaport sets Selfridge's into its wider social context, emphasising the role of women in commercial culture, a theme which might also be explored in Sparke and Falk & Campbell. Lancaster's social history of the department store may be supplemented by reference to Ashmore's essay (in which she quotes *The Times* on sinking ships). Nelson's introduction to Zola offers an outstanding analysis of the mechanisms and symbolism of the department store. The quote from Stuart Rose is taken from Grant's article; Underhill (2000) also offers an insider's view as a pioneer observer of behaviour in 'the science of shopping'. For Bluewater see Field. Thorne (1980) provides the indispensable history of Covent Garden Market and its restoration; Rubenhold gives an entertaining account of the eighteenth-century context of *Harris's List of Covent-Garden Ladies*.

Pubs

The standard account of Victorian pubs (and Temperance) by Girouard (1984b) may be supplemented by reference to Spiller and the well-illustrated Brandwood et al., which highlights those pubs with surviving fittings.

Board schools

In addition to the authoritative accounts of Seaborne & Lowe and Weiner, Girouard's account of the Queen Anne movement (1984a) is especially useful.

COMMERCIAL LONDON

As for the London house and flat, the architectural journals are crucial to understanding the development of commercial London. To recap, the most useful are: *The Builder, Building News, The Architect, Architectural Review, Architects' Journal* and *Architect and Building News*. The London volumes of the Royal Commission on Historical Monuments (England) and the *Survey of London* also cover many of the relevant areas of the City, while volume 1 of the London volumes of the *Buildings of England* (*The City of London,* 1997) is indispensable.

Kynaston's history of the City of London from 1815 gives essential background to the constant rebuilding of the Square Mile, while the social relations of early capitalism are laid out in Hancock. Keene provides an overview of the physical setting for the great expansion of the financial sector from the Middle Ages to 1871. A recent study of the Bank of England by Abramson has given a good picture of the City in the eighteenth century, including the work done by Soane. For Sir Robert Taylor also see Binney (1984). Works devoted specifically to commercial architecture of the nineteenth century include Murphy, Stamp & Amery, and Service (1979). Summerson's essay, republished in 1990, is, as always, informative and stimulating.

The architectural journals are a good source for the interwar period, since many of the buildings they illustrate have given way to newer versions. A case in point is what happened to Fleet Street when the newspapers left, recorded in Barson & Saint. The journals too are a good source for tracing the fate of areas such as Paternoster Square and London Wall, and in this context *Building Design* should be added to the list of architectural journals.

For more recent developments in commercial work, see Sudjic and for Docklands, Cox. New commercial developments regenerating areas south of the river are recorded in Powell (2004).

CAPITAL LONDON

King James was referred to as Great Britain's Solomon in the published oration delivered at his funeral. His proclamation is quoted in Brett-James. The principal sources for government buildings in the nineteenth century are Port's monumental study and Physick & Darby's catalogue of an exhibition at the Victoria & Albert Museum. On the New Government Offices and the War Office, see also Service (1977). On the saving of the Foreign Office, see Stamp (1996). On Greenwich, see Bold (2000); for the Painted Hall, see also Walczak. On the Banqueting House, see Palme and books on Inigo Jones by Harris & Higgott and Summerson (1966), the essay by Newman and the exhibition catalogue by Harris, Orgel & Strong. Orgel's brilliant short analysis of theatre presents significant insights into the intellectual context of the court masques. For the Rubens ceiling, see Donovan, Downes (1980) and the fundamental study by Held. On images of King Charles I, see Howarth, Ollard, Roberts and Strong (1972). For nineteenth-century perceptions and images of the Civil War, see Strong (2004) and Valentine. For a barrister's view of the trial of Charles I, see the persuasive Robertson. On public access to the National Gallery, in addition to Port, see especially MacGregor (2004), who has played a crucial public role as Director successively of the National Gallery and the British Museum in championing the role of museums and galleries in the public service. For the physical, social and political context of the National Gallery, see Mace on Trafalgar Square and Cherry on its statues. For the National Theatre and the British Library, the instant criticism required by journalism does not impede measured judgement in *The Architectural Review*: see especially Blundell Jones, Cantacuzino, and Curtis, Girouard et al. (Curtis is the pre-eminent commentator on Lasdun; see also his monograph and the RIBA exhibition catalogue which he edited). The architect of the British Library, Colin St John Wilson, is reflective and restrained in his informative account of the design and construction of his great work.

LONDON CHURCHES

The *Buildings of England* volumes have full, clear accounts of all the churches discussed. For the City churches, see also Jeffery, who assigns responsibilities and determines costs, and RCHME's attractive photographic survey. Wren's letter on churches is among the selection of his writings in Soo's compilation, which includes extensive commentary, and in du Prey, who also reproduces the Commissioners' Rules for the New Churches and Hickes's observations on Vanbrugh's proposals. The latter are published in Downes (*Vanbrugh*, 1977b). The anonymous incumbent is quoted by Colvin in his summary essay on the 'Fifty New Churches', which includes a catalogue of the churches with lists of craftsmen and notes on later works. Downes is the pre-eminent contemporary historian of the English baroque with numerous books on the principal architects – all are recommended but see especially *The Architecture of Wren* (1982/1988), the short *Hawksmoor* (1969/1987), the long *Hawksmoor* (2nd edn 1979) and *Vanbrugh* (1977b). On Wren, see also Whinney (1985); on Hawksmoor's sources, see also Hart. There is no modern monograph on Archer: in addition to Whiffen's short book, see Downes's survey of the period in *English Baroque Architecture*. The opinion of Ralph is quoted by Meller. For the 'vague, indeterminate concept' of taste, see Vickery's essay on wallpaper in Styles & Vickery's excellent collection of essays on the culture of consumption.

For the nineteenth and twentieth centuries, the architectural journals are again essential, but in addition *The Ecclesiologist* from 1841 should be consulted. T. F. Bumpus, though dating from the early years of the twentieth century, is still a good source for nineteenth-century churches. However, the indispensable guide is Clarke, especially his *Parish Churches of London* (1966). More recent is Howell & Sutton, but a really good study of London's nineteenth- and twentieth-century churches has yet to be written. The *Buildings of England* volumes for London continue to be the best source for church architecture and the most informative.

OPEN SPACES

The most substantial accounts of public parks are provided by Chadwick and Conway (1991). On Finsbury Park, see Hayes. On Greenwich Park, see Bold (2000). For London Zoo, see Guillery (1993), and for an account of the competing imperatives at the Penguin Pool, see Shapland & Van Reybrouck. For the German Gymnasium, see Hunter & Thorne. Worpole provides the best account of open-air public space as an aspect of modernity; this might be supplemented by Gordon's compilation, which makes well-illustrated reference to the German cult of the body. Open air and water come together in Smith's illustrated history, which includes comprehensive lists of operating and defunct lidos and open-air pools. Pleasure gardens are discussed in Brewer's immense cultural survey; see also the detailed entries in Weinreb & Hibbert; for the associated decorative paintings, see Allen, Einberg, Uglow and Hallett & Riding. For Canaletto's depictions, see Beddington and Links. For Roubiliac, see Whinney (1964). For eye-witness accounts of pleasure grounds, see the memoirs of Pepys, Boswell and Casanova. On the pleasure gardens at Highbury and the reference to parks as 'the lungs of London' (a saying of William Pitt, 1808, also quoted by Dickens), see Sugden. For Albert Park, see also Hinchcliffe. On sewers and much besides, below ground, see Trench & Hillman.

Sport

The definitive account of football grounds, with authoritative history and informed comment, is provided by Inglis (1996). The labour employed on the building of Arsenal stadium is noted by White (1986) in his social history of a neighbouring street. For Harringay see Norrie; for Walthamstow see Peter; for dog tracks in general see the website track6.com.

MULTIPLE VOLUMES

Booth, C., *Life and Labour of the People in London*, London and New York 1892–7 (and later editions; Booth's investigative notebooks are in the library of the London School of Economics; see also A. Fried & R. Elman, *Charles Booth's London*, New York 1968).

Buildings of England London volumes:

Bradley, S. & N. Pevsner, *London 1: The City of London*, London 1997.

Cherry, B. & N. Pevsner, *London 2: South*, Harmondsworth 1983.

Cherry, B. & N. Pevsner, *London 3: North West*, London 1991.

Cherry, B. & N. Pevsner, *London 4: North*, London 1998.

Cherry, B., C. O'Brien & N. Pevsner, *London 5: East*, New Haven and London 2005.

Bradley, S. & N. Pevsner, *London 6: Westminster*, New Haven and London 2003.

The History of the King's Works, ed. H. M. Colvin, 6 volumes, London 1963–82.

The Oxford Dictionary of National Biography, 60 volumes, Oxford 2004, and online.

Royal Commission on Historical Monuments (England), *An Inventory of the Historical Monuments in London*, 5 volumes, London 1924–30.

Survey of London, 17 monographs and 47 parish volumes, London 1896–2008 (continuing).

SINGLE WORKS

Abercrombie, P. & J. H. Forshaw, *County of London Plan*, London 1943.

Abramson, D. M., *Building the Bank of England: Money, Architecture, Society*, New Haven and London, 2004.

Adams, A., *Architecture in the Family Way*, Montreal and London 1996.

Allen, B., *Francis Hayman*, New Haven and London 1987.

Allinson, K., *London's Contemporary Architecture*, Oxford 2006.

Alpers, S., *The Art of Describing: Dutch Art in the Seventeenth Century*, Chicago 1983.

Amery, C., J. Martin Robinson & G. Stamp (eds), 'Hawksmoor's Christ Church Spitalfields' (AD Profile 22), *Architectural Design*, 49/7, 1979.

Andreae, S., 'From comprehensive development to Conservation Areas', in Hunter, *Preserving the Past*, 1996.

Apollonio, U., *Futurist Manifestos*, London 1973.

Archer, J., *The Literature of British Domestic Architecture, 1715–1842*, Cambridge MA 1985.

Ascot Gas Water Heater Ltd, *Flats, Municipal and Private Enterprise*, London 1938.

Ashmore, S., 'Extinction and evolution: department stores in London's West End, 1945–1982', *The London Journal*, 31/1, 2006, 41–63.

Attoe, W., *Skylines: Understanding and Molding Urban Silhouettes*, Chichester 1981.

Baedeker, K., *London and its Environs 1900*, reprint Moretonhampstead nd.

Baker, C. & T. Henry, *The National Gallery Complete Illustrated Catalogue* (including a history of the Gallery), London 1995.

Barker, T. G. & M. Robbins, *A History of London Transport*, 2 vols, London 1975–6.

Barson, S. & A. Saint, *A Farewell to Fleet Street*, London 1988.

Barthes, R., *Mythologies*, St Albans 1973.

BBC, *Spirit of the Age*, London 1975.

Beattie, S., *A Revolution in London Housing: LCC Housing Architects and their Work 1893–1914*, London 1980.

Beddington, C., *Canaletto in England*, New Haven and London 2006.

Beresford, C., 'Finsbury Park landscape history study' (for Haringey Council), London 1996.

Betjeman, J. & J. Gay, *London's Historic Railway Stations*, London 1972.

Binney, M., *Sir Robert Taylor: From Rococo to Neo-classicism*, London 1984.

Binney, M., *SAVE Britain's Heritage 1975–2005: Thirty Years of Campaigning*, London 2005.

Blatch, M., *A Guide to London's Churches*, London 1978.

Blau, E. & E. Kaufman, *Architecture and its Image*, Montreal 1989.

Blundell Jones, P., 'Speaking volumes' (the British Library), *The Architectural Review*, cciii, June 1998, 34–51.

Bold, J., *John Webb: Architectural Theory and Practice in the Seventeenth Century*, Oxford 1989.

Bold, J., 'The critical reception of Inigo Jones', *Transactions of the Ancient Monuments Society*, 37, 1993, 147–56.

Bold, J., *Greenwich: An Architectural History of the Royal Hospital for Seamen and the Queen's House*, New Haven and London 2000.

Bold, J., 'Comparable institutions: the Royal Hospital for Seamen and the Hôtel des Invalides', *Architectural History*, 44, 2001, 136–44.

Bold, J., 'A Just Weight, a History of Greenwich Market', *Journal of the Greenwich Historical Society*, 3/4, 2007, 140–58.

Bold, J. & C. Bradbeer, 'Finsbury Park: the identification of a suburban entity', *Transactions of the Ancient Monuments Society*, 44, 2000, 63–86.

Bold, J. & E. Chaney, *English Architecture Public and Private*, London and Rio Grande 1993.

Booker, J., *Temples of Mammon: The Architecture of Banking*, London 1990.

Boswell, J., *Boswell's London Journal 1762–1763*, ed. F. A. Pottle, London 1950.

Boumphrey, G. M., 'Flat v. cottage', *The Architects' Journal*, 82, 31 October 1935, 619–20.

Bradley, S., *St Pancras Station*, London 2007.

Branch, M. C., *City Planning and Aerial Information*, Cambridge MA 1971.

Brandwood, G., A. Davison & M. Slaughter, *Licensed to Sell: The History and Heritage of the Public House*, London 2004.

Brett-James, N. G., *The Growth of Stuart London*, London 1935.

Brewer, J., *The Pleasures of the Imagination: English Culture in the Eighteenth Century*, London 1997.

Brook, P., *The Empty Space*, Harmondsworth 1972.

Brown, C. & H. Vlieghe, *Van Dyck 1599–1641*, London 1999.

Bryant, J., *Finest Prospects – Three Historic Houses: A Study in London Topography*, London 1986.

Buchanan, P., 'National Gallery gamble', *The Architectural Review*, clxxii, December 1982, 19–25.

Buchanan, P., 'National Gallery progress report', *The Architectural Review*, clxxv, February 1984, 56–61.

Bumpus, J., 'Going down the line', *RA*, 65, 1999, 48–51.

Bumpus, T. F., *London Churches: Ancient and Modern*, London 1908.

Burke, G., *Townscapes*, Harmondsworth 1976.

Burnett, J., *A Social History of Housing* 1815–1985, London 1986.

Byrne, A., *Bedford Square: An Architectural Study*, London 1990.

Calladine, T., 'A paragon of lucidity and taste: the Peter Jones department store', *Transactions of the Ancient Monuments Society*, 45, 2001, 7–28.

Campbell, C., *Vitruvius Britannicus*, 3 vols, London 1715–25.

Campbell, P., 'Why does it take so long to mend an escalator?', *London Review of Books,* 7 March 2002, 3–7.

Cantacuzino, S., 'Barbican built', *The Architectural Review*, cliv, August 1973, 66–90.

Cantacuzino, S., 'A necessary giant' (the British Library), *The Architectural Review*, clxiv, December 1978, 337–44.

Casanova, G., *History of My Life*, 12 vols, Baltimore and London 1997.

Chadwick, G. F., *The Park and the Town: Public Landscape in the 19th and 20th Centuries*, London 1966.

Cherry, D., 'Statues in the square: hauntings at the heart of empire', *Art History*, 29/4, 2006, 660–97.

Choay, F., *The Invention of the Historic Monument*, Cambridge 2001.

Clarke, B. F. L., *Church Builders of the Nineteenth Century: A Study of the Gothic Revival in England* (1938), reprint Newton Abbot 1969.

Clarke, B. F. L., *Parish Churches of London*, London 1966.

Clout, H. (ed.), *The Times London History Atlas*, London 1991.

Cobbett, W., *Rural Rides* (1830 and 1853), 2 vols, London 1966.

Coe, P. & M. Reading, *Lubetkin and Tecton: Architecture and Social Commitment*, London and Bristol 1981.

Collins, J., *Eric Gill: The Sculpture*, London 1998.

Colonna, F., *Hypnerotomachia Poliphili* (1499), trans. and intro. J. Godwin, London 1999.

Colsoni, F., *Le Guide de Londres* (1693), ed. W. H. Godfrey, Cambridge 1951.

Colvin, H. M., 'Fifty New Churches', *The Architectural Review*, cvii, March 1950, 189–96.

Colvin, H. M., *A Biographical Dictionary of British Architects 1600–1840*, New Haven and London 1995.

Conekin, B., 'Fun and fantasy, escape and edification: the Battersea Pleasure Grounds', in Harwood & Powers, *Festival of Britain*, 2001.

Conway, H., *People's Parks: The Design and Development of Victorian Parks in Britain*, Cambridge 1991.

Conway, H., *Public Parks*, Princes Risborough 1996.

Cork, R. (intro.), *David Bomberg: Spirit in the Mass*, Kendal 2006.

Cormack, P., *Heritage in Danger*, London 1976.

Cosgrove, D. (ed.), *Mappings*, London 1999.

Council of Europe, *European Cultural Heritage* (2 volumes: collected texts; review of policies and practice), Strasbourg 2002.

Council of Europe, *Framework Convention on the Value of Cultural Heritage for Society* (Faro 2005), Strasbourg nd.

Cox, A., *Docklands in the Making*, London 1995.

Croad, S., *London's Bridges*, London 1983.

Croad, S., 'Changing perceptions – a temple to tobacco in Camden Town', *Transactions of the Ancient Monuments Society*, 40, 1996, 1–15.

Croad, S., *Liquid History: The Thames through Time*, London 2003.

Croft-Murray, E., 'The landscape background in Rubens's *St George and the Dragon*', *The Burlington Magazine*, lxxxix, 1947, 89–93.

Cruickshank, D. & N. Burton, *Life in the Georgian City*, London 1990.

Cruickshank, D. & P. Wyld, *London: The Art of Georgian Building*, London 1975.

Cuno, J. (ed.), *Whose Muse? Art Museums and the Public Trust*, Princeton and Oxford 2004.

Curtis, W. (ed.), *A Language and a Theme: The Architecture of Denys Lasdun and Partners* (RIBA exhibition), London 1976.

Curtis, W., *Denys Lasdun: Architecture, City, Landscape*, London 1994.

Curtis, W., M. Girouard et al., National Theatre special issue, *The Architectural Review*, clxi, January 1977.

Darling, E., *Re-forming Britain: Narratives of Modernity before Reconstruction*, London 2007.

Daumier, H., *Honoré Daumier 1808–1879* (The Armand Hammer Daumier Collection), Los Angeles 1981.

Daunton, M. J., *House and Home in the Victorian City: Working-Class Housing 1850–1914*, London 1983.

Daunton, M. J., *A Property-Owning Democracy?*, London 1987.

Davey, P., 'Cricket stand, Marylebone, London', *The Architectural Review*, clxxxii, September 1987, 42–3.

Davies, P. & D. Keate, *In the Public Interest: London's Civic Architecture at Risk*, London 1995.

de Certeau, M., *The Practice of Everyday Life*, Berkeley, Los Angeles and London, 1984.

de Saint-Exupéry, A., *Wind, Sand and Stars* (1939), reprint London 1975.

Defoe, D., *A Tour through the Whole Island of Great Britain* (1724–6), London 1974.

Delafons, J., *Politics and Preservation: A Policy History of the Built Heritage, 1882–1996*, London 1997.

Department of the Environment and Department of National Heritage, *Planning Policy Guidance: Planning and the Historic Environment* (PPG15), London 1994.

Dickens, C., 'Gin-shops' (1835), in *Sketches by Boz* (1839), London 1995.

Dickens, C., 'Greenwich Fair' (1835), in *Sketches by Boz* (1839), London 1995.

Dixon, R. & S. Muthesius, *Victorian Architecture*, London 1978.

Donovan, F., *Rubens and England*, New Haven and London 2004.

Downes, K., *English Baroque Architecture*, London 1966.

Downes, K., *Hawksmoor* (Thames & Hudson) London 1969, reprint 1987.

Downes, K., *Christopher Wren*, London 1971.

Downes, K., *Hawksmoor* (Whitechapel Art Gallery) London 1977a.

Downes, K., *Vanbrugh*, London 1977b.

Downes, K., *Hawksmoor* (Zwemmer), 2nd edn, London 1979.

Downes, K., *Rubens*, London 1980.

Downes, K., *Sir Christopher Wren* (Whitechapel Art Gallery) London 1982a.

Downes, K., *The Architecture of Wren*, St Albans 1982b, York 1988.

Downes, K., *Sir John Vanbrugh: A Biography*, London 1987.

Downes, K., *Sir Christopher Wren: The Design of St Paul's Cathedral*, London 1988.

Downes, K., *St Paul's and its Architecture*, York 1998.

Downes, K., *Christopher Wren*, Oxford 2007.

Draper, C., *Islington Cinemas and Film Studios*, London 1989.

Draper-Stumm, T. & D. Kendall, *London's Shops: The World's Emporium*, London 2002.

Duncan-Sandys, D. E., Introduction, *European Heritage*, 5, 'Policies and problems', London 1975.

du Prey, P. de la Ruffinière, *Hawksmoor's London Churches: Architecture and Theology*, Chicago and London 2000.

Dyos, H. J., *A Victorian Suburb, London: A Study of the Growth of Camberwell*, Leicester 1961.

Edis, R. W., *Decoration and Furniture of Town Houses*, London 1881.

Edwards, B., 'Swinging boutiques and the modern store: designing shops for post-war London', *The London Journal*, 31/1, 2006, 65–83.

Einberg, E., *Manners and Morals: Hogarth and British Painting 1700–1760*, London 1987.

Elmes, J., see Shepherd & Elmes, *Metropolitan Improvements*.

Englander, D., *Landlord and Tenant in Urban Britain, 1838–1918*, Oxford 1983.

Erlach, J. B. Fischer von, *Entwurff einer historichen Architectur*, Vienna 1721, reprint Dortmund 1978; published in an English limited edition, *A Plan of Civil and Historical Architecture*, 1730.

Evans, J., *How Airliners Fly*, Shrewsbury 2002.

Evans, R., 'Postcards from reality', *AA Files*, 6, 1984, 109–11.

Evans, R., 'Architectural projection', in Blau & Kaufman, *Architecture and its Image*, 1989.

Evans, R., *The Projective Cast*, Cambridge MA and London 1995.

Evelyn, J., *The Whole Body of Antient and Modern Architecture* (English version of Fréart de Chambray, R., *Parallèle de l'Architecture antique et de la moderne*), London 1680.

Evelyn, J., *The Diary of John Evelyn*, ed. E. S. de Beer, London 1959.

Falk, P. & C. Campbell (eds), *The Shopping Experience*, London 1997.

Farr, D., *English Art 1870–1940*, Oxford 1978.

Farrelly, E. M., 'The Venturi effect', *The Architectural Review*, clxxxi, June 1987, 32–7.

Field, M., 'Tragedy in the chalkpit', *Blueprint*, 161, May 1999, 42–5.

Fishman, W. J., *East End 1888*, London 2001.

Flanders, J., *The Victorian House: The Private Face of Public Life*, London 2003.

Forty, A., *Objects of Desire: Design and Society since 1750*, London 1995.

Foskett, D., *Samuel Cooper 1609–1672*, London 1974.

Fowler, P. J., *The Past in Contemporary Society: Then, Now*, London 1992.

Fox, C. (ed.), *London – World City 1800–1840*, New Haven and London 1992.

Friedman, T., *James Gibbs*, New Haven and London 1984.

Friedman, T., E. Silber et al., *Jacob Epstein Sculpture and Drawings*, Leeds 1989.

Galinou, M. & J. Hayes, *London in Paint: Oil Paintings in the Collection at the Museum of London*, London 1996.

Gay, J., *Trivia: Or The Art of Walking the Streets of London* (1716), in V. A. Dearing & C. E. Beckwith (eds), *John Gay Poetry and Prose*, I, Oxford 1974.

Geddes, P., *Cities in Evolution* (1915), reprint London 1968.

George, M. D., *London Life in the Eighteenth Century* (1925), reprint London 1992.

Girouard, M., *The Return to Camelot: Chivalry and the English Gentleman*, New Haven and London 1981.

Girouard, M., *Sweetness and Light: The Queen Anne Movement 1860–1900*, New Haven and London 1984a.

Girouard, M., *Victorian Pubs*, New Haven and London 1984b.

Girouard, M., *Big Jim: The Life and Work of James Stirling*, London 1998.

Glancey, J., *London: Bread and Circuses*, London 2001.

Glendinning, M. & S. Muthesius, *Tower Block: Modern Public Housing in England, Scotland, Wales and Northern Ireland*, New Haven and London 1994.

Godfrey, W. H., *Our Building Inheritance: Are We to Use or Lose It?*, London 1944.

Goldberger, P. (on the Venturi extension design), *New York Times*, 16 April 1987; (on museums as public squares) 'Architecture, museums and authenticity', Morgan Library, 14 November 2003.

Goldhill, S., *The Temple of Jerusalem*, London 2006.

Gordon, M., *Voluptuous Panic: The Erotic World of Weimar Berlin*, Los Angeles 2000.

Grant, L., 'And the brand played on', *The Guardian Weekend*, 12 August 2006, 18–25.

Griffiths, A. & G. Kesnerova, *Wenceslaus Hollar Prints and Drawings*, London 1983.

Gropius, W., *The New Architecture and the Bauhaus* (1935), reprint London 1965.

Grunenberg, C. & M. Hollein, *Shopping: A Century of Art and Consumer Culture*, Frankfurt and Liverpool 2002.

Guillery, P., *The Buildings of London Zoo*, London 1993.

Guillery, P., *The Small House in Eighteenth-Century London*, New Haven and London 2004.

Hallett, M. & C. Riding, *Hogarth*, London 2006.

Halliday, S., *Underground to Everywhere*, Stroud 2001.

Hamnett, C., *Cities, Housing and Profits: Flat Break-Up and the Decline of Private Renting*, London 1988.

Hamnett, C. & B. Randolph, 'The rise and fall of London's purpose-built blocks of privately rented flats: 1853–1983', *The London Journal*, 11/2, 1985, 160–75.

Hancock, D., *Citizens of the World, London Merchants and the Integration of the British Atlantic Community, 1735–1785*, Cambridge 1995.

Hardingham, S., *London: A Guide to Recent Architecture*, London 2002.

Harris, E., *British Architectural Books and Writers 1556–1785*, Cambridge 1990.

Harris, J., *Sir William Chambers: Knight of the Polar Star*, London 1970.

Harris, J., *The Artist and the Country House*, London 1979.

Harris, J., *Echoing Voices: More Memories of a Country House Snooper*, London 2002.

Harris, J. & G. Higgott, *Inigo Jones: Complete Architectural Drawings*, London 1989.

Harris, J., S. Orgel & R. Strong, *The King's Arcadia: Inigo Jones and the Stuart Court*, London 1973.

Harris, J. & M. Snodin (eds), *Sir William Chambers: Architect to George III*, New Haven and London 1996.

Hart, V., *Nicholas Hawksmoor: Rebuilding Ancient Wonders*, New Haven and London 2002.

Harwood, E., *England: A Guide to Post-War Listed Buildings*, London 2003.

Harwood, E. & A. Powers (eds), *Festival of Britain*, London 2001.

Harwood, E. & A. Powers, *The Heroic Period of Conservation*, London 2004.

Harwood, E. & A. Saint, *London*, London 1991.

Hawksmoor, N., *Remarks on the Founding and Carrying on the Buildings of the Royal Hospital at Greenwich* (1728), reprint Wren Society, vi, Oxford 1929.

Hayes, H., *A Park for Finsbury: Finsbury Park at the Millennium*, London 2001.

Heathcote, D., *Barbican – Penthouse over the City*, Chichester 2004.

Hebbert, M., *London: More by Fortune than Design*, Chichester 1998.

Held, J., 'Rubens's Glynde sketch and the installation of the Whitehall ceiling', *The Burlington Magazine*, cxii, May 1970, 274–81. Republished in the collection of Held's essays edited by A. Lowenthal, D. Rosand & J. Walsh, *Rubens and his Circle*, Princeton 1982.

Hendy, P., *The National Gallery London*, London 1964.

Hewison, R., *The Heritage Industry: Britain in a Climate of Decline*, London 1987.

Hibbert, C., *London: The Biography of a City*, London 1969.

Hibbert, C., *London's Churches*, London 1988.

Hinchcliffe, T., 'Highbury New Park: a nineteenth-century middle class suburb', *The London Journal*, 7/1, 1981, 29–44.

Hind, A. M., *Wenceslaus Hollar and his Views*

of London and Windsor in the Seventeenth Century, London 1922.

Hobhouse, H., *Lost London: A Century of Demolition and Decay*, London 1971a.

Hobhouse, H., *Thomas Cubitt: Master Builder*, London 1971b.

Hobhouse, H., *A History of Regent Street*, London 1975.

Hobhouse, H., *London Survey'd: The Work of the Survey of London 1894–1994*, Swindon 1994.

Holden, C. & W. Holford, *The City of London – A Record of Destruction and Survival*, London 1947.

House, J., 'The Thames transfigured: André Derain's London', in Courtauld Institute of Art Gallery, *André Derain: The London Paintings*, London 2005.

Howarth, D., *Images of Rule: Art and Politics in the English Renaissance, 1485–1649*, Berkeley and Los Angeles 1997.

Howell, P. & I. Sutton, *The Faber Guide to Victorian Churches*, London 1989.

Hunter, M. (ed.), *Preserving the Past: The Rise of Heritage in Modern Britain*, Stroud 1996.

Hunter, M. & R. Thorne, *Change at King's Cross*, London 1990.

Hutchison, S. C., *The History of the Royal Academy 1768–1986*, London 1986.

Inglis, S., *Football Grounds of Britain*, London 1996.

Inglis, S., *Sightlines: A Stadium Odyssey*, London 2000.

Inwood, S., *A History of London*, London 2000.

Jackson, A. A., *Semi-Detached London: Suburban Development, Life and Transport 1900–39*, London 1973.

Jeffery, P., *The City Churches of Sir Christopher Wren*, London and Rio Grande 1996.

Jeremiah, D., *Architecture and Design for the Family in Britain, 1900–70*, Manchester 2000.

Jerrold, B. & G. Doré, *London: A Pilgrimage* (1872), reprint London 2005.

Jones, E. & C. Woodward, *A Guide to the Architecture of London*, London 1983.

Keene, D., 'The setting of the Royal Exchange: continuity and change in the financial district of the City of London, 1300–1871', in A. Saunders (ed.), *The Royal Exchange*, London 1997.

Keene, D., A. Burns & A. Saint, *St Paul's: The Cathedral Church of London 604–2004*, New Haven and London 2004.

Kerr, J. & A. Gibson, *London: From Punk to Blair*, London 2003.

Kynaston, D., *The City of London*, 3 vols, London 1999.

Lancaster, B., *The Department Store: A Social History*, London and New York 1995.

Lawrence, D., *Underground Architecture*, Harrow 1994.

Le Corbusier, *Aircraft* (1935), reprint London 1987.

Lingard, J., 'Cyril A. Farey: a personal tribute to St Paul's Cathedral and the City of London, 1940–44', in Bold & Chaney, *English Architecture*, 1993.

Links, J. G., *Canaletto*, Oxford 1982.

London County Council, *Housing*, London 1928, 1931, 1937.

London County Council, *Fire over London 1940–41*, London 1941.

London, J., *The People of the Abyss* (1903), reprint London 2001.

Long, H. C., *The Edwardian House*, Manchester 1993.

Loudon, J. C., *Suburban Gardener and Villa Companion …*, London 1838.

Lowenthal, D., *The Heritage Crusade and the Spoils of History*, London 1997.

MacCarthy, F., *Eric Gill*, London 1989.

MacGregor, A. (ed.), *The Late King's Goods*, London and Oxford 1989.

MacGregor, N., 'The Hampton Site II', *The Burlington Magazine* (editorial), cxxv, February 1983, 67.

MacGregor, N., 'The perpetual present', *Oxford Today*, Michaelmas 2002, 23–5.

MacGregor, N., 'A Pentecost in Trafalgar Square', in Cuno, *Whose Muse?*, 2004.

McKellar, E., *The Birth of Modern London: The Development and Design of the City 1660–1720*, Manchester 1999.

McKibbin, R., *Classes and Cultures: England 1918–1951*, Oxford 1998.

Mace, R., *Trafalgar Square: Emblem of Empire*, London 1976.

Mann, E., 'In defence of the City: the gates of London and Temple Bar in the seventeenth century', *Architectural History*, 49, 2006, 75–99.

Meller, H., *St George's Bloomsbury*, London 1975.

Millar, O., *The Age of Charles I: Painting in England 1620–1649*, London 1972.

Millar, O., *Sir Peter Lely 1618–80*, London 1978.

Millar, O., *Van Dyck in England*, London 1982.

Millar, O., 'Rubens's Whitehall ceiling', *The Burlington Magazine*, cxlix, February 2007, 101–4.

Mitchell, S., *Gilgamesh: A New English Version*, London 2004.

Morris, R. J., 'The middle class and the property cycle during the industrial revolution', in T. C. Smout (ed.), *The Search for Wealth and Stability*, London 1979.

Morrison, A., *A Child of the Jago*, London 1896.

Morrison, K., *English Shops and Shopping*, New Haven and London 2003.

Murphy, S. J., *Continuity and Change: Building in the City of London*, London 1984.

Muthesius, S., *The High Victorian Movement in Architecture 1850–1870*, London and Boston MA 1972.

Muthesius, S., *The English Terraced House*, New Haven and London 1982.

Nairn, I., *Nairn's London*, Harmondsworth 1966.

National Gallery, *The National Gallery January 1973–June 1975* (including Michael Levey's 'Director's Report'), London 1975.

Nead, L., *Victorian Babylon: People, Streets and Images in Nineteenth-Century London*, New Haven and London 2000.

Newman, J., *Somerset House: Splendour and Order*, London 1990.

Newman, J., 'Inigo Jones and the politics of architecture', in Sharpe & Lake, *Culture and Politics*, 1993.

Nicholson, D., *The Londoner*, London 1944.

Norrie, C., 'Harringay Greyhound Stadium Totalisator and George Alfred Julius', *London's Industrial Archaeology*, 5, 1994, 24–34.

North, R., *Autobiography*, ed. A. Jessopp, London 1887.

Nuti, L., 'Mapping places: chorography and vision in the Renaissance', in Cosgrove, *Mappings*, 1999.

Olechnowicz, A., *Working-Class Housing in England Between the Wars: The Becontree Estate*, Oxford 1997.

Oliver, P., I. Davis & I. Bentley, *Dunroamin: The Suburban Semi and its Enemies*, London 1981.

Ollard, R., *The Image of the King: Charles I and Charles II*, London 1993.

Olsen, D., *Town Planning in London*, New Haven and London 1982.

Olsen, D., *The City as a Work of Art: London, Paris, Vienna*, New Haven and London 1986.

Orgel, S., *The Illusion of Power: Political Theater in the English Renaissance*, Berkeley and Los Angeles 1975.

Palladio, A., *I quattro libri dell'architettura*, Venice 1570, facsimile reprint Milan 1980; modern English translation by R. Tavernor and R. Schofield, *Andrea Palladio – The Four Books of Architecture*, Cambridge MA and London 1997.

Palme, P., *Triumph of Peace: A Study of the Whitehall Banqueting House*, London 1957.

Pawley, M., *Eva Jiricna: Design in Exile*, London 1990.

Peacock, T. L., *Headlong Hall* (1816), in *Novels of Thomas Love Peacock*, London 1967.

Pearman, H., '£100m National Gallery facelift to be launched', *The Sunday Times*, 3 November 2002.

Pepys, S., *The Diary of Samuel Pepys*, ed. R. C. Latham & W. Matthews, 11 vols, London 1995.

Perks, S., *Residential Flats of all Classes, Including Artisans' Dwellings*, London 1905.

Peter, B., *Form Follows Fun: Modernism and Modernity in British Pleasure Architecture, 1925–1940*, London 2007.

Pevsner, N., *An Outline of European Architecture*, Harmondsworth 1968.

Pevsner, N., *A History of Building Types*, London 1976.

Physick, J. & M. Darby, *'Marble Halls': Drawings and Models for Victorian Secular Buildings*, London 1973.

Pliny the Elder, *Natural History: A Selection*, trans. and intro. J. F. Healy, London 2004.

Port, M. H., *Imperial London: Civil Government Building in London 1851–1915*, New Haven and London 1995.

Porter, R., *London: A Social History*, London 1994.

Porter, S., *The Great Fire of London*, Godalming 1996.

Powell, K., 'Modern movement: London's Jubilee Line extension', *Architecture Today*, 105, February 2000, 36–55.

Powell, K., *City Reborn, Architecture and Regeneration in London, from Bankside to Dulwich*, London and New York 2004.

Pozzo, A., *Perspective in Architecture and Painting* (c.1707), reprint New York 1989.

Preston, H., *London and the Thames: Paintings of Three Centuries*, London 1977.

Pritchett, V. S., *London Perceived*, London 1962.

Pugin, A. W. N., *Contrasts: Or a Parallel between the Noble Edifices of the Fourteenth and Fifteenth Centuries and Similar Buildings of the Present Day ...*, London 1836.

Pugin, A. W. N., *The True Principles of Pointed or Christian Architecture*, London 1841.

Rapp, J., 'Multiple view perspective and the creativity of Giovanni Battista Piranesi', Architecture Diploma dissertation, University of Westminster 2007.

Rappaport, E., *Shopping for Pleasure: Women in the Making of London's West End*, Princeton 2000.

Rasmussen, S. E., *London: The Unique City*, London 1937.

Ravetz, A., *Council Housing and Culture: The History of a Social Experiment*, London 2001.

Read, B., *Victorian Sculpture*, New Haven and London 1982.

Reddaway, T. F., *The Rebuilding of London after the Great Fire*, London 1940.

Reilly, C. H., 'The Bush buildings New York and London', *Architecture*, 2/18, 1924, 283–96.

Report of the Committee Appointed to Consider Questions of Building Construction in Connection with the Provision for the Working Classes (The Tudor Walters Report), Cd. 919, VII, London 1918.

Richards, J. M., *The Bombed Buildings of Britain*, Cheam 1942.

Riddell, J., *Pleasure Trips by Underground*, Harrow 1998.

Roberts, J., *The King's Head – Charles I: King and Martyr*, London 1999.

Robertson, G., *The Tyrannicide Brief*, London 2005.

Rogers, M., *William Dobson 1611–46*, London 1983.

Rose, D., *The London Underground: A Diagrammatic History*, 7th edn, Harrow nd.

Ross, M., *Planning and the Heritage: Policy and Procedures*, London 1991.

Rothenstein, J., *The Tate Gallery*, London 1966.

Royal Commission on the Historical Monuments of England (RCHME) (P. Guillery & D. Kendall), *The City of London Churches: A Pictorial Rediscovery*, London 1998.

Royal Parks, *Buildings and Monuments in the Royal Parks*, London 1997.

Rubenhold, H., *The Covent Garden Ladies*, Stroud 2005.

Ruskin, J., *The Seven Lamps of Architecture*, London 1849.

Ruskin, J., *The Stones of Venice*, 3 vols, London 1851–3.

Ruskin, J., *Sesame and Lilies: Two Lectures*, London 1865.

Saint, A., *Richard Norman Shaw*, New Haven and London 1976.

Saint, A. (ed.), *Politics and the People of London: The London County Council 1889–1965*, London and Ronceverte 1989.

Saint, A., 'How listing happened', in Hunter, *Preserving the Past*, 1996.

Saint, A. (intro.), *London Suburbs*, London 1999.

Saint, A., 'Diary' (on the Jubilee Line), *London Review of Books*, 20 January 2000.

Samuel, R., *Theatres of Memory: Past and Present in Contemporary Culture*, London 1994.

Samuel, R., *Island Stories: Unravelling Britain – Theatres of Memory, Volume II*, London 1998.

Sargent, A., 'RCHME 1908–1998: a history of the Royal Commission on the Historical Monuments of England', *Transactions of the Ancient Monuments Society*, 45, 2001, 57–80.

Scharf, A., *Art and Photography*, Harmondsworth 1974.

Schofield, J., *Medieval London Houses*, London and New Haven 1994.

Scouloudi, I., 'Panoramic views of London 1600–1666', Corporation of London, typescript Guildhall Library 1953.

Seaborne, M. & R. Lowe, *The English School: Its Architecture and Organisation Volume II, 1870–1970*, London 1977.

Sebald, W. G., *On the Natural History of Destruction*, London 2003.

Sennett, R., *The Fall of Public Man* (1974), reprint New York and London 1992.

Service, A., *Edwardian Architecture*, London 1977.

Service, A., *The Architects of London*, London 1979a.

Service, A., *London 1900*, St Albans 1979b.

Shapland, A. & D. Van Reybrouck, 'Competing natural and historical heritage: the Penguin Pool at London Zoo', *International Journal of Heritage Studies*, 14/1, January 2008, 10–29.

Sharpe, K. & P. Lake, *Culture and Politics in Early Stuart England*, Stanford 1993.

Sheard, R., *Sports Architecture* (foreword by S. Inglis), London and New York 2001.

Shepheard, P., *The Cultivated Wilderness*, Cambridge MA 1997.

Shepherd, T. & J. Elmes, *Metropolitan Improvements* (1827–31), reprint New York 1978.

Sheppard, F., *London: A History*, Oxford 1988.

Silverstone, R. (ed.), *Visions of Suburbia*, London 1997.

Simon, R. & A. Smart, *John Player Art of Cricket*, London 1983.

Smith, J., *Liquid Assets: The Lidos and Open Air Swimming Pools of Britain*, London 2005.

Soar, P. & M. Tyler, *Arsenal: The Official Illustrated History*, London 1986 (and later editions).

Sontag, S., *On Photography*, London 1978.

Soo, L. M., *Wren's 'Tracts' on Architecture and Other Writings*, Cambridge 1998.

Sparke, P., *As Long As It's Pink: The Sexual Politics of Taste*, London 1995.

Spiller, B., *Victorian Public Houses*, Newton Abbot 1972.

Stamp, G., *The Great Perspectivists*, London 1982.

Stamp, G., 'The art of keeping one jump ahead: conservation societies in the twentieth century', in Hunter, *Preserving the Past*, 1996.

Stamp, G., 'The South Bank site', in Harwood & Powers, *Festival of Britain*, 2001.

Stamp, G. & C. Amery, *Victorian Buildings of London, 1837–1887*, London 1980.

Stancliffe, M., Memorandum on St Paul's Heights Code (TAB 46), The United Kingdom Parliament website (Select Committee on Transport, Local Government and the Regions), accessed 2005.

Stater, B., 'War's greatest picture: St Paul's Cathedral, the London Blitz, and British national identity', MSc Architecture dissertation, University College London 1996.

Stevenson, C., *Medicine and Magnificence: British Hospital and Asylum Architecture, 1660–1815*, New Haven and London 2000.

Stevenson, C., 'Robert Hooke, monuments and memory', *Art History*, 28/1, 2005, 43–73.

Stevenson, C., 'Occasional architecture in seventeenth-century London', *Architectural History*, 49, 2006, 35–74.

Stevenson, J. J., *House Architecture*, 2 vols, London 1880.

St John Wilson, C., *The Design and Construction of the British Library*, London 1998.

Stow, J., *A Survey of London* (1598, revised 1603), reprint Oxford 1971.

Strong, R., *Van Dyck: Charles I on Horseback*, London 1972.

Strong, R., *Painting the Past: The Victorian Painter and British History*, London 2004.

Styles, J., & A. Vickery, *Gender, Taste and Material Culture in Britain and North America 1700–1830*, New Haven and London 2006.

Sudjic, D., *New Architecture: Foster, Rogers, Stirling*, London 1986.

Sugden, K., *History of Highbury*, London 1984.

Summerson, J., *Inigo Jones*, Harmondsworth 1966.

Summerson, J., *The Life and Work of John Nash*, London 1980.

Summerson, J., *Architecture in Britain 1530–1830*, Harmondsworth 1983.

Summerson, J., *Georgian London*, London 1988.

Summerson, J., 'The London suburban villa, 1850–1880', in *The Unromantic Castle*, London 1990a.

Summerson, J., 'The Victorian rebuilding of the City of London, 1840–1870', in *The Unromantic Castle*, London 1990b.

Summerson, J. (intro.), *50 Years of the National Buildings Record 1941–1991*, Beckenham 1991.

Swenarton, M., *Homes Fit for Heroes: The Politics and Architecture of Early State Housing in Britain*, London 1981.

Tarn, J. N., *Working-Class Housing in 19th-Century Britain*, London 1971.

Tarn, J. N., *Five Per Cent Philanthropy. An Account of Housing in Urban Areas between 1840 and 1914*, London 1973.

Thorne, J., *Handbook to the Environs of London* (1876), reprint Chichester 1983.

Thorne, R., *Covent Garden Market: Its History and Restoration*, London 1980.

Trench, R. & E. Hillman, *London under London: A Subterranean Guide*, London 1993.

Trollope, A., *The New Zealander* (1855–6), reprint Oxford 1972.

Uglow, J., *Hogarth: A Life and a World*, London 1997.

Underhill, P., *Why We Buy: The Science of Shopping*, New York 2000.

Underhill, P., *Call of the Mall*, New York 2004.

Valentine, H., *Art in the Age of Queen Victoria: Treasures from the Royal Academy of Arts Permanent Collection*, London 1999.

Venturi, R., *Complexity and Contradiction in Architecture*, New York 1966 and London 1977.

Vickery, A., 'Neat and not too showey: words and wallpaper in Regency England', in Styles & Vickery, *Gender, Taste*, 2006.

Walczak, G., 'The man that workt for Sr. J. Thornhill – Dietrich Ernst Andreae (c.1695–1734) in England', *The British Art Journal*, III/2, 2002, 8–19.

Walsh, C., 'Shops, shopping, and the art of decision making in eighteenth-century England', in Styles & Vickery, *Gender, Taste*, 2006.

Warner, M., *The Image of London: Views by Travellers and Emigrés 1550–1920*, London 1987.

Weiner, D., *Architecture and Social Reform in Late-Victorian London*, Manchester 1994.

Weinreb, B. & C. Hibbert, *The London Encyclopaedia*, London 1983.

West, R., *Black Lamb and Grey Falcon: A Journey through Yugoslavia* (1942), reprint Edinburgh 2006.

Wheelock, A. K. Jr, S. J. Barnes & J. S. Held, *Anthony van Dyck*, Washington, DC 1990.

Whiffen, M., *Thomas Archer: Architect of the English Baroque* (1950), reprint Los Angeles 1973.

Whinney, M., *Sculpture in Britain 1530–1830*, Harmondsworth 1964.

Whinney, M., *Wren* (1971), reprint London 1985.

Whinney, M. & O. Millar, *English Art 1625–1714*, Oxford 1957.

White, J. F., *The Cambridge Movement*, Cambridge 1962.

White, J., *The Worst Street in North London: Campbell Bunk, Islington, Between the Wars*, London 1986.

White, J., *London in the Twentieth Century: A City and its People*, London 2001.

White, J., *London in the Nineteenth Century: 'A Human Awful Wonder of God'*, London 2007.

Whitfield, P., *London: A Life in Maps*, London 2006.

Wiener, M., *English Culture and the Decline of the Industrial Spirit, 1850–1980*, Cambridge 1981.

Wilk, C. (ed.), *Modernism: Designing a New World 1914–1939*, London 2006.

Wilson, D., *Our Protestant Faith in Danger*, London 1850.

Wilson, M., *A Guide to the Sainsbury Wing at the National Gallery*, London 1991.

Wilton, A., *Turner in the British Museum*, London 1975.

Winder, R., *Bloody Foreigners: The Story of Immigration to Britain*, London 2004.

Wolmar, C., *The Subterranean Railway*, London 2005.

Woodham, J. M., *Twentieth-Century Design*, Oxford 1997.

Woodley, R., *London* (The Blue Guides series), London 2002.

Worpole, K., *Here Comes the Sun: Architecture and Public Space in Twentieth-Century European Culture*, London 2000.

Wotton, H., *The Elements of Architecture* (1624), reprint Farnborough 1969.

Wren, C., *'Tracts' on Architecture*, see Soo, *Wren's 'Tracts'*, 1998.

Wright, P., *On Living in an Old Country: The National Past in Contemporary Britain*, London 1985.

Wright, P., *A Journey through Ruins: The Last Days of London*, London 1991.

Yelling, J. A., *Slums and Slum Clearance in Victorian London*, London 1986.

Yorke, F. R. S. & F. Gibberd, *The Modern Flat*, London 1937.

Zola, E., *The Ladies' Paradise* (*Au Bonheur des Dames*, 1883), trans. and intro. B. Nelson, Oxford 1995.

INDEX